eleventh edition

Building Classroom Discipline

C. M. Charles
Emeritus, San Diego State University

Collaboration by:

Gail Senter
California State University San Marcos

Marilyn Charles
Cajon Valley Unified School District

D1509710

Boston   Columbus   Indianapolis   New York   San Francisco   Upper Saddle River
Amsterdam   Cape Town   Dubai   London   Madrid   Milan   Munich   Paris   Montréal   Toronto
Delhi   Mexico City   São Paulo   Sydney   Hong Kong   Seoul   Singapore   Taipei   Tokyo

Vice President and Editorial Director:
    Jeffery W. Johnston
Vice President and Publisher: Kevin Davis
Editorial Assistant: Lauren Carlson
Vice President, Director of Marketing:
    Margaret Waples
Senior Marketing Manager: Joanna Sabella
Senior Managing Editor: Pamela D. Bennett
Project Manager: Kerry Rubadue

Senior Art Director: Jayne Conte
Cover Designer: Karen Noferi
Cover Photo: © nagib / Shutterstock
Full-Service Project Management: Jean L. Smith,
    S4Carlisle Publishing Services
Composition: S4Carlisle Publishing Services
Printer/Binder: STP Courier
Cover Printer: STP Courier
Text Font: ITC Giovanni Std

Credits and acknowledgments for material borrowed from other sources and reproduced, with permission, in this textbook appear on the appropriate page within the text.

Every effort has been made to provide accurate and current Internet information in this book. However, the Internet and information posted on it are constantly changing, so it is inevitable that some of the Internet addresses listed in this textbook will change.

Photo Credits: Jean Piaget Society, p. 3; Courtesy of aha! Process, Inc., p. 9; Walter Reuther Library, Wayne State University, pp. 52, 53, 56; ASSOCIATED PRESS, p. 53; Courtesy of The William Glasser Institute, pp. 54, 183; Courtesy of Alice Cohn, p. 57; KLETT-COTTA, p. 59; Dawn Bryan Photography, p. 63; Courtesy of Jane Nelsen, p. 63; Courtesy of Barbara Coloroso, p. 64; Photo by Jason Threlfall, courtesy of Alfie Kohn, p. 66; Courtesy of Ronald Morrish, p. 72; Courtesy of Craig Seganti, p. 94; Harry K. Wong Publications, Inc., p. 116; Courtesy of Fred Jones, p. 138; Courtesy of Marvin Marshall, p. 160; Courtesy of Spencer Kagan, p. 205; Courtesy of Paula Cook, p. 226.

Library of Congress Cataloging-in-Publication Data
Charles, C. M.
  Building classroom discipline / C.M. Charles, Emeritus, San Diego State University. — Eleventh edition.
        pages cm
  ISBN 13: 978-0-13-309531-9
  ISBN 10: 0-13-309531-2
  1. School discipline. 2. Classroom management. I. Title.
  LB3012.C46 2014
  371.5—dc23

                                                                        2012030866

10 9 8 7 6 5 4 3 2 1

ISBN 10:   0-13-309531-2
ISBN 13: 978-0-13-309531-9

PREFACE

A WORD ON HIGH-QUALITY TEACHING

In February 2012, the Grattan Institute released a report on teaching practices that prevail in four of the five top-performing school systems in the world, based on achievement in reading, mathematics, and science. The four were Asian schools: Shanghai, Hong Kong, Singapore, and South Korea. Finland was the other school system in the top five, now ranked second behind Shanghai (see Jensen, B., Hunter, A., Sonnemann, J., and Burns, T. [2012] Catching up: learning from the best school systems in East Asia, Grattan Institute).

The high-performing Asian schools did not rely on special facilities, advanced technology, small class size, high levels of financing, or new curricula, but rather on teachers' continual efforts to identify and make use of factors that result in higher student learning. The report does not specify what teachers say or do when working with students, but it seems to suggest that school learning is most strongly influenced by the interactions between teacher and students. As a means of identifying productive practices and integrating them into teaching, the Asian schools require all teachers, even the most senior, to mentor fellow teachers and be mentored by them. Teachers meet regularly in groups to share practices they find most effective, and all teachers must conduct ongoing research into what actually produces higher levels of learning for their students.

The Grattan Institute's findings are much in harmony with the point of view put forth in this text—that effective teaching and quality learning hinge primarily on the interactions between teacher and students. One of teachers' most important duties is to help students learn to accept responsibility, do the right thing, and relate positively with others, all conducive to success in school and a productive and satisfying life. Motivation may be the most important factor in learning, but also highly important are the development of trusting relationships with others and finding within oneself the desire to do well, accept responsibility, and exhibit civil behavior. This text is dedicated to helping you foster those important qualities in your students.

WHAT'S IN THIS PREFACE

In this preface, you will find indicated or explained:

- Audience for this text
- What is new to this edition
- Goals of this text
- Organization of the text and sequence of chapters
- Chapter topics and organization
- Glossary and references

- A planning rubric for developing a personalized system of discipline
- A listing of discipline authorities who have advised and/or contributed to this text
- The array of supplementary materials available to instructors and students

AUDIENCE FOR THIS TEXT

This text is designed for use by university students who are preparing to become teachers, as well as by teachers already in service. It is comprehensive, intended to be used as a single or primary text in discipline and classroom management, yet it is compact enough to be used in conjunction with other texts or as a primary reference text. It is typically used in courses in discipline, classroom management, learning and instruction, methods of teaching, and educational psychology, and in teacher institutes and inservice programs.

NEW TO THIS EDITION

This 11th edition of *Building Classroom Discipline* has been thoroughly reorganized for greater effectiveness in helping users develop discipline skills and personalized systems of discipline. Readers familiar with previous editions will find the following important changes in the text:

- The text is organized into four sequential phases that progressively guide users to high levels of competence.
- Chapter 12 provides a comprehensive review of the best tactics and strategies in today's discipline, organized to enable users to reflect on and answer the "eight great questions in discipline."
- Chapter 13 follows by presenting self-assessment activities that help users refine their capabilities across a comprehensive array of concepts and tactics. The chapter can be used for review, for personal assessment of knowledge and skills, and for further strengthening of understanding and skills.
- A planning rubric that appears later in this preface and again in Chapters 2 and 14 helps users organize high-quality discipline approaches that meet their particular needs as well as those of their students.
- Self-tests included in most chapters can be used for pre- and post-chapter review, self-appraisal, and group discussions.
- Insightful commentaries are provided by an anonymous elementary teacher and an anonymous secondary teacher, both with many years' experience.

GOALS OF THIS TEXT

This text has two main goals. The first is to help readers understand and become highly competent in today's major concepts, terminology, approaches, and strategies in discipline. Toward that end, information is presented on the nature of behavior and misbehavior, students' behavioral traits, teachers' obligations in discipline, and the goals and procedures of today's most respected approaches in discipline. Later in the text, a comprehensive review of outstanding concepts and tactics is presented, followed by directions for self-appraisal and follow-up review as might be needed.

The second goal is to assist teachers in organizing systems of discipline that best meet their needs and those of their students. The rationale for this emphasis is that any given system of discipline is unlikely to fit the needs of teachers and students everywhere. Students are different at various age levels, and they come from many different social and cultural groups. They vary substantially in personalities, traits, and needs, and they behave and respond differently in accordance with maturation and experience. Teachers vary as well, in personality, philosophy, and styles of interacting and communicating. For those many reasons, a discipline system that works well for one teacher and group of students often does not work well for others. This text acknowledges those realities and, accordingly, provides information and guidance for developing effective, well-rounded systems of discipline that suit any given class. Guidance in personalizing one's approach to discipline remains a unique feature of this text.

ORGANIZATION OF THIS TEXT AND SEQUENCE OF CHAPTERS

As indicated, the text is organized to guide users through four phases of development that lead to excellence in discipline. Each phase is supported by chapters of information and suggested activities related to important aspects of discipline. Although they may be studied independently, the phases are sequenced so that each phase prepares readers for moving easily into the next. Here are the phases:

Phase I: Conceptual Grounding in Discipline in Which You Encounter and Explore in Some Detail the Nature of Classroom Misbehavior, Teachers' Obligations in Discipline, and the General Premise, Mindset, and Terminology of Modern Classroom Discipline

Chapters in Phase I

Chapter 1 discusses the nature of human behavior in general, the realities of student behavior and misbehavior, the meaning of misbehavior, what causes misbehavior, the definition and purpose of discipline, and what it means to exert positive influence on students.

Chapter 2 introduces a number of basic terms in discipline and explains schools' and students' mutual obligations; teachers' professional obligations, including discipline; and how one goes about organizing an effective system of discipline.

Chapter 3 reviews the development of modern discipline and summarizes the contributions and terminology of 20th-century authorities who set the foundations for today's discipline.

↓

Phase II: Preparing Yourself to Take Charge in the Classroom in Which You Learn What Is Needed in a Discipline Plan, the First Things You Should Teach, and How You Establish and Maintain Calm, Purposeful Student Behavior

Chapters in Phase II

Chapter 4 reviews Ronald Morrish's views on what you should include in your system of discipline and how you should present your plan to students.

Chapter 5 explains how Craig Seganti establishes control in classes that are usually thought of as hard to manage.

Chapter 6 reviews Harry and Rosemary Wong's suggestions concerning class procedures and scripting the first minutes and days of a new class.

↓

Phase III: Activating Motivation and Engaging with Your Students in Which You Learn How to Engage Your Students Actively, Involve Them in High-Quality Learning Experiences, Release Their Internal Motivation, Help Them Make Responsible Choices, and Manage Atypical Behavior

Chapters in Phase III

Chapter 7 explains how Fred Jones helps students maintain focus and stay on task.

Chapter 8 explains how Marvin Marshall helps students learn to make positive choices and take responsibility for their behavior.

Chapter 9 explains how William Glasser uses noncoercive choice to promote student self-control and high-quality learning.

Chapter 10 explains how Spencer Kagan enables teachers and students to work together on the same side rather than at cross purposes.

Chapter 11 describes how Paula Cook promotes success for students with neurological-based behavior.

↓

Phase IV: Perfecting and Personalizing Your Approach to Discipline in Which You Bring Everything Together, Strive for Excellence, and Organize a Discipline Approach That Is Optimized for You and Your Students

Chapters in Phase IV

Chapter 12 reviews discipline authorities' opinions on eight fundamental questions in discipline and then helps you answer those questions in your own words.

Chapter 13 guides you in assessing and improving your capabilities in discipline as you reach for mastery.

Chapter 14 guides you in composing a customized approach to discipline that best meets your needs and those of your students.

CHAPTER TOPICS, STRUCTURE, AND SEQUENCE

Previous users of the text may notice that changes have been made in chapter topics, structure, and sequence. These changes have been made to ensure greater clarity and help readers move more easily through the four phases of development. As always, chapter organization and style of writing aim for readability, understanding, and applicability. Their general structure is as follows.

Chapters 1 through 3

With some variations, Chapters 1 through 3 are organized as follows:

- Short introduction to the chapter
- Brief biographical sketches of contributing authorities and their principal publications
- Questions the chapter will answer
- Informational content related to given discipline topics
- Commentaries from an anonymous elementary teacher and an anonymous secondary teacher
- Activities for individuals or study groups, including true/false self-tests, multiple-choice self-tests, "explain this" self-tests, and various other activities

Chapters 4 through 11

Chapters 4 through 10 review seven different commercial approaches to discipline that are attracting wide attention today. "Commercial" means programs that are being disseminated for profit by their originators, through paid workshops, speaking engagements, sale of texts and materials, and consultancies with schools. The commercial programs reviewed in these chapters vary in nature and indicate a range of approaches and points of view.

Chapter 11 presents Dr. Paula Cook's suggestions for working successfully with students who exhibit neurological-based behavior (NBB), a condition that makes it difficult for students to control their behavior.

As for organization, Chapters 4 through 10 reflect the same organization as Chapters 1 through 3, with the following additions:

- "Concept Cases" for practice in applying authorities' suggestions,
- "You Are the Teacher" scenarios that ask you how you would resolve certain discipline situations.

Chapter 11 has exercises interspersed in the body of the chapter.

Chapters 12 through 14

Chapters 12 through 14 guide users in organizing information about discipline, assessing and strengthening their personal levels of accomplishment, and composing a personalized system of discipline. This feature provides greater guidance and direction than did previous editions of this text.

Glossary and References

Following Chapter 14, you will find the *Glossary of Terms Related to Discipline*. The terms were presented in **boldface** when they first appeared in chapters. In the glossary, they appear in alphabetical order. In many cases, authorities who first used or popularized certain terms are identified. Following the glossary, you will find an alphabetized listing of references cited in the text.

FOR SUGGESTED USE: A PLANNING RUBRIC TO HELP YOU ARTICULATE A PERSONALIZED SYSTEM OF DISCIPLINE

All teachers need a system of discipline that works well for them and their students. Nothing is more important to teaching and learning. Teachers are most effective when their discipline systems are concordant with their personalities and preferences, as well as with the needs and other traits of the students they serve. Ordinarily, if teachers are to have such approaches, they must construct them for themselves.

This text encourages practice and provides needed guidance in the form of a planning rubric, introduced here and revisited in Chapters 2 and 14. This text provides all the information you need for completing the rubric in detail. Here are the major topics in the rubric:

Topic 1. My philosophy of discipline, explained in my *conception of discipline*, the *purposes for which I will use discipline*, *my main duties in discipline*, and *my students' main duties in discipline*.

Topic 2. My theory of discipline, explained in what I consider to be *the necessary components of a system of discipline* and *the purposes of each component*.

Topic 3. The professional and ethical demeanor I will display, explained in *how I will comply with the legal, professional, and ethical obligations associated with discipline and teaching*, and *what I will do to establish positive relations and develop trust with students and colleagues*.

Topic 4. The student behavior I will endeavor to promote and the rules that support it, explained in a description of *behaviors I will foster in my classes*, and the *specific rules, if any, I will use to support those behaviors*.

Topic 5. What I will do proactively to prevent or reduce misbehavior, explained in the *specific steps I will take, in advance, to organize instruction and prevent or limit the known causes of misbehavior* that might otherwise occur in my classes.

Topic 6. How I will support my students' efforts to participate and persevere, explained in *how I will speak with and relate to my students*, *how I will make sure students know what they are expected to do*, the *types of activities I will emphasize*, *how I will engage students actively when I am providing instruction*, *how I will monitor and help students when they are doing independent work*, *how I will use my personal charisma*, *how I will use body language to influence behavior*, and *how I will otherwise influence students to do high-quality work*.

Topic 7. How I will redirect students when they misbehave, explained in *how I will influence students to behave acceptably through positive tactics that preserve personal dignity*, *how I will stop misbehavior and help students return willingly to appropriate behavior*, *how I will deal with minor misbehavior* such as talking or distracting others, *how I will deal with more disruptive behavior* such as disrespect and abusiveness, and *how I will deal with refusal to comply with directions or do acceptable work*.

Topic 8. How and when I will communicate my discipline approach to students, administrators, and students' caregivers, explained in *narrative or outline form,* including *how I will seek support from administrators and students' caregivers.*

The Rubric and a Suggested Journal

It is strongly suggested that you keep a journal of ideas and information as you proceed through the text. Make journal headings that correspond to the topics in the rubric, leaving four or five blank pages between rubric headings. On those pages, make notes of information you find especially helpful. When you complete the text, your journal will be filled with information you may wish to include in your personalized system of discipline.

INSTRUCTOR'S MANUAL TO THE TEXT FOR UNIVERSITY AND WORKSHOP INSTRUCTORS

An instructor's manual is available for download from the Instructor Resource Center at www.pearsonhighered.com/irc. The manual includes a wealth of ideas and activities for use in teaching the course.

PARTICIPATION OF DISCIPLINE AUTHORITIES FEATURED IN THIS TEXT

Major ideas from the following discipline authorities are featured in this text. The author has been able to interact with most of the modern-day authorities, who have kindly helped ensure that their concepts are accurately presented herein. Those who participated are indicated with an asterisk; those who are deceased are indicated with a dash. Please refer to the references section for complete documentation.

*Michele Borba on building moral intelligence in our classrooms
*Lee Canter and Marlene Canter on the techniques of assertive discipline
*Barbara Coloroso on self-discipline and combating bullying
*Paula Cook on neurological-based behavior
–Stephen Covey on the habits of highly effective people
*Richard Curwin on discipline with dignity
*Tom Daly on working with students with ADHD
–Rudolf Dreikurs on democratic teaching and discipline
*Ed Ford on the responsible thinking process
*P. M. Forni on promoting civility
–Haim Ginott on congruent communication
*William Glasser on choice theory and quality teaching and learning
*Benna Golubtchik on multisensory classrooms
*Diane Gossen on self-restitution theory
*Fred Jones on body language and keeping students engaged
*Spencer Kagan on the principles of Win-Win Discipline
*Alfie Kohn on in-depth education and classroom communities
–Jacob Kounin on techniques of lesson management

*Lynn Lott on tactics of effective communication
*Marvin Marshall on inner discipline and student responsibility
*Allan Mendler and Brian Mendler on the principles of discipline with dignity
*Ronald Morrish on teaching proper behavior
*Jane Nelsen on tactics of effective communication
*Ruby Payne on how poverty influences behavior
–Jean Piaget on how children behave as they mature and develop intellectually
–Fritz Redl on group dynamics in the classroom
*Craig Seganti on effective teaching in hard-to-manage classrooms
–B. F. Skinner on shaping behavior through reinforcement
–William Wattenberg on group dynamics in the classroom
*Harry and Rosemary Wong on how procedures affect behavior

ACKNOWLEDGMENTS

The author gratefully acknowledges the valuable contributions made to this and previous editions by the following teachers and administrators:

Roy Allen, Constance Bauer, Karen Barr, Linda Blacklock, Tom Bolz, Michael Brus, Gail Charles, Ruth Charles, Tim Charles, Diana Cordero, Keith Correll, Tom Daly, Barbara Gallegos, Nancy Girvin, Kris Halverson, Leslie Hays, Charlotte Hibsch, Elaine Maltz, Colleen Meagher, Nancy Natale, Linda Pohlenz, Lillian Schafer, David Sisk, Deborah Sund, Mike Straus, and Virginia Villalpando.

The author also acknowledges the valuable critiques provided by notable reviewers: Linda Albert, researcher; Dale Allee, Southwest Missouri State University; Michele Borba, researcher; Terrell Brown, University of Central Missouri; James D. Burney, University of North Alabama; Lee Canter and Marlene Canter, educator-researchers; Barbara Coloroso, researcher; Paula Cook, University of Manitoba; Richard Curwin, discipline with dignity; Tom Daly, teaching specialist and author; Philip DiMattia, Boston College; Karen M. Dutt, Indiana State University; Carolyn Eichenberger, St. Louis University; Anne Rene Elsbree, California State University San Marcos; James D. Ellsworth, Northern Arizona University; Ed Ford, director of the Responsible Thinking Process, Inc.; P. M. Forni, director of Civility Initiative, Johns Hopkins University; Sara S. Garcia, Santa Clara University; Robert E. Gates, Bloomsburg University; William Glasser, researcher; Thomas Gordon (deceased), Effectiveness Training International; Diane Gossen, researcher; Marci Green, University of South Florida at Ft. Myers; Gail Gregg, Florida International University; C. Bobbi Hansen, University of San Diego; Fredric Jones and JoLynne Jones, researchers; David I. Joyner, Old Dominion University; Deborah Keasler, Southwestern Oklahoma State University; Spencer Kagan and associates, researchers; Alfie Kohn, researcher; Thomas J. Lasley, University of Dayton; Malcolm Linville, University of Missouri–Kansas City; Lawrence Lyman, Emporia State University; Bernice Magnus-Brown, University of Maine; Marvin Marshall, researcher; Vick McGinley, West Chester University; Susan Mintz, University of Virginia; Janey L. Montgomery, University of Northern Iowa; Ronald Morrish, researcher; Janice L. Nath, University of Houston; Jane Nelsen and associates, researchers; Merrill M. Oaks, Washington State University; Linda Pincham, Roosevelt University; Jack Vaughan Powell, University of Georgia; Elizabeth Primer, Cleveland State University; Craig Seganti, teacher and author, Los Angeles City Schools; Gail Senter, California State University San Marcos; Mary C. Shake, University of Kentucky; Alma A. Shearin, University of Central Arkansas; Terry R. Shepherd, Southern Illinois University at Carbondale; Alina Slapac, University of Missouri–St. Louis; JoAnne Smatlan, Seattle Pacific University; Kay Stickle, Ball State University; Marguerite Terrill, Central Michigan University; Sylvia Tinling, University of California, Riverside; Eileen VanWie, New Mexico State University; Bill Weldon, Arizona State University; Kathleen Whittier, State University of New York at Plattsburgh; and Harry Wong and Rosemary Wong, educator-researchers.

The author would also like to thank the following reviewers of this 11th edition: Deborah Burris, Southern Illinois University–Carbondale; Aubrey Fine, California State Polytechnic University, Pomona; Robert Harrington, University of Kansas; Linda Pincham, Roosevelt University; Madalina Tanase, University of North Florida; Margaret Torrie, Iowa State University.

BRIEF CONTENTS

CONTENTS

PHASE II   Preparing Yourself to Take Charge in the Classroom   71

4   Ron Morrish on Organizing and Presenting a Basic Discipline Plan   72

PHASE III   Engaging with Your Students and Activating Their Internal Motivation   137

7   Fred Jones on Keeping Students Willingly Engaged in Learning   138

8 Marvin Marshall on Fostering Responsible Behavior   160

9   William Glasser on Releasing the Power of Positive Choice   183

10   Spencer Kagan on Working on the Same Side with Students   205

11   Paula Cook on Helping Students Who Exhibit Neurological-Based Behavior   226

PHASE IV   Perfecting and Personalizing Your Approach to Discipline   247

13 Striving for Personal Excellence in Discipline   267

---

14   Building Your Personalized Approach to Discipline   290

PHASE ONE

Conceptual Grounding in Discipline

In Which You Encounter and Explore in Some Detail the Nature of Classroom Misbehavior, Teachers' Obligations in Discipline, and the General Premises, Mindset, and Terminology of Modern Classroom Discipline

CHAPTERS IN PHASE I

CHAPTER 1 Discusses the realities of student behavior and misbehavior, the nature of human behavior, the types and causes of misbehavior, the definition and purpose of discipline, and what it means to exert positive influence on students.

CHAPTER 2 Introduces a number of basic terms in discipline and explains schools' and students' mutual obligations, teachers' professional obligations in discipline, and how one goes about organizing an effective system of discipline.

CHAPTER 3 Reviews the development of modern discipline and summarizes the contributions and terminology of 20th-century authorities who set the foundations for today's system of discipline.

1

Classroom Discipline: The Problems and the Promise

Would You Like to Understand Discipline, Wrinkles and All, and Become Really Good at It?

WHAT, YOU ASK, IS THIS TEXT GETTING ME INTO?

The answer is, this text is getting you into the most important thing you can learn about teaching, which is how to establish and maintain a pleasant learning environment in which students behave civilly and responsibly and you are able to teach without disruption. Such environments are essential to high-quality teaching and learning. Unfortunately, in many of today's classrooms, civil and responsible behavior is not much in evidence. Numbers of students show little respect for teachers. Some make almost no effort to learn, and a few wantonly disrupt learning for everyone in the class. Such behavior harms both teaching and learning. Teachers in disruptive classrooms find little pleasure in their chosen profession, and often burn out early and either leave teaching or struggle on miserably. As for students, persistent misbehavior keeps them distracted and sometimes fearful, both of which are destructive to learning.

But there's bright promise of better things to come. In these pages, you will learn how to minimize misbehavior so you can work enjoyably with well-behaved students. Many students behave civilly most of the time, but altogether too many do not. Given that fact, your first step is to acknowledge five realities of misbehavior and discipline and learn to address all of them. Here are the five realities:

1. *Students are inclined to misbehave.* Many are going to behave nicely most of the time, but a few are going to misbehave so severely that they cheat and damage themselves, their classmates, their teachers, their parents, and the society that depends on (and pays for) their education as citizens.

2. *To be successful in teaching, you must learn how to promote responsible behavior in the classroom.* You must learn how to influence students in a positive manner to behave civilly and considerately *even when they don't want to.* Unless you learn to do that, you will never be able to teach well, and even students who want to learn in your classes will have difficulty doing so.

3. *Fostering responsible behavior is the greatest challenge you will face in teaching.* Bluntly speaking, your success and the well-being of your students depend on it. Unless you have exceptional natural talents, you must work to

develop the skills that promote good classroom behavior. We are happy to say that this book puts you in touch with suggestions offered by the foremost authorities in classroom discipline.

4. *Students who develop responsible behavior have a great advantage in life.* Most people cannot come close to realizing their potential unless they conduct themselves responsibly. Many students receive the help they need only in school, with little support from home or community.

5. *You have to teach many students how to behave responsibly.* You actually have to teach your students how to behave, how to be successful, and even how to be likeable, all of which are very important if they are to enjoy quality lives. This is one of your great challenges. It is of paramount importance. What you need to know in order to be successful is available to you in this book.

CAN I ANTICIPATE HOW MY STUDENTS WILL BEHAVE?

Yes. With effort, you can gain quite a good understanding of how students at various age levels in various segments of society tend to behave individually and in groups. Virtually all conscious behavior, proper or improper, has a motive behind it. Some of those motives are genetically determined and reside within us, some occur and change as part of the maturation process, some are learned, some are triggered by environmental and social situations, some are set off by emotion, and many occur because we become able to make better choices as we develop intellectually. A bit later, we will examine 26 conditions that underlie student misbehavior, but first let's review what is considered typical or "natural" behavior at different levels of development. Keep in mind that these depictions are general and do not always apply.

Behavior in the Primary Grades (Ages 5 to 8)

Have a look at primary-grade children on the playground. They are full of life and very eager to learn. Most of them have loving dispositions. They particularly enjoy stories, music, and rhythmic activities. They have an enormous facility in learning language, which often makes them appear intelligent beyond their years. Children at this age don't like to sit still for long—in fact you can hardly make them do so.

And yet these students, precocious though they seem, have limited capabilities in some regards, which has important implications for teachers. Before the approximate age of 7, most function intellectually at what Swiss psychologist Jean Piaget (shown here) called the *preoperational stage*, where they reason not on the basis of logic but rather on impressions obtained from their surroundings (see Charles, 1974; Piaget, 1951). Piaget found that during the preoperational phase, students are poor at remembering the order of events, understanding rules, explaining cause–effect relationships, comprehending number relationships, and understanding other speakers accurately, including the teacher. Socially, they get along reasonably well with each other, although they often squabble. They tire easily, get fussy, and require frequent rest. They make little distinction between work and play.

An important change occurs in children at around age 7, give or take a year or so. They move into an intellectual stage Piaget called *concrete operations,* where brain development enables them to begin understanding concepts that they interpreted differently only weeks earlier. Importantly, they become able to consider the relationship of parts to whole and to reason in terms of cause and effect. Where previously they reasoned and explained on the basis of appearances or intuition (e.g., "The sun moves because the wind blows it along"), they can now understand number relationships and many concepts in science, such as the cause of day and night.

Socially, they are learning to play well together. By second grade, they are enjoying games such as tag and hide and seek. They like puzzles, riddles, and guessing games. Although able to learn rules for games, they are not so good at following them. They accept adult authority with little question. They tell fabrications routinely but seldom in a malicious way. They are highly imitative of each other. For them, misbehavior is whatever adults don't like, and guilt is understood in terms of getting caught.

By the time they complete the primary grades, students are usually well socialized to understand that raising hands, standing in lines, taking turns, and waiting patiently are expected behaviors. They continue to respond well to affection and personal attention. All through this stage, students enjoy music, art, rhythms, stories, and activities that have to do with plants and animals.

Behavior in the Intermediate Grades (Ages 9 to 11)

As students move into grade 4, they become increasingly able to function independently, although they still want attention and affection from teachers. Holding hands with the teacher replaces hugging. Their interest in animals and the natural world continues strongly.

Intellectually, they continue to use concrete language and images for thinking (as indeed do most of us adults). Teachers need to realize that students cannot yet think by using pure abstractions. For example, they do not conceptualize "minus" numbers per se, such as –4, but can think of four real items being removed from a group.

Socially, these students increasingly want to share each others' company. They like group names and begin to form cliques and clubs. Their individual behavior begins to reflect peer norms. They recognize the need for rules and rule enforcement, both in games and class behavior. They like to play group games. And they are beginning to enjoy competition, provided they win. Losing is a different matter, which they find difficult to accept; it causes many to cry and lose their tempers.

Verbally, these students tend to be highly argumentative. Many are loud and vocally aggressive, yet increasingly they rely on reason and efforts to persuade others. No longer is teacher authority blindly accepted. Students may argue with the teacher, talk back, and be uncooperative.

Ethically, they show a growing awareness of honesty and its importance in relationships. Although most stretch the truth frequently, they see that the more a lie intends to deceive, the worse it is. Conscience is developing along with respect for others. A growing sense of right and wrong is evident.

Behavior in the Middle School Grades (Ages 12 to 14)

At this level, student behavior becomes somewhat more erratic, and teachers require great skill in order to teach well and build supportive relationships. Bodily changes worry, perplex, excite, and dismay these students. New realities associated with sex stir and baffle. Psychological weaning from parents leaves them feeling lost and cut off. They crave adult support, yet the emerging need for independence leads to conflict with adults. These realities often act as serious distractions to school learning.

At the same time, students are becoming increasingly rebellious and disposed to probing the boundaries of rules and customs. Their awe of the teacher has waned, but has been replaced with respect and affection for teachers who show understanding and helpfulness. Intellectually, most of these students have acquired a great new power—the ability to think abstractly. Their minds work as quickly as do those of adults, although they lack adult perspective and wisdom. Students can make use of concepts such as love, hate, honesty, loyalty, negative numbers, force, speed, time, and atomic particles. They have become able to think about thought.

Behavior in the High School Grades (Ages 15 to 18)

Before entering high school, students have developed the capacity for deeper thinking. They now show a proclivity for theorizing. They try to find a cause, a purpose, and a place for everything. They think about the *possible* as much as the *actual* and have acquired a strong concern for right and wrong. Their rational power produces the idealism characteristic of adolescence. Propositional thinking emerges: "If I do so and so, then so and so will result." Interest in people and society in general is growing rapidly.

Lies are now seen as anything intentionally false. Punishment must take into account factors such as intent to break a rule, age of the violator, and previous record of behavior. Many rules and laws are seen as unfair or irrelevant, so breaking them is no longer considered absolutely wrong. Socially, these students can see various groups' points of view, which they like to weigh, clarify, and evaluate against each other. They can't see why everything is not ideal—politics, institutions, human relations, and so forth—which makes them overly critical of the way institutions and people actually function. Students may scathingly reject existing social arrangements and values, but for the most part their personal behavior complies reasonably well with social norms.

As they near the end of high school, students begin to settle down emotionally. They understand themselves better and have reached a truce with their bodies and feelings. They have begun to think about what they hope to do in the future. Some, lamentably, become further alienated from the educational mainstream.

A new relationship with adults also emerges. The love–hate attitude of earlier years fades, while respect for adults grows as students recognize their own interdependence with the community. Teachers can interact with these students as fellow adults, and students see teachers as mentors and role models.

HOW DO STUDENTS' NEEDS AND HABITS AFFECT THEIR BEHAVIOR?

All students have needs that prompt them to behave in certain ways. A **need** is a vague condition within us that strongly and persistently urges us to seek out certain satisfactions. We cannot directly observe a need—that is why psychologists refer to needs as mental constructs, meaning imaginary "somethings" that help us explain motivation and behavior. A desire that is long-lasting, recurrent, and seemingly part of the human psychological makeup is deemed to reflect a "need." A need is a bit different from a "want," which is more societally influenced and transient. When we are unable to satisfy a need, we feel more than disappointed—we feel uneasy, distraught, or incomplete over longer periods of time.

Psychologists generally agree we have inborn **basic needs** for safety, comfort, and positive relations with others. Abraham Maslow (1954) provided the first widely acknowledged model of needs, which he depicted hierarchically. For teachers, the following list of needs is more useful than Maslow's hierarchy because it identifies what students require in order to benefit fully from their educational program. This list is drawn from ideas set forth by Rudolf Dreikurs (1995), William Glasser (1998b), and C. M. Charles (2008), among others:

- *Security.* To feel safe without worry.
- *Association.* To be with and interact with others.
- *Belonging.* To feel a part of things, be valued, have a place in the class.
- *Dignity.* To feel respected and worthwhile.
- *Hope.* To believe that experiences in school and elsewhere are worthwhile and success is possible.
- *Power.* To have some control over and input into events in which one participates.
- *Enjoyment.* To experience pleasurable emotions of anticipation, intrigue, fun, and interest.
- *Competence.* The capability to do many things well, including the expected schoolwork.

Educators can help students meet these basic needs by removing threat from learning activities and social interactions, permitting students to work together, insisting on courteous treatment of others, involving students in planning and making decisions, ensuring that learning activities and personal interactions are satisfying, and making sure students learn important information. When teachers do these things well, student behavior is seldom a serious problem.

Habits also play strong roles in student behavior, but they are different from needs and wants. Habits are patterns of willful behavior, ingrained through practice to the point that we repeat them without having to think. They are quite useful when they help us behave considerately and productively, but harmful when they interfere with our progress or offend others. Thus we hear the expressions "good habits" and "bad habits."

In teaching, we try to help our students establish productive habits, such as automatically sitting down and getting to work, following directions, treating others with consideration, and striving for high quality. Classrooms become efficient and relatively free from disruption when students learn to follow class routines automatically.

What Do Students Need and Want in Their School Experience?

Now let's turn more specifically to what students need and want in their teachers and schools. When students receive these things, they behave better. Although preferences vary somewhat from group to group and change steadily with maturation, virtually all students want the following:

- A sense of safety and importance as a class member.
- A teacher who is friendly, interesting, helpful, and supportive.
- Interesting learning activities in topics of obvious value.
- Camaraderie or enjoyable association with classmates.
- Opportunity for and likelihood of success and accomplishment.
- Acknowledgment for what they do right and help with what they do wrong.

Provide those things and it is quite likely you will be a successful teacher. On the other hand, most students (but not all) dislike the following, which they will avoid if they can:

- Sitting still for long periods of time.
- Keeping quiet for long periods of time.
- Working alone.
- Memorizing facts for tests.
- Completing lengthy reading and writing assignments.
- Doing repetitive work.
- Engaging in competition when they have no chance of winning.

It is suggested that you discuss these matters with your students and explain how you will, as often as possible, provide conditions and activities they appreciate, while you will keep to a minimum those they dislike. Remember, however, that students vary somewhat in preferences. Some students like activities such as working alone and memorizing information. They will tell you if you ask.

HOW DO SOCIOCULTURAL REALITIES INFLUENCE BEHAVIOR?

Today's rapidly changing demographics bring together students from many different economic and cultural groups. Each group displays certain values, outlooks, habits, customs, aspirations, and ways of interacting. Teachers are often criticized for being insensitive to the differences among various groups.

Despite the mistakes teachers might inadvertently make, virtually all genuinely want to serve their students well and equitably. To do so, they need information that helps them understand the traits and mannerisms of students from various backgrounds, especially backgrounds different from their own. Let's take a moment to examine a few of the general differences they encounter.

Values and Associated Behaviors: What Do Schools Emphasize?

The majority of schools and teachers in the Western world reflect values, beliefs, and behaviors that stem from the Judeo-Christian ethic, influenced by a capitalistic outlook, future orientation, and interpersonal equality. Following are examples of such beliefs and behaviors:

- *Time orientation.* Promptness is valued; orientation is toward the future.
- *Planning ahead.* Plans are made ahead of time to serve as guides for action.

- *Relations with others.* A general sense of equality prevails; other people are to be treated with consideration and respect.
- *Personal achievement and competition.* Individuals are urged to aspire to personal achievement; it is considered good to compete and try to rise above the norm.
- *Child-to-adult relations.* Adults are shown respect but are not seen as infallible.
- *Adult-to-child relations.* Children require guidance but are not to be treated subserviently.
- *Opportunity.* Potential advancement in life is available to everyone; one has only to seize the opportunity and follow through.
- *Verbal learning.* Much learning in school is expected to occur verbally through listening, reading, and discussing.
- *Success.* Success in life is seen as performing well, getting a good job, providing a good home, and acquiring a degree of wealth.
- *Personal behavior.* We are all responsible for our own behavior; most people behave ethically; laws and regulations are to be obeyed.

Areas of Conflict: How Do Group Values Differ?

Human behavior and values across all groups are far more similar than different; yet, students from various cultural and economic groups may display certain values and behaviors that are somewhat inconsistent with expectations in school. Sometimes those differences are misunderstood by teachers, and sometimes teacher behavior is misunderstood by students.

For example, some cultural groups do not prize individual achievement and recognition; although they want the group as a whole to do well, they consider it improper for individuals to stand out. Some groups place strong emphasis on traditions from the past. Some see little purpose in working at school activities that do not appear useful or are not inherently interesting. Students in some cultures adopt a subservient manner when interacting with teachers and are made uncomfortable by eye contact. Many do not think it proper to voice opinions that disagree with the teacher. Failure to recognize and adjust to such differences can lead to misunderstandings between teachers and students, making teaching and learning more difficult than anticipated.

Economic Realities: Do They Affect Student Behavior?

Today, large numbers of our students come from economically disadvantaged backgrounds. *Economic disadvantage* is a term used synonymously with *living in poverty.* Students are considered to be **living in poverty** if they are members of households that must spend more than one-third of their disposable income for food adequate to meet the family's nutritional needs. About one-fourth of all students in the United States are judged to fall in that category (Payne, 2001). Karen Pellegrino (2005) has identified poverty as a major factor that limits student success in school. Ruby Payne (2001, 2003) maintains that poor children are much more likely than nonpoor children to suffer developmental delay and to drop out of school early.

What Does Ruby Payne Say About the "Hidden Rules" of Students in Poverty?

Ruby Payne's investigations have led her to conclude that each economic class has its own set of **hidden rules** that help it survive. The hidden rules for schools, teachers, and about half of the school population are concordant with the predominant school values listed previously. But the hidden rules for students from *generational poverty* (meaning long-term poverty) are different. Payne urges teachers to learn those rules because they provide keys to understanding, communicating, and working productively with students.

Payne (2001) says that for people in poverty, the major driving life forces seem to be survival, personal relationships, and entertainment. Students in poverty tend to value relationships more than achievement. It can be disquieting for an individual to acquire too much education because the educated person might leave the community. Conflict is often resolved by fighting, and respect is accorded to those who can defend themselves. School discipline is more about penance and forgiveness than behavior change, and students often save face by laughing when they are disciplined. One's sense of personal value is tied up with the ability to entertain others. Money is to be used and spent, not saved. Destiny and fate are believed to determine most matters; individuals feel they have relatively little control over their lives.

Payne adds that students in poverty often use a casual, informal style of speech that contrasts with the more formal style emphasized in school and business. Teachers should clarify the difference between formal and informal speech and help students learn to use language that is appropriate for given situations. Noise level among people of poverty may tend to be high, with frequent displays of emotion. At home, the television may mix with participatory conversation, in which two or more people talk at the same time. The classroom, in contrast, is expected to be quieter, with speakers taking turns.

How Can I Work More Effectively with Students of Various Societal and Economic Groups?

That's a question most teachers ask. The following is a composite of suggestions from various authorities on working more effectively with students from various backgrounds:

- Learn as much as you can about the **value systems** of students from backgrounds different from your own. Pinpoint what those students consider important, how they relate to each other and to adults, and how they relate to teachers and school in general.
- Become knowledgeable about the hidden rules that affect group and personal behavior.
- Show acceptance of your students, their families, and their lifestyles.
- Show solidarity with students and be eager to help them learn and find success.
- Emphasize the knowledge, skills, and values needed for school success and for a strong personal and cultural identity.

- Communicate your genuine conviction that all students can succeed in school and indicate how you will help them do so.
- Link curriculum content to students' out-of-school experiences.
- Attempt to mentor students, an especially effective tactic for improving motivation and building personal relations.
- Establish standards of class behavior that are sensitive to all cultures while emphasizing responsibility and respect.
- Demonstrate for students the behavior that helps them succeed in school and have them practice that behavior.
- Teach students how to speak and write in a formal manner.
- Keep family members informed about their child's performance and behavior and ask them to work with you for the child's benefit.

Commentary from Anonymous Teacher 1

I teach in a Title 1 school that receives federal assistance for students in low-income families. Several of my students are in generational poverty as described by Ruby Payne. I encounter a number of conditions among my students that Dr. Payne alluded to. There is a good deal of fighting. They do not engage well in class work. They do not structure their sentences as we try to teach in Standard English. Some of them wear tattered clothing, and other students pick on them and make comments about their appearance.

The majority of my students qualify for free or reduced-price lunches. Food is a big issue for them. They often come to school without breakfast. I know that some of them eat bags of chips while walking to school. At recess, it is common to see and hear students asking for snack handouts from their classmates.

In the area where I teach, the proportion of students living in poverty has steadily increased over the past two decades. The faculty at my school discusses this matter often. We are very concerned about it, but see little promise of anything in the near future that will make that condition better for our students.

LET'S EXAMINE *MISBEHAVIOR*: WHAT EXACTLY IS IT?

Misbehavior in school is behavior that violates class rules, demeans others, or is otherwise incompatible with the legal or social norms of the society. Most classroom misbehavior falls into two categories—student unwillingness to work as directed and students' causing unwarranted distractions. Within those two categories we can identify 13 specific kinds of misbehavior that require teacher attention. You will encounter many of them on a daily basis. Some are far more serious than others, yet even the benign ones require attention because they hinder learning. The 13 types, listed generally from less serious to more serious, are:

1. *Inattention.* Daydreaming, doodling, looking out the window, thinking about things irrelevant to the lesson.

2. *Apathy.* A disinclination to participate, sulking, not caring, fearful of trying, not concerned about doing well.
3. *Needless talk.* Chatting during instructional time about things unrelated to the lesson.
4. *Moving about the room.* Getting up and wandering around without permission or congregating in parts of the room.
5. *Annoying others.* Provoking, teasing, picking on others, calling names.
6. *Disrupting.* Shouting out during instruction, talking and laughing inappropriately, using vulgar language, causing "accidents."
7. *Lying.* Falsifying to avoid accepting responsibility or admitting wrongdoing, or to get others in trouble.
8. *Stealing.* Taking things that belong to others.
9. *Cheating.* Making false representations for personal benefit or wrongly taking advantage of others.
10. *Sexual harassment.* Making others uncomfortable through touching, sex-related language, or sexual innuendo.
11. *Aggression and fighting.* Showing hostility toward others, threatening, shoving, pinching, wrestling, hitting, bullying.
12. *Malicious mischief.* Doing intentional damage to school property or the belongings of others.
13. *Defiance of authority.* Talking back to the teacher, ignoring the teacher, or refusing to do as requested.

All of these types of misbehavior have a dampening effect on teaching, learning, personal feelings, and motivation to learn. Many of them occur regularly. Psychologist Fred Jones (1987) reported the frequency of misbehavior in hundreds of classrooms he studied. In the better-behaved classes, one or more of the above misbehaviors occurred every 2 to 3 minutes. In less well-behaved classes, the frequency was more in the order of three or more misbehaviors per minute. You can imagine the amount of time teachers must spend dealing with that amount of misbehavior. More recently, psychiatrist William Glasser (2001) concluded that fewer than half of America's high school students were making any real effort to learn. He found the majority did not take education seriously, rarely paid attention or did the assigned work, and were often disruptive. Many students told him they made little effort in school not because school was too hard, but because school was too boring.

WHAT CAUSES STUDENTS TO MISBEHAVE?

Many conditions promote or "cause" students to misbehave. By addressing those causes, you can significantly reduce inappropriate behavior in your classes. At this point, we will note 26 specific conditions that tend to promote misbehavior in school. You will see that you can take steps proactively to limit, or even eliminate, most of these conditions. For our review, the conditions are grouped in accordance with the locations in which they seem to reside, or from which they seem to emanate.

Causal Conditions That Reside in Individual Students

Ten conditions that often promote misbehavior reside within individual students. Those conditions are: unmet needs, thwarted desires, expediency, urge to transgress, temptation, inappropriate habits, poor behavior choices, avoidance, egocentric personality, and neurological-based behavior. Here we note each of the 10 conditions and indicate how you can address them.

1. *Unmet needs.* Both in and out of the classroom, students continually try to meet strongly felt needs for security, association, belonging, hope, dignity, power, enjoyment, and competence. Everyone, almost without exception, strives to meet these needs. When unsuccessful in doing so, students become unsettled, distracted, and more likely to behave inappropriately.

   Suggestions: Keep these needs in mind, and plan in advance how you will address them. Write them on an index card you keep on your desk to remind yourself they are in play all the time. By observing students and talking with them, you can usually identify needs that are prompting misbehavior and can usually help with them.

2. *Thwarted desires.* When students fail to get something they badly want, they may complain, become destructive, sulk, pout, or act out.

   Suggestions: When appropriate, discuss with students the fact that all of us occasionally get to have things the way we want them, but very often we do not. When students show keen disappointment, compliment them for working hard. Ask them if there is anything you can do to help. Be sympathetic, but don't dwell on the problem. Promote an attitude of "Let's move ahead and keep trying." Do something to draw them back to productive work, such as posing a challenge or creating a mystery for them to solve.

3. *Expediency.* Anticipate that all students will, on occasion, look for shortcuts to make their lives easier or more enjoyable. In doing so, they will break rules and sometimes behave dishonestly.

   Suggestions: Discuss that fact openly, while stressing that the best procedure for all of us is to do things correctly, even when it is inconvenient. That is how we make genuine progress and get others to trust us. Ask students why they sometimes take the easy way, such as reading book summaries or reviews rather than the assigned book, rushing through a writing assignment, or copying the work of others. If they are comfortable enough to answer honestly, they will probably say they do so because they don't like the work, don't see the point in it, or don't want to spend the time it requires. Ask them what would encourage them to give their best effort. Listen to their suggestions and make use of them if you can.

   By the way, expedient behavior is not so evident in classes that students find interesting, but it appears often in classes they find difficult or boring.

4. *Urge to transgress.* Many of us have a natural aversion to rules imposed by others, and we seem to find it a challenge to break them, despite knowing there is a chance we'll get caught or even harm ourselves or others. Students succumb to this urge frequently, especially when class activities are not appealing, and they cheat, take shortcuts, tell lies, break class rules, and annoy others.

Suggestions: Anticipate this urge and plan ways to counter it. When talking with your students about expected behavior, discuss the urge, its effects, and how it can be controlled sensibly. Tie this in with the reasons for rules and their value in keeping us comfortable, equalizing opportunity, and helping us live together harmoniously. If students are old enough, ask if they understand what ethics, ethical conduct, and personal character mean. Ask why they think ethical people are so widely admired.

5. *Temptation.* Students regularly encounter objects, people, situations, and behaviors they find powerfully attractive. This phenomenon is evident in students' taste in music and lyrics, ways of speaking, clothing fashions, lifestyles, and in cutting corners on assignments. Although students know they are sometimes misbehaving when succumbing to these temptations, they nevertheless find them so attractive they often adopt, mimic, acquire, or tolerate them, even when the acts are not condoned by adult society.

   Suggestions: Conduct discussions with your students to analyze temptation and seek to understand why certain objects, styles, and opportunities are so seductive. Help students foresee the undesirable consequences of following disapproved styles and manners. Help them clarify the lines that separate appropriate behavior from inappropriate and urge them to resist involvement in activities likely to do them harm.

6. *Inappropriate habits.* Inappropriate habits are ingrained ways of behaving that transgress established standards and expectations. Jason uses profanity at school. Maria is discourteous and calls others names. Larry shirks his assignments. Some of these habits are learned in school, but most become established outside of school.

   Suggestions: When first discussing desirable behavior in school, raise this topic. Tell your students there are certain requirements for behavior at school, even though those requirements might not prevail outside of school—that there are certain ways we must conduct ourselves and treat and speak with others in school. Be careful not to single out individuals as examples. Identify unacceptable behaviors such as cursing, calling names, and showing disregard for others. If necessary, show students how you expect them to act. When they fail to comply, call it to their attention and ask them if they remember how that particular thing is done in school. Ask them courteously to show you they know.

7. *Poor behavior choices.* The behaviors students use in attempting to meet their needs are sometimes acceptable, sometimes not. In most cases, students choose to behave as they do. For example, Alicia, when seeking attention, pesters others so much they avoid her. Alan, seeking to augment his sense of power, refuses to do what his teacher requests. Assuming those behaviors are under their control, we say that Alicia and Alan are making poor behavior choices.

   Suggestions: Help your class recognize that when they choose to misbehave, they are hindering the likelihood of being successful in school. To help such students, you might address the class as a whole and pose the following questions:

   ■ What are some of the things you have seen students do to [get attention, be acknowledged, get better grades than they deserve, get out of work, become members of certain groups]?

- Does their behavior usually get them what they want?
- What could those students do that would probably bring better and more satisfying results?

8. *Avoidance.* No one likes to face failure, intimidation, ridicule, or other unpleasant situations. One way to escape those things is to avoid activities or places where they might occur, or if that is not possible, simply refuse to participate. But in school, students' reasons for avoidance are not always evident to teachers. Norona, when refusing to participate in a group assignment, seems to show disrespect for the teacher, but her real reason is that she doesn't want to appear inept in front of her peers.

    Suggestions: To help students such as Norona, show your class how to face unpleasant situations and work through them. You might ask them to work in pairs or small groups and together answer questions such as the following:

- Are there things you try to avoid in school, such as people, events, or activities you find frightening or embarrassing?
- Which of those things could best be dealt with through avoidance (e.g., staying away from a clique that is maligning other students)?
- Which of those things cannot be dealt with through avoidance (e.g., giving an oral report in front of the class)?
- What is the worst thing that can happen in class if we make a mistake? Are mistakes valuable? Can they help us learn?
- What could we do as a class to keep others from feeling embarrassed when they make mistakes?
- What might a person do to reduce his or her fear of mistakes or being involved in unpleasant situations?

9. *Egocentric personality.* Students with egocentric personalities focus primarily on themselves, believe they are superior to others, and usually think they do little wrong. Most classes contain one or more students with such personalities.

    Suggestions: To help these students behave more appropriately, ask questions of your entire class such as the following:

- Are the needs and interests of all students important, or do only certain students deserve attention?
- Is one person often entirely right and everyone else entirely wrong?
- Is everyone entitled to an equal opportunity in the class? How should you and I react to a person who always wants to dominate, be first, be right, and quarrel with those who don't agree? (Make sure the proffered suggestions are positive in nature, not negative.)

10. *Neurological-based behavior (NBB).* A few students behave undesirably not through intent or thoughtlessness but because their brains call forth behavior they cannot fully control. In Chapter 11, you will see a discussion of certain behavior diagnoses referred to as "neurological-based behaviors," which include learning disabilities, attention-deficit hyperactivity disorder (ADHD), and a number of other issues. Frequently, students with these diagnoses do not respond reliably to normal discipline tactics. Chapter 11 will explain these conditions and provide information to help you teach students diagnosed with NBB.

Suggestions: Teachers who have students with NBB need help from specialists. That help will usually be provided by the school. But regular classroom teachers can do many things on their own, as will be indicated more comprehensively in Chapter 11. Mel Levine (2003) urges teachers to explain to the class that some people function in such a way that they lose control at times (are "wired up," if you prefer), more often than others do. Other authorities ask teachers to (1) always model the calm, soothing behavior we want students to display and make sure students feel loved and respected as human beings; (2) be careful about making eye contact, which stimulates upper-cortex activity and is often interpreted as a challenge or threat; (3) react to situations calmly (a raised voice tends to make students with NBB raise their voices in return); and (4) provide considerable structure to activities (meaning directions and procedures) because a lack of structure often makes learning difficult for students with NBB.

Conditions That Seem to Reside in Peers and Groups

Two significant causes of misbehavior—*provocation* and *contagious group behavior*—seem to reside in class peers and groups. Here are suggestions for dealing with them.

1. *Provocation.* A great amount of misbehavior results from students' provoking each other through teasing, petty annoyance, put-downs, sarcastic remarks, and aggression or bullying. Heather is trying to study, but Art is bent on teasing her incessantly until she reaches the bursting point. Marty calls Jerry a name and Jerry responds hotly.

   Suggestions: Provocation often produces strong emotions that overwhelm self-control and increase combativeness. Discuss this phenomenon with your class. Ask:

   - Is provoking others or bullying them consistent with the class character we are trying to build or with the kind of person you truly want to be?
   - Can you name some things people say or do that upset you so much you want to retaliate?
   - If you retaliate, what do you think will happen? Will that put an end to the conflict?
   - What are some positive things we can do to stop provocation in the class?

2. *Contagious group behavior.* Students sometimes succumb to peer pressure or get caught up in group emotion and as a result may misbehave in ways they would not consider if by themselves. It is difficult for students to disregard peer pressure, easy to get swept up in group energy and emotion, and easy to justify one's misbehavior as "only what others were doing." Because Kerry and Lee want to look cool to their peers, Kerry defaces school property, and Lee bullies a weaker member of the class. Neither of the boys does those things when alone.

   Suggestions: Discuss this phenomenon with your class. For example, tell the class about some event in which a friend of yours, let's say Sarah, behaved badly just because others were doing so. Indicate that Sarah is now very embarrassed about her behavior and wishes no one knew about it. Ask your students if they know any stories like Sarah's they would be willing to share, without mentioning names the class might recognize. (Tell them they must not mention family matters or members—doing so is a sure way to get parents upset at you.) If they share stories, guide the class in analyzing one or two of them. If they don't contribute a story, have a fictional one ready for their consideration. After hearing or recounting the story, ask questions such as:

- Is the behavior something the person will be proud of later?
- Why do you suppose the person behaved that way (e.g., for fun, comradeship, testing limits, being seen as clever or cool)?
- What do you think the long-term results will be for that person (e.g., an unpleasant story to remember, regret, guilt, getting caught, being found out, worry, disappointing one's family, possible punishment, living with knowing you did the wrong thing)?
- How do you believe the possible benefits compare with the probable dangers?
- If you are caught doing something you are truly ashamed of, is there any way to make amends and save your reputation?
- How can you stay away from, or keep out of, group activities that are unlawful, hurtful to others, or against the rules?

Conditions That Seem to Reside in Instructional Environments

Four conditions that promote misbehavior are associated with instructional environments. They are *physical discomfort, tedium, meaninglessness,* and *lack of stimulation.* All are easily avoided.

1. *Physical discomfort.* Students often become restless when made uncomfortable by inappropriate temperature, poor lighting, or unsuitable seating or workspaces.

   Suggestions: Attend to comfort factors in advance and ask students about them. Make modifications as necessary.
2. *Tedium.* Students begin to fidget after a time when an instructional activity requires continued close attention, especially if the topic is not appealing.

   Suggestions: For such activities, break the work into shorter segments or add something that increases the level of interest.
3. *Meaninglessness.* Students grow restless when required to work at topics they do not comprehend or for which they see no purpose.

   Suggestions: Make sure the topic is meaningful to students—that they understand it and see its relevance and importance in their lives.
4. *Lack of stimulation.* The topic and learning environment provide little that is attractive or otherwise stimulating. Students take no interest in the lesson.

   Suggestions: Select topics and activities in which students have natural interest. When that is not possible, introduce elements students are known to enjoy, such as novelty, mystery, movement, group work, group competition, and role-playing.

Conditions That Seem to Reside in Teachers and Other School Personnel

You won't hear it discussed often, but teachers and other school personnel sometimes misbehave in school and in so doing influence students to misbehave. Here are 10 examples of **teacher misbehavior** (and school personnel behavior) that sometimes promote student misbehavior:

1. *Poor habits.* Personnel in the schools sometimes use inappropriate ways of dealing with students or each other, such as using unseemly language and speaking in a sarcastic or bossy manner.

   Suggestions: Reflect regularly on how you interact with and speak to your students. Self-monitor your behavior and make sure it is as you want it to be. If you see or hear colleagues treating students in an unprofessional manner, and if you believe it is having a harmful effect on the students, consider speaking about the matter in private with your school administrator. Don't identify the colleague or cast blame. Simply describe the situation. The administrator may, or may not, wish to follow up.

2. *Unfamiliarity with better techniques.* Some educators have not had occasion to learn some of the newer, more effective ways of teaching and relating with today's students.

   Suggestions: It is important that you keep yourself informed about topics and activities that are well received by students. Don't be reluctant to approach popular teachers at your school and ask them what seems to work best for them. You can also find innumerable outstanding ideas and suggestions on the Internet and in professional books and journals that might be available at your school.

3. *Presenting poor models of behavior.* At times, all of us behave inconsistently and irresponsibly, especially on days when for whatever reason we are short on self-control. On those occasions, we sometimes treat students discourteously. We can't expect to be perfect, but we must realize that when we treat students poorly—which is to say, in ways we would not want to be treated—we leave a lasting impression that not only damages relationships but also encourages students to imitate our bad behavior.

   Suggestions: Always be the best model you can for your students, who watch you very closely and often pattern their behavior after yours (especially when you misbehave). If you do something that is inappropriate, call attention to it, explain why it was wrong, and apologize if necessary.

4. *Showing little interest in or appreciation for students.* We sometimes fail to show interest in students or appreciation for them as individuals, despite knowing they want our attention. If we disregard them repeatedly, students become hesitant to approach us or may seek our attention in disruptive ways.

   Suggestions: Give each student as much personal attention as possible. Greet them by name, exchange a friendly word, and show you are open to discussing any challenges they might be facing in school. Acknowledge their accomplishments and try to help them feel at ease.

5. *Succumbing to personal frustration.* Some educators get beaten down from continually having to deal with misbehavior, inconsiderate parents, or a surfeit of

meetings and paperwork. The stress may at times make it difficult for them to work with students in a kind, helpful manner.

Suggestions: Educators often try unsuccessfully to force students to comply with expectations. If you use encouragement and enticement rather than force, you will see students become more cooperative, considerate, and willing to make an effort. Also, go out of your way to communicate with caregivers and show appreciation for their children.

6. *Reacting badly to provocation.* Students may do and say things intentionally to get under your skin. You know you should keep your composure, but find yourself becoming upset and saying or doing something that is not professional.

Suggestions: When students try to provoke you, disregard their comments and actions and proceed as if nothing has happened. If you feel the need to respond, only say, "Something is causing violations of our agreement about being considerate of others. I don't like that in our class. I'm wondering what we can do so that won't happen."

7. *Providing ineffective guidance and feedback.* In the absence of guidance and feedback, students sometimes do not understand what is expected of them, how much progress they have made, or how they can improve.

Suggestions: Make sure students understand clearly what they are supposed to do and how they should go about it. During and after assigned activities, tell students what they have done well and what they can do to improve. Emphasize that making mistakes is almost always a part of learning. Ask them for their appraisals of the activity and the efforts they have made.

8. *Using ineffective personal communication.* Some educators are not adept at communicating with students on a personal level. This may result in students' becoming uneasy and reticent about approaching their teachers.

Suggestions: Speak regularly with students in a friendly way. Students want you to know their names and exchange pleasantries with them. Often they want to tell you their views on various matters and would like to know yours. Speaking with students as social equals (i.e., as a friend) validates them personally. You just need to make sure to avoid comments that hurt feelings or dampen enthusiasm. Without overdoing it, say things honestly that increase students' optimism and bolster their confidence.

9. *Failure to plan proactively.* Many educators do not adequately plan their instructional program in advance or anticipate problems that might arise. Then, when unexpected things happen, they are not prepared to respond effectively.

Suggestions: Think carefully about your curriculum and instructional activities and how your students are likely to respond to them. By anticipating difficulties, you can avoid most problems and prepare yourself to deal with whatever might happen. Think through what you will do when people are injured or become suddenly ill, grow defiant, or get into fights. Decide what you will do and say if an unauthorized visitor approaches you, if a parent berates you, if the class groans when you announce an assignment, and so forth. Determine how you can respond decisively to such eventualities, yet maintain your composure and ability to relate positively with others.

10. *Using coercion, threat, and punishment.* Students don't like to be threatened or forced to do anything. If you treat them abrasively, they keep a watchful eye on

you, fearful of being scolded, embarrassed, or demeaned, and will very likely develop negative attitudes toward you and school.

Suggestions: Give up coercion and threat and replace them with considerate helpfulness, personal attention, and good communication. Explain to students how they should behave, demonstrate those behaviors, and have students practice the behaviors. When you see students behave responsibly, thank them for doing so. For older students, express your appreciation privately or to the class as a whole.

AND NOW AT LAST, WHAT IS CLASSROOM DISCIPLINE?

Through most of the history of education, discipline was thought of as what teachers do to make students behave themselves in school. The tactics teachers used in previous times were essentially two in number: (1) Teachers would tell students what to do and what not to do, such as complete work on time and don't bother others; and (2) teachers would punish students who failed to comply with those directives, usually through scolding or detention after school, and sometimes through extra homework or even corporal punishment. In that approach, misbehavior and discipline were treated as crime and punishment. We now call that approach "coercive discipline."

Authorities no longer support coercive discipline, even though, except for corporal punishment, it is still seen in a great many classrooms. You are urged to take a different and more modern approach—one in which you use organization, communication, and personal influence to foster and support proper behavior. In this newer approach based on positive influence, misbehavior is thought of as student mistakes, and discipline is thought of as teacher help. This newer approach to discipline employs three major strategies, each of which involves a number of specific tactics. The three strategies are:

1. First, remove or limit the conditions that tend to promote misbehavior.
2. Second, teach students how to behave appropriately and support their efforts to do so.
3. Third, intervene helpfully when students misbehave by directing them back to proper behavior.

These newer tactics also help students move toward "self-discipline" in which they voluntarily conduct themselves in ways that bring success in school. Again, the process abandons teacher exhortation and replaces it with positive *influence and persuasion.* Teachers speak with students in a kind and helpful manner, teach them how to follow procedures, have them practice kindness and civility, and provide feedback that is helpful, not punitive. Virtually all of today's discipline authorities advocate this approach.

What Are the Three Main Objectives of Discipline Today?

Here are the outcomes we now expect from discipline:

- First and foremost, discipline maintains a safe and civil environment in which high-quality teaching and learning can occur.

- Second, discipline promotes civility and responsible behavior as major character traits in the young.
- Third, discipline helps students develop and use inner motivation and ongoing self-control.

Because you are expected to use discipline for these three purposes, you would probably like to know how to prepare yourself to do so. As luck would have it, a plan for you lies just ahead. It is revealed in the outline that follows. Please read the outline carefully. It shows the three great objectives of discipline and provides a picture of what fine teachers do, as you will come to appreciate. Let your mind play over each of the bulleted headings. Details will be added to the outline as we progress in the book.

1. First objective: To provide a high-quality learning environment for students through:

   - Teacher exercising class leadership by being in charge democratically.
   - Adjusting instruction in accordance with students' traits and needs, which vary with genetics, maturation, and experience.
   - Teaching students to abide by class expectations and procedures.
   - Establishing effective communication with and among students.
   - Providing engaging instruction and interacting helpfully with students.
   - Monitoring student work effectively.
   - Ensuring that you and your students recognize and discharge your specific duties in class.
   - Recognizing and addressing the identifiable causes of misbehavior.
   - Providing ongoing support for proper behavior in class.
   - Redirecting misbehavior humanely and effectively, while preserving personal dignity.

2. Second objective: To pursue and achieve civil, respectful, cooperative behavior by:

   - Practicing and expecting civil and considerate behavior by all members of the class and school community.
   - Eliminating bullying, verbal put-downs, and ethnic and social stereotyping.
   - Fostering a sense of community in the classroom, emphasizing interaction and cooperation.
   - Continually modeling the behavior you expect students to display.

3. Third objective: To promote a sense of personal responsibility among students for learning and behaving acceptably by:

   - Exploring with students the relationships and requirements of freedom, choice, and responsibility.
   - Helping students reflect on how to become the persons they really want to be.
   - Giving students experience, when they are sufficiently mature, with choices, decision making, restitution, and foreseeing and dealing with consequences.

Eight Fundamental Questions in Discipline: How Will They Be Answered?

The eight fundamental questions in discipline follow. Look them over now, just so you know what they are. We have already briefly touched on some of them. You are not expected to answer them yet, but the questions are:

1. What kind of behavior can we expect of students, and what is *classroom misbehavior?*
2. How does misbehavior *damage* teaching and learning?
3. What are the purpose and nature of *classroom discipline?*
4. What does discipline *require of me* legally, professionally, and ethically?
5. What *attitude* toward discipline will serve me best?
6. What are the most effective things I can do, in advance, to *prevent or reduce* misbehavior in my classes?
7. What are the most effective things I can do to *support proper behavior* in my classes?
8. What are the most effective things I can do to *redirect misbehavior* humanely and effectively?

The road ahead will take you into many aspects of these eight questions and how they are answered most effectively. We will look at the questions from various points of view and will examine an abundance of excellent advice from the most respected authorities in discipline.

WHERE ARE WE GOING FROM HERE AND HOW WILL WE GET THERE?

The chapters that follow provide a great deal of the latest and best information on classroom discipline, which you will certainly find enlightening and helpful. But the book's greater purpose is to help you formalize your own personal system of discipline that is carefully attuned to your preferences and to the traits, realities, and needs of the students you teach. The remainder of the book provides guidance and information for accomplishing that task. The effort required for the journey is to be provided by you, the esteemed reader. You will find the journey quite helpful and rather interesting—so the author doth hope and believe.

So that is what you can expect. Of course you don't have to follow the sequence of topics as presented in the text, but under normal circumstances it would be best to do so because the book is designed to take you through four sequential phases of development that lead to high competence in discipline. You may or may not have seen these phases depicted in the preface to this book. The progression is described next.

FOUR PHASES IN YOUR DEVELOPMENT

The phases through which you will be guided are shown in Figure 1.1. The first phase, supported by three chapters, helps you become *conceptually grounded,* meaning you learn quite a number of fundamental things about behavior, misbehavior, discipline, teacher responsibilities, and the concepts, problems, philosophy, and terminology that are prominent in today's system of discipline.

The second phase, supported by three chapters, helps you *get started on the right track* in teaching, with emphasis on organizing discipline, beginning a class, and taking charge in the classroom.

The third phase, supported by five chapters, teaches you how better to *engage your students*, through relating with them personally, obtaining their cooperation, and helping them learn to behave responsibly.

Figure 1.1   Four Sequential Phases in Developing Expertise in Discipline

Phase I: Conceptual Grounding in Discipline
In Which You Encounter and Explore in Some Detail the Nature of Classroom Misbehavior, Teachers' Obligations in Discipline, and the General Premises, Mindset, and Terminology of Modern Classroom Discipline

Chapters in Phase I
Chapter 1 (which we are just now completing) discusses the realities of student behavior and misbehavior, the nature of human behavior at different levels of maturity, the types and causes of misbehavior, the definition and purpose of discipline, and what it means to exert positive influence on students.
Chapter 2 introduces a number of basic terms in discipline and explains schools' and students' mutual obligations, teachers' professional obligations in discipline, and how to go about organizing an effective system of discipline.
Chapter 3 reviews the development of modern discipline and summarizes the contributions and terminology of 20th-century authorities who established the foundations for today's discipline system.

↓

Phase II: Preparing Yourself to Take Charge in the Classroom
In Which You Learn What Is Needed in a Discipline Plan, the First Things You Should Teach, and How You Establish and Maintain Calm, Purposeful Student Behavior

Chapters in Phase II
Chapter 4 reviews Ronald Morrish's views on what you should include in your system of discipline and how you should present your plan to students.
Chapter 5 reviews Harry and Rosemary Wong's suggestions concerning establishing routines and scripting the first minutes and days of a new class.
Chapter 6 explains how Craig Seganti establishes control in classes that are usually thought of as hard to manage.

**Phase III: Activating Motivation and Engaging with Your Students
In Which You Learn How to Release Students' Internal Motivation,
Engage with Them Personally, Involve Them in High-Quality
Learning Experiences, and Manage Atypical Behavior**

Chapters in Phase III
Chapter 7 explains how Marvin Marshall helps students learn to make positive choices and take responsibility for their behavior.
Chapter 8 explains how Fred Jones helps students maintain focus and remain on task.
Chapter 9 explains how William Glasser uses noncoercive choice to promote quality learning and student self-control.
Chapter 10 explains how Spencer Kagan enables teachers and students to work together on the same side rather than at cross purposes.
Chapter 11 describes how Paula Cook promotes success for students with neurological-based behavior.

**Phase IV: Perfecting and Personalizing Your Approach to Discipline
In Which You Bring Everything Together, Strive for Excellence,
and Organize a Discipline Approach That Is Optimized
for You and Your Students**

Chapters in Phase IV
Chapter 12 reviews outstanding authorities' answers to the eight fundamental questions in discipline and then helps you answer those questions in your own words.
Chapter 13 guides you in assessing and improving your capabilities in discipline as you reach for mastery.
Chapter 14 guides you in composing a customized approach to discipline that meets your needs and those of your students.

And the fourth phase, supported by three chapters, helps you organize and perfect your knowledge and skills, thus helping you reach for excellence in discipline. First, it will provide a review of outstanding information pertinent to the eight fundamental questions in discipline. Second, it will take you through a substantial self-assessment that shows your areas of strength and provides remediation for any areas of weakness. And third, it will show you in detail how to design a *personal approach* to discipline that suits both you and your students. In that culminating effort, you will specify exactly what you intend to do to prevent misbehavior, support proper behavior, and redirect misbehavior positively and humanely.

WHAT YOU HAVE LEARNED IN THIS CHAPTER

You have acquired an understanding of the aim and structure of this book and what it will help you do. You have reviewed behavior in general and have an idea of the typical behavior of students at different age levels. You have examined some of the needs, preferences, and habits that prompt students' behavior and you know how to attend to them. You have seen how social and cultural realities influence behavior and what you can do to make schooling more comfortable and productive for all students. And, finally, you have examined the nature, types, and causes of misbehavior you will encounter in teaching, and you have begun to understand how positive influence is used to help students behave responsibly.

Activities

Self-Test: True/False

1. Professional educators agree fairly closely on what constitutes student misbehavior.
2. Any given student will behave somewhat differently over time, as he or she passes through different stages of development.
3. "Needs" and "wants" are synonymous terms that can be used interchangeably when referring to motives that drive student behavior.
4. It was suggested in the chapter that it is fairly useless to discuss needs, wants, interests, and habits when talking with students about their behavior.
5. The status known as "in poverty" is defined in terms of the portion of a family's income needed for food to satisfy its nutritional requirements.
6. It was suggested in the chapter that you should make yourself knowledgeable about the hidden rules that might influence group and personal behavior among your students.
7. "Basic needs" that affect student behavior were depicted as residing in physical conditions that exist in the classroom.
8. One recommended way to make students feel appreciated is for teachers to chat with them individually fairly frequently.
9. According to the author, the first objective of discipline is to use tactics that make it virtually impossible for students to misbehave.
10. It was stressed that the fundamental questions in discipline are five in number.

Self-Test: Multiple Choice

1. Of the following, which type of student misbehavior is considered the most serious?
   (a) inattention
   (b) apathy
   (c) disruption
   (d) aggression
2. Students become able to use cause–effect thinking at the approximate age of
   (a) 5.
   (b) 7.
   (c) 10.
   (d) 12.
3. Behavior seems to be most erratic for students at which age level?
   (a) preschool
   (b) primary grades
   (c) middle school
   (d) secondary school
4. Which of the following usually remains strongest over long periods of time?
   (a) particular need
   (b) particular want
   (c) particular interest
   (d) particular preference
5. What is the approximate percentage of students in the United States said to be "living in poverty"?
   (a) 13%
   (b) 20%
   (c) 25%
   (d) 31%

6. Inappropriate habits are said to reside within
   (a) the learning environment.
   (b) the family structure.
   (c) students.
   (d) poverty.
7. Which of the following is a cause of misbehavior that might stem from the physical environment?
   (a) student need
   (b) physical discomfort
   (c) fear of rejection
   (d) neurological-based behavior
8. Expedient behavior is seldom a problem in classes that are
   (a) demanding.
   (b) interesting.
   (c) teacher-dominated.
   (d) student-dominated.
9. The contention that teachers sometimes "misbehave" in class is
   (a) unfounded.
   (b) a logical nonsequitur.
   (c) an injustice to teachers.
   (d) reasonable and useful.
10. The main purpose of this first phase of your development is for you to become
   (a) conceptually grounded.
   (b) erudite.
   (c) open to possibilities.
   (d) logically minded.

Self-Test: Explain This

1. What is meant by a "psychological need," and how does it differ from an interest or want?
2. What does it mean to say that a condition "causes" misbehavior?

3. If you pinpoint a condition that "causes" misbehavior, what can you do about that condition?
4. What are the major changes in students' intellectual capability between the ages of 5 and 15?
5. Give two examples of how cultural values and economic realities affect behavior.

Additional Suggested Activities

1. Name three ideas in this chapter that you'll give attention to when planning your discipline approach.
2. In pairs or with small groups of colleagues, refer to the values that are typically emphasized in school. Indicate to what extent your own values correspond to those typical of schools. Refer to the general suggestions for working with students from all ethnic and economic groups, then select three of those suggestions that you feel would be most important to your students' success.
3. In pairs or small groups, review the 26 conditions that often promote misbehavior in school. Select five of them you believe are most in need of attention in typical classrooms.
4. Review the section on "conditions that reside in teachers and other school personnel." As a teacher or paraprofessional, have you experienced school personnel who misbehaved in any of those ways? What do you think they could have done to improve their behavior? Share your conclusions with your classmates.

2

Recognizing Your Obligations and Charting the Course Ahead

What Are Your Legal and Professional Obligations, How Do Fine Teachers Communicate with Students, and How Should You Plan for the Future?

WHAT ARE THE SCHOOLS' OBLIGATIONS TO STUDENTS?

In the United States and many other countries, schools by law and common agreement have the obligation to provide the following for students:

- Opportunity for a free or low-cost well-rounded education;
- Curriculum, instruction, and materials that enable students to acquire the knowledge and skills necessary for success in today's world;
- A safe and supportive environment for learning; and
- A corps of well-trained teachers, administrators, and other professional and support staff to assist students in becoming educated.

Almost all schools meet these obligations. Any that do not are usually referred to as poor schools or ineffective schools.

WHAT ARE MY OBLIGATIONS TO STUDENTS?

You have the following obligations to students:

- Display a professional demeanor at all times.
- Maintain a safe, secure, and supportive environment for learning.
- Show sensitivity to and understanding of students' personalities, backgrounds, and needs.
- Help students acquire important knowledge, skills, and attitudes.
- Provide interesting, worthwhile instructional activities.
- Help students learn to behave responsibly and strive for excellence.

Teachers who fail to meet these obligations may be referred to as poor or ineffective teachers. Even when they are ineffective or derelict in their duties, teachers are rarely said to be "misbehaving," but we will use that term when referring to their unprofessional behavior.

WHAT ARE STUDENTS' OBLIGATIONS TO TEACHERS, FELLOW STUDENTS, THE COMMUNITY, AND TAXPAYERS?

Students who attend school incur many important obligations, yet they rarely think of them as such. They usually look upon education as something expected of them or forced on them—something to be endured, rather than enjoyed as one of the greatest opportunities of their lives. Not much is demanded of students—for the most part, they are only asked to make a modest effort to learn and behave properly. When you speak with students about the roles they are expected to fill in class, consider stressing these points:

- Students have the obligation to make a reasonable effort to learn. They fulfill this obligation by attending classes, paying attention, cooperating with the teacher, participating considerately in class activities, and doing the assigned work.
- Students are obliged to refrain from interfering with class work or the progress of others. They must not unnecessarily disrupt the teacher or instructional activities, or interfere with other students' efforts to learn.
- Students are obliged to display acceptable behavior, which includes abiding by class rules, behaving civilly, and showing consideration for others.

When students meet these obligations, their behavior is considered appropriate, and they are almost always successful in school. When students do not meet these obligations, their behavior is considered to be misbehavior or improper behavior, and a great many of those students do poorly in school. You might wish to emphasize this point in your classes.

WHAT DOES DISCIPLINE REQUIRE OF ME LEGALLY?

Certain teacher behavior is required by law, and certain teacher behavior is prohibited by law. For example, you are legally required to exercise due diligence in overseeing students under your care. And you are prohibited by law from dating students below the age of consent. Further, you must not engage in illegal activities or immoral activities that might impinge on your teaching. (The meaning of "immoral activities" is not entirely clear in the law. Check your school district handbook and follow its guidelines.*)

The basic legal requirements you must be sure to observe relate to due diligence, negligence, breach of duty, and expectations associated with *in loco parentis*, a term that will be explained momentarily:

You Must Exercise Due Diligence. **Due diligence** refers to paying close and reasonable attention to students who are under your supervision. You and other school personnel must oversee students at school and take reasonable care to protect them from harm (Goorian & Brown, 2002). Many teachers are unaware

*Note: The author of this book is not a lawyer, and what you read in these pages is not to be considered legal advice. It is the author's interpretation of the general sense of the law.

they are required by law to keep a diligent eye on students. Please remember that your mere presence around students is not sufficient. You must watch over them carefully. You must follow established school policies and conduct yourself as would a reasonable and prudent professional in similar circumstances.

You Must Avoid Negligence and Breach of Duty. **Negligence** is the failure to maintain careful watch over students under your supervision. It is considered to be a serious **breach of duty**, meaning a serious failure to comply with one of your legal obligations at school. If a student is injured emotionally or physically at school and the teacher on supervisory duty did not exercise due diligence, the teacher and school may be sued for negligence (Drye, 2000). You can protect yourself against charges of negligence and breach of duty by adhering to the following guidelines:

- Perform your assigned duties ethically and conscientiously as directed by school policy, even when those duties might seem boring or unnecessary.
- Carefully oversee your students. Be attentive in monitoring their behavior. Do not leave them unattended in your classroom, shop, or instructional area.
- For activities that involve physical risk, provide thorough precautions and safety instructions before you have students undertake the activities.
- Be vigilant for signs that students might be inclined to harm themselves. Pay attention to what they do, say, and write. Be alert to changes in behavior. If you have concerns, speak with your administrator or school counselor.
- Be alert to any signs that a student is being bullied or otherwise abused. Follow your school guidelines to familiarize yourself with signs of abuse and how you should respond.
- Exercise special caution regarding physical contact with students. Don't allow yourself to be alone in the classroom with a student unless you are in plain sight of others. Refrain from touching students, other than on the hands or arms or with pats to the shoulders or head (Note: Pats to the head are considered offensive in some cultures). If students frustrate or anger you, never strike them or grab any part of their bodies, as it is very difficult to justify physical contact motivated by anger. Also make sure you never throw pencils, pens, erasers, books, desks, or chairs, no matter how strongly you are provoked.

You Must Act In Loco Parentis. **In loco parentis** is not an allusion to crazy parents. It is a legal term that means "in place of parents." It requires you to exercise the same duty at school as do parents at home in overseeing children's safety and security. In actual practice, you should watch over students even more carefully than their caregivers sometimes do.

The doctrine of *in loco parentis* is not limited to watching over students. It also gives you and other school officials *authority over students* in matters of academics and discipline. It permits you to take many actions that a reasonable parent would take under similar circumstances. (Physical or verbal abuse is not allowed, even though parents might use it on their children.)

WHAT ARE MY PROFESSIONAL OBLIGATIONS?

For teachers, the term **professionalism** refers to displaying the fairest, most considerate, and most ethical ways of fulfilling the duties of the teaching position. Where discipline is concerned, your primary professional obligation is to establish and maintain a safe and productive learning environment for your students. That means keeping the environment physically and emotionally safe, keeping students on task, fostering positive relationships among members of the class, and minimizing behavior that interferes with your teaching or your students' learning. Take the following suggestions seriously, and make absolutely sure you abide by them:

Regarding Professional and Ethical Behavior. You must always conduct yourself ethically. You must treat students and colleagues fairly, honestly, kindly, and supportively. You must be honest with them, but at the same time avoid, when possible, saying or doing things that hurt their feelings or stifle their desire to learn or cooperate.

Regarding Effort. You must give your genuine best effort to the profession. Your obligation is to do all you reasonably can to help students profit from their educational experience and find satisfaction in doing so. You should give that same effort to relations with administrators, colleagues, and students' caregivers.

Regarding Teaching. You must teach in a manner that is conducive to success for every one of your students. You must give careful attention to selecting appropriate subject matter, providing interesting and worthwhile learning activities, relating effectively and helpfully with students, adjusting instruction to students' abilities and personalities, and insisting on considerate, humane treatment by and for everyone in the class.

Regarding Helpfulness. Always do what you can to help students, collectively and individually. Help them succeed academically. Help them relate well with others. Help them find satisfaction in school and learning. As Haim Ginott (1971) said so many years ago, always ask yourself what you can do, at a given moment, to be most helpful to your students. He referred to continual helpfulness as "teachers' hidden asset."

Regarding Respect. Show genuine respect for your students. Treat all of them as your social equals, worthy of your time and attention. Speak with each of them in a kindly manner as often as you can. Learn their names quickly and remember significant things about them. Show genuine approbation for effort and work done well (but skip the insincere or undeserved praise). Spread your attention around evenly. Do not attack students' dignity or disparage them in any way. As best you can, always treat them as you would like to be treated in similar circumstances.

Regarding Cooperation. Help your students understand that you and they must accept each other and work together in order to achieve expectations in a satisfying manner. Emphasize that you have a plan that will help them learn and enjoy themselves. Reassure them you will be considerate of their desires and feelings. Sincerely invite them to cooperate with you and each other, and give them some responsibility in making the class enjoyable and productive. Make sure they feel part of the process.

Regarding Communication. Students need to know clearly what is expected of them. Be helpful and encouraging but don't preach or moralize. Don't grill students about improper behavior or otherwise put them on the defensive. When they speak, listen attentively and try to understand their points of view. When you reply to them, do not criticize their points of view. If necessary, simply say your comments are intended to help them be more successful in school.

Regarding Your Charisma. Charisma is a quality of attractiveness that draws attention and makes others want to be in your presence and interact with you. You acquire charisma by making yourself personally interesting and by being upbeat and pleasant, with a touch of wit (don't try to be overly witty—just a little works best). Occasionally share tidbits about your interests, experiences, and talents. Don't act silly. Don't use sarcasm, even when you think it is very funny. It is too easily misinterpreted. In short, smile, be helpful, and treat students considerately.

WHO ESTABLISHES PROFESSIONAL AND ETHICAL EXPECTATIONS?

Professional expectations reflect agreements that have been established over time within various professions. They are made specific by groups that wish to promote and maintain high standards of conduct. Over the years, various individuals, groups, and agencies have worked to codify the professional conduct expected of educators. The most widely acknowledged of those efforts was set forth in 1975 by the National Education Association (NEA). Those standards are still in place. Summarized here, they, in part, stipulate that the educator: Should honestly represent his or her professional qualifications, should use discretion when making statements about fellow educators, should take care in accepting gifts, should transparently report students' progress, and should help students maintain dignity. See www.nea.org for a complete listing of the educators' Code of Ethics.

In addition to the NEA stipulations, it is generally agreed that, as a teaching professional, you should abide by the following:

- Dress professionally, as an adult in a professional situation.
- Use appropriate language for the educational setting, with correct speech patterns and complete avoidance of obscenities.
- Be attentive to others and treat them with respect and courtesy.

Today, much attention is also given to professional teacher competencies as articulated by the Interstate New Teacher Assessment and Support Consortium, called InTASC (2011), which has formalized 10 standards that pertain to teaching in general. The standards are grouped into four categories: (1) The Learner and Learning; (2) Content; (3) Instructional Practice, and

(4) Professional Responsibility. Here are the InTASC standards, presented with permission. (You will find that this book gives considerable attention to categories 1, 3, and 4.)

The Learner and Learning

Standard #1: Learner Development. The teacher understands how learners grow and develop, recognizing that patterns of learning and development vary individually within and across the cognitive, linguistic, social, emotional, and physical areas, and designs and implements developmentally appropriate and challenging learning experiences.

Standard #2: Learning Differences. The teacher uses understanding of individual differences and diverse cultures and communities to ensure inclusive learning environments that enable each learner to meet high standards.

Standard #3: Learning Environments. The teacher works with others to create environments that support individual and collaborative learning, and that encourage positive social interaction, active engagement in learning, and self motivation.

Content

Standard #4: Content Knowledge. The teacher understands the central concepts, tools of inquiry, and structures of the discipline(s) he or she teaches and creates learning experiences that make the discipline accessible and meaningful for learners to assure mastery of the content.

Standard #5: Application of Content. The teacher understands how to connect concepts and use differing perspectives to engage learners in critical thinking, creativity, and collaborative problem solving related to authentic local and global issues.

Instructional Practice

Standard #6: Assessment. The teacher understands and uses multiple methods of assessment to engage learners in their own growth, to monitor learner progress, and to guide the teacher's and learner's decision making.

Standard #7: Planning for Instruction. The teacher plans instruction that supports every student in meeting rigorous learning goals by drawing upon knowledge of content areas, curriculum, cross-disciplinary skills, and pedagogy, as well as knowledge of learners and the community context.

Standard #8: Instructional Strategies. The teacher understands and uses a variety of instructional strategies to encourage learners to develop deep understanding of content areas and their connections, and to build skills to apply knowledge in meaningful ways.

Professional Responsibility

Standard #9: Professional Learning and Ethical Practice. The teacher engages in ongoing professional learning and uses evidence to continually evaluate his/her practice, particularly the effects of his/her choices and actions on others (learners, families, other professionals, and the community), and adapts practice to meet the needs of each learner.

Standard #10: Leadership and Collaboration. The teacher seeks appropriate leadership roles and opportunities to take responsibility for student learning, to collaborate with learners, families, colleagues, other school professionals, and community members to ensure learner growth, and to advance the profession.

For each of the standards presented above, InTASC provides recommendations concerning the essential knowledge teachers should possess and the related performances that characterize highly effective teaching. To see a full presentation of the InTASC recommendations complete with many examples, consult http://www.ccsso.org/Resources/Publications/InTASC_Model_Core_Teaching_Standards_A_Resource_for_State_Dialogue_(April_2011).html.

The Interesting Case of Miss Gusperson

Miss Gusperson was one of the most popular teachers, if not *the* most popular teacher, on the faculty of Clines Middle School. Her elective classes were always filled to overflowing and students gravitated to her wherever she went on campus. They called her "Miss Gus," and she could often be seen "high-fiving" students and pretending to dance with them. On most days, she invited at least five of her favorite students to have lunch with her in her classroom.

Her usual attire was a dark sweatshirt, knee-length pants, and tennis shoes. She was conversant with students' slang expressions and used them liberally when interacting with students. She usually made time to talk with students about their personal and social concerns, and often used class time for doing so.

Despite her popularity with students—or perhaps because of it—she was often the object of criticism. A few fellow teachers considered her to be too chummy with students. More than a few parents commented about her somewhat slovenly attire and grooming, and her principal, Mr. Clarke, was uneasy about her open reluctance to participate in groups working to update the school curriculum.

In view of what you have read so far about professionalism, what is your overall appraisal of Miss Gusperson's conduct at school? What do you consider laudatory? Might you have any concerns about her conduct? What changes in behavior, if any, do you think she should make?

ARE YOU READY TO CAPTURE THIS CHANGE IN THE WIND?

A change is occurring in discipline. Educators are now accepting that it is very difficult to promote desirable behavior in today's students by using criticism, admonishment, or punishment. They are realizing they have a better chance of getting the results they want by using "influence tactics" that are positive and helpful. Such tactics attract students, encourage cooperation, and make learning more enjoyable. Some of the tactics activate students' internal inclination to do what they know is right. You will encounter numbers of such tactics as you proceed through this book.

Learning about these newer approaches is of no value unless you understand and master their application. You must make an effort to grasp the ideas, understand their purpose, and become comfortable with them. When possible, discuss the approaches with others and practice applying them in realistic situations. You will find guidance for doing these things in the activities at the end of chapters in this book.

The tactics you will be learning also help students move toward "self-discipline," in which they voluntarily conduct themselves in ways that bring success in school. Teachers exert positive influence by demonstrating the behavior they expect, speaking with students in a kindly and helpful manner, teaching students how to follow procedures, having students practice kindness and civility, and providing feedback that is helpful, not punitive.

INTRODUCING SOME NEW TERMS: WHAT DO THEY MEAN?

As we proceed, you will encounter a number of concepts and terms that are used in the conversation about discipline. You saw some of them in Chapter 1, including: **classroom discipline, behavior, misbehavior, appropriate behavior, limits,** and **positive influence**. Whenever you see a new term in bold type, that means it is listed and defined in the glossary near the end of the book.

Classroom discipline refers to teachers' efforts to establish and maintain four conditions of fundamental importance in all classrooms:

1. Teachers are allowed to teach in a professional manner without being disrupted.
2. Students are allowed to learn as intended without being hindered by others.
3. Students learn how to cooperate, work together, and get along with each other.
4. Teachers and students experience satisfaction and pleasure in their school experiences.

Discuss these four conditions with your students. They help students see the difference between appropriate behavior (which helps them succeed) and inappropriate behavior (which hinders their progress). It is your duty to make those things clear to students.

How do you do so? In former times, teachers told students they were to "act like civilized human beings" or "behave like ladies and gentlemen." Laudable as those suggestions sound, you must be more specific about your expectations. Students need to see, understand, and practice various behaviors that will help them be successful, such as:

Raise your hand before speaking.

Begin work immediately when you enter the classroom.

Treat others as you would like them to treat you.

Don't interrupt or disrupt.

Anticipate that you will have to teach students how to comply with such expectations, through explanation, demonstration, and practice.

In addition to clarifying expectations, you need to have in mind several helpful comments or questions to use when students fail to display acceptable behavior. Those comments and questions *do not scold or criticize*, but instead call on students to reflect and make choices. Here are examples of questions you might ask, using a pleasant facial expression and neutral tone of voice:

That is against our rules. Would you do it again, please, correctly this time?

Is that what you intended to do (or say)?

Let's remember to give everyone a chance to speak.

Which of our class expectations does that violate?

Is that in keeping with the kind of person you truly want to be?

How would your parents or caregiver want you to conduct yourself in this situation?

As we move ahead, we will examine many such ways of responding to misbehavior. None of them scolds the student.

Behavior is the totality of one's physical and mental activities. Although it includes everything we do, in classroom discipline, we are only concerned about actions over which students and teachers have *voluntary control*. We will be working toward influencing students to *choose* to behave in ways that benefit themselves and the class.

Misbehavior (also called **disruptive behavior** and **inappropriate behavior**) refers to actions that disrupt teaching, interfere with learning, demean others, or otherwise violate the moral codes of society. Make sure students understand the meaning of misbehavior by using examples to which they can relate. (And let's recognize that students are not the only ones who misbehave in school. As we noted earlier, school personnel, including teachers, also misbehave at times.)

Appropriate behavior (also called **acceptable behavior** or **responsible behavior**) refers to student behavior that is consistent with class expectations and does not interfere with learning, demean others, or violate the moral codes of society.

Limits are the imaginary boundaries that separate acceptable behavior from misbehavior. Those boundaries are generally established by cultural traditions and are made explicit by teachers. In actual classrooms they vary somewhat from teacher to teacher. To be fair to your students, you should make very clear just where your limits are set—that is, where the lines are that separate acceptable behavior from misbehavior.

Positive influence is what we do, noncoercively, to invite or entice students to conduct themselves in accordance with class expectations. It is exerted through various acts and comments, positive in nature, that open up possibilities and provide helpful assistance rather than negative criticism. Positivity is important because it minimizes student resistance while supporting appropriate actions. Better yet, it often activates students' inner motivation to do what is proper.

WHAT PROFESSIONAL COMMUNICATION SKILLS SHOULD TEACHERS DISPLAY?

In discipline—indeed in all of teaching—the ability to communicate effectively is paramount. It always comes into play when we want students or others to feel welcome, be receptive to us, take in new information and make sense of it, follow directions, or stop behaving in a counterproductive manner. Both verbal communication and nonverbal communication play key roles. Our effectiveness depends on *what* we say or do, *how* we say or do it, how we *look* when saying or doing it, and how we *respond* to what the other person says or does. Let's see what some of the great authorities have said about these aspects of teacher communication.

What Did Haim Ginott Say About Congruent Communication?

Haim Ginott (1972) was the first authority to focus heavily on improving the effectiveness of communication between teachers and students. He identified *congruency* as the most important aspect of communication. He used the term **congruent communication** to mean communication that is harmonious with students' feelings about situations and themselves. For example, when third-grade Johnny disrupts your lesson by riding the classroom broom as his pony, Ginott would have you say,

■ "Johnny, the broom belongs in the closet, please."

Ginott also urged teachers to use **sane messages** when speaking with students. By sane messages he meant messages that address *situations* rather than students' character or past behavior. Thus, with Johnny and the broom horse, he would *not* want teachers to say, "This is the fourth time today you've disobeyed our rule."

Ginott emphasized that teachers *at their best*, using congruent communication, do not preach, moralize, impose guilt, or demand promises. Instead, they confer dignity on their students by respectfully treating them as capable of making good decisions. For example:

■ "Johnny, could I ask you to help by getting the broom back into the closet, please?"

In contrast, teachers *at their worst* label students, belittle them, and denigrate their character:

■ "Johnny, you are disturbing the class again. I've had about enough of your poor manners."

Ginott added that effective teachers invite cooperation from their students. They do so, when a problem occurs, by describing the situation and what needs to be done. Further, they use **laconic language**—short and to the point—when responding to or redirecting student misbehavior. "Johnny, the broom belongs in the closet. Thanks." They do not dictate to students or boss them around—acts that sometimes demean students and provoke resistance. Ginott also said teachers should feel free to express their concerns, even anger, but when doing so should use **I-messages** rather than **you-messages**.

■ Using an I-message, the teacher might say "I'm troubled about the disruption."
■ Using a you-message, the teacher might say "Johnny, you are being very rude."

You can see that the I-message is less offensive to the student, leaving him or her more open to suggestions you might make.

How would Ginott have us correct a student's misbehavior? He says we should simply teach the student how to behave appropriately. That might require reteaching the student two or three times. Even though the process might take time, it is much better than causing the student to react negatively or hostilely.

One more thing: Ginott especially urged teachers to refrain from asking *why* **questions** when discussing behavior—for example, "Why did you get that broom out again?" He said such questions almost always make students feel guilty and put them on the defensive. Instead of asking *why* questions, simply ask the student to take the appropriate action.

What Did Stephen Covey Say About Frames of Reference?

Stephen Covey (2004) says one of the most important things he ever learned about communication was that in order to communicate well, you have to understand your listener's **frame of reference** as well as your own. The listener's frame of reference, he says, is often different from yours.

For teachers, that means being perceptive of students' deeper hopes, fears, realities, and difficulties. When you understand those things, you adjust what you wish to communicate so it aligns with the student's child or adolescent frame of reference, rather than your adult or teacher frame of reference. What the student sees as reality often differs substantially from your perception of reality, and matters you consider important may be trivial in students' view. Covey suggests that to work well with students, you need to know not just their thoughts but what those thoughts mean in their personal existence.

Earlier, Covey wrote that highly successful people attempt to understand their listeners *before* they try to make listeners understand them. As he put it: "If I were to summarize in one sentence the single most important principle I have learned in the field of interpersonal relations, it would be this: *Seek first to understand, then to be understood*. This principle is the key to effective interpersonal communication" (Covey, 1989, p. 237).

Covey uses the term *empathic listening* to refer to attempting to read and understand the emotions of others. He acknowledges that empathic listening takes time, but not nearly as much time as does having to back up and correct misunderstandings and unexpressed and unresolved problems. Students want to be understood, and you influence them much more strongly when you understand them.

What Did William Glasser Say About Seven Connecting Habits?

Renowned psychiatrist and educational authority William Glasser (2001) put great emphasis on communication between teachers and students. He identified **seven deadly habits** that inhibit teachers' ability to establish optimal relationships with students. The deadly habits are *criticizing, blaming, complaining, nagging, threatening, punishing,* and *rewarding students to control them*. He said that if teachers are to establish and maintain good relationships with students and gain their willing cooperation, they must eliminate these deadly habits.

Glasser contends that as teachers stop using the seven deadly habits, their relations with students will begin to improve. The improvement continues further when teachers replace the deadly habits with **seven connecting habits**, which Glasser identifies as *caring, listening, supporting, contributing, encouraging, trusting,* and *befriending*. Glasser believes—and the success of his quality schools supports his conviction—that all students who come to school can do competent work. In order to ensure acceptable competence, teachers must connect strongly with their students. This means you use the seven connecting habits and *give up* trying to use external controls to make students behave.

Glasser makes his point by describing how we relate to friends (and he does indeed urge teachers to befriend their students). He notes that we do not criticize, blame, or speak harshly to our friends. Rather, we use connecting habits when relating with them.

Please take a moment at this point to do the following, preferably with a partner:

> **?** For each of the following, think of a specific example in a realistic situation. Then indicate what you might say instead, using a connecting habit.
>
> Give an example of <u>criticizing</u> . . . what might you say instead?
>
> Give an example of <u>blaming</u> . . . what might you say instead?
>
> Give an example of <u>complaining</u> . . . what might you say instead?
>
> Give an example of <u>nagging</u> . . . what might you say instead?
>
> Give an example of <u>threatening</u> . . . what might you say instead?
>
> Give an example of <u>punishing</u> . . . what might you say instead?
>
> Give an example of <u>rewarding students to control them</u> . . . what might you do instead?

What Did Fred Jones Say About Nonverbal Communication?

Fred Jones (2007), a widely followed psychologist and expert in teaching and discipline, believes nonverbal communication—which he refers to as **body language**—is even more effective than verbal statements in promoting good behavior in the classroom. He puts special emphasis on eye contact, physical proximity, body carriage, and facial expressions, as follows:

Eye Contact. Suppose Miss Remy is explaining the process of multiplying fractions. She sees Jacobo has stopped paying attention. She pauses. The sudden quiet causes Jacobo to look at Miss Remy and discover that she is looking directly at his eyes. He straightens up and waits attentively. Jones says few physical acts are more effective than eye contact for conveying the impression of being in control. He adds that turning and pointing the eyes and the feet toward students who disengage or disrupt shows teacher commitment to discipline.

Physical Proximity. Miss Remy has finished her demonstration and has directed students to complete some exercises on their own. After a time, she sees from the back of the room that Jacobo has stopped working and has begun talking to Jerry. She moves toward him. When Jacobo senses her presence, he immediately gets back to work, without Miss Remy having to say anything. Jones emphasizes that teachers who use physical proximity rarely need to say anything to the offending students to get them to behave.

Body Carriage. Jones also concluded that posture and body carriage are effective in communicating authority. Good posture and confident carriage suggest strong leadership, whereas a drooping posture and lethargic movements suggest resignation or fearfulness. Students read body language and are able to tell whether the teacher is feeling in charge or is tired, disinterested, or intimidated. Effective teachers, even when tired or troubled, know to stand tall and move assertively.

Facial Expressions. Teachers' facial expressions communicate a great deal. They can show enthusiasm, seriousness, enjoyment, and appreciation, all of which encourage good behavior; or they can reveal boredom, annoyance, and resignation, which may prompt lethargy or misbehavior among students. Facial expressions such as winks and smiles demonstrate a sense of humor and personal connection, traits students appreciate in teachers.

Commentary from Anonymous Teacher 1

I am an elementary teacher with 18 years of experience in grades 2, 3, and 5. I prepared for teaching at a large reputable university and later earned a master's degree there.

I was asked if, during my training and graduate studies, I had heard of, or had experience with, any of the teachings of Ginott, Covey, Glasser, or Jones. I'm not absolutely certain, but I don't remember ever hearing or reading about Ginott, Covey, or Glasser, although I realize now they are widely recognized. A few years ago, I attended an inservice workshop directed by Dr. Jones. He influenced me a great deal and I now regularly use his suggestions on eye contact, physical proximity, and facial expressions to help my students stay on task and conduct themselves properly. For me, Jones's nonverbal tactics work about 90% of the time.

One thing struck me as I read Dr. Ginott's views on using *why* questions to correct misbehavior. I realized that throughout my career I have been doing just what he says not to do. I had a boy, Jason, who always turned in sloppy papers and another, Ahmed, who talked all the time without permission during seat work. I must have asked Jason a dozen times why he couldn't turn in neater work, and Ahmed dozens of times why he was talking. Jason always looked away and answered with a shoulder shrug. As for Ahmed, he would answer by saying he didn't know why he was talking. Neither my *why* questions nor my mild reprimands seemed to improve things at all. Yet I kept on nagging. I actually believed that by asking "why?" I could cause them to think about their behavior and decide to improve it. It never did work, so I'll have to say I fell short in those cases.

WHAT ADDITIONAL THINGS MIGHT I DO TO EXERT POSITIVE INFLUENCE?

There are many suggestions for exerting positive influence on students in a systematic way. For now, please open your mind to maintaining a positive attitude, attending to the "neglected 50%" in teaching, avoiding the pitfall of arguing with students, and using positive influence to replace criticism. Here we briefly examine those four topics.

Establish and Maintain a Positive Attitude

You will probably love dealing with students who are nice to you, but you may find it distasteful and troubling to deal with those who misbehave. But doing so is necessary, and you need to do it well. Following are some suggestions.

First, look at your misbehaving students. Allow your mind to sweep across them and see them as individual human beings, many of them striving for recognition from you and from their classmates, perhaps showing off or pestering others or just carrying on in preference to being involved in the lesson.

Second, think this thought and do your best to truly mean it (paraphrased from an unknown source): *I am grateful to each and every one of my students for being here, for trusting themselves to my care, and for enabling me to have this important job. I appreciate the challenge of helping them. I appreciate the opportunity to assist them in becoming better persons. I appreciate their testing and strengthening my capabilities. Because I am truly grateful for this opportunity, I will do the very best for them I can.*

Third, if you feel like it, you might tell your students what has just gone through your mind. It can't hurt, and it will probably help if you only do it once in a great while. You might add that you will support them in school and would like for them to support you in return.

Attend to the "Neglected 50%" in Teaching

You should always give your best effort on behalf of your students, but today many beginning (and experienced) teachers do not understand fully how to do so. Let's look at this matter for a moment. Suppose you take the most brilliant scholar in a given field and put her in charge of teaching your students who have virtually no interest in the subject she is to teach. What does that scholar need to do in order to teach the students well? Which of these three things do you think should be at the top of her list?

1. Emphasize her strong knowledge of the subject matter.
2. Organize a structure that will help students understand the subject matter, see how its main points are interconnected, and understand what it is good for.
3. Influence students by using personal charisma, intriguing questions, interesting demonstrations, and personal attention.

All three of those aspects—knowledge, structure, and influence—are essential for successful teaching. But of the three aspects, the one for which teachers usually receive the *least* preparation is the last of the three. Occasionally a teacher knows intuitively how to approach and work with students—teachers with that ability are often called "natural teachers." But most beginning teachers have focused mostly on learning their subject matter and learning how to organize it for student learning. Unfortunately, they have not been taught very much about how to interact with students and influence them in a positive manner.

That aspect of teaching is what is here called the **neglected 50%** in teaching. At this point in your career you are knowledgeable in subject matter. You know how to organize material so students can access it easily. But you may not have had much instruction in how to influence students to cooperate and make an effort—hence the term the *neglected 50%*. To be a highly effective teacher, you must be able to engage your students, rally them to your side, and get them to work in tandem with you. That's what makes school satisfying for everyone.

Avoid the Pitfall of Arguing with Students

It is self-defeating to argue with students, or anyone else for that matter. It is worse than a waste of time, because telling them (or anyone) they are wrong doesn't change their minds. It often makes them even more resistant to your point of view. They will usually clam up or get defensive or angry, and after a time so will you. Remember this adage:

> *People convinced against their will*
> *Are of the same opinion still.*

Dale Carnegie included that saying in his marvelous book *How to Win Friends and Influence People* (1981 revision), in which he pointed to the pitfalls of arguing. He said he had listened to, participated in, and analyzed thousands of arguments and had concluded that arguing was invariably detrimental to your cause. You should avoid it, he said, as you would avoid rattlesnakes. Why? Because you can't win an argument. It is impossible. If you make the weaker case, you lose. If you make the stronger case, you also lose, because you have made the other person feel inferior and have wounded his or her pride. Wounded pride does not seek to cooperate.

Carnegie says that when you disagree with another person but need to discuss a situation, here's what to do: Control your temper, listen, look for areas of agreement, and promise to think carefully about what the other person has said. He further advises that when you express your view, try saying, "I may be wrong. I often am. Let's see if we can examine the facts together." Never tell the other person he or she is wrong. If it turns out you are wrong, admit it quickly and sincerely.

Replace Criticism with Positive Influence

Let's suppose you are teaching a lesson and come face to face with the moment of truth in discipline: A student, or group of students, has misbehaved—perhaps offended you personally. You feel you can't overlook this behavior; you feel you must respond. What do you do?

Here is a suggestion: At that point in time, hesitate (with a thoughtful expression on your face) just long enough to hold in check your natural reaction to find fault, criticize, admonish, or lash back. Those reactions won't accomplish anything positive, nor will they ever convince the student he or she was wrong. They may well make the student shut up or answer back, but that student will never thank you for the correction. She will not consider that she might be wrong. Or he will think you are browbeating him. Students who become embarrassed or resentful or angry are far more inclined to withdraw or subvert your efforts than to cooperate.

Instead of scolding or criticizing, select a response that does not threaten or demean the student's sense of self. Your actions or comments should lead the offender back to positive behavior, with no damage to the fragile ego. How, exactly, do you do so? Following are two suggestions.

First, if the misbehavior is relatively benign, just pause a moment and look at the offenders, making eye contact if you can. If the misbehavior seems to stop, continue on with your lesson in a smooth flow.

Second, if the misbehavior continues or is repeated, follow the suggestion of either Marvin Marshall or Diane Gossen. Marshall (2001/2007), whose work you will encounter later, might ask the misbehaving student,

- "At what level is that behavior?" He would have taught students the characteristics of four different levels of behavior. Merely asking the student to identify the level of his or her behavior is not very threatening. By honestly categorizing the level of behavior, the student is influenced to return to an acceptable level.

Or Gossen (2004), an authority on restitution theory, might ask the offending student,

- "Is that behavior in keeping with the kind of person you want to be?" If the student answers "yes," ask him or her to stay for a moment after class to speak with you (at which time you might say, "If that is truly how you want to be, we need to do some thinking. It is simply not acceptable for anyone in the class to interfere with the lesson and other students' learning"). If the student says it is not how he or she wants to be, Gossen would ask, "Then, what could you do that would be?"

Such questions do not criticize the student or ask students to criticize themselves. Remember: criticism almost never works. Who among us seeks it? Or appreciates it? Although we may enjoy criticizing others, we hate being on the receiving end.

Then what do we like to receive from others? How do we like to be made to feel? In five minutes, you could make a list that would fill the next two pages, but one thing stands out above all the others. It is this:

We want to feel appreciated and important. ■

Simple as that. If you want to draw students to you, if you want them to cooperate with you and support you, just say and do things that make them feel appreciated.

One way to make students feel appreciated is to ask them privately if they will help you with something. Another way is to offer them support and encouragement. Another is to give them individual help. Another is simply to listen to them when they confide in you. Another is to learn and remember something of importance to each student—their siblings, pets, or favorite activities outside school. And a surprisingly powerful one is simply to find a minute or two each day to chat with them individually about anything at all *except* their misbehavior. But what you say to them must be genuine. Insincere flattery doesn't do the job. Not for long. Students see through it.

Commentary from Anonymous Teacher 2

I have learned that just as we encourage our students to develop scholarly habits to make learning easier, we can develop "teacherly" habits that make teaching and learning easier and more enjoyable. Three of my favorites are:

1. *Greet students as they enter the classroom.* I stand at the door, smile, use first names, and offer a quick comment or question to each student. This is quick, easy, and fun. It helps students feel "seen" and valued, and I can model friendliness and caring. I see less misbehavior arising from students who otherwise feel unnoticed.

2. *Use lesson planning as a key tool in behavior management.* Variety is the name of the game to keep students interested, engaged, and just a little off-balance. I like to use different groupings of learners, offer choices in activities and tasks, and feature assignments using all learning modalities. Planning carefully for variety makes the class more fun and cuts down on misbehavior stemming from boredom.

3. *Keep students and caregivers informed of expectations, assessments, and evaluations.* In my experience, parents don't like surprises at report card time and students are poor at guessing how they are doing in a class. For all projects, reports, oral presentations, and the like, I use grading rubrics. I design the rubric to reflect my expectations, then spend time teaching it to the students before they begin the assignment. I have students practice peer evaluations using the rubric. They soon understand what is expected and how to go about meeting the requirements. My district, and all others that I know of, uses a Web-based computer grading program that offers parent access. I make it a priority to keep up with my grading and to post grades at least once weekly. In addition, I print out monthly progress reports for all students. This habit ensures students receive guidance in successfully completing assignments and that they receive accurate and timely feedback.

I'd also like to tell you about my struggles with a student I'll call Brendan. Our ongoing battle started the first day of school. He and all other students in our French class were asked to choose French names from lengthy lists. They would be called by those names in class. Brendan insisted on "Mozambique" for his name. I asked him to consider a normal name such as "Philippe" or "Guillaume" or "Jacques." He refused and began chanting, "Mozambique! Mozambique! Mozambique!" I relented, smiling, in order to avoid an unpleasant standoff on the first day.

That was the beginning of my unending difficulties with Brendan. I soon saw him not as a quirky kid but as an absolute contrarian. You'd have thought his mission in life was to plague me by doing the opposite of what I asked or expected. Hardly a threat to the eye, he was cute with dark brown curls, bright eyes, and a cheerful smile, liked by his peers, especially girls. But his actions and attitudes flustered me and put me off my game. Worse, the two of us produced a negativity that affected the entire class.

There was nothing explosive or violent from him, but before long his ceaseless resistance wore me down.

To illustrate with but one example, we began each class with 5 to 7 minutes of bell work. Once the procedure was established, all the students except Brendan complied without grumbling. Brendan didn't grumble, but he stalled. "I don't have a pencil/study guide/piece of paper." I would supply him with what he needed, accompanied by a frown or look of exasperation. Those exchanges sometimes lasted through bell work. If any time was left, he would say, "I don't understand this." If the assignment was to practice French greetings and good-byes with table partners, Brendan was certain to remark: "I don't speak French." And "I don't know these people."

If the assignment was to respond with correct answers about days and months, Brendan would call out, "Paris! Notre Dame! Haiti! New Orleans!" We had a rule to keep chair legs flat on the floor with no leaning back: Brendan would lean back as far as he could, balancing precariously. If I said, "Please don't lean back in your chair," he would say, "My bad." In less than 3 minutes he'd be leaning back again.

I didn't know how to handle that or relate to him. I nagged, complained, criticized, reasoned, counseled, muttered, and shook my head in disgust and resignation. None of that changed Brendan. But it changed me. I retreated behind clenched jaws and grinding teeth. I suspended bell work for that class. I used fewer and fewer groupings for oral practice. I started to pretend I didn't see when he leaned back in his chair. I came to dread that class and rejoice when he was absent.

I soon learned Brendan was not motivated by grades, good or bad, or by parent phone calls, good or bad. He didn't care about privileges or the loss of same. He was not intimidated by threats, by referrals, by chats with the assistant principal. He was always smiling. He kept me frowning and itchy. He won. I finally asked to have him removed from my class.

I think now I could do better. But back then, I took his behavior personally. His defiance offended me and kept me on the defensive. I wish I would have just smiled and chatted with him about his pets and his music, the two most important things in his life. I got that information from him the first day on "inventory" sheets I use for students to introduce themselves to me. I wonder, too, if we might have chatted about geography or French history or anything he liked in school. But I didn't think of it. I was stubborn. My pride was on the line. I gave it priority over taking the time to get to know a bright and challenging student in my care.

SHALL WE EXAMINE A PLANNING RUBRIC FOR BUILDING A PERSONALIZED SYSTEM OF DISCIPLINE?

Like all teachers, you need a system of discipline that works well for you and your students. Nothing else is more important to your success. You may be able to find a ready-made approach provided by one of the various great authorities in discipline.

But it is unlikely you will find one that fully meets your particular needs and also those of all your students.

If you don't find an existing system that suits you well, you can construct one for yourself. It will actually further your competence if you do. This book provides guidance for you in the form a planning rubric, which you will soon see. Chapters in the book contain the information you need for completing the rubric. You are certain to find many suggestions in later chapters that resonate with you, along with some that don't. The rubric presented here will help you select, modify, and reorganize tactics to bring everything in line with your students' needs and your beliefs and situations.

The rubric was also presented in this book's preface, which you may or may not have seen. It will be revisited in Chapter 14. It calls on you to answer certain questions for yourself, and for others if necessary. Now as you move ahead, just keep this summary point in mind:

> Today, discipline is not about "making" students behave. It is about teaching them how to behave properly and "influencing" them to do so in a kind and positive manner. ■

The Rubric and Its Contents

Here are the topics you should address when formulating a personalized approach to discipline. The remainder of the book will provide what you need for completing this task. As you proceed through the chapters that follow, please refer to this rubric and make notes in your journal (another item to be suggested presently) as you consider these elements.

Topic 1. My philosophy of discipline.

My definition of discipline.

The purposes for which I will use discipline.

My main duties in discipline.

My students' main duties in discipline.

Topic 2. My theory of discipline.

What I consider to be the necessary components of an effective system of discipline.

What I consider to be the purpose of each component.

Topic 3. The professional and ethical demeanor I will display.

How I will comply with the legal, professional, and ethical obligations associated with discipline.

What I will do to establish positive relations and develop trust with students, colleagues, and my students' caregivers.

Topic 4. The kind of behavior I will endeavor to promote and the rules that support it.

Generally speaking, the behaviors I will promote in my classes.

The specific rules, if any, I will use to support the desired behaviors.

Topic 5. What I will do proactively to prevent or reduce misbehavior.

Specific steps I will take to prevent or limit the known causes of misbehavior that might otherwise influence my classes.

Topic 6. How I will support my students' efforts to participate and persevere.

How I will speak with and relate to my students.

How I will make sure students know what they are expected to do.

The types of activities I will emphasize in teaching.

How I will engage students actively when I am providing instruction.

How I will monitor and help students when they are doing independent work.

How I will use my personal charisma.

How I will use body language to influence behavior.

How I will influence students to do high-quality work.

Topic 7. How I will redirect students when they misbehave.

How I will influence students, using positive tactics that preserve personal dignity.

How I will stop misbehavior and help students return willingly to appropriate behavior.

How I will deal with minor misbehavior such as talking or distracting others.

How I will deal with more disruptive behavior such as disrespect and abusiveness.

How I will deal with students' refusal to comply with directions or do acceptable work.

Topic 8. How and when I will communicate my discipline approach to students, administrators, and students' caregivers.

How and when I will explain my discipline plan to students.

How and when I will communicate my discipline plan to my administrator and seek support.

How and when I will communicate my plan to students' caregivers and request support.

A SUGGESTED JOURNAL TO ACCOMPANY THE PLANNING RUBRIC

It is strongly advised that you keep a journal as you develop your rubric. A notebook serves well. Make journal headings that correspond to the topics in the rubric. Allow space for notes between rubric headings. When you encounter appealing information related to the various topics, jot notes underneath the appropriate heading. When you have completed your studies, your journal will contain the information you need for articulating a personalized system of discipline. Then, you only have to organize that information as guided by the questions in the rubric.

WHAT YOU HAVE LEARNED IN THIS CHAPTER

You have reviewed your important legal and professional obligations to students and have noted students' obligations to you. You have examined some of the major communication tactics that are effective with students today, and you have learned additional ways of exerting positive influence. You have learned the meanings of several important terms—discipline, behavior, misbehavior, appropriate behavior, limits, influence tactics, due diligence, negligence, breach of duty, professionalism, sane messages, congruent communication, laconic language, *why* questions, I-messages, you-messages, frames of reference, seven deadly habits, seven connecting habits, and the neglected 50%. You have examined the three main categories of tactics that are used in effective discipline—prevention of misbehavior, support of appropriate behavior, and redirection of improper behavior—and you have at hand a planning rubric to guide your progress in articulating your personal views on discipline.

Activities

Self-Test: True/False

1. "Modern discipline" is characterized as relying on teacher persuasion rather than stern enforcement to help students conduct themselves properly in school.
2. "Coercion" refers to trying to make students do what they don't want to do, whereas "influence" refers to persuading students to want to do what we want them to do.
3. "Limits" in discipline refer to how far teachers are willing to go in order to enforce their rules of behavior in the classroom.
4. Stipulations concerning teachers' exercising due diligence are considered to be professional obligations, not legal obligations.
5. The InTASC stipulations lay out the 10 areas of legal requirements with which teachers must comply.
6. The term *communication skills* has the same meaning as *verbal skills*.
7. "Sane messages" as described and advocated by Haim Ginott are legally required of teachers.
8. The "neglected 50%" of teaching refers mainly to actions teachers use to exert positive influence on students.

9. Argumentation is not an effective activity for causing people to change their minds when they are wrong.
10. William Glasser's "connecting habits" are things a teacher can do and say that increase students' inclination to cooperate with the teacher.

Self-Test: Multiple Choice

1. Classroom discipline is most accurately thought of as
   (a) raucous misbehavior.
   (b) rules, rewards, and punishments.
   (c) teacher efforts to maintain good behavior.
   (d) a joint effort by teacher, parent, and administrator.
2. Which was *not* listed among the main objectives of discipline?
   (a) self-improvement
   (b) security and safety
   (c) civil behavior
   (d) personal responsibility
3. The boundaries that separate appropriate behavior from misbehavior are referred to as
   (a) parameters.
   (b) rubrics.
   (c) limits.
   (d) rules.

4. For teachers, *"in loco parentis"* is what kind of requirement?
   (a) ethical
   (b) legal
   (c) professional
   (d) ubiquitous

5. Professional and ethical standards for teachers have been articulated by the
   (a) GOP.
   (b) CEO.
   (c) CLU.
   (d) NEA.

6. "Congruent communication" was popularized by
   (a) Stephen Covey.
   (b) Haim Ginott.
   (c) William Glasser.
   (d) Fred Jones.

7. Nonverbal communication received greatest attention from
   (a) Stephen Covey.
   (b) Haim Ginott.
   (c) William Glasser.
   (d) Fred Jones.

8. The "neglected 50%" in teaching refers to
   (a) good communication.
   (b) frames of reference.
   (c) exerting positive influence.
   (d) teacher–parent cooperation.

9. Who is noted for insisting that you cannot win an argument?
   (a) Dale Carnegie
   (b) Bill Clinton
   (c) Mohandas Gandhi
   (d) Oprah Winfrey

10. What did Haim Ginott call ever-ready teacher help?
    (a) professional imperative
    (b) sane message
    (c) hidden asset
    (d) velvet-covered hammer

Self-Test: Explain This

1. How would you define "classroom discipline," and why is it so important in school?

2. Explain the terms *professionalism, ethics,* and *legalities*. Give an example of each in relation to teaching.

3. What does it mean to "exert positive influence" on students, and why is that approach deemed better than using criticism and coercion?

4. What did Ginott mean by the term *congruent communication;* what did Glasser mean by *connecting habits;* what did Covey mean by *frames of reference;* and why did Jones put so much emphasis on nonverbal communication?

Additional Suggested Activities

1. In your journal, enter ideas from this chapter you might wish to incorporate in your personal approach to discipline.

2. Provide and discuss examples of teacher behaviors that (a) comply with, and (b) violate:
   - two things expected of teachers professionally
   - two legal obligations of teachers

3. With regard to teachers' personality traits:
   - Identify two personality traits that seem to promote better student behavior.
   - Identify two personality traits that often seem to make student behavior worse.
   - Explain how you will emphasize your effective traits and downplay the less effective.

4. Think back to one of the best teachers you ever had and one of the poorest teachers you ever had. Now respond to these questions:
   - What did the good one do that pleased you?
   - What did the poor one do that displeased you?
   - Rank the following qualities of your favorite teacher beginning with what you liked best:
     a) Knowledge of subject matter
     b) Personal charisma
     c) Ability to organize and present the material to be learned
     d) Personal interest directed to you and your progress
   - To what extent is your ranking (in the item above) similar to the chapter commentary on the "neglected 50%" of teaching?

3

The Development
of Modern Discipline

*Which 20th-Century Authorities Set the Foundations
for Today's Discipline, and What Did They Advocate?*

Prior to the 1950s, discipline was thought of as an ongoing struggle between demanding teachers and disobedient students. The teachers' job was to make students learn, and although many students complied with that expectation, many others resisted work and caused disruptions. Altogether, discipline was a mélange of demands, rules, misbehavior, insubordination, punishments, detention, suspension, and paddles at the ready. Yet, no one really objected. Those conditions were accepted by students, parents, and teachers, often smilingly, as natural and necessary in schooling.

That picture began to change around the middle of the 20th century. With the end of World War II, newer attitudes toward behavior and discipline were becoming evident. Society was growing more tolerant of behavior a bit outside the norm, and with that tolerance came an inclination to treat students more considerately and humanely. Bit by bit, threat, corporal punishment, and other forceful means of controlling misbehavior began to fall from favor.

At the same time, society began asking schools to assume a stronger role in teaching students to be civil, responsible, and self-controlled, traits that were traditionally taught in the family and sometimes in the churches. The schools accepted the challenge, more or less by default, and by the end of the 20th century, the sternly coercive teacher had almost disappeared, replaced by teachers of gentler demeanor who relied on "friendly persuasion" to get students to behave themselves. In this chapter, we review the nature of those changes and see how they came about.

CHAPTER PREVIEW

Following this paragraph, you will see a timeline of major developments in discipline, beginning with the first systematic discipline approach set forth in 1951 and running up through the year 2010, which gives a picture of the 60-year transformation in discipline. Incorporated into the timeline are commentaries about contributions from great educators, psychologists, and psychiatrists between 1951 and 2001, showing how discipline evolved in the last half of the 20th century.

Those powerful ideas, which opened new lines of thought about discipline, are then reviewed succinctly in this chapter. Newer contributions that appeared or grew in strength after 2001 are listed in the overall timeline but are described in greater detail in Chapters 4 through 10.

A TIMELINE OF DEVELOPMENTS IN MODERN DISCIPLINE

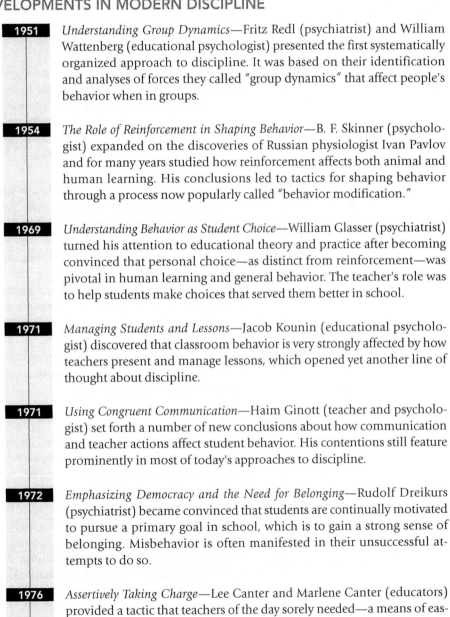

1951 *Understanding Group Dynamics*—Fritz Redl (psychiatrist) and William Wattenberg (educational psychologist) presented the first systematically organized approach to discipline. It was based on their identification and analyses of forces they called "group dynamics" that affect people's behavior when in groups.

1954 *The Role of Reinforcement in Shaping Behavior*—B. F. Skinner (psychologist) expanded on the discoveries of Russian physiologist Ivan Pavlov and for many years studied how reinforcement affects both animal and human learning. His conclusions led to tactics for shaping behavior through a process now popularly called "behavior modification."

1969 *Understanding Behavior as Student Choice*—William Glasser (psychiatrist) turned his attention to educational theory and practice after becoming convinced that personal choice—as distinct from reinforcement—was pivotal in human learning and general behavior. The teacher's role was to help students make choices that served them better in school.

1971 *Managing Students and Lessons*—Jacob Kounin (educational psychologist) discovered that classroom behavior is very strongly affected by how teachers present and manage lessons, which opened yet another line of thought about discipline.

1971 *Using Congruent Communication*—Haim Ginott (teacher and psychologist) set forth a number of new conclusions about how communication and teacher actions affect student behavior. His contentions still feature prominently in most of today's approaches to discipline.

1972 *Emphasizing Democracy and the Need for Belonging*—Rudolf Dreikurs (psychiatrist) became convinced that students are continually motivated to pursue a primary goal in school, which is to gain a strong sense of belonging. Misbehavior is often manifested in their unsuccessful attempts to do so.

1976 *Assertively Taking Charge*—Lee Canter and Marlene Canter (educators) provided a tactic that teachers of the day sorely needed—a means of easily and effectively taking charge in their classrooms and dealing with misbehavior. Their approach, called "assertive discipline," dominated discipline practice for 20 years thereafter.

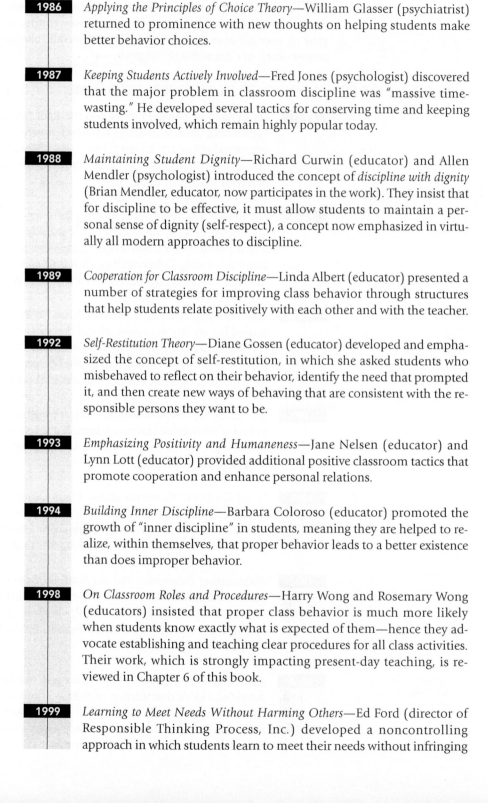

1986   *Applying the Principles of Choice Theory*—William Glasser (psychiatrist) returned to prominence with new thoughts on helping students make better behavior choices.

1987   *Keeping Students Actively Involved*—Fred Jones (psychologist) discovered that the major problem in classroom discipline was "massive time-wasting." He developed several tactics for conserving time and keeping students involved, which remain highly popular today.

1988   *Maintaining Student Dignity*—Richard Curwin (educator) and Allen Mendler (psychologist) introduced the concept of *discipline with dignity* (Brian Mendler, educator, now participates in the work). They insist that for discipline to be effective, it must allow students to maintain a personal sense of dignity (self-respect), a concept now emphasized in virtually all modern approaches to discipline.

1989   *Cooperation for Classroom Discipline*—Linda Albert (educator) presented a number of strategies for improving class behavior through structures that help students relate positively with each other and with the teacher.

1992   *Self-Restitution Theory*—Diane Gossen (educator) developed and emphasized the concept of self-restitution, in which she asked students who misbehaved to reflect on their behavior, identify the need that prompted it, and then create new ways of behaving that are consistent with the responsible persons they want to be.

1993   *Emphasizing Positivity and Humaneness*—Jane Nelsen (educator) and Lynn Lott (educator) provided additional positive classroom tactics that promote cooperation and enhance personal relations.

1994   *Building Inner Discipline*—Barbara Coloroso (educator) promoted the growth of "inner discipline" in students, meaning they are helped to realize, within themselves, that proper behavior leads to a better existence than does improper behavior.

1998   *On Classroom Roles and Procedures*—Harry Wong and Rosemary Wong (educators) insisted that proper class behavior is much more likely when students know exactly what is expected of them—hence they advocate establishing and teaching clear procedures for all class activities. Their work, which is strongly impacting present-day teaching, is reviewed in Chapter 6 of this book.

1999   *Learning to Meet Needs Without Harming Others*—Ed Ford (director of Responsible Thinking Process, Inc.) developed a noncontrolling approach in which students learn to meet their needs without infringing on the rights or comforts of others, thereby reducing conflict in the classroom.

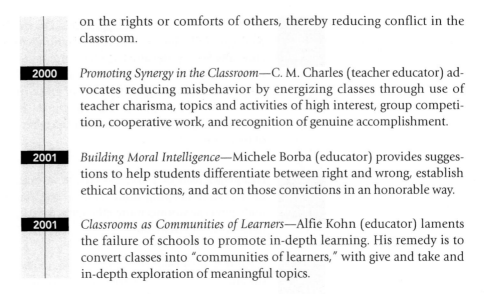

2000 *Promoting Synergy in the Classroom*—C. M. Charles (teacher educator) advocates reducing misbehavior by energizing classes through use of teacher charisma, topics and activities of high interest, group competition, cooperative work, and recognition of genuine accomplishment.

2001 *Building Moral Intelligence*—Michele Borba (educator) provides suggestions to help students differentiate between right and wrong, establish ethical convictions, and act on those convictions in an honorable way.

2001 *Classrooms as Communities of Learners*—Alfie Kohn (educator) laments the failure of schools to promote in-depth learning. His remedy is to convert classes into "communities of learners," with give and take and in-depth exploration of meaningful topics.

The works noted up to this point have been pivotal in the development of modern thought on discipline. Those that now follow depict today's strongest influences in discipline. Most, but not all, will be discussed in separate chapters, as indicated.

1998 to present *How to Be an Effective Teacher*—Harry Wong and Rosemary Wong's ideas grow in popularity. Their book *The First Days of School: How to Be an Effective Teacher* (revised edition, 2009) is the best-selling education book of all time. The Wongs' highly influential teachings are presented in detail in Chapter 6 of this book.

2001 to present *Every Student Can Succeed*—William Glasser (psychiatrist and education consultant) established yet another major approach to discipline, which promotes high levels of student learning and positive behavior. His contribution is described in Chapter 9 of this book.

2001 to present *Raising the Level of Student Responsibility*—Marvin Marshall (educator) developed and disseminated a highly popular approach to humane discipline that he calls *Discipline Without Stress*. As described in Chapter 8 of this book, Marshall's approach makes strong use of a four-level "Hierarchy of Social Development," with teachers helping students learn to function at the highest level.

2002 to present *Promoting Civility in the Classroom*—P. M. Forni (director of the Civility Initiative at Johns Hopkins University) launched and continues a push to popularize civil behavior in schools and society. A synopsis of Forni's work is presented in Chapter 13 of this book.

2002 to present

Teacher-Student Same-Side Approach to Discipline—Spencer Kagan (psychologist and educator), in collaboration with Patricia Kyle (educator) and Sally Scott (educator), explains the strategy and tactics of *Win-Win Discipline*, which calls on teachers and students to work together on the same side, learn to identify states of emotion in students who misbehave, and employ appropriate "structures" that help students conduct themselves appropriately. *Win-Win Discipline* is described in Chapter 10 of this book.

2003 to present

Fred Jones's Tools for Teachers— Fred Jones enjoys growing popularity for his tactics in keeping students meaningfully involved in lessons and managing classrooms more efficiently. His ideas are examined in detail in Chapter 7 of this book.

2005 to present

What Is Real Discipline?—Ronald Morrish (behavior specialist and consultant) answers this question in a website article (see references) and two popular books. He describes basic tactics for promoting responsible behavior that ring true to all teachers. His ideas are presented in detail in Chapter 4 of this book.

2008 to present

Discipline Through Clear Expectations, Leverage, and Student Accountability— Craig Seganti (teacher) worked for 20 years in inner-city Los Angeles schools, where he developed tactics for getting the best from students who are often considered to be difficult to manage. His work is described in Chapter 5 of this book.

Now, we proceed to review in a bit more detail the earlier-20th-century contributions in discipline (1951–2001) and note the specific influences they have had on today's discipline.

GROUP DYNAMICS: WHAT DID FRITZ REDL AND WILLIAM WATTENBERG EXPLAIN ABOUT GROUP BEHAVIOR?

In 1951, psychiatrist Fritz Redl (left) and educational psychologist William Wattenberg (top, next page) developed and disseminated the first theory-based approach to humane classroom discipline. Their conclusions, described in their book *Mental Hygiene in Teaching* (1951), helped teachers understand **group behavior** and how it affects individual behavior. Redl and Wattenberg contended that much student misbehavior is caused by forces detectable only in larger groups. They called those forces **group dynamics** and said if teachers are to understand student behavior, they must first understand group dynamics. Their ideas marked the beginning of what we now think of as "modern discipline."

Redl and Wattenberg explained that group dynamics account for phenomena such as group spirit, group norms and expectations, imitative behavior, desire to excel, scapegoating of certain students, and providing hiding places for nonachievers. They said students take on **student roles** such as leader, follower, clown (who shows off), instigator (who provokes misbehavior), and scapegoat (on whom blame is placed even when not deserved). They urged teachers to be watchful for these roles, bring them to the class's attention, and be prepared to encourage or discourage them as appropriate.

They also pointed out that students expect teachers to fill certain **teacher roles**, such as role models, sources of knowledge, referees, judges, and surrogate parents. Teachers must be aware that students hold these expectations and should discuss the implications with students.

Redl and Wattenberg urged teachers to behave toward students in a helpful manner, remain as objective as possible, show tolerance, keep a sense of humor, and help students maintain positive attitudes toward school and the class. All these things, they said, should be thought of as **influence techniques**, to be used instead of threat and punishment to promote desirable behavior. They also advised teachers to involve students in setting class standards and deciding how misbehavior should be handled, both of which are now widely used practices.

> **The Redl and Wattenberg Model.**   To control misbehavior, (1) identify and soften typical causes of misbehavior; (2) clarify and discuss student roles and teacher roles; (3) involve students in deciding how misbehavior should be handled; and (4) maintain responsible student behavior by using "influence techniques" such as encouragement and support of self-control rather than demands and reprimands. ■

SHAPING BEHAVIOR: WHAT DID B. F. SKINNER DISCOVER ABOUT HELPING STUDENTS LEARN AND CONDUCT THEMSELVES PROPERLY?

In the 1940s and early 1950s, Harvard behavioral psychologist Burrhus Frederic Skinner (1904–1990) was investigating how our voluntary actions are influenced by what happens to us immediately after we perform an act.

Skinner reported his conclusions in a number of publications, two of which were his book *Science and Human Behavior* (1953) and his article "The Science of Learning and the Art of Teaching" (1954). His findings convinced him that much if not most of our voluntary behavior is shaped by reinforcement (or lack thereof), which we receive immediately after performing an act. Simply put, when we perform an act and are reinforced immediately afterward, we become more likely to repeat that act or a similar one and even to try harder in the future.

For purposes here, reinforcement can be thought of as reward, although reward is a term Skinner never used. The term he used was **reinforcing stimulus**. He learned that a stimulus (something the individual receives) can strengthen a particular behavior, but only if it is received very soon after that behavior occurs. In the

1960s, teachers frequently used reinforcers such as candy, popcorn, and tangible objects, but that practice died out once teachers learned that students often worked mainly to get the reward, leaving unsatisfactory residual learning once the rewards were removed. Reinforcing stimuli now commonly used in classrooms include knowledge of results, peer approval, awards, free time, and teacher smiles, nods, and praise.

Constant reinforcement, given every time a student behaves as desired, helps new learning become established quickly. *Intermittent reinforcement*, given occasionally, is sufficient to maintain desired behavior once it is established, whereas behavior that is not reinforced tends to disappear over time.

Shaping behavior is accomplished through **successive approximation**, in which behavior is reinforced as it comes closer and closer to a pre-set goal. This process is helpful in building skills incrementally.

Although Skinner did not concern himself with classroom discipline per se, his discoveries affected it strongly. In the early 1960s, his followers organized his principles into the procedure called **behavior modification**, which became very popular in discipline and teaching. By the mid-1960s, many primary-grade teachers were using behavior modification as their entire discipline system, rewarding students who behaved properly and ignoring those who misbehaved. (Skinner did not use punishment in shaping behavior. He considered its effects unreliable.)

But before many years passed, teachers abandoned behavior modification as a main approach to discipline, considering it akin to bribing students to get them to behave acceptably. Moreover, teachers found the process cumbersome to use and inefficient in teaching students what *not* to do. Teachers quickly realized it was far easier just to teach students how they *should* and *should not* behave.

That said, it is nevertheless true that teachers still use reinforcement tactics dozens of times every day, principally through praise and approval to motivate and support students.

The Skinner Model.   When students conduct themselves acceptably, provide immediate reinforcement to increase repetition of good behavior and shape behavior in desired directions. ■

CHOICE THEORY: WHAT DID WILLIAM GLASSER SAY ABOUT CHOICES AND FAILURE?

William Glasser is unique among the authorities featured in this book, in that he was both a pioneer in the earlier movement toward modern discipline and, later, the contributor of an exemplary approach in modern discipline. In Chapter 2, you saw descriptions of "seven deadly habits" he observed in teachers and "seven connecting habits" that produced much better results.

Glasser gained instant fame in educational circles with the publication of his blockbuster *Schools Without Failure* (1969). That was his second major book in four years and was later acclaimed as one of the most influential education books of the 20th century.

Glasser was already widely known for his prior book, *Reality Therapy: A New Approach to Psychiatry* (1965). In that book, he urged psychotherapists to move their main focus *away* from probing into what had happened to troubled individuals in the past (the classical approach) and *toward* helping individuals resolve their problems within the context of present reality.

Glasser, when counseling delinquent adolescents, found that they responded especially well to reality therapy. That experience led to a long career of writing about education, working with educators, and striving to apply his ideas in schools. Glasser believed a great many of our personal problems are due to unsatisfactory or nonexistent connections with people upon whom we depend. Reality therapy provides a means for troubled people to connect or reconnect with others important in their lives, such as teachers. Glasser's suggestions for working effectively with students include:

- *Focus on the present.* Don't waste time dwelling on the past, complaining, or discussing symptoms. Instead, focus on the here and now and seek ways to resolve problems.
- *Avoid criticizing and blaming.* These are harmful external control behaviors that destroy relationships.
- *Remain nonjudgmental and noncoercive.* Appraise everything in terms of the results. If actions are not providing the desired results, the old behaviors are not working. New ones are needed.
- *Don't get bogged down in excuses.* Whether legitimate or not, excuses prevent one from making needed connections with others.
- *Put together specific workable plans for connecting with people important to you.* Implement the plans and evaluate your efforts and the results. Be ready to revise or reject plans if they do not work (The William Glasser Institute, 2009).

In addition to the principles of reality therapy, Glasser introduced three new ideas that gained educators' immediate attention:

1. *The Problem with Failure.* Sense of failure is one of the most disheartening things that can happen to students. School should be organized to promote genuine success for all.
2. *The Power of Choice.* Students choose to behave as they do. Nothing forces them to misbehave and no one can force them to learn. Teachers must recognize that all they can do is *influence* students to make better choices in how they behave, which leads to greater success in school.
3. *The Value of Classroom Meetings.* Classroom meetings are a superb vehicle for interacting with students and involving them in meaningful discussions.

Glasser also proposed an approach to discipline that emphasized rules of behavior linked to consequences for breaking them. Students, themselves, were to assume responsibility for proper behavior. When students misbehaved, they were asked in a friendly tone to state what they had done and to evaluate the effect their actions had on themselves, their classmates, and teacher. They were further asked to identify and commit themselves to subsequent behavior that would be more appropriate.

Glasser acknowledged that this process was a bit tedious. But he insisted that students who saw themselves as failures were not likely to improve unless they had ongoing supportive involvement with successful people, such as teachers, who provided positive influence and accepted no excuses for improper behavior.

The Early Glasser Model.   (1) Involve students in reflecting on difficulties they encounter in school. (2) Have students suggest how they might help resolve the problems they face. (3) Ask them to take positive action by consciously choosing how they will behave in various circumstances. (4) Remove the notion of failure; judge students in terms of their positive efforts. ∎

Commentary from Anonymous Teacher 1

From what I have seen in the past several years, I'd say most of the teachers at my school pretty much follow Glasser's principles when interacting with students. However, I doubt that many of us, if any, credit those skills to Dr. Glasser. We have picked up on them somehow or another. Maybe they have become part of the climate of teaching. Anyhow, most of us have good rapport with our students, and best I can tell most of the students seem to have a feeling of connectedness with teachers.

Personally, I think Glasser's ideas are right on the mark. I, for one, find that using them makes my teaching days go more smoothly and leaves me with fewer behavior problems to deal with.

On the other hand, I don't see much evidence that teachers I know follow Glasser's suggestions in their personal lives. When we interact informally among ourselves, mostly what we do is criticize, make excuses, and blame other people and other conditions for the difficulties we face. I'm guessing, too, that we teachers do not use the principles as we should when dealing with our family members. I wonder about that. I'm as guilty as anyone. What's going on here, when we certainly know better? I think our personal existence could be much improved if we would only make a conscious effort to employ the principles of reality therapy in our personal lives. That's my opinion, without anything scientific to back it up.

LESSON MANAGEMENT: WHAT DID JACOB KOUNIN DISCOVER ABOUT TEACHING STYLE AND STUDENT BEHAVIOR?

In the late 1960s, Jacob Kounin, an educational psychologist at Wayne State University, conducted an extensive investigation into how highly effective teachers dealt with classroom misbehavior. But as reported in his 1971 book *Discipline and Group Management in Classrooms*, he didn't find much at first, as his research failed to uncover the information he was seeking.

And yet it remained evident that some teachers seemed to promote excellent class behavior while others did not. Kounin analyzed his data again and this time made a surprising finding—that good discipline was not so much dependent on what teachers did when misbehavior occurred, but on how teachers presented lessons and dealt with various groups in the class. Their success came from what they did before misbehavior occurred, rather than from what they did to correct it after it occurred.

Specifically, Kounin noted that the more effective teachers managed their lessons so that students were kept alert, on task, and involved. He found that those teachers used identifiable procedures for gaining student attention and clarifying expectations. Of particular interest was what he called **group alerting**, where teachers obtained students' full attention before giving directions or making explanations. Then, during lessons, the teachers maintained student **accountability** by calling on students from time to time to respond, demonstrate, or explain.

Kounin also found that teachers of well-behaved classes displayed a constant awareness of what all students were doing in the classroom at all times. He used the term **withitness** to refer to such awareness. Teachers with higher levels of withitness were able to monitor and interact with students doing independent work even while those teachers were presenting lessons to smaller groups. Kounin used the term **overlapping** to refer to teachers attending to two or more classroom events simultaneously. He concluded it was one of the most important of all teaching skills.

Other important qualities Kounin discovered included lesson **momentum**— referring to a forward movement of the lesson, with no confusion or dead spots; **smoothness**, meaning a steady progression in the lesson without abrupt stops and starts; and **satiation**, meaning students getting their fill of a particular topic or activity and becoming bored or frustrated, causing them to disengage from the lesson.

The connection Kounin identified between teaching and student behavior led to a new line of thought concerning how teaching style affects student behavior. Most systems of discipline now place heavy emphasis on that connection.

> **The Kounin Model.**   Know what is going on in all parts of the classroom at all times. Learn to attend to multiple issues simultaneously. Carefully organize and conduct interesting lessons that (1) move forward smoothly without dead spots or abrupt changes, (2) hold students accountable for attention and participation, and (3) stop before reaching students' point of satiation. ■

CONGRUENT COMMUNICATION: WHAT DID HAIM GINOTT TEACH US ABOUT COMMUNICATING WITH STUDENTS?

In the same year that Kounin published his work, another small book appeared that had immediate and lasting influence on teaching. The book was Haim Ginott's *Teacher and Child* (1971), in which Ginott explained the critical role of communication in teaching and discipline. One of Ginott's main contentions was that learning and behavior are greatly influenced by the way teachers talk with students. His teachings had enormous effect in establishing the personal, caring tone that prevails in discipline today. In Chapter 2, reference was made to Dr. Ginott's views on "congruent communication," which for your convenience are revisited in this chapter.

Ginott, a classroom teacher early in his career, later held professorships in psychology at Adelphi University and New York University Graduate School. He also served as UNESCO consultant in Israel, was resident psychologist on NBC's *Today,* and wrote a weekly syndicated column entitled "Between Us" that dealt with interpersonal communication.

In *Teacher and Child,* Ginott reminds us that learning always takes place in the "present tense" and is intensely personal to students. He said teachers must not pre-judge students and must remember that each learner is an individual who requires much personal attention.

Ginott coined several terms to help convey his messages about communication. Those terms included **congruent communication,** meaning communication that is harmonious with students' feelings about situations and themselves; **sane messages,** which address *situations* rather than the students' character or past behavior; **teachers at their best,** as when they use congruent communication and do not preach, moralize, impose guilt, or demand promises, but instead **confer dignity** on their students by treating them as social equals; and **teachers at their worst,** as when they label students, belittle them, and denigrate their character.

Effective teachers also **invite cooperation** from their students by describing the situation when a problem occurs and indicating what needs to be done. They do not dictate to students or boss them around—acts that demean students and provoke resistance. Above all, teachers have a **hidden asset** on which they can always rely, which is to ask themselves, "How can I be most helpful to my students right now?"

Ginott had a great deal to say about praise as well, and his contentions came as a surprise to most teachers. He insisted that **evaluative praise** is worse than no praise at all and should never be used. An example of evaluative praise is "Good boy for raising your hand." Instead of evaluative praise, which comments on student character, teachers should use **appreciative praise,** which comments on effort or improvement (e.g., "Thank you for remembering to raise your hand.")

With regard to correcting inappropriate behavior, Ginott advised simply teaching students how to behave properly, instead of reprimanding them when they misbehave. He urged teachers to avoid asking *why* **questions** when discussing behavior, such as, "Why did you do that to Thomas?" *Why* questions make students feel guilty and defensive.

Ginott acknowledged that his suggestions do not produce instantaneous results. They have to be used repeatedly over time for their power to take effect. Ginott said that misbehavior can be squelched, but **genuine discipline** (meaning self-discipline) rarely occurs instantaneously. Rather, it develops as a series of small steps that lead to genuine changes in student attitude. He placed great emphasis on the teacher's role in the overall process:

> As a teacher I have come to the frightening conclusion that I am the decisive element in the classroom. It is my personal approach that creates the climate. It is my daily mood that makes the weather. As a teacher I possess tremendous power to make a child's life miserable or joyous. I can be a tool of torture or an instrument of inspiration. I can humiliate or humor, hurt or heal. In all situations it is my response that decides whether a crisis will be escalated or de-escalated, and a child humanized or dehumanized. (1971, p. 13)

> **The Ginott Model.**   Use congruent communication and sane messages when helping students with their behavior. Sincerely confer dignity on students and invite them to cooperate with you. Use appreciative praise and avoid tactics students might see as punishment. ■

NEEDS AND DEMOCRATIC TEACHING: WHAT WERE RUDOLF DREIKURS'S CONTENTIONS ABOUT STUDENT NEEDS AND THE BEST WAY TO TEACH?

In 1972 (the year he died), psychiatrist Rudolf Dreikurs put forth two ideas that were new to discipline. The first was that students—indeed all humans—have a powerful inborn need for **belonging**. He believed that when students in school are unable to satisfy this prime need (the **genuine goal** of their behavior) they turn by default to certain **mistaken goals** such as attention-seeking, power-seeking, revenge-seeking, and withdrawal.

Dreikurs's second major idea was that learning occurs best in **democratic classrooms** that emphasize active student involvement, promote a sense of belonging, and foster self-discipline. He characterized democratic classrooms as those where students participate in class decision making and are treated as social equals by their teachers.

Dreikurs (1897–1972) was born in Vienna, Austria, and died in Chicago, Illinois. After receiving his medical degree, he entered into a long association with renowned Austrian psychiatrist Alfred Adler. Dreikurs immigrated to the United States in 1937 and became director of the Alfred Adler Institute in Chicago and professor of psychiatry at the Chicago Medical School. His involvement in child and family counseling prompted his interest in discipline practices in families and schools.

Dreikurs said the best way for teachers to deal with misbehavior is to identify and address the mistaken goal it reflects and discuss with students, in a friendly and nonthreatening manner, the faulty logic in that goal. Dreikurs suggested calmly asking, "Do you need me to pay more attention to you?" or "Could it be that you want to show that I can't make you do the assignment?"

Dreikurs also has much to say about the nature and importance of democratic classrooms. In such classrooms, teachers help students develop self-control based on **social interest**, which includes showing responsibility to oneself as well as to and for members of the group in matters of work, friendship, and self-significance. Students gain self-control as they become able to show initiative, make reasonable decisions, and assume responsibility in ways that benefit themselves and others.

Dreikurs contrasted democratic classrooms with autocratic classrooms and permissive classrooms as follows: In **autocratic classrooms**, the teacher makes all decisions and imposes them on students, which does nothing to help students show personal initiative and accept responsibility. In **permissive classrooms**, the teacher overlooks students' failure to comply with rules or conduct themselves humanely, which suggests the teacher accepts those behaviors. In democratic classrooms, teachers are seen to do the following:

- Always speak in positive terms, never negative.
- Encourage students to strive for improvement, not perfection.
- Emphasize students' strengths while minimizing their weaknesses.
- Help students learn from mistakes, which are valuable elements in the learning process.
- Encourage independence and responsibility.
- Show faith in students; offer them help in overcoming obstacles.
- Encourage students to help each other.
- Show pride in student work; display and share it with others.
- Be optimistic and enthusiastic—a positive outlook is contagious.
- Use encouraging remarks such as, "You have improved." "Can I help you?" "What did you learn from that mistake?" (Dreikurs & Cassel, 1995 [originally published in 1972], pp. 51–54)

The Dreikurs Model.   Help all students meet their need for belonging in the class. When they misbehave by pursuing mistaken goals, discuss the fallacy in a nonthreatening manner. Strive to maintain a democratic classroom that emphasizes group well-being. Such classrooms provide the best venue for promoting sense of belonging and helping students make positive choices and exercise responsibility. ■

TAKING CHARGE: HOW DID LEE AND MARLENE CANTER ADVISE TEACHERS TO ESTABLISH CONTROL IN THEIR CLASSROOMS?

In 1976, Lee and Marlene Canter, both classroom teachers, published a book entitled *Assertive Discipline: A Take-Charge Approach for Today's Educator*. In that book, they introduced a discipline approach called assertive discipline, which took education by storm and for the next 20 years was far and away the most popular discipline system in American schools.

As the title of their book suggests, the Canter approach urged teachers to "take charge" in the classroom and showed them how to do so—just what teachers were looking for at a time when permissiveness throughout society was fostering student behavior that made teaching ever more difficult. The Canters provided a simple but well-structured plan that enabled teachers to interact with students in a calm, insistent, and consistent manner. In the rationale for their plan, the Canters insisted that students had a **right to learn** in a calm, orderly classroom, and teachers had a **right to teach** without being interrupted by misbehavior.

Assertive discipline prompts students to make positive behavior choices. Its approach requires the following:

1. A clear set of rules for class behavior.
2. Positive consequences such as recognition and praise applied intermittently when students comply with the rules.

3. Negative consequences applied consistently when students break the rules. The negative consequences are organized into a hierarchy that becomes progressively more unpleasant if students continued to break rules. Misbehavior ends when teachers apply a consequence that is distasteful enough that students would choose to comply with class rules rather than endure the consequence.

The Canters wanted all teachers to function as **assertive teachers**, who clearly, confidently, and consistently model and express class expectations, build trust, and teach students how to behave appropriately.

Assertive discipline was enthusiastically accepted at first, but gradually over time it began receiving criticism for being overly controlling. To address that complaint, the Canters added provisions for talking helpfully with students and working to establish mutual trust and respect. After some 20 years of dominance, assertive discipline as a major discipline strategy faded away, but vestiges of it are still seen in classrooms everywhere.

The Canter Model.   Establish five or six rules for class behavior. Make a list of positive consequences you will apply when students comply with rules. Make a list of negative consequences you will apply when students break the rules. Organize the negative consequences from less severe to more severe. As students continue to break rules, apply more severe consequences until the misbehavior ceases. ∎

THE COOPERATIVE APPROACH: HOW DOES LINDA ALBERT ADVISE TEACHERS TO WORK WITH STUDENTS?

Linda Albert, author and disseminator of *Cooperative Discipline* (1989/1996), is a counselor, syndicated columnist, university professor, and former classroom teacher who works nationally and internationally with educators and parents. She has authored regular columns in *Working Mother* and *Family* magazines and has made featured appearances on NBC's *Today*, CBS's *This Morning*, and CNN's *Cable News*.

Albert's main focus is on helping teachers and students cooperate with each other in a manner that removes most of the adversarial relationship that so often exists between teacher and student. Albert believes cooperation occurs more easily when students truly feel they have an important place in the class. To make sure students gain that feeling, she gives heavy attention to what she calls the **Three C's**—helping all students feel *capable, connect* with others, and make *contributions* to the class and others.

To increase student sense of *capability*, Albert advises teachers to consider the following:

1. *Make mistakes okay.* The fear of making mistakes undermines students' sense of capability, and when they are fearful, many stop trying. To minimize this fear, Albert asks teachers to talk with students about what mistakes are, help them understand that everyone makes mistakes, and show students that mistakes are a natural part of learning.

2. *Build confidence.* In order to feel capable, students must have confidence that success is possible. To help students gain this confidence, teachers should convey that learning is a process of improvement, not an end product.

3. *Make progress tangible.* Teachers should provide tangible evidence of student progress. Grades are ineffective because they tell little about specific accomplishments. Albert suggests using devices such as accomplishment albums and portfolios along with talks about specific progress students have made and improvements they will make in the future.

4. *Recognize achievement.* Albert believes that sense of capability increases when students receive attention for what they've accomplished. She suggests that teachers have class members acknowledge each other's accomplishments, recognize students at awards assemblies, set up exhibits, and make presentations for other classes and parents.

Albert also feels it is essential that all students *connect,* meaning they establish and maintain positive relationships with peers and teachers. As students make these connections, they become more cooperative and helpful with each other and more receptive to teachers. Albert would have teachers facilitate making connections by practicing the **Five A's**—acceptance, attention, appreciation, affirmation, and affection.

The third "C" refers to *contributing.* Students who do not feel accepted or needed often see school as purposeless. Albert suggests that one of the best ways to help students feel they are needed is to make it possible for them to contribute. Some of her suggestions are:

1. *Encourage student contributions in the class.* Ask students to state their opinions and preferences about class requirements, routines, and other matters. Students can also furnish ideas about improving the classroom environment.

2. *Encourage student contributions to the school.* Albert suggests creating *Three C Committees* whose purpose is to think of ways to help all students feel more capable, connected, and contributing. Teachers and administrators can assign school service time, in which students perform such tasks as dusting shelves, beautifying classrooms, and cleaning the grounds, all of which help build a sense of pride in the school.

3. *Encourage student contributions to the community.* Albert suggests:

   ■ Adopting a health care center and providing services such as reading, singing, and running errands for residents of the center.
   ■ Contributing to community drives such Meals on Wheels, Toys for Tots, and disaster relief funds.
   ■ Encouraging random acts of kindness, such as opening doors for people and providing help with their packages.

The Albert Model.   The key to good classroom behavior lies in close cooperation between teacher and students. Help students grow in the Three C's: personal *capability, connections* with others, and *contributions* to school and society. Continually show students—and ask them to show each other—the Five A's of acceptance, attention, appreciation, affirmation, and affection. ■

POSITIVITY AND HUMANENESS: HOW DO JANE NELSEN AND LYNN LOTT HELP TEACHERS BRING THOSE QUALITIES INTO THE CLASSROOM?

Jane Nelsen (top) and Lynn Lott are educators who disseminate their views on discipline through lectures, workshops, printed material, and video material. Their goal is to help adults and children learn to respect themselves and others, behave responsibly, and contribute to the betterment of the groups of which they are members. Their book *Positive Discipline in the Classroom* (2000 [originally published in 1993]) explains how to establish classroom climates that foster responsibility, mutual respect, and cooperation. They believe such climates do away with most discipline problems because they teach students to value respect and helpfulness. Nelsen and Lott have authored a number of books and teaching materials that can be previewed on the Positive Discipline website at www.positivediscipline.com and on the Empowering People website at www.empoweringpeople.com.

Nelsen and Lott assert that teachers foster positive discipline when they establish classroom climates of acceptance, encouragement, respectfulness, and support. Such classrooms enable students to behave with dignity, self-control, and concern for others. Nelsen and Lott contend that virtually all students can learn to behave in that manner.

The key lies in helping students see themselves as *capable, significant,* and *able to control their own lives.* These qualities are best promoted in classrooms where students are treated respectfully and taught the skills needed for working with others. In such classrooms, students (1) never experience humiliation when they fail, but instead learn how to turn mistakes into successes; (2) learn how to cooperate with teachers and fellow students to find joint solutions to problems; and (3) are provided an environment of firmness, kindness, and excitement for life and learning. Such environments reflect dignity and mutual respect, thereby replacing fear, discouragement, and feelings of inadequacy.

Nelsen and Lott especially emphasize the value of classroom meetings as venues for developing social skills of listening, taking turns, hearing different points of view, negotiating, communicating, helping one another, and taking responsibility for one's own behavior. When teachers involve themselves as partners in class meetings, a climate of mutual respect develops. Teachers and students listen to one another, take each other seriously, and work together to solve problems for the benefit of all. Antagonisms often seen in most classrooms tend to fade away.

Nelsen and Lott's Significant Seven

Nelsen and Lott identified three perceptions and four skills that contribute to the special benefits of *Positive Discipline in the Classroom.* They call these perceptions and skills the **Significant Seven**, which they describe as follows.

The Three Empowering Perceptions

Within a positive environment, students develop **three perceptions** about themselves that lead to success in life. Those three perceptions are:

1. Perception of *personal capability.* (I have ability; I can do this.)
2. Perception of *significance in primary relationships.* (I am needed; I belong.)

3. Perception of *personal power* to influence one's own life. (I have control over how I respond to what happens to me.)

The Four Essential Skills

In their approach, Nelsen and Lott strive to help students develop **four essential skills** that contribute significantly to success in life:

1. Intrapersonal skill. (I understand my emotions and can control myself.)
2. Interpersonal skill. (I can communicate, cooperate, and work well with others.)
3. Strategic skill. (I am flexible, adaptable, and responsible.)
4. Judgmental skill. (I can use my wisdom to evaluate situations.)

The Nelsen and Lott Model of Discipline.   Make sure the tone of your classroom is accepting, encouraging, respectful, and supportive. Discuss the Significant Seven with students and incorporate them into daily practice. ■

INNER DISCIPLINE: WHAT DOES BARBARA COLOROSO SAY ABOUT HELPING STUDENTS ACCEPT RESPONSIBILITY AND MAINTAIN SELF-CONTROL?

Barbara Coloroso believes that a major goal of education is to teach students to conduct themselves in a socially acceptable manner. She wants students to develop an inner sense of responsibility and self-control, and she thinks the school must help them do so. Responsibility and self-control enable students to take positive charge of their lives while respecting the rights of those around them. This process can be made to occur when students are given responsibility for making decisions and for managing the outcomes of those decisions.

Classrooms are ideal places to learn this process, and teachers are in an ideal position to help. The paragraphs that follow present Coloroso's suggestions for helping students in this manner. Most of the material presented here comes from her book, *Kids Are Worth It: Giving Your Child the Gift of Inner Discipline* (1994/2002). To see more of Coloroso's contributions, consult her website at www.kidsareworthit.com.

Teachers help students learn self-control by taking the following steps when students misbehave:

1. Show students what they have done wrong.
2. Give students **ownership of the problems** involved.
3. When necessary, guide them to strategies that might solve the problems.
4. Make sure students' dignity remains intact.

These steps help students acquire integrity, wisdom, compassion, and mercy, all of which contribute to inner discipline.

Teachers must make sure they never speak hurtfully to students or provoke anger, resentment, or additional conflict. When misbehavior is sufficiently serious, Coloroso would have teachers quickly guide students through a process of *restitution, resolution,* and *reconciliation*. **Restitution** means doing what is necessary to repair whatever damage was done. **Resolution** means identifying and correcting whatever caused the misbehavior so it won't happen again. **Reconciliation** establishes healing relationships with people who were hurt or offended by the misbehavior. The offending student is asked to make decisions concerning future behavior, follow up accordingly, and then learn from the results of those decisions, even if they bring discomfort.

The teacher intervenes in student decisions only when they are physically dangerous, morally threatening, or unhealthy. Otherwise, students deal with matters on their own.

You give students ownership of discipline problems when you ask them, "What do you intend to do about the situation?" That causes them to realize it is up to them to make matters better. Teachers are there to offer advice and support, but not to provide solutions. Inner discipline is acquired through learning how to think, not just what to think. The following are additional points that Coloroso emphasizes:

- Students have the right to be in school, but they also have the responsibility to respect the rights of those around them. Rights and responsibility go hand in hand.
- Teachers should never treat students in ways they, the teachers, would not want to be treated.
- Rather than rescuing students or lecturing them when they misbehave, give students opportunities to solve their problems in ways that everyone finds acceptable.
- Students who consistently experience realistic consequences for misbehavior learn that they themselves have positive control over their lives. In contrast, students who are bribed, rewarded, and punished become dependent on others for approval. They work to please the teacher and try to figure out how to avoid getting caught when they misbehave.

The Coloroso Model.   Place heavy emphasis on helping students develop responsibility and self-control. When students misbehave, you should (1) have them state clearly what they have done wrong; (2) give them ownership of the problem by asking, "How will you fix the problem?"; (3) suggest options for resolution if the student needs them; (4) hold the student responsible for following through. ■

Commentary from Anonymous Teacher 2

Here is something I recently learned about making assumptions. I decide on students' seating assignments through the year, but promise that when June arrives I will allow them to sit with special friends to work on projects we have planned. I enjoy their happy reactions when I unveil my carefully considered final seating chart.

A while back, Monica, upon learning where she was to sit, slammed her backpack down on the table and vulgarly exclaimed, "I am not sitting here with that (bleep)!" She was referring to Chloe, who stood with a stricken look on her face. It caught me off guard because I knew Monica and Chloe often referred to themselves as "BFFs" (best friends forever).

Celina quickly whispered to me, "Chloe stole Monica's boyfriend." I then took a new tack and said to the class, "Let's sit down calmly for a moment and I'll pass out half-sheets of paper. Will you please list classmates you would like to sit next to, and also any you might have a conflict with? By tomorrow I will have a seating chart ready that should work better for us."

Just a comment, too, on a different matter: Cleaning up after art projects used to be unpleasant for all of us. I was prone to say, "Oh, what a mess! We only have 2 minutes to get it cleaned up! We've got to leave this place spotless, right now!" It was not a good way to end a pleasant experience.

Somehow I learned it was much better to say, "Your projects look great! I love seeing what you come up with. Now it's cleanup time! Let's see how fast we can get the room back to normal. Anybody want to vacuum up the glitter? Can somebody help me gather the glue sticks and scissors?" I invariably have a couple of students who grew up watching *Barney* start singing, "Cleanup, cleanup, Everybody, everywhere..." I guess this is an example of a "builder" approach that shows respect for students. It works far better than my admonitions ever did.

LEARNING COMMUNITIES: HOW DOES ALFIE KOHN SUGGEST WE INVOLVE STUDENTS MORE CLOSELY IN GENUINE LEARNING?

Alfie Kohn has been deeply troubled by teaching that tries to force students to behave compliantly. He often begins his workshops for teachers by asking, "What are your long-term goals for the students you work with? What would you like them to be—to be like—long after they've left you?" (Kohn, 1996/2001, p. 60).

When you ask most teachers, they say they want their students to be caring, happy, responsible, curious, and creative. Unfortunately, says Kohn, there is a yawning chasm between what we teachers want and what we are doing to get it. We say we want children to continue reading and thinking after school has ended, yet we focus on testing and grading, which does little to make students want to learn. We want students to be critical thinkers, yet we feed them predigested facts and conclusions—partly because of pressure from various constituencies to pump up standardized test scores. We act as though our goal is short-term retention of right answers rather than genuine understanding (Kohn, 1996/2001).

Kohn, a former teacher, is now a full-time writer and lecturer with a number of influential books to his credit. He is critical of many of today's educational practices and is the foremost proponent of converting ordinary classrooms into caring, supportive communities of learners, where students work together as they delve into topics that capture their attention. He stresses these views in his addresses, workshops, appearances on radio and television programs, and books such as *Punished by Rewards: The Trouble with Gold Stars, Incentive Plans, A's, Praise, and Other Bribes* (1993/1999) and *Beyond Discipline: From Compliance to Community* (1996/2001). He speaks at major conferences and has appeared on well over 200 radio and television programs, including *Oprah* and *Today*. His website is www. alfiekohn.org.

Kohn thinks traditional instruction—the type in which the teacher selects the curriculum; does the planning; delivers the lessons through lecture, demonstration, guided discussion, reading assignments, worksheets, and homework; and then uses tests to evaluate progress—is falling disastrously short of the expectations we hold for education.

That kind of instruction is aimed at getting students to demonstrate behaviorally certain specific objectives, usually on tests. But it gives little attention to exploring ideas, seeking new solutions, looking for meaning or connections, or attempting to gain deeper understanding of the phenomena involved.

In the style of instruction most commonly used today, students remain relatively passive most of the time. They listen, read assignments, answer questions when called on, and complete worksheets, all with little give and take. Instruction and learning are deemed successful in the extent to which students show on tests they have reached the stated objectives. But this approach, says Kohn (1999), makes students focus on outcomes that are shallow, relatively insignificant, and of little interest or relevance to them. Students come to think of correct answers and good grades as the major goals of learning. They rarely experience the satisfaction of exploring interesting topics in depth and exchanging views and insights with others.

Kohn goes on to say that students taught in this way often develop poor attitudes toward learning. To them, learning is not an exciting exploration, but just a way of getting the work done. Once they have done the "stuff," they quickly forget much of it as they move on to learn more new stuff. They strive to get the right answers, and when they do not, or if they don't make top scores on the test, they experience a sense of failure that is out of place in genuine learning, where making mistakes is the rule. And even when students seem to be learning well, they may actually be doing poorly because they are not thinking widely and exploring ideas thoughtfully.

Kohn argues for instruction that is different from the traditional. He says, first, that students must be taken seriously, meaning teachers must honor them as individuals and seek to determine what they need and enjoy. Further, teachers must recognize that students construct their knowledge and skills from a basis of experience. When students explore, grapple with ideas, and try to make sense of them, they make many mistakes, but mistakes are always part of learning. Teachers in that approach facilitate learning by seeking out students' interests and finding what lies behind their questions and mistakes.

Kohn (1996/2001) says the kind of schooling he would like to see is best promoted by transforming schools and classrooms into **learning communities**, meaning places in which students feel cared about and are encouraged to care about each other. There they experience a sense of being valued and respected; they matter to one another and to the teacher. They come to think in the plural. They feel connected to each other; they are part of an "us." And, as a result of all this, they feel safe in their classes, not only physically but emotionally.

Kohn suggests the following as ways to develop a greater **sense of community** in schools and classrooms:

- *Show respect for students.* Students behave more respectfully when important adults in their lives behave respectfully toward them. They are more likely to care about others if they know they are cared about.
- *Help students connect with each other.* Connections among students are established and enhanced through activities that involve interdependence. Familiar activities for enhancing connections include cooperative learning, getting-to-know-you activities such as interviewing fellow students and introducing them to the class, and finding a partner to check opinions with on whatever is being discussed at the moment. Kohn also suggests using activities that promote **perspective taking**, in which students try to see situations from another person's point of view.
- *Use classroom meetings.* Kohn says the overall best activity for involving the entire group is the class meeting. He suggests holding class meetings at the beginning of the year to discuss matters such as, "What makes school awful sometimes? Try to remember an experience during a previous year when you hated school, when you felt bad about yourself, or about everyone else, and you couldn't wait for it to be over. What was going on when you were feeling that way? How was the class set up?" Kohn says not enough teachers use this practice, particularly in elementary schools, where an aggressively sunny outlook prevails.
- *Provide classwide and schoolwide activities.* To develop a sense of community, students need many opportunities for the whole class or the whole school to collaborate on group endeavors. This might involve producing a class mural, producing a class newsletter or magazine, staging a performance, taking care of the school grounds, or doing some community service.
- *Reflect on academic instruction.* In class meetings, talk about how the next unit in history might be approached, or what the students thought was best and worst about the math test. Academic study pursued in cooperative groups enables students to make connections while learning from each other, and units of study in language arts and literature can be organized to promote reflection on helpfulness, fairness, and compassion.

The Kohn Model.   Think of your students as serious learners who construct knowledge from a variety of experiences. Organize the class into a community of learners, interconnected and concerned with each other. Use classroom meetings to address concerns about instructional matters and personal behavior. ■

WHAT YOU HAVE LEARNED IN THIS CHAPTER

In this chapter, we covered the following:

- How discipline changed during the second half of the 20th century.
- How Redl and Wattenberg launched the change with their work in group dynamics.

- How Skinner contributed to the change with his principles of reinforcement.
- How Glasser used reality therapy to help students make better choices.
- What Kounin discovered about lesson management and its effects on student behavior.
- Ginott's techniques to help teachers communicate more effectively with students.
- Dreikurs's contentions about "belonging" and democratic teaching.
- The Canters' tactics for helping teachers take charge in the classroom.
- Albert's suggestions for helping teachers and students cooperate more closely.
- Nelsen and Lott's efforts to make discipline more humane and positive.
- Coloroso's prescriptions for helping students develop inner discipline and responsibility.
- Alfie Kohn's suggestions for involving students more deeply in meaningful learning.

Activities

Self-Test: True/False

1. Fritz Redl and William Wattenberg were concerned primarily with the types of communication that occur between teachers and students.
2. B. F. Skinner did not concern himself with classroom discipline *per se*.
3. William Glasser believed that failure had relatively little effect on students' motivation to achieve in school.
4. Jacob Kounin made discoveries about how lesson management affected student behavior.
5. Haim Ginott's term *congruent communication* refers to teachers' efforts to speak with students at their level of intellectual development.
6. Rudolf Dreikurs believed that the prime motive for student behavior in classrooms is students' need to feel they "belong."
7. Lee and Marlene Canter referred to their system of discipline as a "take-charge" approach.
8. Barbara Coloroso is noted for being one of the foremost advocates of behavior modification to shape student behavior.
9. Linda Albert, Jane Nelsen, and Lynn Lott worked to make classrooms more humane and positive.
10. Alfie Kohn exerted considerable influence in helping schools use standardized testing as a means of establishing accountability.

Self-Test: Multiple Choice

1. The term *group dynamics* refers mainly to
   (a) individuals in groups.
   (b) forces in groups.
   (c) peer pressure in groups.
   (d) leaders in groups.
2. In this chapter, "behavior shaping" was depicted as resulting from
   (a) reinforcement.
   (b) group dynamics.
   (c) choice theory.
   (d) lesson management.
3. Which of the following focused his or her research on investigations into lesson management?
   (a) Coloroso
   (b) Albert
   (c) Ginott
   (d) Kounin
4. Language described as brief and to the point is called _____ language.
   (a) congruent
   (b) laconic
   (c) positive
   (d) assertive

5. Strong advocates of "cooperative discipline" include which of the following?
   (a) Linda Albert
   (b) Rudolf Dreikurs
   (c) Lee and Marlene Canter
   (d) Jane Nelsen and Lynn Lott
6. Which of the following authorities wrote about moving education away from compliance and toward community?
   (a) Kounin
   (b) Kohn
   (c) Canter
   (d) Coloroso
7. The only authority discussed in this chapter to write about students' prime need was
   (a) Kounin.
   (b) Ginott.
   (c) Coloroso.
   (d) Dreikurs.
8. Which of the following husband-and-wife teams was featured in this chapter?
   (a) Harry and Rosemary Wong
   (b) Eddie Singer and Elsie Canter
   (c) Rudolf Dreikurs and Pearl Cassel
   (d) Sam Abbot and Louise Costello
9. Which of the following authorities featured in this chapter made both pioneering and modern contributions to discipline?
   (a) Glasser
   (b) Kounin

   (c) Dreikurs
   (d) Ginott
10. Which of the following authorities championed the notion of "inner discipline"?
    (a) Canter
    (b) Coloroso
    (c) Redl and Wattenberg
    (d) Skinner

Self-Test: Explain This

1. What was the single most important change in discipline that occurred between 1951 and 2001?
2. Which ideas (if any) of the authorities featured in this chapter are now considered to be invalid?
3. Define the following terms, and note who advocated each of them: congruent communication; reinforcement; choice theory; overlapping; group dynamics; prime need; assertive discipline; democratic teaching; inner discipline; learning communities.

Additional Suggested Activities

1. In your journal, enter items of information from this chapter that you might wish to include in your personal system of discipline.
2. In small groups, discuss your appraisal of the relative merits of the various contributions presented in this chapter and rank them in terms of their applicability in classrooms today.

Preparing Yourself to Take Charge in the Classroom

In Which You Learn What Is Needed in a Discipline Plan, the First Things You Should Teach, and How You Establish and Maintain Calm, Purposeful Student Behavior

CHAPTERS IN PHASE II

4

Ron Morrish on Organizing and Presenting a Basic Discipline Plan

What Does Ronald Morrish Include in a System of Discipline, and How Does He Present It to Students?

Ronald Morrish says we have to teach students how to behave properly because many of them do not learn how to do so at home. Our ultimate goal is for students to develop self-control, but that only happens over time, and almost never without the help of supportive adults. Unfortunately, supportive adults are missing from many students' lives today. We teachers are in an ideal position to offer that support, and it is our duty to do so.

Morrish's approach to discipline is straightforward, sensible, and easy to teach and learn. It consists of four main components: (1) rules of behavior; (2) compliance training, in which students are taught how to comply with expectations; (3) a few carefully chosen things you will do and say when students break rules; and (4) when students are old enough, a provision for allowing and helping them to make choices in a responsible manner.

As for rules of behavior, Morrish says teachers, not students, should make them. He believes it a major mistake for teachers to involve students in making rules before students have sufficient maturity and wisdom to do so.

Once teachers have established clear rules (about five will usually do), they should teach them carefully to students, emphasizing what the rules mean and why they are needed. After that, students must be taught why and how they are to comply with the rules. This is done over time and involves **compliance training**, in which you begin by helping students understand the difference between right and wrong behavior in general. From that point, you move to teaching the difference between right and wrong behavior in school. You teach these concepts through explanation, examples, demonstration, and guided practice. The compliance training process not only clarifies expectations, but also promotes students' acceptance of your authority. When those two understandings become established, students usually follow class rules consistently without hesitation.

Although rules and compliance training will prevent most problems, Morrish acknowledges that students will still misbehave at times. When that happens, you must be able to redirect student misbehavior in positive directions, in a manner that leaves no residue of resentment. How is that best done? Simple, says Morrish. You make sure students understand that when they break a rule, you will ask them to *redo* the behavior in question, in a correct manner. Insist on that, he says, and you will get acceptable behavior from your students almost all of the time.

Finally, after compliance has been well established, you should teach students how to manage choice, provided they are sufficiently mature to do so. That final step will enable them to develop genuine self-discipline.

Components of Morrish's Approach.   (1) Teacher-made rules; (2) compliance training; (3) redo misbehavior correctly; and (4) later, make choices. ■

WHO IS RONALD MORRISH?

Ron Morrish, an independent consultant in discipline, was for many years a teacher and behavior specialist in Canada. He now writes, makes conference presentations, conducts professional development programs, presents courses for teachers, and works with parent groups and child care providers around the world. He has authored three books. The first, *Secrets of Discipline* (1997), was also produced as a video. In that work, Morrish discusses 12 keys for raising responsible children without engaging in deal making, argumentation, or confrontations. His second book, *With All Due Respect* (2000), focuses on improving teachers' discipline skills and building effective schoolwide discipline programs through a team approach. In 2003, he published *FlipTips*, a mini-book of discipline tips and maxims excerpted from his books and presentations. To see Morrish's own description of his program, called "Real Discipline," consult his 2005 article "What Is Real Discipline?" posted on his website at www.realdiscipline.com.

WHAT QUESTIONS WILL THIS CHAPTER ANSWER FOR ME?

- ■ What does Morrish believe is wrong with today's discipline?
- ■ What does Morrish mean by "Real Discipline"?
- ■ What does Morrish say is needed for an effective system of discipline?
- ■ What are the four main components or phases in Morrish's Real Discipline?
- ■ Why is it important to train students to comply with expectations?
- ■ Why is it important to teach students how to behave?
- ■ What does Morrish say about fostering student self-esteem?
- ■ What does Morrish suggest we do when students do not comply with directions or expectations?

WHAT IS THE MORRISH MODEL OF DISCIPLINE?

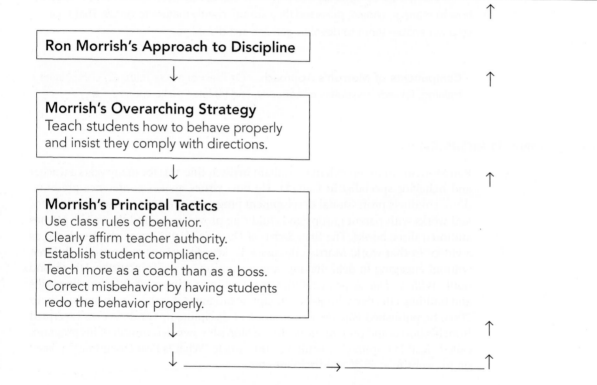

**The Common Goal of All Approaches
to Discipline** *Responsible, Civil Classroom Behavior
That Becomes Habitual and Lasts over Time*
Responsible means paying attention, making a strong
effort, and doing what is proper without being told.
Civil means respectful, polite, cordial, and well-mannered.

Ron Morrish's Approach to Discipline

Morrish's Overarching Strategy
Teach students how to behave properly
and insist they comply with directions.

Morrish's Principal Tactics
Use class rules of behavior.
Clearly affirm teacher authority.
Establish student compliance.
Teach more as a coach than as a boss.
Correct misbehavior by having students
redo the behavior properly.

IN MORRISH'S VIEW, HOW AND WHY HAS MODERN DISCIPLINE GONE WRONG?

Morrish (2005) fully agrees with other authorities that discipline continues to be a major problem in schools, with students frequently trying to manipulate teachers and refusing to cooperate fully. He assigns some of the blame to undesirable trends in society, such as "me-first" attitudes and a general disinclination to accept responsibility, but he also assigns much of it to bad advice teachers get in many of today's popular systems of discipline.

All too often, he says, today's authorities urge teachers to involve students in decision making before the students are mature enough to do so responsibly. Consequently, teachers waste large amounts of time negotiating and haggling with students about behavior. Morrish says that for decades, experts have erroneously claimed that plentiful student choice leads to self-esteem, responsibility, and motivation to achieve. As those experts see it, the teacher's role is to encourage good choices and discourage poor ones.

That approach has failed, Morrish contends, for three reasons. First, it does not demand proper behavior from students, but instead allows them, if they don't mind the consequences, to choose to behave discourteously and irresponsibly. Systems based on fear of consequences, he explains, cannot be effective unless students truly find the consequences intolerable, which is virtually never the case today.

Second, many discipline approaches do not adequately teach students how they are to behave in school.

And third, many approaches leave teachers stuck with bargaining and negotiating endlessly, and often fruitlessly, to get students to cooperate.

Morrish contends that if discipline is to be effective, a different approach is required—one in which students are taught what is acceptable and what is unacceptable before they are given latitude to make choices. Otherwise, he says, they are likely to choose whatever appeals to them at the time, and teachers will find it difficult to live with many of those choices.

Although all of us want students to be successful, the discipline approaches we use often allow students to underachieve, behave discourteously, engage in high-risk behaviors, contribute little or nothing of value to the school environment, and use intimidation and violence in dealing with others. Clearly, says Morrish, such discipline is not producing the results we want.

WHAT IS THE "REAL DISCIPLINE" MORRISH ADVOCATES?

Morrish calls his approach **Real Discipline**. He explains that it is not a new theory, but an organized set of techniques that great teachers and parents have used for generations in teaching children to be respectful, responsible, and cooperative. It emphasizes careful teacher guidance to ensure that children learn how to conduct themselves in an acceptable manner.

Morrish feels teachers have been sidetracked into focusing on what he calls "behavior management" rather than real discipline. Both management and discipline are needed, he says, but they are not one and the same. **Behavior management** is about making the learning environment functional, keeping students on task, and minimizing disruptions. It attempts to deal with whatever behavior students bring to school. Although important in teaching, behavior management is not very effective in helping students learn to behave responsibly.

Real Discipline, on the other hand, explicitly teaches students how to behave properly. It requires them to show courtesy and consideration. It helps them develop needed social skills and trains them to work within a structure of rules and limits. It does these things while protecting students from self-defeating mistakes they are otherwise likely to make. As Morrish (1997, p. 33) puts it:

> Real Discipline is a lot more than simply giving choices to children and then dealing with the aftermath. We have to teach them right and wrong. We have to

teach them to respect legitimate authority. We have to teach them the lessons that have been learned by others and by ourselves. Then, and only then, will we enjoy watching them develop into adults.

Morrish says these provisions are necessary because children, in their early years, are by no means wise and tolerant. They are frequently the opposite—impulsive and self-centered. If they are to develop into contributing members of society, they must learn to cooperate, behave responsibly, and show consideration for others.

Some young students are fortunate to have good caregivers and role models who teach them these things. But many children today are overly indulged and rarely called to account for their behavior. They remain self-centered and grow up concerned only with their own interests. They want things their way, they cooperate in school only when they feel like it, and they show little consideration for teachers and fellow students. For many, lack of effort, abusive language, and bullying are rules of the day.

Morrish says this condition has come about, at least in part, because the society in which we live stresses individual rights and freedom, but has lost sight of the personal responsibility that must accompany rights and freedom. Without responsibility, rights and freedom mean little. Personal responsibility is too important to leave to chance. Life requires us to live within certain constraints that limit individual freedom. We accept those constraints in exchange for life that is safer, more secure, and more orderly.

Morrish does believe students should be allowed to make choices and helped to make good ones, but only when they are sufficiently mature to do so intelligently. Students do not innately know how to do so, nor can they do so early in their lives. They first have to develop respect for, and a degree of compliance with, authority.

WHICH MAXIMS HELP US UNDERSTAND THE NATURE OF REAL DISCIPLINE?

As noted, Morrish also published a small book called *FlipTips* (2003), which contains comments and maxims from his various publications and presentations. They reflect the mindset that Morrish would like teachers to acquire. Here are a few of the tips that illustrate Morrish's ideas on discipline. How would you explain, in your own words, what each of them means or suggests?

- Discipline is a process, not an event.
- Discipline is about giving students the structure they need for proper behavior, not the consequences they seem to deserve for misbehavior.
- Discipline comes from the word *disciple*. It's about teaching and learning, not scolding and punishing.
- Discipline isn't what you do when students misbehave. It's what you do so they won't.
- Discipline isn't about letting students make their own choices. It's about preparing them properly for the choices they will be making later.

- Don't let students make choices that are not theirs to make.
- Train students to comply with your directions. Compliance precedes coopera- tion. If you bargain for compliance now, you'll have to beg for it later.
- Always work from more structure to less structure, not the other way around.
- To prevent major behavior problems, deal with all minor behavior problems when they occur.
- Students learn far more from being shown how to behave appropriately than from being punished.
- The best time to teach a behavior is when it isn't needed, so it will be there when it is needed. Today's practice is tomorrow's performance.
- If you teach students to be part of the solution, they're less likely to be part of the problem.
- When dealing with adolescents, act more like a coach and less like a boss.
- A single minute spent practicing courtesy has more impact than a 1-hour lecture on the importance of it.
- To stop fights, stop put-downs. Verbal hits usually precede physical hits.
- Discipline should end with the correct behavior, not with a punishment.
- Rapport is the magical ingredient that changes a student's reluctance to be controlled into a willingness to be guided.

WHAT ARE THE THREE PROGRESSIVE PHASES THROUGH WHICH WE SHOULD GUIDE STUDENTS?

Morrish explains that rather than approaching discipline from the perspective of choice, Real Discipline asks teachers to guide students through three progressive phases he calls *training for compliance, teaching students how to behave,* and *managing student choice.* Each of these **three phases** is aimed at a particular goal and involves the use of certain strategies, as explained in the following paragraphs.

Phase 1: Training for Compliance

Note: In a September 2012 memo to the author of this text, Mr. Morrish said some people react a bit negatively to the word "compliance." He wants teachers to think of compliance as meaning "following directions," which students must do if teach- ing is to be effective. When explaining this point to teachers, Morrish uses driver training as an illustration, where it is clear that the driving instructor will be giving directions that the learner must follow. In the same way, teachers teach routine behaviors that students are to follow. Doing so consistently results in a classroom that runs smoothly.

Morrish strongly urges teachers to train their students to comply with rules, limits, and authority. *Rules* are descriptions of how students are to behave. An example might be "Show courtesy and respect for others at all times." *Limits* spec- ify behavior that will *not* be allowed. An example would be, "No name-calling in this room." *Authority* refers to power that has been assigned to certain individuals. By custom and law, teachers are given legitimate authority to control and direct students in school, and they should use that power to set and maintain standards of conduct.

Teachers' first task is to train their students to accept authority and comply with it automatically. Compliance should be taught as a *nonthinking activity.* Nonthinking activities are habits you don't have to reflect on or make choices about, such as stopping at red lights or saying "thank you" when a person does something nice for you.

Begin by telling your students straightforwardly that one of your most important jobs is to help each and every one of them be successful in school and life. Success comes from behaving in approved ways, with limits set on what people are allowed to do. He says he finds it astonishing that compliance receives virtually no attention in most approaches to discipline, even though compliance helps students learn to conduct themselves properly and at the same time provides the basis for later decision making.

Further explain to your students that in order to find success, they must learn to behave courteously, show self-control, and do what is expected of them to the best of their ability. Point out that as a professional teacher, you have been trained to help students accomplish those things, and that you have a clear plan for doing so that will bring success for everyone in the class. Indicate that you will begin by training your students to pay attention, follow directions, and speak and act respectfully to others. Those things will be practiced until they occur automatically, without anyone having to think about them.

As you proceed, use direct instruction and close supervision to teach students exactly how you want them to behave. For example, if you want students to raise their hands before speaking, tell them what you expect and show them how to do it. Then have them practice it until it becomes habitual. When students make mistakes, show them again how to do the act properly and, again, practice it. Morrish says to start small, and you will see a general attitude of compliance grow out of many small acts of compliance.

Because compliance is so important, you should address all instances of misbehavior. Do not overlook small misbehaviors, as suggested in many discipline programs. If you do, you will soon be overwhelmed with explaining, negotiating, and tending to consequences. This overload will cause you to "pick your battles" and not "sweat the small stuff." Thus, you might allow students to put their heads on their desks during opening routines, talk during announcements, throw their jackets in the corner instead of hanging them up, and wander around the room instead of getting ready to work.

Such minor misbehavior might seem unimportant, but it should never be overlooked. Poor habits easily expand into poor behavior overall. If you walk by students who are doing something wrong and you say nothing, they interpret that as meaning you don't care, and the next thing you know they are engaged in disruptive behavior.

Don't get the idea you can't manage such behavior, but do understand that you can't manage it by scolding and doling out consequences. Morrish repeats again and again that the most effective approach is to tell students what you want them to do and then insist they do it properly. When they do something wrong, have them do it right. That is how you establish good practices and habits in your classes. Students get the picture quickly.

What Role Do Rules Play in Training for Compliance?

Just as we need rules for structure and predictability in everyday living, so do we need rules for classroom behavior. Teachers should make the rules. There is no need to ask students if they agree with them. Students are supposed to learn rules, not determine them. Teach students why we have rules and why they are made by people in positions of authority. Explain your rules to students and take their opinions into account, but don't pretend they are helping decide what the class rules are to be.

Once you've established rules, you must commit to ensuring they are obeyed. Even after you've stated your rules, you really don't have them unless you can enforce them. Your enforcement should be consistent, even for misbehavior that seems incidental, such as carelessly dropping rubbish on the floor or talking during quiet study time. As noted earlier, small infractions have a way of growing into large infractions.

Morrish says **insistence** is the best strategy for enforcing rules. Punishment is rarely if ever needed. You must be absolutely determined that students will do what you want them to, and you must be willing to persist until they do. You should develop the mindset that once you give an instruction, there is no question about students doing what you say.

Morrish does not suggest you give up punishment altogether, even though he points out that punishment does not encourage cooperation or responsibility and that it sometimes produces unwanted side effects. However, he maintains that punishment can do two things well. First, it can teach that "no means no," a message that students need to learn quickly. Second, punishment can bring misbehavior to a stop when other tactics can't.

> **?** Students usually enter Mrs. James's class casually, talking and joking among themselves. Mrs. James doesn't mind because she likes to use the first few minutes of class time to review her lesson plans and chat with individual students whose assignments have not been completed correctly.
>
> What do you think Ron Morrish would say about her approach?
>
> What do you think he would have her do differently, if anything?

What Role Do Limits Play in Training for Compliance?

Morrish uses the term *rule* to refer to what students should do (e.g., "Raise your hand before speaking"). He uses the term *limit* to refer to what students should not do (e.g., "Absolutely no bullying allowed"). Rules and limits are set and enforced by teachers, in accordance with established standards. Teachers do not negotiate them with students. Morrish says the first secret of good discipline is: *Never give students a choice when it comes to limits.*

You set limits in many ways, formally and informally. For example, you may work with students so they know that when they arrive in the classroom, they are to hang up their jackets and get ready for work immediately (these are rules). They also know they are not allowed to scuffle or swear (these are limits). You present the rules and limits and have your students practice the behaviors. Students do not have any say in them. If they have questions about limits, you should select a time to explain the reasons behind them, but in no case are students allowed to ignore your directions. Your word is final.

Morrish laments that limits in today's classrooms are so often compromised by bargaining between teacher and students. He says that the more teachers give special privileges in exchange for behaving properly, the more students are likely to misbehave. Bargaining simply does not produce the results teachers want.

Teachers expect that once the bargaining is done, students will assess the possible outcomes of their behavior choices and thus make good choices automatically. However, things don't work that way. The main result for students is not better choice making, but feeling that everything in the class is decided through bargaining. All that does is give students power in decisions they are ill-prepared to make.

What Role Does Teacher Authority Play in Training for Compliance?

Morrish insists we need to reestablish teacher authority in the classroom, and he reminds teachers that their authority is based in law, custom, and professionalism. The power of teacher authority comes from teachers' knowing their responsibilities, knowing why they are setting limits, and knowing what they expect students to learn. It is conveyed by tone of voice, choice of words, and the way teachers present themselves.

Teachers should clearly communicate what they expect of students and then accept nothing less. They should make clear that no negotiation is involved. They do this without threatening or raising their voices. They simply say, with confidence and authority, "This is what you must do. This is the job you are here for. Now let's get on with it" (Morrish, 1997, p. 65).

If, in this process, students question your authority, tell them, "It is my job." If they challenge your right to make demands, tell them, "It is my job." Morrish says not to worry if your students don't like some of the things you expect them to do. It is respect you need at this point, not appreciation. Appreciation will come later, provided respect comes first.

Morrish acknowledges that many teachers become uneasy when asked to train their students for compliance. They fear automatic compliance will make their students passive, submissive, and unable to think for themselves. But as you have seen, Morrish disagrees, insisting that today's discipline gives students too much freedom of choice, not too little. What we need, he says, is a balance, which is achieved through the three phases of Real Discipline. Now we move ahead to the next phase.

Phase 2: Teaching Students How to Behave

The second phase in Real Discipline involves teaching students the skills, attitudes, and knowledge they need for cooperating, behaving properly, and assuming responsibility. When beginning this phase, you will have already established class rules and limits, which you will have taught through explanation, demonstration, practice, corrective feedback, and repetition. Students understand the need for rules and limits, and they will comply with them if they accept your authority.

Now you begin to teach them how to be courteous, work and play together harmoniously, resolve conflicts, set personal goals, organize tasks, and manage time. Most teachers erroneously assume students will somehow learn those skills from experience. You can't wait for experience to produce this desired result, even if it were capable of it. If you are to have order and acceptable behavior in your classes, you will have to prepare your students. The best way to teach what they need to know is through direct instruction and supervised practice.

Again, here is the basic operating principle you should follow: When students fail to comply with expectations, don't scold or punish them. Simply have them redo the behavior in an acceptable manner. Do this as often as necessary. You can expect them to show improvement very quickly.

Now we proceed to the third phase.

Phase 3: Managing Student Choice

The third phase of Real Discipline is called *choice management*. It helps students move toward greater independence by gradually allowing them the opportunity to make more choices as they show they are able to handle them intelligently. At this point, a basic operating principle is that when students make choices, they must take into account the needs and rights of fellow students and school personnel. They also need to begin learning exactly who has the right, or duty, to make a particular choice. Teachers have to make certain choices. Students can be allowed to make others.

As a rule of thumb, if students don't care about the outcome of a particular concern, they should not be allowed to make choices about it. Many teachers think students who do poor class work should receive low marks, which will motivate them to do better in the future. This may work for some highly motivated students, but it does nothing for those who don't care and are perfectly willing to accept the low grades. If Alana indicates she doesn't care about her performance in school, then you don't let her make choices about it. You say to her, "That's okay, Alana. I do care how well you do, so I'll make the decisions for you. Someday, when you care how well you do, you can make your own choices" (Morrish, 1997, p. 101). If Alana turns in poor work, you say to her: "Alana, your work is disorganized and incomplete. I'm not accepting it. Take it back, please, and fix it up. I'll mark it when it is done properly" (Morrish, 1997, p. 105).

You should never suggest that Alana can choose to do poor work if she wants to. Morrish says this is one area where we truly need to get back to basics, meaning we should expect students to do quality work and accept nothing less. Remember that the goal of Real Discipline is to help students become self-disciplined. You don't promote self-discipline by allowing students to do whatever they please instead of what is right.

In his book *Secrets of Discipline: 12 Keys for Raising Responsible Children*, Morrish (1997, pp. 93–94) relates a classroom incident that epitomizes self-discipline. Morrish was visiting a combination grade 2/3 class when the teacher told her students she would be leaving the classroom for a few minutes. The students were to continue working quietly. She asked them, "What does this mean you need?" Hands were raised. A student answered, "Self-discipline." The teacher continued,

"What does self-discipline mean?" Another student answered, "It means we behave when you're not with us, exactly the same way we behave when you are standing right next to us."

The teacher and Morrish both left the room but Morrish stopped in the hallway to watch the students from a distance. He observed that the students continued to work as if the teacher were in the room with them. Later he asked the teacher how she had accomplished that result. She said she had the class practice the skill from the first day. She would stand next to them and ask them to show their best behavior. Then she challenged them to continue behaving that way as she moved farther and farther away. Before long, the students had learned how to maintain their behavior when the teacher left the room.

As students become older and move toward independence, Real Discipline will have already taught them three things about making independent choices: (1) independence requires balancing personal rights with personal responsibility; (2) the rights and needs of others must always be taken into account; and (3) students should look at every unsupervised situation as an opportunity to demonstrate personal responsibility. Morrish reiterates that independence isn't "doing your own thing": It's doing what's right when you are on your own.

SPECIFICALLY, WHAT DOES MORRISH ADVISE IN REGARD TO PLANNING AND IMPLEMENTING A GOOD DISCIPLINE PROGRAM?

For discipline to be effective, teachers must plan proactively, meaning they anticipate problems, keep them from occurring if possible, and prepare carefully for attending to problems that might occur. Morrish (2000) suggests teachers follow these 11 steps when organizing their discipline system:

1. *Decide in advance how you want your students to behave.* Think through matters such as the following: How students will demonstrate courtesy, the words and tone of voice they will use, how they will speak to you, what other signs of courtesy they will show, how they will treat visitors, how they will welcome new students to the class, how they will listen to you and other students, how they will contribute to class discussions, how they will help substitute teachers, what they will do when upset or when they disagree with you or others, how they will respond to other students who need assistance, how they will deal with losing, how they will comply when you tell them what to do, how they will respond when you correct them, and how they will behave when you step out of the room.

2. *Design a supporting structure.* When you have in mind how you want students to behave, design a structure that will support your goals. This structure will consist mostly of procedures you teach students to follow, such as how students will enter and exit the room, what they will do if they arrive late, how they will handle completed work, how they will request assistance, what they should do about missed assignments, what they should do if they finish work early, what they should do if the teacher does not appear on time, how they will learn the class rules and enforcement procedures, and what the specific limits on behavior are.

3. *Establish a threshold for behavior at school.* You must not allow students to bring negative behaviors to the class from home and the community. You must create a clear separation between school and outside school. Say to students, "You're now at school. Remember how you behave when you are here." Then enforce the courtesy and work habits required in your class.

4. *Run a 2-week training camp.* Effective teachers work hard the first 2 weeks in establishing class expectations and procedures. They give particular attention to behavior standards, clear limits, routines, and compliance. Morrish maintains that the investment you make in discipline during these first 2 weeks determines how the rest of the school year will unfold. This does not suggest you overlook academic work, but in the early stages, academic work is of lower priority than proper behavior. As students acclimate to Real Discipline, academic work moves to highest priority.

5. *Teach students how to behave appropriately.* Morrish believes students should be taught a number of skills necessary for school success, not only in the classroom but also in school assemblies, on school buses, and in the school cafeteria. They should practice courtesy and be taught how to treat new students and be good role models for younger students. They should be taught how to help substitute teachers. They should be taught to recognize and suppress incidents such as teasing and name-calling that escalate into conflicts in class. They should be taught always to take others into account, to help someone every day, and to acknowledge people who have helped them. And they should be taught to be good ambassadors for the class and school, displayed through behavior in public that brings credit to themselves, their school, and their families.

6. *Set the stage for quality instruction.* Discipline cannot succeed in an environment where students must be coerced to endure boring, tedious lessons and activities. You must make your classes interesting and worthwhile. Ask questions that force students to expand their thinking. Increase the amount of hands-on activities. Make use of group learning activities. Include activities based on sports, music, drama, and crafts. Ask students to make presentations to the class and to younger students. These approaches keep students interested and less likely to behave disruptively.

7. *Provide active, assertive supervision.* Good discipline requires that you take certain steps to forestall misbehavior. Remind students of rules and expectations ahead of time. Remind them of limits that might apply. Be specific and don't oververbalize. Govern and correct small misbehaviors. Reinforce good social skills when you see them. Move briskly around the classroom. Talk briefly with various students, provided it doesn't interrupt their work. Let everyone see your presence. Move with a sense of purpose. Make eye contact with students.

8. *Enforce rules and expectations.* Most teachers believe they should make students aware of unpleasant consequences that will be applied when students misbehave. They use the consequences as warnings. But neither warnings nor consequences are very effective in getting students to conduct themselves properly. Success depends on the teacher's ability to *require* good behavior. You must be willing to establish your natural authority and take charge of students. There is no game playing involved. Don't allow them to decide whether or not to comply with rules. Don't allow them to call you by your first name, talk back, run around

the room, or throw things at each other. Teachers worry that some students will confront them over expectations and rule enforcement they don't like. You can limit that concern by addressing all small infractions such as discourteous language or failure to clean up. When students learn to comply on small matters, they will continue to comply on larger matters. Meanwhile, connect with your students on a personal basis. Listen to them and take their concerns into account. Capitalize on their interests. Be understanding and supportive when a student is going through a hard time. Establish rapport, but combine it with insistence.

9. *Focus on prevention.* Real Discipline goes to lengths to prevent misbehavior. Remember, discipline isn't as much what you do when students misbehave as it is what you do in advance so they won't misbehave. Use the suggestions presented earlier for making classes interesting and engaging. Emphasize civil behavior and do not allow verbal put-downs. Discuss potential behavior situations with students and devise ways of avoiding them.

10. *Set high standards.* Don't allow underachievement to be a student choice. You must make it clear you will not accept underachievement in any form, whether academic or social. When students do something inadequately or improperly, have them do it over again. Challenge your students and get them excited about improving everything they do in school.

11. *Treat caregivers as partners.* Keep caregivers informed about serious incidents and repetitive misbehavior involving their child, but don't worry them with minor matters—take care of those things yourself. When you need to communicate with caregivers, do so by email or by phone if possible. Don't send notes. Suggest ways they might help the student do better in school, but never suggest punishment. Talk *with* caregivers, not down to them. Reassure them that you and they both want success for their child and that you want to work together with them to make that happen.

Commentary from Anonymous Teacher 1

As I read Mr. Morrish's suggestions, I was aware I already do some of the things he recommends and find them effective. For example, I do deal with minor problems when they occur in order to keep them from escalating into bigger problems. I endeavor to provide a good model for students concerning helping others, speaking to them in a kindly way, and avoiding saying things they might find personally hurtful. I often have them repeat their behavior properly when they misbehave. I also got some ideas from Mr. Morrish that I will begin using. My students are young (third grade) and I think I may have been involving them too much in giving input into the rules of behavior for the class. I think in reality my efforts have been more along the lines of leading them to suggest the kind of behavior I want to see from them in the first place. I think I might spend too much time on that. I like Morrish's suggestion about my making rules for the class and then talking with students to help them see how those rules will help them be successful in class, stay safe from harm, get along better with other members of the class, and better enjoy their experience in school.

I also became more aware of a few things I'd like to emphasize more with my students. For example, I will try spending more time teaching my students how to speak invitingly and encouragingly with each other during cooperative work activities. I think that might increase participation by all members of the group. I think I will also teach them to make positive comments about each other and avoid put-downs in other class activities. I think I sometimes just tell my students what is expected of them while not actually teaching them how to do things properly or efficiently. Usually I get good cooperation from my students. I treat them nicely and show them personal attention, and I get the feeling they want to please me—not always, but at least most of the time.

HOW DOES ONE DEVELOP POSITIVE RELATIONS WITH STUDENTS?

No approach to discipline is going to accomplish what you hope unless you can establish and maintain good personal relations with your students. If students like you, they will want to please you and not disappoint you. They will be inclined to comply with your requests and will understand and accept that the rules you establish ensure security and proper treatment for everyone. Morrish offers a number of suggestions for strengthening relationships between you and your students:

- *Consistently focus on the positive.* Look for things students do right. If they make a mistake, help them improve. No need to criticize.
- *Wipe the slate clean after students make behavior mistakes.* Deal with the mistake in a positive manner and move on. Don't hold grudges; they don't help in any way. The important thing is what the student does next.
- *Don't back away from discipline.* Students sometimes don't like having to obey rules or practice appropriate behavior. That doesn't mean they don't want discipline. They understand it is important. They expect it and interpret the effort you expend on it as a sign of concern for them. Later, they will remember you with appreciation.
- *Lead the way.* Students learn more from watching you than from hearing what you say they should do. Model civilized behaviors and attitudes. Listen to students. Speak kindly to them. Be helpful and give credit when it is due.
- *Never humiliate students when correcting their misbehavior.* Morrish says teachers unintentionally humiliate students more than they imagine, as when they scold students in front of their friends or correct mistakes in an unpleasant manner. Whenever students need to be corrected, just make sure they know how to behave properly and then insist they do so.
- *Don't accept mediocrity.* Some teachers fail to set standards of learning and behavior, believing they need only to befriend students in order to obtain their cooperation. Standards are essential if students are to recognize success and maintain their determination to improve. If you willingly accept mediocrity, that is what you will get. Reasonable standards tell students you believe they are bright and sensitive enough to learn and behave properly.

WHAT ABOUT CONSEQUENCES FOR MISBEHAVIOR?

Morrish believes students should face consequences when they misbehave. He maintains that consequences, when structured and applied correctly, are very helpful in discipline. But the consequences he advocates are not punishments. Instead, they involve teaching students to behave properly and then having them show they can do so. We have seen that Morrish's favorite consequence is to have the student repeat the behavior in a correct manner. But he uses other consequences as well, and would have you explain to students why they are applied and how they help students conduct themselves more responsibly. Here are some consequences he suggests you use when students push at boundaries or do something that hurts others:

- *Make an improvement plan.* Have the student make a plan for handling the situation better in the future. Keep track to ensure the student follows through.
- *Provide compensation.* Have the student do something positive to make up for negative behavior. This might include making the offended person feel better or the school or classroom look better.
- *Write a letter.* Have the offending student write a letter to the person who was offended, including a statement of commitment for better behavior in the future.
- *Teach younger children.* Have the offending student write and illustrate a story about the incident to read to younger children, emphasizing what was done wrong and what was learned from the experience. (Morrish, 2000, p. 66)

WHAT ABOUT MOTIVATION AND REWARDS?

Many experts in discipline assert that we can't *make* students do anything—that the best we can do is provide an environment and activities so appealing that students will naturally work and otherwise conduct themselves appropriately. Morrish doesn't entirely agree. He says we should certainly provide enticing learning opportunities, but it is ridiculous to believe we cannot make students do anything. The very purpose of discipline, he says, is to make students do what they don't want to do. He points out that students ordinarily do not want to obey rules, don't want to stay quiet, don't want to do homework, don't want to study for tests, and so forth. We use discipline to ensure that they set aside their natural desires and accept education's plans for helping them succeed in life.

He goes on to say that good discipline teaches students how to persevere and work through activities that are not especially appealing. To the extent you can make instructional activities interesting, do so, and everyone will enjoy school more, including you. But when that is not possible, don't shy away from teaching students what they need to know, even when lessons are tedious.

Morrish also advises teachers to forego praise and reward when students merely do what is expected of them. He says occasional rewards are fine, because they give special recognition when it is needed. But overall, rewards are vastly overused and students often see them as ends in themselves. Teachers have two powerful natural rewards at their disposal, but they are not stickers, points, or special privileges. They are what you always have with you—your personal attention and your approval.

Teachers these days typically dispense copious quantities of praise. Some of them really spread it on thick. But Morrish says we must be cautious about that, too. Beyond a certain point, praise actually reduces motivation and increases dependency. Students develop healthier attitudes if teachers praise student work and behavior only when they truly merit recognition.

> **?** Suppose Carmelo has defaced a bulletin board in the room.
>
> What sort of consequence do you think Morrish would apply for that behavior?
>
> Suppose Carmelo helps Anthony resolve a personal problem with another student.
>
> What sort of reward, if any, would Morrish suggest for that behavior?

WHAT DOES MORRISH SAY ABOUT FOSTERING SELF-ESTEEM?

Many educators believe low self-esteem is the root cause of antisocial behavior. Morrish sees the picture differently. He acknowledges that students who do poorly in school and get into trouble sometimes (but not always) have low self-esteem, whereas those who do well tend to have higher self-esteem. But self-esteem does not determine success or failure. It is the other way around, he says—success in school or lack thereof influences self-esteem. If you are competent and successful, you usually think better about yourself than if you are incompetent and unsuccessful.

Morrish goes on to say that teachers who try to build student self-esteem directly may actually do more harm than good, especially if they never allow failure, never put pressure on students to excel, and permit students to express themselves freely without fear of rebuke. These things remove students from the helpful criticism that normally follows misbehavior or lack of effort, and as a result, students become more self-indulgent. They gradually lose their sense of shame and begin to rationalize their misdeeds with explanations such as "I just felt like it" or "It made me feel good."

Genuine self-esteem comes from increased competence in academic and social matters and the ability to overcome obstacles. If we teach students academic and social skills, and if we help them achieve the high expectations we hold of them, we will see them come to think well of themselves. Competence is the goal; it comes first, then self-esteem follows.

WHAT SHOULD YOU DO WHEN STUDENTS FAIL TO COMPLY WITH YOUR DIRECTIONS?

Occasionally a student may fail to comply with your directions or may, in the heat of the moment, display other inappropriate behavior. Suppose one of your students has behaved discourteously toward you in class. Many teachers will send the offending student to time-out for an indefinite period before allowing him or her to rejoin the class. That does very little positive for the student. Instead of time-out or some other consequence, you should insist on a **do-over**. Have the student repeat the behavior in an acceptable manner. If a student speaks to you disrespectfully, tell him or her to start over and do it courteously this time.

The same procedure applies any time a student fails to follow directions or comply with class standards. Many teachers make the mistake of using *if–then statements,* such as, "If you speak to me in that manner again, then you will be going to the principal's office." Teachers should not use such statements with misbehaving students. They should give students no choice in the matter. They should say, "We don't speak that way in this class. Start over." Most of the time, that is all you need to do.

Remember, your most important and powerful tool is *insistence.* You must convey to students they have no choice in the matter, other than to do as you direct. Morrish says that students who are never required to act appropriately seldom will.

If a student still refuses to do as you direct, repeat your instruction in a serious tone of voice. If that doesn't work, use a mild punishment such as time-out to get across the message that you mean what you say. Then after a short time, bring the student back to do the task correctly. The discipline procedure does not end with the time-out. The student is still expected to show proper behavior, and only positive practice ensures that. As discussed previously, punishment is rarely necessary if you persistently help students behave properly.

Commentary from Anonymous Teacher 2

Some of Dr. Morrish's suggestions may sound like advice to parents, but the fact is I now usually have students in class who have not had the benefit of decent parenting. Sometimes I need to help students with a "reality check" of how things work in the real world. This past year, for example, I was challenged by the following students. I have changed their names:

- ✓ Venus, whose family had disintegrated, leaving her in foster care, uncertain and untrusting.
- ✓ Tristan, the only child of older parents, who hadn't yet learned to take no for an answer.
- ✓ Josh, treated as a peer by his parents, felt entitled to question my every decision.
- ✓ Sammy, an excellent student and charming to adults, who wielded her cell phone as a saber, slicing and dicing her classmates with rumor and innuendo on various social networking sites.
- ✓ Dimitri, who studied me with the intensity of a profiler, figuring out my buttons and waiting for the optimal occasion to push them, purely for the sport of it.

The truth is, students expect teachers to be in charge and keep order in the classroom, even though many don't act like it. With a strong structure in place and a strong teacher in authority, students feel safer, more confident, and more secure. At least that's what I believe. If you don't assume leadership of your students and of your classroom, some of your students will step up to fill the void. Personally, I found the following suggestions from Dr. Morrish to be right on target:

✓ Don't make rules you are not prepared to enforce.

✓ Plan interesting lessons and challenge students to achieve.

✓ Stay on your feet, stay on the move, and stay on top of things.

✓ Be patient, pleasant, persistent, and pragmatic.

✓ Cut down on the lecturing, preaching, and scolding, which students quickly tune out.

✓ Model your expectations and always try to show kindness, courtesy, respect, and appreciation in interactions with students.

WHAT YOU HAVE LEARNED IN THIS CHAPTER

This chapter explained and advocated the following:

■ Real Discipline is a process that leads to cooperation and responsible behavior. It takes time. There are no shortcuts.

■ From the beginning, communicate to your students that you are committed to providing a classroom in which they can learn easily, without threat or put-downs, and where everyone, teacher and students alike, courteously and willingly does the jobs expected of them.

■ Tell students about duties in the class—what your job is and what their job is. You might wish to explain that your job is to provide a quality learning environment, teach students the best you can, and treat everyone with respect and courtesy, while their job is to follow your directions, do the best they can to learn, and treat everyone with respect and courtesy.

■ Make it plain that you will steadfastly help students make the most of their opportunities to learn. Inform them why it is necessary they follow your directions, every time. Show them how you will teach directions for simple activities such as beginning work when entering the classroom and handing in homework or class assignments.

■ Project an image of friendly authority as you introduce the rules of behavior for the class. Discuss the rules thoroughly and make sure students understand how rules help everyone learn things they need to know in life. Tell the students you will insist they follow the rules, but you will teach them how to do so and always help them. Follow through and have students practice proper behavior.

■ During the first days of school, ask in advance if students remember the rules for beginning work, have only school materials on their desks, and so forth.

Activities

Self-Test: True/False

1. Morrish's Real Discipline invites students to play a strong part in formulating the rules of behavior that apply in the classroom.

2. The best way to correct misbehavior is to require students to repeat the improper behavior in an acceptable manner.

3. If you require students to comply with the class rules you establish, you will be asking for trouble later on when you expect them to make decisions for themselves.

4. The best way to improve students' self-concept is to help them succeed in challenging situations.

5. "Limits" is synonymous with "rules," in that both terms refer to what students are forbidden to do in the classroom.

6. Teaching students to comply with teacher authority is one of the best things you can do to help students be successful in school.

7. Teachers should furnish evident rewards to students almost every time students conduct themselves in accordance with class rules.

8. When students misbehave, they should experience the consequences established for improper behavior.

9. A very effective way to help students behave appropriately is to teach them to follow procedures you have established for class activities.

10. Strong emphasis should be placed on clarifying the teacher's main roles and the students' main roles in class and how those roles are to be carried out.

Self-Test: Multiple Choice

1. Morrish believes you should teach younger students to
   (a) fend for themselves.
   (b) accept responsibility.
   (c) comply with teacher directions.
   (d) work with a buddy.

2. In Morrish's view, Real Discipline
   (a) encourages choice.
   (b) focuses on management.
   (c) teaches students how to behave.
   (d) involves students in formulating class rules.

3. In Morrish's view, punishment
   (a) should never be used.
   (b) can do certain things well.
   (c) has no role in Real Discipline.
   (d) is the resort of the weak teacher.

4. Students will usually try to please you if they
   (a) aren't afraid of you.
   (b) fear you.
   (c) like you.
   (d) understand your role.

5. Many outstanding authorities say you can't make students do anything they don't want to do. Morrish
   (a) agrees.
   (b) equivocates.
   (c) disagrees.
   (d) demurs.

6. With regard to clarifying teachers' and students' jobs, Morrish says
   (a) it's a waste of time.
   (b) you definitely should.
   (c) don't expect too much.
   (d) use common sense.

7. Morrish thinks discipline should teach students to
   (a) become self-analytical.
   (b) survive.
   (c) relish the moment.
   (d) persevere.

8. When students break a rule, you should insist on
   (a) a do-over.
   (b) an appropriate apology.
   (c) a clarification.
   (d) self-restitution.

9. Morrish advises that when students do what is expected of them, you should
   - (a) give positive reinforcement.
   - (b) praise them.
   - (c) smile at them.
   - (d) skip the praise.
10. As you introduce rules of behavior, you should project an image of friendly
    - (a) empathy.
    - (b) authority.
    - (c) concern.
    - (d) adversity.

Self-Test: Explain This

1. Why does Morrish believe you must teach students to comply automatically with teacher directives?
2. Why is Morrish opposed to allowing younger students to make choices as to what they will do or how they will behave?
3. What does Morrish mean when he says discipline is a process, not an event?
4. What does Morrish believe about fostering student self-esteem?
5. What does Morrish think you should do in order to get along well with students and entice them to follow your lead?

Additional Suggested Activities

1. Make entries in your journal concerning ideas from Morrish's Real Discipline that you might wish to include in your personal system of discipline.
2. Refer back to the section "What Questions Will This Chapter Answer for Me?" at the beginning of this chapter. For each item listed there, test yourself to see if you understand what Morrish was advising or teaching.
3. Morrish makes some interesting contentions about the role of student choice in discipline. Outline your understanding of his points and indicate whether you agree with them or not, and why. Discuss your conclusions in class, if possible.

Concept Cases

CASE 1   Kristina Will Not Work

Kristina, a student in Mr. Jake's class, is quite docile. She socializes little with other students and never disrupts lessons. However, despite Mr. Jake's best efforts, Kristina will not do her work. She rarely completes an assignment. She is simply there, putting forth no effort at all. *What would Ronald Morrish suggest to help Kristina and Mr. Jake?*

Morrish would have Mr. Jake remind Kristina of the class rule about everyone doing their best to learn. He would insist that Kristina begin her work and follow through. Mr. Jake might need to stand beside her to help her get started. He would not punish her, but would continue to press her to comply with the assignment. He might ask questions such as, "Do you know what you are supposed to do in this activity?" "Do you understand why it needs to be done?" "Can I count on you to do your part?" As Kristina improves, Mr. Jake might make comments to her such as, "You made a good effort today. I can see you are trying. Thank you for that." If more intervention was required, Morrish would consider assigning Kristina to the school's study hall or keeping her in the classroom for additional time (a productive extension of her day, rather than a punitive detention). He might also have her create a daily plan for accomplishing her schoolwork, involve her caregivers in the process, or assign an older student to mentor her.

CASE 2   Sara Will Not Stop Talking

Sara is a pleasant girl who participates in class activities and does most, though not all, of her assigned work. She cannot seem to refrain from talking to classmates, however. Her teacher, Mr. Gonzales, has to speak to her repeatedly during lessons, to the point that he often becomes exasperated and loses his temper. *What suggestions would Ronald Morrish give Mr. Gonzales for dealing with Sara?*

CASE 3   Joshua Clowns and Intimidates

Joshua, larger and louder than his classmates, always wants to be the center of attention, which he accomplishes through a combination of clowning and intimidation. He makes wise remarks, talks back (smilingly) to the teacher, utters a variety of sound-effect noises such as automobile crashes and gunshots, and makes limitless sarcastic comments and put-downs of his classmates. Other students will not stand up to him, apparently fearing his size and verbal aggression. His teacher, Miss Pearl, has come to her wit's end. *Would Joshua's behavior be likely to improve if Ronald Morrish's techniques were used in Miss Pearl's classroom? Explain.*

CASE 4   Tom Is Hostile and Defiant

Tom has appeared to be in his usual foul mood ever since arriving in class. On his way to sharpen his pencil, he bumps into Frank, who complains. Tom tells him loudly to shut up. Miss Baines, the teacher, says, "Tom, go back to your seat." Tom wheels around, swears loudly, and says heatedly, "I'll go when I'm _____ good and ready!" *How would Ronald Morrish have Miss Baines deal with Tom?*

You Are the Teacher

HIGH SCHOOL BIOLOGY

You teach an advanced placement class in biology to students from middle- to upper-income families. Most of the students have already made plans for attending college. When the students enter the classroom, they know they are to go to their assigned seats and write out answers to the questions of the day that you have written on the board. After that, you conduct discussions on text material that you assigned students to read before coming to class. During the discussion, you call randomly on students to answer questions and require that they support their answers with reference to the assigned reading. Following that, students engage in lab activity for the remainder of the period.

A TYPICAL OCCURRENCE

You have just begun a discussion about the process of photosynthesis. You ask Sarolyn what the word *photosynthesis* means. She pushes her long hair aside and replies, "I don't get it." This is a comment you hear frequently from Sarolyn, even though she is an intelligent girl. "What is it you don't understand?" "None of it," she says. You say, "Be more specific! I've only asked for the definition!" Sarolyn is not intimidated. "I mean, I don't get any of it. I don't understand why plants are green. Why aren't they blue or some other color? Why don't they grow on mercury? The book says plants make food. How? Do they make bread? That's ridiculous."

You gaze at Sarolyn for a while, and she back at you. You ask, "Are you finished?" Sarolyn shrugs. "I guess so." She hears some of the boys whistle under their breath; she obviously enjoys their attention. You say to her, "Sarolyn, I hope someday you will understand that this is not a place for you to show off." "I hope so, too," Sarolyn says. "I know I should be more serious." She stares out the window. For the remainder of the discussion, which you don't handle as well as usual, you call only on students you know will give proper answers. Now that the discussion is completed, you begin to give instructions for the lab activity. You notice that Nick is turning the valve of the gas jet on and off. You say to Nick, "Mr. Contreras, would you please repeat our rule about the use of lab equipment?" Nick drops his head and mumbles something about waiting for directions. Sarolyn says calmly, "Knock it off, Nick. This is serious business."

She smiles at you. After a moment, you complete your directions and tell the students to begin. You walk around the room, monitoring their work. You stand behind lab partners Mei and Teresa, who are having a difficult time. You do not offer them help, believing that advanced placement students should be able to work things out for themselves. But as they blunder through the activity, you find yourself shaking your head in disbelief.

CONCEPTUALIZING A STRATEGY

If you followed the suggestions of Ronald Morrish, what would you conclude or do with regard to the following?

- Pinpointing the problems in your class
- Preventing the problems from occurring in the first place
- Putting an immediate end to the misbehavior
- Maintaining student dignity and good personal relations
- Using the situation to help the students develop a sense of greater responsibility and self-control

5

Craig Seganti on Taking Charge in the Classroom

How Does Craig Seganti Establish Control, Especially When Students Are Hard to Manage?

Today, most teachers reluctantly accept that their students will misbehave much of the time. They are more or less resigned to it. But Craig Seganti insists you should not settle for that, although it's probably what you'll get if you don't immediately establish one understanding with your students—that you are in charge and are a professional who knows what you're doing.

WHO IS CRAIG SEGANTI?

For more than 20 years, Seganti was a teacher in inner-city Los Angeles schools, where he not only survived but flourished. He describes how he did so in his 2008 book *Classroom Discipline 101: How to Get Control of Any Classroom.* He believes the approach he developed will solve discipline issues for all teachers and will save the careers of many who've been beaten down by resistant, uncooperative students.

Mr. Seganti taught middle school and high school English and English as a second language (ESL) to students from many different backgrounds. He also taught juvenile offenders of both sexes in probation camps and interim schools for Los Angeles County. He now is devoted full time to disseminating his ideas on discipline. Seganti describes his approach as reality based rather than theory based, and says his tactics work with students in the real world. He invites you to examine his approach thoroughly. It will, he says, free you to teach, free your students to learn in a positive environment without disruptions and turmoil, and bring you the overall success you always hoped for.

In this chapter, we explore Seganti's main concepts and procedures. It is suggested that you also review the short articles he has posted at http://ezinearticles .com/?expert=Craig_Seganti (Seganti, 2008b). Those articles include the following:

- How to Get Any Student to Behave Well All of the Time
- How to Avoid Useless Arguments with Students
- Eliminating the Middle Man—the Myth of Giving Warnings
- The Role of Accountability in Classroom Management

WHAT QUESTIONS WILL THIS CHAPTER ANSWER FOR ME?

- What does Seganti do when he first meets a new class?
- What does Seganti mean by "stopping problems before they get into the classroom"?
- What teacher attitude tends to promote the best student behavior in the classroom?
- How does Seganti ensure that students will comply with class rules?
- What does Seganti mean by *teacher leverage* and *student accountability*?
- What rules or rule topics best promote student accountability in the classroom?
- What sort of "leverage" ensures that students will conduct themselves responsibly?
- How do leverage and accountability work together to promote learning and desirable behavior?
- Which management efforts best enhance the classroom experience for students and teacher?

THE SEGANTI MODEL OF DISCIPLINE

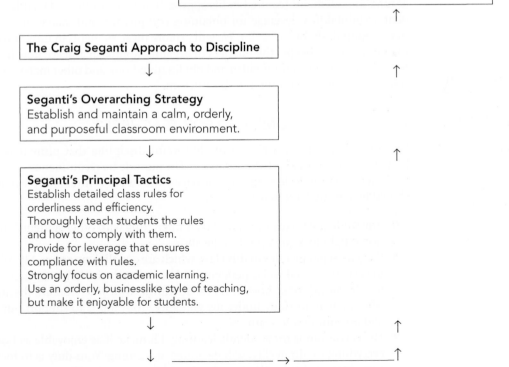

The Common Goal of All Approaches to Discipline *Responsible, Civil Classroom Behavior That Becomes Habitual and Lasts over Time*
Responsible means paying attention, making a strong effort, and doing what is proper without being told.
Civil means respectful, polite, cordial, and well-mannered.

↑

The Craig Seganti Approach to Discipline

↓   ↑

Seganti's Overarching Strategy
Establish and maintain a calm, orderly, and purposeful classroom environment.

↓   ↑

Seganti's Principal Tactics
Establish detailed class rules for orderliness and efficiency.
Thoroughly teach students the rules and how to comply with them.
Provide for leverage that ensures compliance with rules.
Strongly focus on academic learning.
Use an orderly, businesslike style of teaching, but make it enjoyable for students.

↓   ↑

↓ ——————— → ——————↑

WHAT DOES SEGANTI SAY ABOUT DISCIPLINE?

Here is a preview of some of Seganti's main points of advice. We will examine them further throughout the chapter:

- Adopt and share with students the attitude that your class is, first and foremost, for academic learning.
- Emphasize that behavioral disruptions interfere with all students' right to a good education.
- Make it your first priority to teach all students to understand and comply with class rules of behavior. Then hold all students accountable for complying with those rules.
- Establish "leverage" that ensures you can enforce the rules. (Seganti recommends as very effective a 15-minute detention that misbehaving students must attend after school.)

In short, you can manage a productive class even for "difficult" students if you establish and clarify rules of behavior, teach the rules, and establish leverage that ensures student compliance with rules.

At first glance, Seganti's approach may appear a bit harsh. But he maintains it works wonders in fostering respectful behavior and motivating effort to learn. He contends it is exactly what hard-to-manage students need, and that there is nothing better you can do for students than help them develop responsibility and gain a good education in a classroom that is focused on learning.

We now proceed to examine Seganti's core ideas and suggestions, organized around four elements featured in his approach: teacher attitude, class rules for student accountability, leverage for obtaining compliance, and management tactics that support desirable behavior. We will explore these elements in turn. If you wish to examine more deeply the nuances of Seganti's approach and see how he makes his points, you can view his video and obtain his e-book and other materials on the Internet at www.classroomdiscipline101.com.

WHAT ATTITUDE DOES SEGANTI RECOMMEND FOR TEACHERS?

Seganti says it is the teacher's attitude toward discipline that ultimately affects how students behave, for better or worse. The attitude he recommends is conveyed to students via the following four messages, which are central and powerful and should be repeated as often as necessary:

- Any student who disrupts the class is interfering with other students' constitutional right to a good public education.
- We have separate roles in this class, which are equally important. My role: I am the expert, trained and experienced in how to teach and help you learn. I make the decisions about how to do those things. Your role: You are the students who are here to study under my guidance. Your job is to support our efforts and do your best to learn.
- The classroom is for academic learning. I'll make it as enjoyable as I can, but everything we do in class will be aimed at learning. Your duty is to focus and participate and learn. That is what I will always expect of you.

■ I know you want to enjoy school and feel good about yourselves. I will help you do just that. But you need to understand that self-esteem doesn't come from messing around in the classroom. It comes from doing hard work to acquire the knowledge and skills that will enable you to enjoy a good life.

Seganti suggests many principles for greatly improving teacher effectiveness. For example:

■ *Rely on Actions.* When dealing with students, make your points through actions, which speak far louder than words. It is worse than useless to spend time cajoling, arguing, and continually trying to justify your decisions to students. Just make good rules and enforce them without fail. No explanations are needed. If you don't enforce your rules, students will act as though your rules don't exist.

■ *Don't Give Warnings.* Giving students warnings is self-defeating and it wastes time. Students beyond first or second grade know when they are misbehaving, so there is no need to warn them about it or say you are thinking of doing something about it. You can spend your day (week, month, career) giving warnings instead of teaching. If you don't want students to manipulate you, don't give warnings. (Seganti does give students one warning, on the first day of class only, as we will see when we review his rules.)

■ *Don't Give Superfluous Rewards.* Don't spend time doling out rewards for learning. Learning is what students are supposed to do. Of course you want your students to enjoy your classes and you will help them do so, but their reward for doing the assigned work lies in seeing their abilities expand as part of a good education. Emphasize that principle and help students keep track of what they have learned. Recognition of genuine progress is the only reward that truly counts. If you try to motivate students with gimmicks, pep talks, and tangible rewards, you send a poor message about education—that it is of so little value you need to bribe students to endure it. If students ask you what the reward will be for behaving properly, tell them the reward will be a good education, which is priceless.

■ *Provide for Enjoyment.* All the while, you must do what you can to make the class enjoyable for students. Provide numerous fun activities. Treat students with kindness and consideration. Give them personal attention. Be helpful. Celebrate learning and show there can and should be some fun and enjoyment in the classroom.

■ *Speak Effectively.* Learn how to talk effectively with students. (The suggestions presented here have to do with teaching information and proper behavior. If you were counseling students or commiserating with them, you would speak in a different manner.) Look at the following exchange as an example of what *not* to do:

Teacher: Stop talking, Johnny.
Johnny: I wasn't talking.
Teacher: You were talking—I just saw you talking to Henry.
Johnny: Well, Jason was talking. He was doing it first.
(and so forth, on and on)

Seganti comments, "What's your strategy here? Are you going to stand there arguing with Johnny about whether or not he was talking? That only perpetuates the problem." The following shows how Seganti would interact with Johnny:

Teacher: There is no talking in my class, Johnny—stay after school 15 minutes today for detention.
Johnny: But I wasn't talking!
Teacher: Show up for detention. If you don't want another 15 minutes, stop disrupting now.

RULES: HOW DO THEY PROMOTE STUDENT ACCOUNTABILITY?

Seganti insists on holding students accountable for their behavior. There should be no getting around it. Class rules of behavior provide the specifics of accountability. You, the teacher, must establish effective rules and make sure students understand them clearly. Compose the rules yourself, before you see your students, and make copies to hand out. Every possible behavior that concerns your class, positive or negative, should be addressed somewhere in the rules. You are the professional and you know how students should behave. Don't waste time asking students to help you decide what the rules should be.

Right away when students arrive at your door for the first day of class, teach them the rules for your class and exactly what those rules mean. This is to be done so no misunderstanding is possible. The students' first assignment in class is to copy the rules neatly, sign their copy, and hand it in. From that point onward, students are held accountable for their actions in class. They can no longer claim they didn't know the rules. If they try that ploy, have them once again copy the rules, sign the copy, and give it to you.

The following are rule topics Seganti advocates. The first two are given in Seganti's words. After that, additional topics for rules are presented with brief suggestions. In Seganti's book *Classroom Discipline 101* (Seganti, 2008a), you can find his exact wording for his 11 rules and the procedures he uses for teaching them to students.

Seganti's Rule 1 and Rule 2

Rule 1

You are to enter the classroom calmly and quietly and go immediately to your assigned seat. You are to sit at a 90-degree angle to your desk with your feet on the floor, showing good posture and a straight spine.

How to Teach Rule 1 to Students.   Stand in the door on the first day and teach this rule to each student in turn. This procedure is immediately established as a rule, not an option. A student who enters the room improperly has defied a rule and is subject to the consequence you have established for violating rules (Seganti's 15-minute detention consequence will be explained later). Once all students are seated, explain this rule again to the class as a whole.

Rule 2

Students are to show respect at all times and in all manners toward staff, others, and themselves. This includes all verbal and nonverbal forms of communication, including body language, facial expression, and tone of voice.

How to Teach Rule 2 to Students.   When all students are in the room, read this rule once. Even in the wildest schools there is usually a window of time the first day when students are curious and will listen. Now, read it again, piece by piece.

This can become a good lesson on nonverbal communication. Tell the students that most communication is nonverbal. Take your time here. Be a teacher— give examples and demonstrate. Tell the students, "If I give you a direction and you roll your eyes, it is just as disrespectful as if you insult me verbally, and you will get detention." Act it out—"Suppose I say: Jack, open your book to page 134." Pretend to be Jack and roll your eyes. Explain again that eye rolling and other disrespectful actions are just as unacceptable as saying something rude and will be met with the same consequences.

Additional Topics Seganti Suggests for Rules

Working on Task

This topic centers on clarifying when students should be on task, how they should be working, what they should do when they have completed their assigned work, and when and how they may talk.

Begin by clarifying exactly what *being on task* and *paying full attention* mean. Act out for students what these requirements look like and *do not* look like. Then, have selected students demonstrate behavior that complies with and violates the rule.

You absolutely must train your students to get their materials out immediately and be quietly at work by the time the bell rings. You must insist on this, or else students will begin to dawdle more and more when entering the room. In addition, you must help students identify productive and respectful activities they can do when they have completed their work. This heads off the future manipulation technique in which students say "I'm done with my work."

Eliminating Distractions

This topic centers on potential distractions, such as food, playthings, electronic media, and the like that students might intentionally or inadvertently bring to class. Seganti provides a list of potential distractions and carefully explains exactly what he will do if any of those distractions appear in noncompliance with the class rule. He explains again to students that class time is devoted entirely to learning and strongly reiterates that nothing will be permitted to interfere with that time.

One of the distractions Seganti highlights is chewing gum. He says he is famous for his "no-chewing" rule, which helps make him manipulation-proof. Students sometimes appear to be chewing, but claim they are not, sticking their tongues out to prove it. Seganti says this act can earn two detentions—one for chewing gum and one for lying. As Seganti explains it, here is how this situation usually plays out:

Teacher: Spit out the gum, Jane, and come after school for 15 minutes.

Jane: I'm not chewing gum.

Teacher: Well, there's no chewing in my class, even if you aren't chewing any-thing, so come to detention.

Jane: But I'm not chewing anything!

Teacher: I don't argue with students. You can either spit out the gum or get suspended for defiance.

(Jane then either spits out the gum or the teacher suspends her from the class.)

Seganti says you won't have to do this often. Once or twice and everyone gets the idea you are manipulation-proof. Caregivers or administrators may complain if you suspend a student from class for merely chewing gum. If that happens, point out that the student has violated two rules—one for chewing gum and another for noncompliance with teacher directions. This point will be addressed again when we explore the roles of administrators, counselors, and caregivers.

Beginning the Period

This topic centers on what students must be doing when the bell rings at the begin-ning of class and what will happen to them if they violate the rule. Simply explain to students what the rule requires of them when the beginning bell rings. Although Seganti does not say so explicitly, it would be a good idea to have students practice moving into full compliance with the rule at least several seconds before you pre-tend to ring the tardy bell.

Being Ready for Work

This rule centers on how students should be prepared for class, which includes bringing any materials they need for immediate class participation. It also stipu-lates what students will not be allowed to do once the bell rings. This admonition covers several matters that might seem trivial, but are serious because they take away time for learning.

For example, your students may be accustomed to coming to class without having at hand all the materials they need for successful learning. They may have the feeling that missing an item or two is not very bad. Seganti would have you quickly correct that misconception. He says you should insist to students they are old enough to take responsibility for this requirement. He advocates firm regula-tions regarding pencil sharpening in particular, because students often use sharpen-ing as a distraction and manipulation tactic. Unless you are insistent on compliance with the readiness rule, your more disruptive students will be asking for various school-related materials all period long.

Attending to Miscellaneous Behavior

This topic centers on matters such as students calling out, leaving their seats, and dealing with the scrap paper and other trash that accumulates around desks and elsewhere in the room. Have students act out the behaviors associated with speaking out improperly, raising their hands, getting permission, and keeping the classroom environment neat. Show them the wrong way of doing things—such as raising their hands as they begin to speak—and the right way, such as raising their hands, waiting for permission, and then speaking. Have them practice everything you expect of them.

Remind them that you cannot get around to answering each and every question promptly—sometimes they will have to wait a minute when you are busy.

Regarding Procedures

This topic centers on procedures for various activities, including leaving the room when necessary. You might be surprised at what Seganti requires of students who request restroom passes, but he says his tactic has worked wonders in stopping the debates between teacher and students on whether or not the student really has to go. If a student begs and squirms to prove the need is real, do the following:

> **Teacher:** Sure, here's the pass—but you have to make up 10 minutes after school.
> **Student:** Huh? Why 10 minutes?
> **Teacher:** (Don't say anything; just hold the hall pass and wait. The procedure has been stated and clarified. No need to repeat it.)

Regarding Teacher Requests and Directions

This topic centers on how students are to conduct themselves when the teacher asks them to do anything, such as change seats or pick up trash. Seganti has a steadfast way of interacting with students in these cases—he doesn't argue. Instead, he tells students that if they feel the direction is unreasonable, they may arrange to discuss it with the school counselor, vice principal, or in a conference involving student, parent, and teacher. He does not use class time for arguing with students, insisting the limited time for learning is too valuable to waste in that way.

As before, in teaching the rule, he advises you to read the rule aloud, then go back, explain, and have students practice complying in the manner expected. This rule must make it abundantly clear that you do not argue or debate discipline issues or directions with students. The focus is always on actions, not words.

End of Class

This topic centers on what students are to do when the bell rings at the end of class. Have students practice the procedure you require. Seganti suggests you make a bell noise and have students pack up their materials, then wait for you to say, "Okay, you are dismissed." Don't fall for the old "that's not my paper" retort when it's time to make sure the floor is clean. Students are accountable for their area.

Clarifying the System of Consequences

This topic centers on what will happen to students who violate any of the class rules. This system, once it is presented so students understand it, is the only warning Seganti gives. If students who have violated any of the prior rules do not abide by the indicated consequences, they are suspended from class and not allowed to reenter until they have fulfilled the requirement.

By this time, you have carefully gone through how you expect students to conduct themselves in class. You and your students will be tired of reading and talking about the rules, but rules must be stressed hard the first day so there is no room for doubt about what is expected. The time investment is very productive in making sure things go smoothly the rest of the year.

Leverage: How Do You Get Students to Follow the Rules?

The purpose of rules is to make sure your class operates responsibly and efficiently. But remember—rules are of no value unless you can enforce them and do so consistently. For that reason, you must create the mindset in all your students that breaking class rules is not going to get them what they want. To establish that mindset, you need some kind of **leverage** that makes students choose to follow the rules.

Seganti has determined that the most effective leverage for his classes is "Mr. Seganti's famous **15-minute detention** after school." This detention is only slightly inconvenient for students, but nevertheless they dislike it. And it works because they can't get out of it. Seganti calls this detention the "lever that can move boulders." It promotes psychological compliance while causing very little resentment. It doesn't punish teachers, either, because they usually have to stay after school for a while anyway.

A student who comes to your detention is tacitly agreeing that you are in position of authority. Once you have established that understanding, behavior problems dwindle. But what if students simply don't appear at detention as directed? That rarely happens, Seganti says, but if it does, suspend the student from class, in accordance with the class rules. Don't let the student back into your class until (1) his or her parents or caregiver have been notified, (2) the student has once again copied all the class rules, and (3) the student has served the detention. Students quickly realize they simply cannot escape the detention.

In a 2008 personal communication with the author of this book, Mr. Seganti made these further observations about students adjusting to the 15-minute detention:

> Some students who are difficult to manage will not come to detention the first time you assign it unless they are convinced they cannot get out of complying with the consequence. Therefore, they all must learn very quickly that it is better to show up than not. The whole system depends on the idea that testing the rules will bring more discomfort than simply following them. You must make it clear that if students do not show up for detention when it is assigned, they will be suspended from your class and not allowed to attend until they do so. They must see that you will indeed follow through on this requirement. Once this is clear, you will seldom be tested.

If you suspend a student from class, you will need to inform your administrator and the student's parent or caretaker. Preparations for doing so should be made in advance.

Figure 5.1 presents Seganti's protocol for calling caregivers.

Figure 5.1   Craig Seganti's Protocol for Calling Caregivers

"Hello, Mrs. Smith? I'm Mr. Jones, James's history teacher. James was disrupting my lesson today and I assigned him a 15-minute detention after school, but he didn't come. As he knows, that means he is suspended from my class until he does two things—copy the class rules and come to detention for 15 minutes. Can you make sure he copies the rules for me and comes to detention tomorrow so he can return to class?"

Sometimes the parent will take the student's side and say, "What exactly did he do?" Then you can say, "He was disrupting the lesson by talking," or "He defied instructions to change his seat," or whatever. Sometimes a parent will misunderstand and say, "You are suspending him for talking in class?" Answer like this: "No. I am suspending him for defiance of my rules and refusing to come to his 15-minute detention. As soon as he makes up his 15 minutes, he can return to class. Can you ensure that he does this and copies the rules for me?"

If you get the parent's assurance that James will come to detention the next day, you might delay the suspension until you see if he does. If James comes to class the next day, you should say in front of the class, "James, as you know I talked to your mother last night and she assured me you are coming to detention today—is that correct?" (James says, "Yes.")

"Okay, then I will hold off the suspension until tomorrow. But let's be clear that if you don't show today, you are suspended." This exchange lets the rest of the class know what will happen if they don't show up.

Source: Seganti, C. (2008). *Classroom discipline 101: How to get control of any classroom* (pp. 89–90), retrieved from http://www.classroomdiscipline101.com. Reproduced with permission.

Seganti maintains that detention of 10 to 15 minutes is the most effective leverage available to most teachers, but he recognizes that after-school detention is difficult or impossible in many schools because students have to catch buses. He advises teachers who encounter an obstacle to discuss with their administrator ways in which after-school detention can be managed. If no solution is evident, Seganti suggests three alternatives:

- Arrange for students to serve detention during school time by going to a fellow teacher's room for 10 or 15 minutes to copy rules—this could be done as a favor or as an exchange.
- If most of class is misbehaving, stop and have everyone spend 15 minutes copying the rules. The well-behaved students seldom complain about this because they intuitively realize you are trying to help everyone.
- In cooperation with four fellow teachers, work out a detention schedule during lunch time. Each teacher can stay 20 minutes or so one day a week. This has the added advantage of establishing a consistent behavior code that involves other classes.

MANAGEMENT: WHAT SHOULD YOU DO TO SUPPORT DESIRABLE BEHAVIOR?

Seganti has identified several things teachers can do, both before and after they meet their students, to make this discipline approach more effective. Here are some of his suggestions:

Organize the room arrangement. The success of your program is affected by how you arrange your room physically. Have your desks in rows and, if you think students might deface the furniture, number each chair and desk so they remain together and students are accountable for them. Have everything in the room, including your materials, neat and organized—a sloppy room encourages sloppy behavior. Place one or two desks adjacent to your desk for students who are most likely to be disruptive. Put one desk in the back corner facing the wall, to use for in-class suspensions. If a student doesn't show up for detention, but is not usually disruptive, put him or her in the back of the room facing the wall to copy the rules. Then if he or she comes to detention that afternoon, permission is given to rejoin class the next day.

Cultivate quiet. Cultivate a quiet classroom for a week or two with no group work and minimal talking—give a lot of reading and written work to acclimate the students to the idea that this classroom is quiet. The resultant habits are very powerful. When students get used to them, you can move into more vocal lessons.

Be at the ready. Have your referrals, detention logs, teaching props, and parent phone numbers at hand.

Dress professionally. In various walks of life, people who are leaders dress differently from those with whom they work. You see this, for example, in the military, religious institutions, and even the workaday world. Seganti believes the way you dress helps determine the impact you have on students by separating you from them psychologically, just as a priest looks different from the congregation or a general from a private. Seganti advises male teachers to wear ties and female teachers to dress in a professional manner. A professional appearance projects authority; but if you dress in a way that says, "I am one of you," then students will tend to treat you as one of them. When you establish a psychological separation from your students, they are less likely to challenge your authority.

Make eye contact. Looking students in the eye and having them look you in the eye reinforces your authority. When you give a direction, and it looks as though your students are not committed to it, get their undivided attention. Say, "Look at me. Did you understand?" Remember, you are looking for full nonverbal and verbal compliance with your directions.

Give something back to students. Teach in a way you can be truly proud of. Teach useful information in an engaging manner all period long. Students are not eager to cooperate with teachers who show little sparkle and assign meaningless tasks. If you teach as though you are just going through the motions, students will think you don't care about learning and are using rules as a power trip.

But when you combine tight boundaries with teaching that is interesting and valuable, students see that you care enough about them to work hard for their benefit. They will be thankful there is an adult around who can take charge and help them become more competent.

Organize your procedures. Good organization is your best friend. Make sure you have procedures for everything. Clarify them for students—seating charts, labeled desks, referrals, detention, what you will do when students try to manipulate you, and so on. Everyone should know exactly what they should be doing from bell to bell and what you are likely to do.

Listen to students. Listen attentively to students. Don't listen merely to *what* students say. Listen for the *motivation* behind their words.

Speak in statements. When speaking with students about discipline matters, use statements, not questions—for example, "This is work time," rather than "Why aren't you working?"

Educate students. Recognize that your job is to educate students, not to counsel them or deal with emotional problems they may have. That's what counselors are for.

Hold students accountable for proper behavior. After a few years in school, your students know how to behave properly. Except for new procedures, you don't have to teach them how to behave. Your rules for the class are simply to make students accountable. Your main job is to educate. Every student can understand that message.

Prepare. Know in advance exactly what action you will take every time a student breaks a rule.

Hold the line. Do not settle for anything less than a quiet, respectful, focused classroom. Repeat all procedures as often as necessary to maintain that kind of classroom. Make sure students stay on task and complete their work. It is not enough just to be quiet.

Keep 'em busy. Keep your students busy from bell to bell. Don't have any downtime and don't leave any time for talking.

Review the rules. You can have a near-perfect classroom if you continue having students review the required rules and procedures. Do this every day if necessary until they get it. In a personal communication with the author of this text, Mr. Seganti commented that feedback he has received from teachers confirms the powerful effect of teaching class rules two days in a row. You may say to your students, "Everybody got this yet? No?" (Laughingly) "Okay, we will go over the rules again tomorrow."

Assess yourself. Review your performance every day. Identify mistakes you have made and decide what you can do next time to get better results.

Take care of things. Don't count on administrative or parental support except to ensure that your established consequences are enforced.

Don't be manipulated. Students will invariably manipulate you if you allow them to do so. To students, it's a game. They will argue, waste time, cause you to become exasperated, and so forth. Seganti devotes much attention to this matter and shows teachers how to avoid being manipulated. The dialogs that follow indicate what you should do when students try to manipulate you. Notice that Seganti responds by stating a rule, rather than arguing with students. This tactic keeps attention on the teacher's agenda (in this case, following the rules) instead of moving attention to the student's agenda (such as wasting time, getting the better of the teacher, or trying to get out of detention).

Violation of Rule 1. Miguel is talking during quiet study time.

You: "Miguel, that's a 15-minute detention for talking."
Miguel: "I wasn't talking."
You: "I don't argue with students."

Violation of Rule 2. Megan is chewing gum.

You: "Megan, that's a 15-minute detention for chewing gum."
Megan: "I'm not chewing gum."
You: "Fine, but since giving the appearance of chewing gum is against the rules, you have detention anyway." Or you might say, "If you don't spit it out I will have to send you out for defiance."

Seganti provides more advice on answering manipulators in a piece called "Mr. Seganti's Big Kahuna Manipulation Destroyer" (Seganti, 2008a, p. 126). The manipulation destroyer he describes is *silence*. Seganti explains that when students make manipulative, irrelevant comments like those in the preceding dialogs, you just look at the students and say nothing. After all, there is no real answer to a manipulative question. A student is talking. You say, "Stop talking." They say, "I wasn't talking." What good can come of arguing back and forth in a silly exchange? So try just saying nothing. Just look at the student, deadpan, showing that you will not engage in the matter. Silence stops most manipulation in its tracks. The student may make a last feeble protestation such as, "Man, I wasn't even talking," but the matter will usually end there. If the student does continue talking, assign detention if you've not already done so.

HOW MIGHT I PUT SEGANTI'S IDEAS INTO EFFECT?

The following are suggestions from Mr. Seganti.

Use Effective Doorway Tactics

Seganti places great emphasis on **doorway tactics**, meaning what you do when students arrive at your classroom door. Before you let students through the door, make sure they are ready to get down to business. Do not wait inside the room for everyone to enter any way they like and then try to calm them down and get their attention afterward. When they approach your room they may be noisy, rude, jumpy, eating, distracted, or doing other things that are not conducive to academics. Don't allow any of this. Make sure that as students walk through your doorway they are moving into a mindset for learning. Be attentive to students' body language, not just their words.

Here are details of his recommendations for interacting with students the *first* time they arrive for class (Seganti, 2008a, pp. 21–34):

- Stand in your doorway and stop *every* student briefly before they enter. You might have to block the entrance with your body.
- Hand each student a copy of the class rules and say, "I want you to go directly to the seat I have assigned you without talking and in an orderly manner. You are to sit down quietly, take out your materials and immediately copy these rules onto a separate sheet of paper. Do this without talking. Do you understand?" Point to the exact seat you want each student to sit in. Make an effort to repeat the part about "being quiet" and "not talking" three times before you let them in. Conveying these messages of "strictness" will help your classroom atmosphere enormously.
- If any students say they already know how to behave or if they ask why they need to copy the rules, or if they do or say anything disrespectful, say, "I gave you a direction. You need to follow it." Do not enter into a discussion or rationalize your requirements. Don't fool yourself by thinking that copying the rules is a small matter that can just be let go. From the beginning, get students to realize they have to comply with *all* your directions, great and small. Before long, that is what they will do.
- If students are disrespectful, or do not have their materials, or in any other way appear unprepared for class, do not let them through the door. They can borrow what they need from a friend, but they can't enter the room until they have all of their materials.
- If their nonverbal cues say they are not ready to study, have them stand to the side. Tell them what you expect and say honestly, "To me, you don't look ready to study." When they manage to meet your standards of a proper attitude for entry to the class, let them in. Otherwise just wait. There is no hurry.
- If any students begin disrupting after entering, call them back to try again. You can say something like, "Now try again—go to your seat quietly, take out your materials without talking, and copy the rules." If the student interrupts while you are speaking, say, "Do not interrupt me again. This is not a conversation but a simple direction you can comply with, or else leave the room for defiance." Do this every day until students enter in a manner that meets your standards for entering and getting to work. Repeat this procedure for as long as necessary. Students do not resent it and they soon respond well. They will even start saying your entry rules before you do.

Watch for and Address Three Types of Behavior on the First Day

There are roughly three types of behavior you can expect to see among your students the first day of school. Seganti refers to them as Type A, Type B, and Type C. He comments on them as follows:

1. Type A behavior—these students are polite, prepared, and ready to enter class. Give them their instructions quickly and send them in.
2. Type B behavior—these students are basically respectful but appear a bit rowdy or distracted. Tell them to stop, take a deep breath, calm down, and then get

ready to enter the class in an orderly manner. Make sure they look you in the eye and are clear about your directions—then send them in.

3. Type C behavior—these students appear disrespectful, arrogant, and/or rowdy. These are the students who are most likely to present problems. Show the class they are not going to be a problem for you. Establish right away that poor behavior in your presence will not go unchallenged. Have these students stand to the side while the rest of the class enters. Every small thing you do here helps or hurts your cause. You save many problems later on when students see that you are on top of everything from the start. Get compliance from all Type C students before you let them enter. Direct them to a specific seat right next to your desk if possible. If they are noncompliant, argumentative, or rude, give them the simple choice of complying or being suspended for defiance. Do this as calmly as possible. You can say, "I don't argue with students. You can follow my directions or be sent out of the room for defiance." This is what sets your authority.

Assign Seats and Begin Learning Students' Names

Once students are all in the room and are busy copying the rules, get their attention and say the following: "I'm going to call roll now and assign new seats. When I tell you where to sit, get up immediately and move to that desk without questioning or complaining. There is no discussion about it, and if you try to engage me in a discussion about your assigned seat you will be sent from the room. Just move to your seat right away. Does everyone understand?"

You should have a class roster with names in alphabetical order. As you call the names, assign the seats and tell students to return to the same seat the next day. When all students are seated and are again copying class rules, do the following: Silently to yourself say the names of the students in the first row. Repeat a few times. Then do the same with students in the next row. Review frequently. Rememorize the ones you forgot by checking the seating chart. Their names will come back to you quickly.

Explain Leverage for Rules and Exclusion from Class Procedures

As noted, Seganti's "leverage" consists of a 15-minute detention. As soon as students have finished copying the class rules, tell them you will enforce the rules through the 15-minute detention. Explain how you will do so. You might enlist two or three students to help you demonstrate enforcement.

In Seganti's approach, only three things call for students to get excluded from the room—defiance, repeated disruption, and gross disrespect. The following scenarios depict those reasons, as Seganti would explain them.

Reason 1: Defiance

I tell Judy to change her seat. She says, "Why?" I reply that I do not argue with students. She does not immediately change her seat and I assign her a 15-minute detention and tell her to change her seat. She continues to argue or just doesn't move. I write up a referral, whether or not she moves at this point, and send her from the class for defiance. She goes to the counselor. I have written on the referral that Judy is suspended for defiance until she comes to detention and copies the class rules.

Five minutes later Judy returns from the counselor's office with a note saying "Student counseled—please re-admit student to class." If I re-admit Judy now, I will be making a big mistake. I say to her, "No, you are suspended from my class. Come to detention after school today for 15 minutes, copy the rules, and you may reenter tomorrow."

At my first opportunity, I explain to the counselor once again how my system works, and that the only help I need from him or her is in enforcing my requirement that Judy comes to detention and copies the rules. If Judy does not meet my requirement, I will send her back again for defiance of my detention rule. I don't care if the counselor provides her counseling or not, so long as Judy comes to detention and copies the rules. Judy can copy rules in the counselor's office or she can be moved to somebody else's class, but will not be re-admitted to my class until she copies the rules and does the 15-minute detention. The matter is simply about the necessity that Judy comply with my class rules.

Reason 2: Repeated Disruption

Disruption is anything that interferes with student concentration in class. It might be a little buzz of talk that I have to try to talk over. It might be a student tapping a pencil on the desk, or rumpling papers, or loudly sighing to show disinterest in the class, or turning away from me while I am talking. Those are all disruptions. They are specified in the class rules and are not allowed.

Let's say there is a lot of buzz in class, an undercurrent of noise I can't pinpoint. I'm not sure where to start—no one is being really bad, it seems, nothing that would normally call for detention. So, not knowing what else to do, I say "Quiet!" to the whole class. They get quiet for a minute, like boiling water does when you cut the heat.

But then it starts to boil again and you say, "Quiet! Okay, quiet down!" This vacillation can go on for awhile—in some cases for an entire teaching career. What do I do? I start with individuals. I pick one student.

"Brian, you are disrupting the class. Be quiet or come to detention."

Brian replies, "Everyone else is talking."

I ignore his comment, write down his name, and say, "Come 15 minutes after school today. If you continue disrupting I will have to suspend you from the class."

I don't wait for the big disruptions. I make students adjust to the boundary being squeaky tight. My standard is no disruption during my lesson—not even a little. Follow this advice and, tomorrow, count the times you say "quiet" to your class. If it is more than once per class or five times per day, it is too much and likely to escalate. So, I have the counselor ensure that Brian will come to detention for 15 minutes that day and copy the rules in the meantime. If he doesn't, I won't re-admit him.

Reason 3: Gross Disrespect

If a student swears at you or insults you or engages in any other highly offensive behavior, immediately suspend the student, send him or her from your class, and demand a parent conference as well as the detention and copying the rules or other consequence you use. Any of these things should include your basic consequence of detention because some students would rather have their caregivers called than have to serve detention. If it looks like a student is going to be a real problem, start a paper trail on him or her right away. You need to minimize the damage these students do to your teaching and other students' education.

OUTSIDE SUPPORT: WHAT DOES SEGANTI WANT OF ADMINISTRATORS, COUNSELORS, AND CAREGIVERS?

Seganti says to make sure you inform your administrator clearly about your discipline plan, including its logic, rules, and procedures. Administrators don't want to be caught off guard if a parent complains, and they need to know how they can help you make your program work. They will usually be pleased to know you are handling discipline problems on your own and only need their help as backup when students are suspended from your class.

As for caregivers, Seganti doesn't believe they will be of much help to you in discipline matters. He says he cannot recall a single instance in his career when a parent conference had a significant long-term effect on a student's behavior. Parent conferences are simply not a consequence that students care about. However, they are useful in establishing a paper trail on students who chronically misbehave and defy the teacher. Most administrators have no objection to your sending a student from your room for defiance, so it is helpful to document your calls to caregivers when you give detention for serious and repetitive breaches of the rules, especially those rules over which caregivers have some control, such as having class materials in hand.

When you talk with caregivers, most will listen to the problem and say something like, "Okay, I'll talk to her/him." Occasionally caregivers will take the student's side and express concern that you are not doing your job properly. When that happens, don't go on the defensive. Explain your rules and ask the parents if they see anything unfair in them (they won't). Explain that their child has not shown up for detention or continually violates the rules, which interferes with your teaching and educational rights of other students.

A CLOSING COMMENT FROM MR. SEGANTI

The following comment was provided to the author by Mr. Seganti:

> Our schools are currently doing things out of sequence—trying to let students know all their rights and encouraging self-expression and independent thought, etc., before working to establish basic respect for others and the environment. Schools seem oblivious of the misery they cause students and teachers by emphasizing things in this order. In a more effective sequence, respect must be established first, as a fundamental principle of all classroom interactions.

Commentary from Anonymous Teacher 1

Most of the time, my third-grade class is not very disruptive, and I would not need the detention leverage that Mr. Seganti describes. However, although his suggestions are new to me, I find I do use many that are similar. In teaching students how they are expected to behave, I make use of role-playing, in which I have them act out how they are to enter and exit the room, clean up after work, keep track of their materials, and so forth. The students actually enjoy acting these things out. Right from the beginning I explain how students are expected to behave. If they fail to do as directed, I have them show me they know the proper way of behaving. This takes a bit of time, but I only have to do it a few times before students get the idea I won't accept their behaving inappropriately. In addition to having them act out the desirable behaviors, I give them oral explanations and sometimes written explanations, too, that include what they are to do when they have completed assigned work earlier than expected. I add reminders now and then just to make sure they remember.

Mr. Seganti explains how he forbids students to bring various "distraction" objects into the room with them. I also have rules about those things—such as erasers, bracelets, hair clips, and so on—which I call "doo-dads." I explain that if they bring such things to class, I will take them and keep them until the end of the school year. I have a collection of doo-dads to prove I mean business. I have informed parents of this rule and that I will return the objects at the end of the year. Everybody knows my expectations, why they are used, and how they will be enforced. The students accept my policies and only rarely does a parent ask about them.

Commentary from Anonymous Teacher 2

I think these suggestions and strategies have merit and reinforce ideas about good classroom management. I especially like the focus on academics, the notion of holding students accountable, the emphasis on teacher consistency in rule enforcement, and most of all the idea of teaching with energy and enthusiasm the entire class period. I think the keys to making this approach work are, as Mr. Seganti suggests, planning, organization, and determination from the teacher along with buy-in from administrators and parents.

One of the aspects of Mr. Seganti's approach that I find particularly valuable is the notion of the teacher taking care of the detentions, parent contacts, and record-keeping. I do think it is important to be seen by your students as being willing and able to manage your own students and their behavior, rather than passing them off to the assistant principal for disciplinary action. I'd just add the caution that a teacher who wants to implement leverage as Mr. Seganti suggests should be sure to consider carefully the requirements for enforcement. For example, in my district, it is necessary to give a parent or guardian 24 hours notice if you want to keep a child after school. We have forms available to use for this parent notification. In my state a teacher can "suspend" a student for up to 3 days from his or her classroom. (If you have a student "hold-out" who refuses to serve detention, you will need to make a plan for that student. Office? Another teacher's room? Have the student sit out in the hallway? All of these solutions end up with the student missing out on class and basically becoming someone else's problem.)

One of my colleagues, Mr. Albert, had very exacting standards for student classroom behavior. He also had stringent requirements for supplies that students were to bring to class daily. If students did not have the required supplies or did not complete a homework assignment, he would write out referrals and send the students to the AP's office for the period. In short order, some students figured out that an easy way to get out of class and spend time with friends in the AP office was to not comply with Mr. Albert's requirements. This practice put a burden on the school administration, office staff, and other personnel. Ultimately, Mr. Albert backed down and gave up. He wouldn't have had to do that if he had used the ideas as presented by Mr. Seganti.

WHAT YOU HAVE LEARNED IN THIS CHAPTER

You have seen how teacher Craig Seganti takes charge in his classes of "hard-to-manage" students by placing priority on academic learning and backing it with rules and leverage. You saw, specifically, what Mr. Seganti does to establish productive rules and gain compliance that leads to student success. You learned about his "leverage" system (the 15-minute detention) that helps keep students on task. You also noted that he uses a charismatic personality and interesting activities to keep students involved and makes sure that, while students have some fun in learning, they master the academic knowledge and skills needed for a productive life.

Activities

Self-Test: True/False

1. By "stopping problems before they get into the classroom," Seganti means informing caregivers by phone or email about your discipline approach and asking for their support.

2. The relationship between leverage and accountability is as follows: leverage is used to ensure student accountability.

3. Seganti emphasizes the importance of involving students in helping establish the rules of behavior for the class.

4. Seganti suggests you introduce class rules through discussion and then have students write from memory as many of the rules as they can.

5. When Seganti sends a student to the counselor, he doesn't expect the counselor to grant permission for the offending student to reenter Mr. Seganti's class.

6. Because after-school suspension damages students' self-concept, Seganti is very reluctant to assign it more than once for any given student.

7. Seganti says to place students' desks facing the front of the room and seat the more unruly students near the teacher's desk.

8. The first thing Seganti does when he first meets a new class is tell the students about his family, hobbies, and favorite pastimes.

9. Although Seganti is reluctant to call caregivers about student misbehavior, he says doing so almost always results in better student behavior.

10. Seganti says administrators are pleased when teachers resolve most of their discipline problems on their own.

Self-Test: Multiple Choice

1. Seganti says any student who disrupts is interfering with other students' constitutional
   - (a) rights.
   - (b) guarantees.
   - (c) protections.
   - (d) freedoms.

2. Seganti's Rule #1 has to do with students'
   - (a) entering the room.
   - (b) completing their work.
   - (c) showing respect.
   - (d) accepting responsibility.

3. Seganti says he is famous for his rule about
   - (a) talking back.
   - (b) restroom passes.
   - (c) chewing.
   - (d) swearing.

4. Seganti suggests that teachers should dress
   - (a) casually.
   - (b) professionally.
   - (c) comfortably.
   - (d) stylishly.

5. Seganti's "leverage" consists of
   - (a) parental consent.
   - (b) administrator backup.
   - (c) provisions for detention.
   - (d) making up any work not completed.

6. Regarding warnings, Seganti says
   - (a) limit them to two.
   - (b) be sure to inform caregivers.
   - (c) make them unpleasant.
   - (d) don't give them.

7. For Seganti, which of the following would *not* warrant excluding or removing a student from the class?
   - (a) defiance
   - (b) repeated disruption
   - (c) gross disrespect
   - (d) inattention

8. In discipline problems, Seganti says he never received much help from
   - (a) caregivers.
   - (b) administrators.
   - (c) fellow teachers.
   - (d) textbooks.

9. Seganti says the first thing you must establish in discipline is
   - (a) understanding.
   - (b) personal relations with students.
   - (c) responsibility.
   - (d) respect.

10. To begin a class, spend a week or so cultivating a climate of
    - (a) excitement.
    - (b) quiet.
    - (c) high activity.
    - (d) give and take.

Self-Test: Explain This

1. What does Seganti do when new students first arrive at his classroom door?

2. What attitude does Seganti attempt to establish in his classes, and what does he say about disruptions?

3. What does Seganti mean by "leverage," and how does he establish it?

4. What roles would Seganti like for administrators, counselors, and caregivers to fill in his approach to discipline?

5. What does Seganti mean by "stopping problems before they get into the classroom"?

Additional Suggested Activities

1. In your journal, enter ideas from Seganti's approach that you might wish to incorporate into your personal system of discipline.

2. With colleagues, if possible, practice Seganti's doorway tactics and his method of responding to students who break class rules.

Concept Cases

CASE 1   Kristina Will Not Work

Kristina, a student in Mr. Jake's class, is quite docile. She socializes little with other students and never disrupts lessons. However, despite Mr. Jake's best efforts, Kristina will not do her work. She rarely completes an assignment. She is simply there, putting forth no effort at all. *How would Craig Seganti deal with Kristina?*

Mr. Seganti provided the following commentary on this particular case: Kristina is required by the rules to be on task at all times. Therefore she will be assigned a 15-minute detention if she does not stay on task. At the detention I will try to determine the root of the problem: It is almost always that the work is too challenging, so in this case I might help her with the work after school a bit and/or contact her caregivers to see if they can help her at home.

CASE 2   Sara Will Not Stop Talking

Sara is a pleasant girl who participates in class activities and does most, though not all, of her assigned work. She cannot seem to refrain from talking to classmates, however. Her teacher, Mr. Gonzales, speaks to her repeatedly during lessons, to the point that he often becomes exasperated and loses his temper. *What suggestions would Craig Seganti give Mr. Gonzales for dealing with Sara?*

CASE 3   Joshua Clowns and Intimidates

Joshua, larger and louder than his classmates, always wants to be the center of attention, which he accomplishes through a combination of clowning and intimidation. He makes wisecrack remarks, talks back (smilingly) to the teacher, utters a variety of sound-effect noises such as automobile crashes and gunshots, and makes limitless sarcastic comments and put-downs of his classmates. Other students will not stand up to him, apparently fearing his size and verbal aggression. His teacher, Miss Pearl, cannot control his disruptive behavior. *Would Joshua's behavior be likely to improve if Miss Pearl implemented Seganti's approach in her class? Explain.*

CASE 4   Tom Is Hostile and Defiant

Tom has appeared to be in his usual foul mood ever since arriving in class. On his way to sharpen his pencil, he bumps into Frank, who complains. Tom tells him loudly to shut up. Miss Baines, the teacher, says, "Tom, go back to your seat." Tom wheels around, swears loudly, and says heatedly, "I'll go when I'm _____ good and ready!" *How would Craig Seganti have Miss Baines deal with Tom?*

You Are the Teacher

CLASS CLOWNS

Your new fifth-grade class consists of students from a small, stable community. Because the transiency rate is low, many of your students have been together since first grade, and during those years they have developed certain patterns of interacting and assuming various roles such as clowns and instigators. Unfortunately, their behavior often interferes with teaching and learning. During the first week of school you notice that four or five students enjoy making smart-aleck remarks about most things you want them to do. When such remarks are made, the other students laugh and sometimes join in. Even when you attempt to hold class discussions about serious issues, many of the students make light of the topics and refuse to enter genuinely into an exploration of the issues. Instead of the productive discussion you have hoped for, you find that class behavior often degenerates into flippancy and horseplay.

A TYPICAL OCCURRENCE

You have begun a history lesson that contains a reference to Julius Caesar. You ask if anyone has ever heard of Julius Caesar. Ben shouts out, "Yeah, they named a salad after him!" The class laughs and calls out encouraging remarks such as "Good one, Ben!" You wait for some semblance of order, then say, "Let us go on." From the back of the classroom, Jeremy cries, "Lettuce and cabbage!" The class bursts into laughter and chatter. You ask for their cooperation and no more students call out or make remarks, but you see several continue to smirk and whisper, with a good deal of barely suppressed giggling. You try to ignore it, but because of the disruptions you are not able to complete the lesson on time or to get the results you hoped for.

CONCEPTUALIZING A STRATEGY

If you followed Seganti's suggestions, what would you do with regard to the following?

- Preventing the problem from occurring in the first place.
- Putting an immediate end to the misbehavior now.
- Maintaining student dignity and good personal relations.
- Using follow-up procedures that would prevent the recurrence of the misbehavior.

6

Harry and Rosemary Wong on the First Things You Should Teach

What Do Harry and Rosemary Wong Say About Scripting the First Minutes and Days of a New Class?

In 2009, Harry Wong and Rosemary Wong, two of the most highly acclaimed educators in America, interviewed four administrators of schools where students were showing unusually high levels of achievement. The Wongs wanted to know what those leaders did to promote such strong learning and outstanding behavior. What they discovered was rather simple—it was just that everyone—students, teachers, and administrators—knew exactly *what they were supposed to do* at all times and *how to do it*. Consequently, they did those things as expected, more or less automatically.

As the Wongs put it, there was no hocus-pocus, bag of tricks, special programs, or funding from multimillion-dollar endowments. There was simply a schoolwide mindset of success, where teachers continually sought to become more effective. Those teachers began by teaching students very thoroughly the roles, procedures, processes, and routines they were expected to follow. That was done schoolwide. Once students understood those requirements and procedures, teachers were left free to focus almost entirely on promoting learning.

That simple process, say the Wongs, opens the royal road to success in teaching. Their view is that the main trouble in classrooms is not discipline, as most people think, but rather teachers' failure to teach students very clearly the roles, responsibilities, and procedures that make classrooms run like clockwork. They point out that everything teachers ask students to do involves a procedure. When students learn to follow procedures automatically, they behave better, learn more, and are far easier to teach.

The beginning of a new class or term is an especially important time. That is when teachers set the structure and expectations of the class. The first few days should be devoted to two matters: (1) clarifying the proper roles and responsibilities of students and teacher, and (2) teaching students exactly how to follow the various procedures expected of them. The result that follows will be good learning, good behavior, and a thoroughly successful school year.

WHAT QUESTIONS WILL THIS CHAPTER ANSWER FOR ME?

- What are Harry and Rosemary Wong's suggestions for establishing classes that run smoothly with little misbehavior?
- What is meant by *procedures,* and what do they have to do with well-functioning classrooms?
- What are examples of the many important classroom procedures students should learn to follow automatically?
- What do the Wongs suggest we do in the first 5 minutes, the first day, and the first 10 days of school?
- What is meant by "scripting," and why it is so strongly recommended?
- What do the Wongs have to say about cooperative group work?

WHAT IS THE WONGS' MODEL FOR CLASSROOM MANAGEMENT?

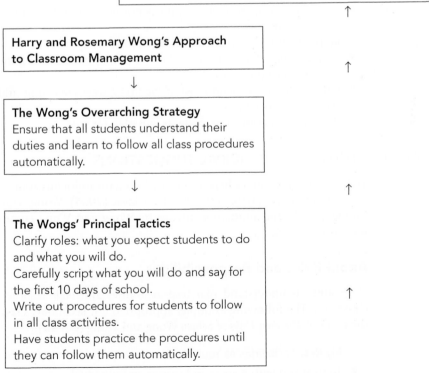

The Common Goal of All Approaches to Classroom Management: *Responsible, Productive Classroom Behavior That Becomes Habitual and Lasts over Time*
Responsible means paying attention, making a strong effort, and doing what is proper without being told. Civil means respectful, polite, cordial, and well mannered.

Harry and Rosemary Wong's Approach to Classroom Management

The Wong's Overarching Strategy
Ensure that all students understand their duties and learn to follow all class procedures automatically.

The Wongs' Principal Tactics
Clarify roles: what you expect students to do and what you will do.
Carefully script what you will do and say for the first 10 days of school.
Write out procedures for students to follow in all class activities.
Have students practice the procedures until they can follow them automatically.

WHO ARE HARRY AND ROSEMARY WONG?

Harry and Rosemary Wong are among today's most widely acclaimed authorities in teaching and classroom management. Harry Wong, now an educational speaker and consultant, previously taught science at the middle school and high school levels. He received numerous awards for outstanding teaching and high student achievement, including the Horace Mann Outstanding Educator Award and the National Teachers Hall-of-Fame Lifetime Achievement Award. *Instructor* magazine named him one of the 20 most admired people in education.

Rosemary Wong taught grades 1–8 and served as media coordinator and student activity director. She was selected as one of California's first mentor teachers and has received numerous awards for her contributions to the profession. She speaks around the world with her husband, Harry.

At the time of this writing, their book *The First Days of School* had sold over 4 million copies, making it the best-selling education book of all time. It has been translated into five languages. They have also produced a video series entitled *The Effective Teacher,* which won the Gold Award in the International Film and Video Festival and the Telly Award as the best educational staff development video. Harry and Rosemary write a monthly column for www.teachers.net that provides easy access to how their ideas have been implemented in classrooms, schools, and school districts. You might wish to peruse that site as well as the Wongs' website at www.effectiveteaching.com.

The Wongs get their points across through maxims such as:

- The main problem in classrooms is not poor discipline, but poor classroom management.
- Responsibilities help clarify what everyone is supposed to do.
- As a teacher, what you do on the first day of school determines your success for the rest of the year.
- Effective teachers spend most of the first 2 weeks teaching students to follow classroom procedures.
- If you do not plan, your students will plan for you.

A QUICK READ OF THE WONGS' PRINCIPAL SUGGESTIONS

The Wongs' ideas you see here are gleaned from the following sources: Starr (1999), Wong and Wong (2004b, 2007, 2009b), Glavac (2005), Wong, Wong, Rogers, and Brooks (2012) and numerous articles by Wong and Wong currently posted on www.teachers.net.

About Roles and Responsibilities

Help students understand *your* responsibilities and *their* responsibilities in the classroom. The following example, appropriate for secondary classes, appears on the cover of *The First Days of School* Wong and Wong (2004b):

My Responsibilities as Your Teacher
- To treat you with respect and care as an individual.
- To provide you an orderly classroom environment.

- To provide the necessary guidance for success.
- To provide the appropriate motivation.
- To teach you the required content.

Your Responsibilities as My Students

- To treat me with respect and care as an individual.
- To attend classes regularly.
- To be cooperative and not disruptive.
- To study and do your work well.
- To learn and master the required content.

About Classrooms and Procedures

- The single most important factor affecting student learning is not discipline; it is how a teacher manages a classroom.
- Your classroom need not be chaotic; it can be a smoothly functioning learning environment.
- A well-managed classroom is task-oriented and predictable.
- *Ineffective teachers* begin the first day of school attempting to teach a subject. They then spend the rest of the school year running after students.
- *Effective teachers* spend most of the first 2 weeks of school teaching students to follow classroom **procedures** that help them become responsible learners.
- What is done on the first day of school or a class—even the first few minutes—can make or break a teacher.
- The very first day, the very first minute, the very first second of school, teachers should begin to establish a structure of procedures and routines for the class.

About School

- School is where students go to learn how to be productive citizens and reach their potential as human beings.
- School should be challenging, exciting, engrossing, and thought-provoking, but its program must have structure to ensure success.
- You cannot give students self-esteem, which has no validity in education, but you can ensure they find success in school.

About Teaching

- Teaching is a craft—a highly skilled craft that can be learned.
- By far the most important factor affecting school learning is the ability of the teacher. The more capable the teacher, the more successful the student.
- Good teachers enhance the life and spirit of the students they teach.
- Stop asking, "What am I supposed to do?" Start asking, "What must I know that will help me accomplish what I need to do?"
- What you do on the first day of school determines your success for the rest of the year.
- When students arrive, start class immediately. Do not take roll until later.

- Learning is often most effective when it takes place in a supportive community of learners.
- The more students work together responsibly, the more they learn.
- Shorter assignments produce higher student achievement.
- Intersperse questions throughout a lesson. Ask a question after you have spoken a few sentences rather than many. By doing so, you significantly increase student learning and retention.
- Students usually learn more from an activity–question approach than from a textbook-lecture approach.
- Teachers go through four stages of development—fantasy, survival, mastery, and impact. Good management moves you quickly from fantasy to mastery.
- You can have your achievements or you can have your excuses.
- Those who teach well never cease to learn.

About Testing and Evaluation

- Use criterion-referenced tests rather than norm-referenced tests to evaluate student performance. Grade on what is learned, not on the curve—a practice that has done great harm.
- Within reason, the more frequent the tests, the higher the achievement.

About Student Behavior

- Classroom rules indicate the behavior you expect from students. In order to provide a safe and effective learning environment, establish and enforce appropriate rules.
- Rules of behavior set limits, just as do rules in games. They create a work-oriented atmosphere in the classroom.
- Behavior associated with rules must be taught through discussion, demonstration, and practice.
- Consequences should be attached to rules—positive consequences for compliance and negative consequences (but not punishment) for noncompliance.
- Explain your management plan to students on the first day of school.

About the First Day of Class

- Have your classroom ready for instruction and make it inviting.
- Organize your class by preparing a written script that covers precisely what you will say and do.
- Plan for more than you can get around to, so there will be no dead time with a chance of losing the students' involvement in the class.
- Stand at the door and greet students as they enter.
- Give each student a seating assignment and a seating chart.
- Position yourself in the room near the students. Problems are proportional to the distance between you and students.
- Post an assignment in a consistent location so students can begin when they enter the room.

- Display your diploma and credentials with pride.
- Dress in a professional manner that models success and suggests you expect achievement.

About the First Week of Teaching

- The two most important things you must teach the first week of school are procedures and rules.
- Explain your management plan to students and put it into effect immediately.
- State your procedures and have students rehearse until they follow them automatically.

More About a Management Plan

Although the Wongs focus mainly on the management of procedures, they remind us that in addition to good management, teachers need an approach that specifies and teaches procedures. This approach helps students know how to be successful in the class. The Wongs have found that most teachers want to begin teaching lessons before procedures are addressed. Then, when misbehavior occurs, those teachers apply harsh measures that are counterproductive. Without an effective classroom management plan that begins the first day, you are setting yourself up for failure.

The Wongs do say you need a discipline plan, but they are not particular about the plan you use, other than to say that you should (1) develop one that is suited to your requirements and your students' needs, and (2) make sure it includes rules of behavior, steps for teaching those rules, and actions that are applied when students comply with or break rules.

As for class rules, the Wongs (2004b) suggest you think carefully about what your students need to do in order to be successful and, when necessary, write those expectations as rules, post them in the class, and go over them with students on the first day. You will have firm confidence in your ability to manage the class if you and your students understand clearly what is expected.

The Wongs suggest you limit the number of rules to a maximum of five, stated in a positive manner (although in some cases it is more effective to state them in a negative manner, such as "No fighting"). Here are five universal rules the Wongs (2004b, p. 146) provide as examples:

- Follow directions the first time they are given.
- Raise your hand and wait for permission to speak.
- Stay in your seat unless you have permission to do otherwise.
- Keep hands, feet, and objects to yourself.
- No cursing or teasing.

Introduce the rules on the first day of class and post them in a prominent place. The Wongs suggest introducing them approximately as follows, using your own language and explanations:

> *Rationale for rules.* The rules are to help you learn in a classroom that is safe and effective. They help make sure nothing keeps you from being successful in this class.

Working together comfortably. We will be working together closely. We need to keep this classroom a place where you will never have fear of being ridiculed or threatened. I care about all of you, and I will not allow anyone to do anything that interferes with someone trying to learn.

My job. My job is to teach you and help you be successful, so I will not allow you to do anything that interferes with my teaching and our group success and enjoyment.

Our class rules. So I can teach and all of us can learn in the best possible conditions, I have prepared a set of rules that help make this classroom safe, orderly, and productive. I'll explain those rules to you now so you understand clearly what they mean, how you are to follow them, and how I will enforce them.

About Planning and Organizing

Begin by acknowledging and accepting the overriding importance of organization. It enables you to keep on schedule, know where things are, and make your time and space work for you. It eliminates chaos, lets you get things done, and allows you some time to enjoy life.

Procedures and What They Entail

Think of procedures as involving what you want students to do in the classroom and precisely how they will do those things. Student behavior and learning will be determined in large part by how well you establish good, workable classroom procedures, beginning the very first day.

Students accept and appreciate procedures that provide security while minimizing confusion. If you don't put those procedures in place, students will likely behave undesirably and develop poor work habits that are difficult to correct later.

To establish good procedures, do three things: First, decide what *routines* are necessary in the activities you intend to conduct; second, list the steps students must follow in order to participate in and benefit from the activities; and third, teach students through explanation, demonstration, and practice in how to follow the procedures.

You will find you end up with a very large number of procedures for students to learn. Don't worry; students can learn them. Just keep in mind that every time you want students to do something, they need to know the procedure to follow—for example, how to enter and exit the classroom; how to begin the period or day; how to come to attention; how to begin and finish work; what to do when the class is dismissed; what to do on returning after being absent; what to do when arriving tardy; how the class is to get quiet when necessary; how to ask for help from the teacher or others; how to move about the classroom; how papers, materials, and supplies are to be distributed and collected; how everyone is to listen to and respond to questions; how to work cooperatively with others; how groups are changed; how to organize student notebook/binder; how directions are given for each assignment and how to find the directions; and how to walk in the corridors. And the list goes on.

The Wongs give specific attention to these matters and many more. Good procedures allow a variety of activities to occur without confusion, often several at the same time. But you have to teach students the procedures, not just talk about them. The Wongs suggest a three-step method for teaching procedures:

1. *Teach.* You state, explain, and demonstrate the procedure.
2. *Rehearse.* The students practice the procedure under your supervision.
3. *Reinforce.* You reteach the procedure, have students rehearse it, and keep repeating it until students follow it automatically.

Examples of Procedures in a Fourth-Grade Classroom

The Wongs provide the following guidelines and procedures for structuring successful classes: which the Wongs credit to teacher Nathan Gibbs, show how one teacher has structured his fourth-grade class for success. This is an example of how a skilled teacher uses procedures to create a safe and caring learning environment. You may teach kindergarten or high school physical education and feel these procedures do not apply to you. But the Wongs remind us that this scheme reflects realities that exist in all classrooms. As you read these procedures, consider how they can assist you in creating procedures for your own classroom.

Make your classroom a place where students feel genuinely cared for. Provide personalized instruction within a warm, relaxed, refined learning environment. On the first day of school give your students a written list of all the classroom procedures, with a cover page that says, "Follow these procedures to reward yourself with complete success."

Spend the first 2 weeks of class teaching the procedures, and expect students to follow them to the letter. The number of procedures may seem overwhelming, but the students soon learn and appreciate them. Here are some of the things you might emphasize (Wong & Wong, 2004a):

"You will be safe in this class. I will do my best for you, and I want you to do your best for yourself. Be ready to begin learning very well."

Morning Entry Procedures

✓ Enter the classroom in a quiet and orderly manner.
✓ Greet your teacher as you enter and say "hi" to your classmates.
✓ Turn in homework or keep at desk if it is to be graded in class.
✓ Begin on your seat work.

Desk Procedures

✓ Only your notebook, assignment book, textbooks, reading book, and supply box belong in your desk. Toys, food, and loose paper do not belong in your desk.
✓ Keep hands, feet, paper, books, and pencils off your neighbors' desks.
✓ Push in your chair every time you get up.
✓ Clean your desk and the area around it before you leave.

Line-Up Procedures

✓ When dismissed, stand in two equal lines and wait quietly.
✓ First excused line goes out of room, and then the second line follows.
✓ Walk quietly in the hallway.

Lunch Procedures

✓ When excused for lunch, get your lunch if you brought it.
✓ Lunch Leaders stand in front with lunch buckets.
✓ Follow the line-up procedures.
✓ When dismissed by teacher, walk to the cafeteria.
✓ If you have brought your lunch, go and sit at the correct table.
✓ If you are buying lunch, get your card from the slot and wait quietly in line.
✓ Talk with a low voice.
✓ Clean up your area and raise your hand when you want to be dismissed.
✓ Put all leftover food and trash in the trashcans.
✓ Place your lunchbox in the bucket when you leave.

Bus Pick-Up Procedures

✓ Walk quickly to bus area.
✓ Quietly wait behind the line for the bus.
✓ Show respect for the teacher on duty.
✓ Show respect for the bus driver.

Car Pick-Up Procedures

✓ Walk to car pick-up area.
✓ Don't walk onto the blacktop where cars park or drive.
✓ Show respect for the teacher on duty.
✓ Quietly wait for your ride.
✓ If your ride is more than 10 minutes late, go sit quietly in the office and wait.

Bicycle Rider Procedures

✓ Walk your bike on campus before and after school.
✓ Lock your bike to the bike rack and leave other bikes alone.
✓ Wear your helmet while riding your bike.
✓ Obey all traffic laws.
✓ Come straight to school and go straight home.

Walker Procedures

✓ Walk straight to school.
✓ Walk straight home.
✓ Obey all traffic laws.

Basic Assembly Procedures

✓ Line up inside or outside our classroom first.
✓ Follow the student council representatives to the correct area.
✓ Pay attention and sit where you are instructed to.
✓ Show respect for the presentation.
✓ Be patient if you have a question for the presenter.
✓ Return to the classroom in a quiet, orderly manner.

End-of-Day Procedures

✓ Copy down the homework assignment in your notebook.
✓ Clean around your desk.
✓ Pack your assignment book and what you need for homework.
✓ Leave only when dismissed.
✓ Remember to tell your family about your day at school.

Restroom Procedures

✓ Only one person at a time may go.
✓ Quietly hold up three fingers and shake your fingers if it is an emergency.
✓ Wash your hands afterward.
✓ Come right back and enter quietly.

Drinking Fountain Procedures

✓ Do not line up at the drinking fountain outside or inside the classroom after the recess bell has rung.
✓ No more than three people at the sink area at any time.
✓ Wipe the sink after you drink.

Computer Procedures

✓ Wash your hands before using the computer.
✓ No more than two people at a computer.
✓ Refer your questions to the technology assistant.
✓ Log out of all programs you have been using.
✓ Shut off the computer at the end of the day if you are the last to use it.

When You Have a Substitute Teacher

✓ Respect and follow the substitute's directions and rules, even if they are not exactly the same as ours.
✓ Remember the substitute is taking my place and is an equal of mine.
✓ Be as helpful as possible. The substitute has a copy of all our class procedures.
✓ Assist the substitute in finding supplies.

Group Work

✓ Be prepared with the necessary tools and resources to be successful.
✓ All members participate, share, learn from, and help one another. Collaboration is the key to being a successful learning club.
✓ Use the same procedures for speaking as you do during class.
✓ Practice active listening.
✓ Cooperate.
✓ Do your best.

To view these procedures and more in detail, access http://teachers.net/wong/MAR04.

WHAT DO THE WONGS SUGGEST FOR BEGINNING A CLASS SUCCESSFULLY?

As we have seen, the Wongs place great emphasis on what teachers should do to begin the term effectively (for review, see Wong & Wong, 2005). New teachers, the Wongs say with a note of irony, often have bags brimming with lesson plans, boxes of activities, the state performance appraisal instrument, five interpretations of educational foundations, nine theories of child development, conflicting advice from a plethora of educational specialists, and a collection of buzzwords and current educational fads. But they have little idea about exactly what to do in the first days and weeks of school.

To help new teachers overcome this problem, the Wongs (2007) present a First Day of School Action Plan, which they credit to teacher Sarah Jondahl. Ms. Jondahl developed a plan of step-by-step procedures having to do with preparing the classroom before students arrive, academic expectations, time frames, lesson plans and activities for first days of school, steps in establishing working relations with students and caregivers, class schedules, maintaining a good learning environment, and procedures for documenting and evaluating student progress.

To illustrate, in preparing the classroom before the first day of school, Sarah lists the following matters that require her attention:

✓ "Be Prepared" sheet
✓ Preparation checklist
✓ Getting organized
✓ "Cooperative Classroom" dry-erase board
✓ Student contract for classroom materials
✓ "Our Class Fits Like a Puzzle" bulletin board
✓ Classroom door decoration
✓ "Brag About Me" bulletin board
✓ "All About Me" bulletin board
✓ Room arrangement

In the section on establishing relationships with students and caregivers, she included the following:

✓ Letter to students
✓ Open house activities
✓ Substitute teacher handbook
✓ New student folder
✓ Parent letter
✓ Homework policy
✓ Homework tip list
✓ Transportation checklist
✓ Rules, consequences, and rewards
✓ Volunteer sheet
✓ "Welcoming Phone Call" planning sheet for caregivers of potential problem students

✓ "Positive phone call" form
✓ Parent conferences outline

For the section on maintaining a good learning climate, she detailed what she would do concerning the following:

✓ Reasons for the behavior management plan
✓ Rules, consequences, and rewards
✓ Procedures in behavior management
✓ First morning greeting and seating arrangement
✓ Housekeeping ideas
✓ "Duty Wheel" for student jobs
✓ Intervention plan packet
✓ Socio-gram
✓ Form used to create a socio-gram
✓ Notes of encouragement
✓ Student postcard
✓ "Special News About a Very Special Student" certificate
✓ "Super Job/Way to Go/Great Day" letter form

In summary: The Wongs stress that teachers should set high expectations on the first day, plan the entire day right down to the minute, and make sure to give attention to establishing routines and learning students' names.

They emphasize that during the first week, the most important thing you can do is provide the security of consistency.

They add that if the furniture is movable, you do best to align all the desks facing the teacher during the first day of school. Keep them that way until there is a purpose for changing the arrangement. Make sure to provide a well-organized, uncluttered, attractive classroom. Have the room ready and inviting when students arrive on the first day.

On a bulletin board or elsewhere, post schedules, rules, procedures, and a preview of what is to come. Also post information about yourself, including a picture and a sign that welcomes students to the class. Wear neat clothing—first perceptions affect how students relate to you. Stand when you speak and use short, clear sentences or phrases. Use a firm but soft voice. When emphasizing something, do not point your finger, as it presents an accusatory image.

Your major mission during the first few days is to establish student routines and classroom procedures. If you have very young students, place their name on their coat hooks, desks, and cubbyholes and tell them to use that particular coat hook, desk, or cubbyhole every day. Set up a seating plan beforehand, as this helps you to get to know your students quickly. Begin addressing your students by name as quickly as you can.

On the first day, go to school early and take time to double-check everything. Have your first bell-work assignment ready (a short assignment that students begin working on when they first arrive in the room). Make it interesting but fairly easy so students will have an initial sense of accomplishment. Students who fail early tend to create problems in the classroom. Before class begins, tell yourself the following:

- I will establish classroom management procedures from the beginning.
- I will convey that this class will be work-oriented, with a competent, and caring teacher.
- I will establish work habits in my students first before teaching content.

As the students arrive, position yourself outside the door to greet them. This establishes rapport and relationships and shows you consider the students important. If young children are to line up before entering, insist on an orderly line. If you pick up your class from another area, don't say: "Follow me" or "Come on." Rather, greet the students, introduce yourself and then teach the procedure you want students to follow as they walk to your room.

WHAT DO THE WONGS SAY ABOUT THE FIRST 5 MINUTES OF CLASS?

The Wongs say you should always have an assignment posted for the students to begin working on the second they walk into the room (Wong & Wong, 2000a). They say if you establish that, you eliminate 90% of the discipline problems that otherwise arise. Engaging students in learning keeps them involved and less prone to off-task behavior. If free time happens for students, then a list of choices should be available for students to always be responsible for selecting something to do in the classroom while waiting for others. It is far better to have too much planned for the class period than too little.

The first few minutes with your students are crucial to maintaining a productive tone in your class. Students must know what they are expected to do. When they come in, explain what you want to have happen at the start of the day or period. For instance, let them know what materials they need that day and that they should have pencils sharpened and paper ready. Explain where the warm up activity will be located each day and they are to start on it even before the bell rings to start class.

As students work, take roll while you walk around and observe. Check homework, if needed, and assure yourself that your students are ready for learning.

WHAT ELSE DO THE WONGS SAY ABOUT THE FIRST DAY OF SCHOOL?

As you have seen, the Wongs suggest you carefully plan your first day of class or school in detail. They describe how art teacher Melissa Pantoja attends to this task (see Wong & Wong, 2000c). They liken Mrs. Pantoja to a football coach who scripts the first several plays of a game. They say a teacher should not "wing it" in a classroom any more than a coach would wing it on a football field or a pilot would wing it on a flight from Baltimore to Kansas City. The effective teacher goes in with a plan and modifies that plan as needed. Each teacher's plan will be different. Here is Mrs. Pantoja's plan for the first day:

Greeting Each Student at the Door

✓ Hand each student a classroom rules sheet (goes in notebook).
✓ Direct the student to his or her assigned seat (alphabetical).
✓ Tell the student to read and follow the instructions that are written on the board.

Welcoming Students to Class and Introducing Myself

✓ My name
✓ My family (spouse, kids)
✓ Where I'm from and where I live
✓ Why I wanted to teach

Establishing Rules and Procedures

✓ Explain and teach the rules, which are posted at the front of the room.
✓ Introduce the daily procedures for arrival and dismissal of class.

Assigning Numbers to Students

✓ Explain that each person will have a number that represents him or her.
✓ The numbers will be on all of their art papers and on their art folders to help all of us keep the papers straight.

Respecting the Classroom and the Art Supplies

✓ Teach students how to be responsible for the art supplies and room.
✓ Teach the procedures for obtaining, using, and replacing art supplies.

Clarifying Teacher's Things and Students' Things

✓ Explain with examples that some things are only for me, while other things are for students to use as needed.

Using the Art Centers

✓ Everyone will get the opportunity to go to all the centers.
✓ The art center board will have names (numbers) that tell us who does what that day.

Keeping Portfolios and Notebooks

✓ Each student will receive a portfolio he or she can take home.
✓ Each student will keep a notebook for recording grades and vocabulary words and for writing a weekly entry about what he or she liked most in the week's work.

WHAT DO THE WONGS SAY ABOUT THE FIRST 10 DAYS OF SCHOOL?

The Wongs (2005) further provide detailed suggestions for procedures to be followed in the first 10 days of school. In that regard, they present a guide they credit to Jane Slovenske, a National Board Certified Teacher. Ms. Slovenske's class uses a *self-manager plan* in which students are taught to manage their own behavior in a responsible manner.

Standards are established through class discussions about responsible behavior, treatment of others, and working promptly to the best of one's ability. Once a list of behaviors is agreed on, the students are presented a *self-manager application* to use as a self-evaluation of their behaviors and standards. When students are able to manage all of the items on the application, they fill in the form and take it home for parental review. When the adults are in agreement with the student's self-evaluation, they sign the form and have the student return it to school.

Ms. Slovenske must then see if she agrees with the student's self-evaluation. She discusses with students any differences of opinion. She reports that most students, with input from the adults at home, are honest about self-evaluating their performance. Here, space limitations preclude the inclusion of Ms. Slovenske's plan in detail. If you wish to examine it you can find it on the Internet at http://teachers.net/wong/JAN05.

WHAT DO THE WONGS SAY ABOUT PROCEDURES FOR COOPERATIVE WORK GROUPS?

The Wongs maintain that, generally speaking, most students do better in school when allowed to work in cooperative learning groups. The Wongs suggest you call your cooperative groups **support groups**, with each member of the group known as a **support buddy**. Instead of isolating children with seat work, consider surrounding them with support buddies and teach them how to support each other. Group procedures must be taught clearly, and it is important that each student in the group has a specific job to do. *Ineffective* teachers divide students into groups and simply expect the students to work together. *Effective* teachers teach the group procedures and social skills needed for functioning in a group. Before you begin your first group activity, teach students how to do the following:

- Be responsible for your own work and behavior.
- Ask a support buddy for help if you have a question.
- Help any support buddy who asks for help.
- Ask for help from the teacher only when support buddies cannot supply it.

As you can see, the Wongs identify a multitude of procedures that come into play every day in the classroom. For further detailed information on how to work with groups, consult Chapter 24 in *The First Days of School* (Wong & Wong, 2005a).

DO THE WONGS' IDEAS WORK FOR SECONDARY TEACHERS?

Secondary teachers sometimes comment that the Wongs' suggestions appear to be too elementary for use in high school, but the Wongs emphasize that their approach works equally well at the high school level. Their website includes testimonials from secondary teachers, many of whom assert that the Wongs' suggestions actually saved their professional careers.

For example, Chelonnda Seroyer (see http://teachers.net/wong/FEB05), a first-year teacher, used the Wongs' ideas as the basis for managing her class and had a very successful year academically. In addition, she was senior class sponsor, homecoming parade assistant, and a member of the support team for the school's efforts related to the No Child Left Behind Act. In recognition of her contributions she received the Bob Jones High School "First Year Patriot Award," which is given to the first-year teacher who is recognized for outstanding accomplishments and achievements in academics, athletics, or co-curricular pursuits.

Jeff Smith (see http://teachers.net/wong/APR04), a teacher of welding at a Career Tech Center in Pryor, Oklahoma, reports he was almost fired during his first year because of his poor classroom management. But he happened to hear one of the Wongs' tapes and later wrote the Wongs to say, "You saved my job, and someday I want to help other beginning teachers just like you helped me." Jeff went on to set the state record for the most Career Tech students certified under the industry standard welding certification. He reports that his former students have the highest pay average for high school graduates in the state. He goes on to say that he always knew his subject matter, but had no clue about classroom management until he encountered the Wongs' ideas.

Ed Lucero (see http://teachers.net/wong/MAR05), a high school teacher of business, marketing, and finance in Albuquerque, New Mexico, wrote, "Last year was my eleventh year of teaching. I was miserable! Students weren't paying attention. I constantly repeated myself. Students would ignore my instructions and at times talk back. Some students would attempt to call me 'bro' instead of Mr. Lucero."

Ed decided if things did not improve, he would leave teaching and return to public accounting. His wife suggested he read the Wongs' *The First Days of School: How to Be an Effective Teacher.* He spent the summer studying their suggestions and when the next school year began he was able to implement them. He reported that very quickly he began enjoying the pleasures of teaching.

Other Examples of Management Success

New teacher Amanda Brooks started her school year with a plan and as she says, "I had no behavior problems. I simply taught and enjoyed my students." See www.teachers.net/wong/AUG10.

Kara Moore succeeded because she started the school year with a plan, even though her assignment was changed a week before school began. See www.teachers.net/wong/AUG12.

One principal created a school with consistent procedures and produced the first public school on an Indian reservation to ever achieve AYP (Adequate Yearly Progress). She did this by teaching her teachers how to start the first day with a script. See www.teachers.net/wong/AUG11.

WHAT YOU HAVE LEARNED IN THIS CHAPTER

- ■ You have particular roles to fill and so do students. Help students understand what you will do and what you expect them to do.

- Smooth-running classes are those in which students understand how to follow the procedures required of them.
- Effective teachers spend most of the first 2 weeks of class teaching students how to follow procedures and comply with expectations.
- Your first 5 minutes with your students set a lasting tone for your class.
- It is helpful to script (write out) exactly what you intend to say, do, and accomplish during the first day or days of class.
- Teaching your students to follow expected procedures is one of the most important things you can do as a teacher.
- Students often learn best in cooperative work groups (support groups). You must teach students how to be contributing members of such groups.

Commentary from Anonymous Teacher 1

Now with many years of teaching under my belt, I have my opening-of-class instructions well memorized, so I don't need to script the first day of school. But I could certainly have used that information (but didn't have it) when I first began teaching. Back then, I sort of began the year with trial and error, plenty of both. I really didn't know quite what to convey to my students or how to do so.

Even now, although I have most things under control, I learn a lot from the Wongs. It is no wonder they have such a large following. I especially like what they suggest we tell students about rules—that rules ensure a calm, respectful classroom where everybody will be safe and successful. I also like their ideas about teaching procedures to the point that students have a complete understanding of what they are to do. That suggestion alone really cuts down on confusion and disorder.

Commentary from Anonymous Teacher 2

Rosemary and Harry Wong are great champions of teachers and of the teaching profession. The suggestions they provide for managing a classroom are uplifting and empowering. The collective wisdom of their experiences and of the many teachers who have used their ideas is readily accessible and inspires pride and self-confidence. Their ideas are not just pretty words; they are practical, classroom-tested solutions to some of the most annoying situations in a classroom. Here are situations I often encounter that are easily controlled with the Wongs' suggestions:

Problem: Students come in very chatty and rambunctious from passing period, recess, lunch.

Solution: Bell work. I, and almost every teacher I know, use this tried-and-true method to achieve a calm and orderly start to the class.

Problem: Students bombard you with the same questions (totally unrelated to subject matter), over and over, the sheer volume of which is exhausting and exasperating.

Solution: Create and teach procedures for all of these common situations:

"May I use the restroom? I really need to pee. Ms. Forsythe wouldn't let me go!"

"Can I go call my mom? I forgot my PE clothes/homework/ project at home!"

"I need to go take my project/model/essay/book to _____. Can I please, please go, really fast?"

"Where do I turn in my late work?"

"I'm done. What do I do with this and what do I do now?"

"I've been absent for 3 days. Did I miss anything important?"

The Wongs' advice does help us make things easier for ourselves and our students. I use PowerPoint presentations to teach my students the processes of creating group posters, murals, role-plays, and skits. Sometimes we make a Jeopardy-style game for reviewing and reinforcing what has been learned. I like the visuals to reinforce the words and also keep everything more interesting for the kids. Also, PowerPoint presentations keep me on track so I don't forget something I intended to say. Power Point slides are easy to move around or replace as needed without redoing an entire presentation. As follow-up, I have students make charts and other displays and sometimes let groups act out what we should be doing when we go out to fire drills or other activities.

Activities

Self-Test: True/False

1. The Wongs believe that more teachers fail because of poor management skills than because of faulty knowledge of subject matter.

2. The Wongs advise teachers to carefully explain their responsibilities as well as students' responsibilities in the class.

3. The Wongs use the term "procedures" to refer only to teachers' carefully thinking through the steps they will follow in presenting lessons.

4. The Wongs, believing testing is overrated, advise teachers instead to evaluate students on the basis of projects they complete.

5. The Wongs maintain that what teachers do during the first few minutes of class is crucial to success in teaching and learning.

6. The Wongs' advise against using cooperative work groups because the less capable students usually get left out of the interaction.

7. How primary students are to use the drinking fountain is one example of a "procedure."

8. "Scripting" refers to writing a description of what happened in a given class for later analysis of strengths and weaknesses.

9. The Wongs maintain that their suggestions work just as well for secondary teachers as they do for teachers at the elementary level.

10. The Wongs urge you, when first meeting your students, to teach a typical academic lesson so students will get a feel for how you teach.

Self-Test: Multiple Choice

1. The Wongs urge you to spend the first days of class
   (a) teaching responsibilities and roles.
   (b) learning students' names.
   (c) reviewing objectives.
   (d) getting acquainted.
2. Your success for the year is most strongly influenced by what you do
   (a) on the first day.
   (b) at the end of first month.
   (c) during the first grading period.
   (d) during the last 2 weeks of the year.
3. The Wongs say effective teachers spend most of the first 2 weeks teaching
   (a) courtesy.
   (b) responsibility.
   (c) procedures.
   (d) subject matter.
4. The Wongs say the main problem in schools today is
   (a) discipline.
   (b) poor class management.
   (c) unmotivated students.
   (d) ineffective administrators.
5. To increase student achievement, teachers should (within reason)
   (a) visit students' homes.
   (b) communicate with caregivers.
   (c) give frequent tests.
   (d) use discovery learning.
6. Ineffective teachers begin the first day of school trying to teach
   (a) subject matter.
   (b) routines.
   (c) the discipline plan.
   (d) roles and responsibilities.
7. You should limit the number of rules of behavior to
   (a) three.
   (b) five.

(c) seven.
(d) none of the above—it depends on the class.

8. The Wongs say their approach works
   (a) better for elementary classes.
   (b) better for secondary classes.
   (c) better for preschool classes.
   (d) equally well for any level.
9. On the first day, you should greet each student
   (a) at his or her desk.
   (b) on the school grounds.
   (c) at the bus drop-off.
   (d) at the classroom door.
10. Throughout lessons, you should intersperse
    (a) questions.
    (b) time for quiet reflection.
    (c) positive reinforcement.
    (d) compliments.

Self-Test: Explain This

1. What do the Wongs mean by "procedures"?
2. What do the Wongs say about "the first 5 minutes of class"?
3. What do the Wongs say about tests and testing?
4. What do the Wongs mean by "scripting"?
5. What do the Wongs say about cooperative student work?

Additional Suggested Activities

1. In your journal, make notes of suggestions from the Wongs that you might wish to incorporate into a personalized system of classroom management.
2. What would you communicate to students concerning your roles and their roles in the class? What would you do to make sure they remembered their roles? How might you tie your management plan into your explanation of their roles?
3. Following the Wongs' suggestions, outline what you would script for the first 10 minutes of your first class.

Concept Cases

CASE 1   Kristina Will Not Work

Kristina, a student in Mr. Jake's class, is quite docile. She socializes little with other students and never disrupts lessons. However, despite Mr. Jake's best efforts, Kristina will not do her work. She rarely completes an assignment. She is simply there, putting forth no effort at all. *What would Harry and Rosemary Wong suggest to help Kristina and Mr. Jake?*

The Wongs would advise Mr. Jake to carefully teach Kristina the procedures associated with completing assignments and other work activities. He should ask her to show him that she understands the procedures. He might consider having Kristina work with a support buddy with whom she feels comfortable. He would supply positive consequences for all improvements Kristina shows. If Kristina does not improve, Mr. Jake should talk further with her privately, and in a positive, supportive tone reiterate that he cares about her, wants her to succeed, will let nothing interfere with her progress if he can help it, and will help correct anything that might be standing in the way of her completing her work.

If Kristina still doesn't improve, Mr. Jake should seek help from school personnel who are trained to assess Kristina and help provide conditions that improve her likelihood of success.

CASE 2   Sara Will Not Stop Talking

Sara is a pleasant girl who participates in class activities and does most, though not all, of her assigned work. She cannot seem to refrain from talking to classmates, however. Her teacher, Mr. Gonzales, has to speak to her repeatedly during lessons, to the point that he often becomes exasperated and loses his temper. *What suggestions might Harry and Rosemary Wong give Mr. Gonzales for dealing with Sara?*

CASE 3   Joshua Clowns and Intimidates

Joshua, larger and louder than his classmates, always wants to be the center of attention, which he accomplishes through a combination of clowning and intimidation. He makes wise remarks, talks back (smilingly) to the teacher, utters a variety of sound-effect noises such as automobile crashes and gunshots, and makes limitless sarcastic comments and put-downs of his classmates. Other students will not stand up to him, apparently fearing his size and verbal aggression. His teacher, Miss Pearl, has come to her wit's end. *Do Harry and Rosemary Wong provide suggestions that might improve Joshua's behavior? Explain.*

CASE 4   Tom Is Hostile and Defiant

Tom has appeared to be in his usual foul mood ever since arriving in class. On his way to sharpen his pencil, he bumps into Frank, who complains. Tom tells him loudly to shut up. Miss Baines, the teacher, says, "Tom, go back to your seat." Tom wheels around, swears loudly, and says heatedly, "I'll go when I'm _____ good and ready!" *What suggestions might Harry and Rosemary Wong offer to help improve Tom's behavior?*

You Are the Teacher

MIDDLE SCHOOL MEDIA CENTER

You are the specialist in charge of the middle school media center. You see your job as serving as a resource person to students who are seeking information, and you are always eager to give help to those who request it. Each period of the day brings different students to your center. Usually, small groups come to do cooperative research. In addition, unexpected students frequently appear who have been excused from their regular classes for a variety of reasons, but often have no particular purpose for visiting the center.

A TYPICAL OCCURRENCE

You have succeeded in getting students settled and working when Tara appears at your side, needing a book to read as makeup work for missing class. You ask Tara what kinds of books interest her. She resignedly shrugs her shoulders. You take her to a shelf of newly published books. "I read this one last night," you tell her. "I think you might like it. It's a good story and fast reading." Tara only glances at it. "That looks stupid," she says. "Don't you have any good books?" She glances down the shelf. "These are all stupid!"

Another student, Jaime, is tugging at your elbow. He is trying to deliver a note to you from his history teacher. You ask Tara to look at the books for a moment while you keep Jaime as your side. At that moment you notice that a group of students, supposedly doing research, are watching Walter and Teo have a friendly pencil fight, hitting pencils together until one of them

breaks. You address your comments to Walter, who appears to be the more eager participant. Walter answers hotly, "Teo started it! It wasn't me!" "Well," you say, "if you boys can't behave yourself, just go back to your class." Teo smiles and Walter feels he is being treated unjustly. He sits down and pouts.

Meanwhile, Tara has gone to the large globe and is twirling it. You start to speak to her but realize that Jaime is still waiting at your side with the note from his teacher. Somehow, before the period ends, Tara leaves with a book she doesn't want and Jaime takes a citation back to his teacher. The research groups have been too noisy. You know they have done little work and wonder if you should speak to their teacher about their manners and courtesy. After the period is over, you notice that profane remarks have been written on the table where Walter was sitting.

CONCEPTUALIZING A STRATEGY

If you followed the suggestions of the Wongs, what would you conclude or do with regard to the following?

- Pinpointing the problems in your class
- Preventing the problems from occurring in the first place
- Putting an immediate end to the misbehavior
- Maintaining student dignity and good personal relations
- Using the situation to help the students develop a sense of greater responsibility and self-control

PHASE THREE

Engaging with Your Students and Activating Their Internal Motivation

In Which You Learn How to Engage with Students Personally, Release Their Internal Motivation, Involve Them in High-Quality Learning Experiences, Influence Them Toward Making Good Choices, and Manage Atypical Behavior

CHAPTERS IN PHASE III

CHAPTER 7 How Does Fred Jones Help Students Focus and Stay on Task?

This chapter explains how Fred Jones helps students maintain focus and stay on task.

CHAPTER 8 How Does Marvin Marshall Help Students Learn to Make Good Choices and Take Responsibility for Their Behavior?

This chapter explains how Marvin Marshall helps students learn to make good choices and take responsibility for their behavior.

CHAPTER 9 How Does William Glasser Use Noncoercive Choice to Promote Quality Learning and Student Self-Control?

This chapter explains how William Glasser uses noncoercive choice to promote quality learning and student self-control.

CHAPTER 10 How Does Spencer Kagan Foster Good Behavior by Working in Tandem with Students?

This chapter explains how Spencer Kagan enables teachers and students to work together on the same side rather than at cross purposes.

CHAPTER 11 What Is Neurological-Based Behavior, How Does It Impact Your Students and You, and How Can You Help Students Who Have It?

This chapter explains how Paula Cook promotes success for students with neurological-based behavior.

7

Fred Jones on Keeping Students Willingly Engaged in Learning

How Does Fred Jones Help Students Focus and Stay on Task?

Some years ago, psychologist Fred Jones conducted large-scale studies of outstanding teachers who were identified as "naturals" by their administrators and colleagues. He hoped to discover what those teachers did that made teaching and discipline seem so effortless. The answer, he found, was that those teachers kept students fully engaged in learning while teaching them to be self-disciplined. Jones decoded what these teachers did and translated the techniques into coachable skills. He then taught a set of struggling teachers in the same school to use these skills. The results showed that disruptions decreased by 87%. To validate that the intervention was what changed the behavior, he did a reversal study wherein the teachers stopped using their new skill set. The students' behavior reverted, indicating that the new skills were the critical factor. In this chapter, we examine Jones's findings and conclusions and see how they are applied in the classroom.

WHO IS FRED JONES?

Dr. Jones, an independent consultant in teaching and classroom management, is the author of Fred Jones's *Tools for Teaching* (2007a), in which he explains tactics for motivating students, instructing them effectively, and helping them develop self-discipline. He first became interested in the nature of better teaching while on the faculties of the UCLA Medical Center and the University of Rochester School of Medicine and Dentistry. He now devotes himself to making presentations and developing materials for educators. In addition to *Tools for Teaching,* Jones is author of *Positive Classroom Discipline* (1987a) and *Positive Classroom Instruction* (1987b). Jones has also developed a video course of study called *The Video Toolbox* (2007b) and has published a number of articles on effective teaching in *Education World.* The manual for *The Video Toolbox* is authored by Patrick T. Jones. Descriptions of these materials, programs, and available presentations are posted on Dr. Jones's website at www.fredjones.com.

WHAT QUESTIONS WILL THIS CHAPTER ANSWER FOR ME?

- What does Jones identify as the main problem in discipline?
- How does Jones keep students actively engaged in learning?

- What does Jones mean by "body language," and how is it used?
- What is Say, See, Do teaching, and how is it done?
- What does Jones mean by "working the crowd," and what does it entail?
- What are visual instructional plans, and how are they used?
- What is preferred activity time (PAT), and what is it used for?
- How can teachers provide help to students most effectively?
- How might I apply Jones's ideas in my own classroom?

THE JONES MODEL

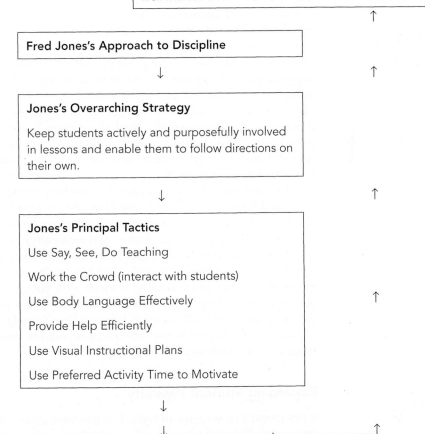

The Common Goal of All Approaches to Discipline
Responsible, Civil Classroom Behavior That Becomes Habitual and Lasts over Time
Responsible means paying attention, making a strong effort, and doing what is proper without being told. Civil means respectful, polite, cordial, and well-mannered.

Fred Jones's Approach to Discipline

Jones's Overarching Strategy

Keep students actively and purposefully involved in lessons and enable them to follow directions on their own.

Jones's Principal Tactics

Use Say, See, Do Teaching

Work the Crowd (interact with students)

Use Body Language Effectively

Provide Help Efficiently

Use Visual Instructional Plans

Use Preferred Activity Time to Motivate

WHAT FIVE PROBLEMS DID JONES BRING TO LIGHT?

Jones and his associates spent thousands of hours observing and recording in hundreds of elementary and secondary classrooms. Their analyses of those recordings pinpointed the misbehaviors that most often occurred in classrooms and located the points in lessons where they usually appeared. The information also revealed many tactics that highly effective teachers used to prevent and deal with misbehavior.

Jones concluded that five major conditions are usually evident in less effective classrooms. They are massive time wasting, student passivity, student aimlessness, "helpless handraising," and ineffective nagging by teachers. Here is how he describes those conditions and how he suggests you can address them. His research showed that by using the skills sets he developed, you can reduce misbehavior, increase learning, make schooling enjoyable for you and your students, and promote positive attitudes for everyone concerned.

Regarding Massive Time Wasting

Jones found that the main problem in less productive classes was simply **massive time wasting**. Even though many of the classrooms he studied were in inner-city schools and alternative schools for students with behavior problems, Jones found relatively little student hostility and defiance—the behavior teachers fear and that many people believe predominates in schools. Instead, students wasted huge amounts of time by talking, goofing off, daydreaming, and moving about. He found they were doing one or more of those things in about 95% of the classroom disruptions that affected teaching and learning.

Jones also determined how frequently disruptions occurred. In well-managed classrooms, one disruption occurred about every 2 minutes. In louder, more unruly classes, the disruptions averaged about 2.5 per minute. He found that the typical class did not get down to business until 5 to 7 minutes after the bell rang, while in-class transitions from one activity to another normally took 5 minutes. The resultant inefficiency contributed to teachers losing almost 50% of the time that could have been devoted to teaching and learning (Jones, 1987a).

Jones described students in the less effective classes as "expert time wasters" who had no vested interest in "hustle" and took every opportunity to dawdle. Jones consequently set out to determine how this time wasting could be reduced. He concluded it could best be remedied by: (1) clearly communicating class requirements to students and following through with class rules, (2) establishing and practicing class routines, (3) increasing students' initial inclination to participate, (4) using tactics and activities that keep students actively involved in lessons, and (5) efficiently providing help to students who need it. Presently we will see Jones's suggestions for making those improvements.

Regarding Student Passivity

Jones found that students in typical classes were passive most of the time, rather than active. Passivity tends to reduce attention, and so students would disengage from lessons and daydream, look out the window, or talk with others. Jones concluded that this passivity was fostered by the teaching methods being used, which only infrequently asked students to participate or show accountability, especially in the early phases of lessons. Students mainly sat and (supposedly) listened while teachers explained and demonstrated.

Jones hastens to add that the teachers who encountered problems were working hard at their jobs—he described their efforts as "bop 'til you drop" and likened their activities to actors performing five matinees a day. Yet, despite all their effort, when the lesson transitioned from teacher input to independent student seat work, waving hands would shoot into the air because students simply didn't know what to do. The hands, Jones noted, usually belonged to the same **"helpless handraisers"** every day. When hands went up, the teachers would begin chasing from student to student, repeating over and over the same information they had tried so hard to impart earlier in the lesson.

Regarding Aimlessness

Another problem Jones found was that students either had scant knowledge of the procedures they were to follow or else chose not to follow them. This lack of knowledge, or disregard, resulted in apathetic inaction. Jones believes students usually know, generally if not specifically, what is expected of them, yet many disregard those expectations.

The students Jones observed did not behave the same in all their classes. They adjusted their behavior to match the standards that each teacher was able to uphold. As Jones put it, if your second-period teacher let you talk and fool around while your third-period teacher did not, you talked in second period and cooled it in third period. The standards in any classroom, he says, are defined by whatever students can get away with. If teachers do not take the time to teach expectations and procedures carefully—and if they fail to ensure compliance with those expectations—they will invariably get whatever the students feel like giving them, which usually is not much. Jones's views correspond with those of Harry and Rosemary Wong (discussed in Chapter 6) that teaching and enforcing classroom procedures is probably the most neglected aspect of classroom management.

Regarding Helpless Handraising

Jones found that when teachers were working hard in the first parts of lessons, students seemed to pay attention and understand well enough. But when students were directed to continue work on their own, hands went up, talking began, students rummaged around or stared out the window, and some got out of their seats. As Jones (1987b) put it, "that was when the chickens came home to roost" (p. 14), meaning the natural results of incomplete student understanding became painfully evident.

Often, teachers did not know what to do at that time other than admonish, nag, or reteach the lesson to the handraisers. That scene, said Jones (1987b), reflected "another day in the life of a typical classroom" (p. 14). Teachers everywhere can relate to that scenario and the frustration it brings. Later we will examine Jones's solution to that problem.

Regarding Ineffective Nagging

Jones's observations revealed that many teachers spend a great deal of time nagging students—telling them over and over what they ought to be doing and admonishing them when they don't comply. Jones calls that the *nag-nag-nag syndrome,* which many teachers use even though experience has repeatedly shown them it doesn't work. Jones says instead of nagging, teachers should calmly show they mean business. As we will see later, Jones believes they can do this more effectively through body language than through verbal language.

HOW WOULD JONES HELP TEACHERS BECOME MORE EFFECTIVE?

Jones says that all the highly touted efforts to improve education—all those policies, mandates, and well-intentioned "solutions"—don't mean a thing until they are translated into workable practices in the classroom. Most teachers try their best not only to maintain reasonable behavior in the room, but also to implement the latest and best teaching practices. And what does that get them? Usually, little more than an increasingly heavy workload that over time becomes more and more difficult to manage.

But, says Jones, there is a much easier way to get things done, and done well. By using a better approach, teachers can raise their effectiveness without working themselves to exhaustion, as many do today. Here we review 11 of Jones's suggestions for promoting active involvement, purposeful behavior, and responsibility.

First, Conserve Time and Don't Allow Students to Waste It

The most effective teachers make maximum use of the time available for instruction. They do this by establishing a classroom structure of rules, routines, and responsibility training that uses time efficiently. The structure puts students on task when the bell rings and allows 30-second transitions from one activity to another. These two tactics alone can save 10 minutes of learning time that is wasted in the usual 50-minute class period.

Second, Arrange Class Seating to Facilitate Active Teaching and Close Proximity to Students

Jones would have you maintain close proximity and eye contact with students and move among them, both during direct instruction and while students are engaged in seat work or cooperative learning. To allow you to move easily among students, classroom seating must provide generous walkways. Jones advocates an **interior loop** arrangement, where desks or tables are set with two wide aisles from front to back, with enough distance between side-to-side rows for you to walk comfortably among the students. Your path of circulation would be along the black loop, as shown in Figure 7.1.

This seating arrangement not only allows you to maintain close proximity to all students, but is especially helpful when you **work the crowd,** as Jones says, meaning you monitor and interact with students who are doing independent or group work. It also allows you to bring body language more effectively into play,

Figure 7.1   Jones's Interior Loop Seating Arrangement.

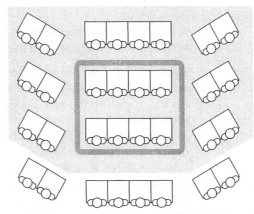

Source: Jones, F. (2007). *Tools for teaching.* Santa Cruz, CA: Fredric H. Jones & Associates.

as will be described later in this chapter. These conditions keep students attentive and actively involved.

Third, Teach Your Students the Meaning and Purpose of Discipline

Jones wants you to make it plain to your students that the purpose of discipline is to help them learn, be successful in school, and have an enjoyable time doing so. Think of discipline in that way—a means of helping students rather than clashing with them. Help students see it that way, too. Jones suggests a number of positive, **unobtrusive tactics** that provide good results in that kind of discipline. Here are three examples:

- Prevent the occurrence of misbehavior. Jones stresses that the best way to manage behavior problems is to prevent their occurrence, and that the best preventive strategy involves setting limits, specifying class rules, giving students class responsibilities, organizing an effective seating arrangement, and establishing a routine for beginning the class.
- Set limits on behavior. In **setting limits**, you clearly demarcate the boundaries that separate acceptable behavior from unacceptable behavior. Those boundaries are then verbalized as class rules, which you must enforce. Jones urges you to begin this process when you first meet your students. At that time, discuss with them the class rules and explain how they ensure behavior that allows everyone to learn and feel safe.
- Use workable class rules. Jones describes two types of class rules—general and specific. **General rules**, fairly few in number, define your broad guidelines, standards, and expectations for work and behavior. Examples of general rules:

  - Do quality work every time; don't settle for anything else.
  - Treat every member of the class as you would like them to treat you.

Rules of this type should be posted, referred to regularly, and reviewed periodically.

Specific rules refer to procedures and routines. They detail exactly what students are to do in various learning activities. Examples:

- When you enter the room, sit down and begin bell work immediately.
- When you wish to speak, raise your hand and wait to be called on.

There will be many specific rules. The behaviors they specify must be taught and rehearsed until they are learned, just like any academic skill. Jones advocates spending the first 2 weeks making sure students understand them thoroughly.

Introduce rules by involving your students in identifying examples of desirable and undesirable classroom behavior. This process helps students recognize the need for rules. You will have formalized your rules in advance, but you should go through them with students until students clearly understand their purpose and the behavior they require. Then you should have students practice complying with rules until doing so becomes second nature.

In your discussions about rules, be sure to explain what you will do to help students abide by the rules. Indicate how you will teach the required behavior when necessary. Explain how you will show your approval and appreciation when students follow rules properly, and also explain what you will do when students break rules.

Fourth, Assign Your Students Specific Responsibilities in Caring for the Classroom

Jones believes in assigning a classroom chore to every student, if possible. This practice helps students develop a sense of personal responsibility and ownership in the class program. The number and type of classroom jobs you assign depends upon your grade level, teaching assignment, and personal preferences. Here are some examples of jobs that many teachers use: teacher assistants, classroom librarians, paper distributors, assignment collectors, zoologists/animal handlers, gardeners, homework monitors, media monitors, computer technicians, bulletin board designers, materials managers, room inspectors, mail carriers, and job managers. You can check the Internet to learn how other teachers have organized their systems for classroom jobs. You will find teachers are very generous in sharing their systems and ideas with fellow educators.

Fifth, Begin Every Class with Bell Work

Class sessions in many schools begin in a fragmented way, with announcements, taking attendance, handling tardies, and the like. This fragmentation causes the loss of 5 to 8 minutes at the beginning of most classes.

You can avoid losing this time simply by beginning lessons promptly. Jones would have you teach students to sit down and begin doing **bell work** immediately upon entering the room. Bell work engages students and focuses their attention. No active instruction from you is required. Examples of bell work are answering review questions, doing warm-up problems, solving brain teasers, doing silent reading, and writing in journals.

Sixth, Keep Your Students Actively Engaged in Learning

To help teachers maintain student involvement, Jones emphasizes a teaching approach he calls **Say, See, Do teaching**. In that approach, the teacher *says* the task, the students *see* the teacher perform the task, and then the students *do* it. This process is used frequently through the lesson.

You can see that Say, See, Do teaching is preferable to the traditional approach in which teachers tell about, explain, and demonstrate a quantity of information before students do anything active. Jones (2007) graphically depicts the old-fashioned approach as follows:

Teacher input, input, input, input, input → Student output

This traditional approach contains some built-in faults, such as:

- The large amount of teacher input produces cognitive overload in students, which makes them want to disengage from the lesson.
- The students sit passively for too long and the urge to do something builds up.
- The teacher does not adequately work the crowd, that is, interact with individual students, particularly in the back of the classroom.

Say, See, Do teaching is different. Teachers present smaller bits of information and then quickly have students do something with it. This approach is *doing oriented*, with activities occurring often and at short intervals. Jones depicts it as follows:

Teacher input → Student output → Teacher input →
Student output → Teacher input → Student output

Seventh, Use Visual Instructional Plans

Say, See, Do teaching becomes even more effective when augmented with **visual instructional plans (VIPs)**. VIPs are graphics or picture prompts that students use as guides in completing processes or activities. They come into play during the second part of the lesson, when students are asked to work on their own. VIPs are displayed in the room, and students are taught to consult them for guidance instead of raising their hands and waiting for the teacher when they get stuck. To illustrate, Fred Jones (2007) asks you to imagine you are teaching a class how to divide 495 by 6. Typically, you would explain and demonstrate the calculation one step at a time, and, when finished, your work on the chalkboard might look like that in Figure 7.2.

Now, Jones says, imagine the helpless handraiser during independent work, stuck on step four. What does the student do? Step four is not evident in the summary graphic in Figure 7.2. Our typical technique of laying one step over another produces only a single *summary graphic*. The helpless handraiser will now call for help and do nothing until the teacher arrives to provide yet another tutoring session.

Jones's remedy is to display a graphic plan that shows one step at a time and a picture for every step. Such plans are easy to consult and follow, allowing students

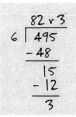

Figure 7.2 Summary Graphic.
Source: Jones, F. (2007). *Tools for teaching.* Santa Cruz, CA: Fredric H. Jones & Associates.

Figure 7.3   Portion of a Step-by-Step Graphic.

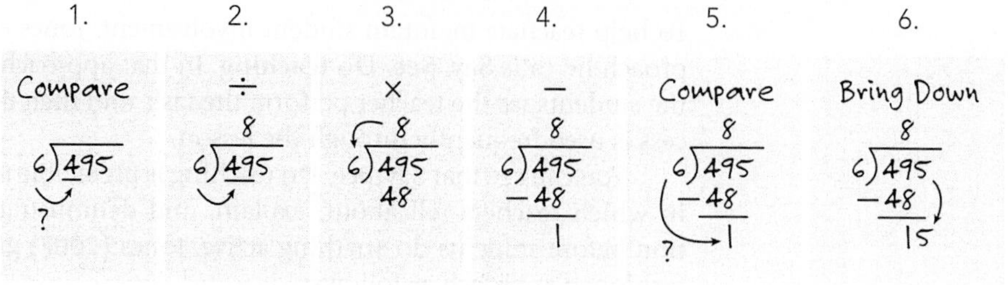

Source: Jones, F. (2007). *Tools for teaching.* Santa Cruz, CA: Fredric H. Jones & Associates.

to continue working on their own. Figure 7.3 shows a guide to helping students who forget the steps in long division. This VIP, with the first six steps shown along the top, offers guidance that is simple, clear, and permanent. A student can refer to it at any time to answer the question, "What do I do next?"

Eighth, Use Body Language to Communicate Pleasantly and Clearly That You Mean Business

It is essential that your students understand that their job is to acquire important learning, while your job is to help them do so in pleasant circumstances. You need to convince them that you will not permit any behavior that interferes with those basic jobs. But, says Jones, you have to show them you mean business, and many teachers don't know how to do so convincingly. If students don't believe that you mean what you say, they will push back at you and you will find yourself nagging and cajoling for compliance—you'd do better to save your breath.

Here is Jones's main suggestion for showing you mean business: Say what you mean and use **body language** to reinforce your words. Body language works nonverbally through body carriage, eye contact, and tone of voice. When used properly, it is low key and nonadversarial, and it eliminates most student backtalk and argumentation. Better yet, it increases learning for those who need it most—the low achievers who typically spend vast amounts of class time goofing off. Jones claims that simply by using body language, you can increase achievement for the bottom half of your class by as much as 50% while eliminating the majority of classroom disruptions—and you hardly have to open your mouth.

Bring body language to students' attention right away. When discussing rules, demonstrate examples of body language you will use to help students stay on task. Include eye contact, facial expressions, gestures, and **physical proximity**. Jones says teachers are most effective in setting limits when they use their bodies correctly but say nothing and take no other action. He emphatically reminds us that we cannot discipline with our mouths—that if we could, nagging would have fixed every kid a million years ago. He warns that when you open your mouth, you often do more harm than good. Jones does not leave to chance the interpretation of what constitutes effective body language. He coaches teachers in every detail. The prompts used for coaching are available free in the study Group

Activity explained later in this chapter. Following are further suggestions Jones makes about body language.

Regarding Body Carriage

Posture and **body carriage** are both very effective in communicating authority. Good posture and confident carriage suggest strong leadership, whereas drooping posture and lethargic movements suggest resignation or fearfulness. Students read body language and are able to tell whether you are feeling in charge or are tired, disinterested, or intimidated. Even when you are tired or troubled, remember to stand tall and move assertively.

Regarding Calm and Proper Breathing

Teachers do well to remain calm in all situations. Calm conveys strength. In part, it is attained and conveyed through proper breathing. The way teachers breathe when under pressure signals how they feel and what they are likely to do next. Teach yourself through practice to breathe slowly and deliberately before responding to annoying situations. Jones noted that some teachers take two deep breaths before turning to a misbehaving student. In doing so, they project an aura of self-control.

Regarding Eye Contact

Suppose you are explaining the process of multiplying fractions. You see that Jacob has stopped paying attention. You pause. The sudden quiet causes everyone to look at you. Jacob sees you are looking directly at his eyes. He straightens up and waits attentively. Jones says few physical acts are more effective than eye contact for conveying the impression of being in control. He adds that turning and pointing the eyes and the feet toward misbehaving students shows your commitment to discipline.

Regarding Physical Proximity

Suppose you have explained a process and have directed students to complete some exercises on their own. After a time, you notice that Jacob has stopped working and has begun talking to Jerry. You move toward Jacob. When he becomes aware of you, he immediately gets back to work. Jones maintains that teachers who use physical proximity rarely need to say anything to get offending students back on task.

Regarding Facial Expressions

Your facial expressions communicate a great deal. They can show enthusiasm, seriousness, enjoyment, and appreciation, all of which encourage good behavior; or they can reveal boredom, annoyance, and resignation, which may promote student lethargy and inattention. Facial expressions such as winks, smiles, and raised eyebrows demonstrate a sense of humor and personal connection, traits students appreciate in teachers.

Ninth, Increase Motivation and Responsibility Through Wise Use of Incentives

An **incentive** is a proffered condition that prompts an individual to act. To illustrate, you promise (as an incentive) to allow students to engage later in a specific activity you know they enjoy, but first they must do their work and behave properly. The incentive is held in abeyance until the behavior occurs acceptably. Examples of incentives include the opportunity to work with a group to present a report or play an instructional game that reviews material pertinent to the subject. Jones features such incentives prominently as a means of motivating students and teaching them to be responsible. He found that some of the most effective teachers use incentives systematically, whereas less effective teachers use them improperly or not at all.

As for effective incentives, Jones says you should discuss with students the kinds you will make available and how you will manage them. He says the incentives should be provided in the form of **preferred activity time (PAT)**, meaning instructional activities students especially enjoy. To obtain them, students must work steadily rather than fool around. The time they save in doing so is then returned to them in the form of the incentive—the activity they enjoy. Jones says those activities must all have instructional value. Don't use any that are simply for play or filling in time.

In elaborating further on PAT, Jones provides comments and reminders related to (1) Grandma's rule, (2) student responsibility, (3) genuine incentives, (4) preferred activities, (5) educational value, (6) group concern and management, (7) omission training, and (8) backup systems. Let us see what is involved in each.

Grandma's Rule

Grandma's rule states: "First eat your vegetables, and then you can have your dessert." Applied to the classroom, this rule requires that students first do their assigned work, and then they can enjoy a favorite activity. It is a fact of life that children—and we adults, too—prefer to dive into the dessert, promising to eat our vegetables afterward. But as we all know, even the best intentions fade away once the motivation behind them is gone. Incentives are of no value unless they are delivered after, and only after, students have done their work in an acceptable manner. If they don't eat their broccoli first, they don't get their ice cream.

Student Responsibility

Jones contends that properly used incentives help foster **student responsibility**, by which students learn to take responsibility for their decisions and actions. For example, one way students can show responsibility is through cooperating with others. However, because cooperation is voluntary, it is difficult to force it on anyone. When asked to cooperate, students who enjoy goofing off and daydreaming can ask themselves, "Why should I? What's in it for me?" Jones argues that when incentives are provided for cooperation, students see they have something to gain by it. At first, they may cooperate primarily to obtain the incentive bonus, but over time, cooperation becomes natural and enjoyable in itself.

Genuine Incentives

There is a wide difference between what many teachers might consider to be incentives (e.g., "Let's all work in such a way that we will later be proud of what we do") and what students consider **genuine incentives** (e.g., "If you complete your work on time, you can have 5 minutes of preferred activity time"). Certainly students are more motivated by specific outcomes they like than by vague outcomes that mean little to them. Jones comments on the different effects promoted by a promise of "free time" versus a promise of "preferred activity time." He says students won't work for long to earn free time, but they will work hard to gain time for an activity they enjoy. Teachers simply have to be sure the incentive is genuine in students' eyes. The following, for example, are *not* incentives for most students:

- "The first person to complete a perfect paper will receive two bonus points."
- "If you really work hard, you can be the best class I have ever had."

The first may motivate a few of the most able students, but all the others know they have little chance to win so they see no point in trying. The second statement sounds good to the teacher but means very little to the students and is not sufficient to get them to make extra effort.

On the other hand, students respond well to the anticipation of activities such as art, games for learning or review, viewing a video, or having time to pursue interesting topics with friends. Such group activities are effective because almost all students desire them sufficiently to make extra effort to obtain them *and* they are available to all students, not just a few.

Tangible objects, awards, and certificates should not be used as incentives. They do not motivate students highly, nor do they have educational value.

Earning Preferred Activity Time

PAT may be earned in a number of different ways. Mr. Jorgensen gives his fourth graders 3 minutes to put away their language arts materials and prepare for math. Any time left over from the 3 minutes goes later to PAT. In Mrs. Nguyen's English class, if everyone is seated and ready when the bell rings, the class earns 2 minutes of additional PAT. However, if some or all of the class continues to be noisy, the class loses PAT commensurate with the amount of time they have wasted. Some classes use PAT on the day it is earned, whereas others accumulate PAT for a future activity.

Educational Value

It has been emphasized that to the extent feasible, class time, including PAT, should be devoted to activities that have educational value. Work that keeps students occupied but teaches them nothing of value can seldom be justified. Although most educators are comfortable in allowing occasional frivolity in the class, the opposite extreme of holding daily or weekly parties as incentives is difficult to condone. What, then, should one use as PAT?

Jones maintains that when teachers introduce PAT to their students, they must make sure of three things: (1) the activity has educational value, (2) students want to participate in the activity, and (3) students understand they earn the activity by conducting themselves responsibly. There are many activities with educational value that students enjoy greatly, both individually and in groups. Among the best activities are learning games and enrichment activities, which are both fun and educational. Examples of such activities are using new vocabulary words to play hangman, completing an art project, or reading a book for pleasure.

In PAT, students are never left to do just anything, nor do they proceed without guidance. The freedom they enjoy lies in being able to choose from a variety of approved activities. Activities can be chosen by vote, with all students engaging in the same activity during the time allotted. Elementary school students often select physical education, art, music, drama, or construction activities, or having the teacher read to them. Secondary students often choose to hold class discussions on special topics, participate in performances by class members, or work together on projects such as a class magazine. Posted on the Jones website (Jones, n.d.) you can find suggestions from teachers for a large number of educationally sound activities that are effective as preferred activities; see www.fredjones.com/PAT/index.html.

Group Concern and PAT Management

Jones also emphasizes the importance of making sure every student has a stake in earning the PAT incentive for the entire class. This **group concern** motivates all students to keep on task, behave well, and complete assigned work. PAT can be managed thus: The teacher agrees to set aside a period of time in which students might be allowed to engage in a preferred activity. The PAT can be at the end of the school day for self-contained classes—perhaps 15 to 20 minutes. For departmentalized classes, the time can be set aside at the end of the week—perhaps 30 minutes on Friday. The students can decide on the activity for their "dessert" time, and to earn it, they have only to work and behave in accordance with class standards.

The teacher keeps track of the time that students earn. Of course, it is possible that a single student, by misbehaving, can prevent the class from earning full PAT. Teachers often think it unfair to penalize the entire class when only a few have transgressed. In practice, this is rarely a problem, because the class quickly understands that this is a group effort, not an individual one. The group is rewarded together and punished together regardless of who misbehaves. A strength of this approach is that it engenders peer pressure in favor of proper behavior.

In ordinary circumstances, a misbehaving student obtains reinforcement from the group in the form of attention or laughter. With proper PAT, the opposite is true. The class is likely to discourage individual misbehavior because it takes away something the class members want. Nevertheless, some students do occasionally misbehave to the detriment of responsible students. When this occurs, the teacher may decide to work with the offending student individually.

Omission Training

Generally speaking, incentives and PAT bonuses are earned by the entire class. Teachers cannot possibly monitor incentives for all students individually. The exception lies in the occasional student whose misbehavior repeatedly ruins PAT for the rest of the class. The following case shows how **omission training** is useful in earning PAT for the entire class:

> Kevin is a student in Ms. VanEtten's class. He disregards the requirements of PAT and is continually late, loud, and unprepared, thus ruining PAT for the others. Ms. VanEtten privately explains to Kevin that he doesn't have to participate in PAT because he doesn't care about it, but she does want him to be successful with his own work and behavior. She explains that she will use a timer, and when Kevin behaves in accordance with class rules, he will earn time for himself individually,

and also extra time for the class. When he misbehaves, he will lose time for himself but not for the class. Kevin soon learns he can gain status in the class by earning PAT for other members of the class.

Backup Systems for Misbehavior

As a last option for students who subvert PAT, Jones suggests **backup systems**, which are hierarchical arrangements of sanctions for putting a stop to unacceptable student behavior. Jones identifies three levels of backup:

1. Small backup responses, conveyed privately or semiprivately to the student: "I expect you to stop talking so we can get on with our work." With such low-key messages, the student knows the teacher means business.
2. Medium backup responses, delivered publicly in the classroom: "Emily, sit in the thinking chair for 3 minutes and think about what you have done that caused me to send you there." Or, "Brian, because you are late again, you will have detention with me tomorrow after school." Other medium backup responses include warnings, reprimands, loss of privileges, and parent conferences.
3. Large backup responses are used to deal with repeated disruptions or other intolerable behavior. They require the involvement of at least two professionals, usually the teacher and an administrator. They include trips to the office, in-school or out-of-school suspension, and occasionally placement in special classes or special schools.

Tenth, Provide Help Efficiently During Independent Work

As noted earlier, Jones puts particular emphasis on how teachers should provide help to students who get stuck during seat work. Suppose Mrs. James is teaching a lesson in determining percentages. She illustrates at the board by showing how to calculate 4% of three different amounts, asks a couple of questions to verify that students are understanding, and then assigns independent exercises for students to calculate a number of percentages ranging from 5 to 120%.

Almost immediately, Arnell raises his hand for help. If he were the only one to do so, there would be little problem. But Mrs. James sees other hands began to wave, as well. She knows most of those students will sit and do nothing productive while waiting for her.

In his research, Jones asked teachers how much time they thought they spent, on average, when providing help to individuals who raised their hands. The teachers felt that they spent from 1 to 2 minutes with each student, but when Jones's researchers timed the episodes, they found that teachers actually spent around 4 minutes with each student. The total amount of time consumed made it impossible for the teacher to attend to more than a few students during the work period. Even if the teacher spent only 1 minute per contact, several minutes would pass while some students sat and waited.

Jones's research led him to conclude that independent seat work is especially susceptible to four problems: (1) wasted time, (2) insufficient time for teachers to answer all requests for help, (3) high potential for misbehavior, and

(4) perpetuation of student dependency on the teacher. Jones determined that all four could be resolved if teachers learned to provide help efficiently, using the following tactics we have examined previously.

First, organize the classroom seating so that all students can be reached quickly. The interior loop seating arrangement previously described is suggested because it allows quick and easy access to all students in the room.

Second, use visual instructional plans, which, as noted, are graphic reminders displayed in the room that provide clear examples and step-by-step instructions for students to consult. The reminders are posted where students can see them and thus continue on their own without needing to call for the teacher.

Third, minimize the time used for giving help to students. To see how this can be accomplished, consider that teachers normally give help through an inefficient questioning tutorial, in which the teacher poses questions and makes comments similar to the following:

> "What's the problem?"
> "All right, what did we say was the first thing to do?" [Waits; repeats question.]
> "No, that was the second. You are forgetting the first step. What was it? Think again." [Waits until student finally makes a guess.]
> "No, let me help you with another example. Suppose . . ."

In this manner, the teacher often reteaches the concept or process to each student who requests help. Four minutes can be spent very easily in each interaction. In place of these tutorials, Jones trains teachers to give help in 20 seconds or less, with an optimal goal of 10 seconds. If the VIP does not help a student know what to do next, Jones would have teachers to do the following when arriving beside the student:

1. (Optional for initial contact.) Quickly find anything that the student has done correctly and mention it favorably: "Your work is very neat." or "Good job up to here."
2. Give a straightforward prompt that will get the student going: "Follow step 2 on the graphic," or "Regroup here." Jones also recommends that, instead of tutoring students through the whole exercise, teachers should prompt students to ask themselves, "What do I do next?"
3. Leave immediately. Don't stay to see if students follow the prompt you have given.

Help provided in this way solves the time problem that plagues teachers during independent work. Students who need help receive it quickly, with little lost time. Rapid circulation also permits the teacher to monitor the work of students who do not raise their hands. When errors are noted in those students' work, the teacher should provide help just as for students who have raised their hands.

Eleventh, Have Stronger Backup Systems Ready for Use If and When Needed

As noted earlier, you will need to organize backup systems for use when students refuse to comply with rules or directives. Discuss and explain them to students. Ordinarily you can limit misbehavior by using benign tactics such as proximity, eye contact, or showing personal interest. But there will be times when those tactics come up short. In those cases, tell the offending student, "If you are not going to do your work, sit there quietly and don't bother others. I'll speak with you later." And for yet more serious defiance or aggression, you need to plan for, stronger backup systems—such as isolating the student or calling for help if needed. You should explain and demonstrate to students these stronger tactics, which you should clear in advance with your administrator.

Commentary from Anonymous Teacher 1

I think I mentioned in a previous context that I use body language quite a bit to keep students on task and behaving properly. However, I said "ouch" when reading Dr. Jones's comments on nagging because, honestly, I do that quite a bit, way more than necessary, I know. It seems I feel it is my teacherly duty to add a lot of verbiage to what I have already accomplished through body language. I realize it sometimes makes students want to answer back, and then I have another problem to deal with. Aside from that, I don't think I waste a lot of time in my classes, except for trying to teach students during seat work what I already taught (I thought). I have my share of helpless handraisers, and spending lots of time with them probably does more harm than good. I'm going to make myself learn to provide adequate help in under 15 seconds. We'll see if I can do it.

WHAT IS JONES'S STUDY GROUP ACTIVITY?

Jones makes available a free Study Group Activity Guide that can be downloaded from his website. It is associated and aligned with *The Video Toolbox* and is for use by small groups of teachers or student teachers who meet regularly to discuss and practice the skills Jones advocates. The Study Group Activity Guide and *The Video Toolbox* also present class activities that you can use immediately to perfect your management skills.

Jones highly recommends meeting and working with colleagues. He suggests the ideal group size is three to eight people. The structure he provides includes focus questions, study-group questions, and performance checklists, with 12 meetings titled as follows:

- Working the Crowd and Room Arrangement
- Praise, Prompt, and Leave
- Visual Instructional Plans
- Say, See, Do Teaching
- Rules, Routines, and Standards
- Understanding Brat Behavior
- Calm Is Strength
- The Body Language of Meaning Business
- Eliminating Backtalk

- Responsibility Training
- Omission Training and Preferred Activity Time
- Dealing with Typical Classroom Crises

IN REVIEW, HOW MIGHT I IMPLEMENT JONES'S APPROACH IN MY CLASSROOM?

Jones (1987a, p. 321) suggests you organize a five-tiered system that gives careful attention to: (1) physical classroom organization; (2) limit setting; (3) Say, See, Do teaching; (4) incentives; and (5) backup systems. The system should be planned in advance and introduced as a whole. In the planning phase, you might wish to keep the following in mind:

- Do what you can to preserve and make wise use of instructional time that is so often wasted. A few simple management techniques will conserve this time.
- Present instruction in a way that maximizes attention, active involvement, and student responsibility.
- Use an effective seating arrangement, establish clear routines, and assign individual chores to students.
- Use Say, See, Do teaching to increase student alertness, involvement, and learning.
- Actively "work the crowd," moving about and interacting frequently with individual students as you teach and monitor their work.
- Use visual instruction plans (VIPs) and other graphic reminders to help students follow procedures.
- Learn to give individual help to students in 20 seconds or preferably less, a tactic that eliminates student dependence on your presence and enables you to provide help as needed to all students quickly.
- Use class incentives to foster student involvement and increase responsibility.
- Use body language and personal-relations skills more than verbal messages to limit misbehavior and help students stay on track.

If you decide to implement Jones's system at midsemester or midyear, it is not absolutely necessary to present it as a full-blown system. You can assess your own behavior and isolate certain of his suggested tactics, and then add them incrementally.

Commentary from Anonymous Teacher 2

When it comes to Fred Jones's ideas for better teaching, seeing is believing. I, along with the rest of our staff, was encouraged by my principal to read Dr. Jones's *Tools for Teaching*. She was impressed with the research behind his ideas as well as with the practicality of his suggestions. I started by taking small steps and then building on those. First, I changed the furniture arrangement to create an interior loop. I really liked the idea of being able to move around the room easily and quickly. I appreciated the notion of being no more than a few steps away from any student. I had a perfect layout in place before classes began, which I then had to modify slightly once actual students were sitting in those chairs. I found I needed a little more room in the aisles so I could walk without getting my feet tangled up in backpacks or tripping over outstretched legs. It was easy to fix that and the students and I both liked the seating arrangement. The principal had already indicated she believed teachers should be on their feet, "moving continuously, like a shark," 80% of the time. She firmly believed in the concept of proximity in maintaining acceptable student behavior.

I improved my lessons with more frequent guided practice and independent practice, as suggested in Say, See, Do teaching. It really did work better for my students and was less frustrating for me. Using graphic organizers and/or picture prompts and reminders became part of my standard operating procedures. I found that I learned better with a visual representation of concepts and steps in a process, and so did many of my students. I even created a few reminders on sticky notes (such as taking two deep breaths before responding to a negative event, and a reminder not to nag!) and placed them on my desk. What I found very useful for the students was to provide them with blank graphic organizers and let them fill in and illustrate their own VIPs as they learned.

For PAT, I just assigned each activity a certain amount of time for successful completion. I would subtract a given amount for noncompliance. I usually had the minutes add up over the course of a week so there would be a reward on Fridays, and then we could start over again the following Monday. My students loved playing Jeopardy, Wheel of Fortune, Who Wants to Be a Millionaire, and other such games. We would play as an entire class at least once a month. I regulated their activities by the choices I offered. Some students liked learning a poem or dialog in French, some loved written games or board games (like Scrabble) where they could use their new vocabulary, and so forth. Everyone's favorite activity, though, was something I offered once each trimester—croissants and hot chocolate for everyone as we practiced French conversation. I admit, that was my favorite PAT as well.

WHAT YOU HAVE LEARNED IN THIS CHAPTER

You have learned that the major discipline problem in most classes is massive time wasting. You have seen why it occurs so frequently and what you can do to avoid it. You have also learned how to counter student passivity, help the "helpless handraisers," and eliminate the ineffective nagging used by many teachers. You have seen Jones's suggestions for improving your teaching by conserving time, using an effective seating arrangement, teaching students the meaning and purpose of discipline, giving students chores in the classroom, and beginning every class with bell work. You learned about the effectiveness of body language and how it is used to help students remain engaged in lessons, and you have seen how to engage students through Say, See, Do teaching. Finally, you have seen how to use visual instructional plans and incentives to strengthen your instructional program.

Activities

Self-Test: True/False

1. According to Jones, the main discipline problem in most classes is simply what he calls "massive time wasting."
2. Astonishingly, most teachers do not tell students what they are supposed to do during independent work time.
3. The "helpless handraisers" to whom Jones refers tend to be different students from day to day and lesson to lesson.
4. Say, See, Do teaching means the teacher tells, the students watch, and then the teacher demonstrates.
5. "Preferred activity time" refers to a segment of regularly scheduled time when students are allowed to do whatever they prefer doing.
6. Jones says when students raise their hands for help, you should provide the help they need in 20 seconds or less.
7. Visual instructional plans that help students know what to do are a major tool Jones advocates for "working the crowd."
8. Jones advises teachers to "sit down and shut up" when students are doing independent seat work.
9. Grandma's rule refers to a cluster of time-honored sayings, such as, "Wash your hands before eating."
10. Incentives can serve to motivate students to complete their assigned work.

Self-Test: Multiple Choice

1. According to Jones, a main problem in classrooms is
   (a) student insolence.
   (b) excessive pressure.
   (c) ineffective communication.
   (d) massive time wasting.
2. *PAT* refers to
   (a) parents and teachers.
   (b) patience and training.
   (c) preferred activity time.
   (d) pause and think.
3. Jones says effective teachers are good at
   (a) conserving time.
   (b) expending abundant energy.
   (c) counseling with caregivers.
   (d) communicating verbally.
4. Physical proximity is an aspect of
   (a) body language.
   (b) taking charge.
   (c) showing concern.
   (d) providing reassurance.
5. "First do what you must do, and then you can do what you'd like to do" is the key idea in
   (a) Grandpa's folly.
   (b) Grandma's rule.
   (c) Molly's dictum.
   (d) Jasper's delusion.
6. Most closely related to procedures and routines are
   (a) general rules.
   (b) alternative rules.
   (c) congruent rules.
   (d) specific rules.
7. "Working the crowd" requires much
   (a) attention to individuals.
   (b) miming by the teacher.
   (c) knowledge of students' backgrounds.
   (d) storytelling ability.
8. Jones says the goal for the amount of time teachers spend helping students who raise their hands is
   (a) 2 minutes or less.
   (b) 1 minute or less.
   (c) 20 seconds or less.
   (d) unspecified.
9. An especially notable feature of classrooms as suggested by Jones is
   (a) bulletin boards.
   (b) materials display.
   (c) a focal area.
   (d) seating arrangement.

10. "Say, See, Do" refers to a style of
    (a) learning.
    (b) thinking.
    (c) teaching.
    (d) analyzing.

Self-Test: Explain This

1. What does Jones mean by "helpless handraisers"?
2. How does Jones advise teachers to deal with helpless handraisers?
3. What is Say, See, Do teaching, and what is its purpose?
4. What does Jones mean by "body language," and how is it used?
5. What is the interior loop, and what purpose does it serve?
6. What does Jones say about teacher nagging?
7. What are PAT and VIP, and how are they used?

Additional Suggested Activities

1. Make notes in your journal concerning elements from Jones's model that you would like to include in your personalized system of discipline.
2. Review the questions listed at the beginning of the chapter. In as few words as possible, write your answers to those questions.
3. Suppose you have decided to implement Jones's discipline system in your classroom. You have determined to use incentives, provide help quickly to students at work, stop directing your students by nagging, and use body language to show you mean business. Does this list leave out any of Jones's major suggestions?

4. Working with a partner, see if you can state the meaning and implications of: backup systems, bell work, body carriage, body language, genuine incentives, Grandma's rule, helpless handraisers, interior loop, massive time wasting, physical proximity, preferred activity time (PAT), visual instructional plans (VIPs), working the crowd, and Say, See, Do teaching.

5. For each of the following scenarios, first identify the problem that seems to promote the undesired behavior, then describe how Jones would have the teacher deal with it.
   - Mr. Anton tries to help all of his students during independent work time but finds himself unable to get around to all who have their hands raised.
   - Ms. Sevier wants to show trust for her class. She accepts their promise to work hard if she will allow them first to listen to a few favorite songs. After listening, the students talk so much that they fail to get their work done.
   - Mr. Gregory wears himself out every day dealing ceaselessly with three class clowns who disrupt his lessons. The other students always laugh at the clowns' antics.
   - Mrs. Swanson, who takes pride in her lectures, is becoming frustrated because students begin to gaze out the window and whisper before she has completed what she wants to tell them.

Concept Cases

CASE 1   Kristina Will Not Work

Kristina, a student in Mr. Jake's class, is quite docile. She socializes little with other students and never disrupts lessons. However, despite Mr. Jake's best efforts, Kristina will not do her work. She rarely completes an assignment. She is simply there, putting forth no effort at all. *What would Fred Jones suggest to help Kristina and Mr. Jake?*

Jones would probably suggest that Mr. Jake take the following steps to improve Kristina's behavior:

- Make frequent eye contact with her. Even when she looks down, Mr. Jake should make sure to look directly at her. She will be aware of it, and it may be enough to encourage her to begin work.
- Move close to Kristina. Stand beside her while presenting the lesson.
- Give Kristina frequent help during seat work. Check on her progress several times during the lesson. Give specific suggestions and then move quickly on.
- Increase the amount of Say, See, Do teaching so Kristina has less information to deal with and is called on to respond frequently.
- Set up a personal incentive system with Kristina, such as doing a certain amount of work to earn an activity she especially enjoys.
- Set up a system in which Kristina can earn rewards for the entire class. This brings attention and support from her peers.

CASE 2   Sara Will Not Stop Talking

Sara is a pleasant girl who participates in class activities and does most, though not all, of her assigned work. She cannot seem to refrain from talking to classmates, however. Her teacher, Mr. Gonzales, has to speak to her repeatedly during lessons, to the point that he often becomes exasperated and loses his temper. *What suggestions would Fred Jones give Mr. Gonzales for dealing with Sara?*

CASE 3   Joshua Clowns and Intimidates

Joshua, larger and louder than his classmates, always wants to be the center of attention, which he accomplishes through a combination of clowning and intimidation. He makes wise remarks, talks back (smilingly) to the teacher, utters a variety of sound-effect noises such as automobile crashes and gunshots, and makes limitless sarcastic comments and put-downs of his classmates. Other students will not stand up to him, apparently fearing his size and verbal aggression. His teacher, Miss Pearl, has come to her wit's end. *What specifically do you find in Fred Jones's suggestions that would help Miss Pearl with Joshua?*

CASE 4   Tom Is Hostile and Defiant

Tom has appeared to be in his usual foul mood ever since arriving in class. On his way to sharpen his pencil, he bumps into Frank, who complains. Tom tells him loudly to shut up. Miss Baines, the teacher, says, "Tom, go back to your seat." Tom wheels around, swears loudly, and says heatedly, "I'll go when I'm _____ good and ready!" *How effective do you believe Fred Jones's suggestions would be in dealing with Tom?*

MRS. WARDES' SCHEME OF DISCIPLINE

You are a student teacher in an inner-city magnet school that emphasizes academics. Half of your students are African American. The other half, of various ethnic groups, have been bused in to take advantage of the instructional program and rich resources. All are academically talented and none has what would be called a bad attitude toward school. Mrs. Warde, the regular teacher of the class, does not seem to rely on any particular scheme of discipline, at least not any that is obvious to you. She simply tells the students what to do and they comply. For the first few lessons you have taught, Mrs. Warde has remained in the room, serving as your aide. The students worked well, and you felt pleased and successful.

WHEN MRS. WARDE LEAVES THE ROOM

Mrs. Warde tells you that she will leave the room during the math lesson so that you can begin getting the feel of directing the class on your own. Mrs. Warde warns you that the class might test you with a bit of naughtiness, although nothing serious is likely to occur. "Just be in charge," Mrs. Warde counsels. The math lesson begins well, without incident. The lesson has to do with beginning algebra concepts, which you approach through a discovery mode. You tell the class, "I want you to work independently on this. Think your way through the following equations and decide if they are true for all numbers."

$$a + 0 = a$$

$$a + b = b + a$$

$$a (b + c) = ab + c$$

$$a + 1 = 1$$

$$a \times 0 = a$$

The students begin work, but within 2 minutes hands are shooting up. You go to help Alicia, who is stuck on the third equation.

"What's the matter?" you whisper.

"I don't understand what this means."

"It was like what I showed you on the board. The same."

"Those were numbers. I don't understand it with these letters."

"They are the same as the numbers. They take the place of the numbers. I showed you how they were interchangeable, remember? Go ahead, let me see. Tell me what you are doing, step by step."

You do not realize it, but you spend almost 5 minutes with Alicia. Meanwhile, a few of the students have finished and are waiting, but most are holding tired arms limply in the air. You rush to the next student and repeat your questioning tutorial. Meanwhile, Matt and Alonzo have dropped their hands and are looking at each other's papers. They begin to talk, then laugh. Others follow, and soon all work has stopped and the classroom has become quite noisy. You repeatedly say, "Shhh, shhh!" but with little effect. Finally, you sternly tell the class how disappointed you are in their rude behavior.

CONCEPTUALIZING A STRATEGY

If you followed Jones's suggestions, what would you do with regard to the following?

- Preventing the problem from occurring in the first place.
- Putting an immediate end to the misbehavior now.
- Maintaining student dignity and good personal relations.
- Use follow-up procedures to prevent the recurrence of the misbehavior.

8

Marvin Marshall on Fostering Responsible Behavior

How Does Marvin Marshall Help Students Learn to Make Good Choices and Take Responsibility for Their Behavior?

Students happily engage in class activities when they find school satisfying, and they come to behave more responsibly when taught how to make responsible decisions. Some teachers seem naturally able to promote satisfaction and responsibility, but many are not, and so they unwittingly teach in ways that leave students disaffected with school and inclined to do as little work as possible. This chapter reviews Marvin Marshall's suggestions for helping students be more successful in school and for restoring the pleasure in teaching. He identifies the ineffective practices that many teachers use and then outlines positive alternatives that produce the results all teachers want.

WHO IS MARVIN MARSHALL?

Dr. Marshall is one of today's most influential authorities in discipline. He is an experienced teacher, counselor, and administrator who has served at all levels of public education. Currently, he devotes himself to writing, helping with staff development in schools, and speaking nationally and internationally. His views on classroom discipline and how it can be improved are set forth in his book *Discipline without Stress, Punishments, or Rewards: How Teachers and Caregivers Promote Responsibility & Learning* (2001, 2007, 2012) and his monthly electronic newsletter entitled *Promoting Responsibility & Learning*, which is available free of charge at www.marvinmarshall.com; and from his foundation, *Discipline without Stress, Inc.*, where any school in the U.S.A. that would like a thoroughly noncoercive—but not permissive—*Discipline without Stress Teaching Model* can receive free books and materials (www.disciplinewithoutstress.org).

Marshall believes classroom discipline improves significantly when students are helped to increase their personal level of responsibility, which occurs naturally when internal motivation (rather than "external" motivation) is activated. Teachers can activate that motivation, he says, by consistently working with students as follows: (1) Teach and practice *procedures*, (2) Infuse *positivity* into communications, (3) *Empower* students by giving *choices*, and (4) Learn to ask *reflective questions* to influence students—rather than trying to force obedience. In this chapter, you will see how these four processes improve both teaching and learning.

WHAT QUESTIONS WILL THIS CHAPTER ANSWER FOR ME?

- What is the difference between obedience and responsible behavior?
- What are McGregor's Theory X and Theory Y, and what do they have to do with teaching?
- What is Marshall's "hierarchy of social development"?
- How does Marshall's hierarchy help students raise their level of responsible behavior?
- How does Marshall teach his hierarchy to students?
- How should teachers and students use Marshall's hierarchy?
- In what ways do teachers unknowingly alienate students?
- How does Marshall differentiate between coercion and influence?
- What does Marshall mean by "empowerment of choice"?
- How does Marshall advise you to intervene when students misbehave?
- How does Marshall's *Discipline without Stress Teaching Model* promote responsibility and learning?

WHAT IS THE MARSHALL MODEL OF DISCIPLINE?

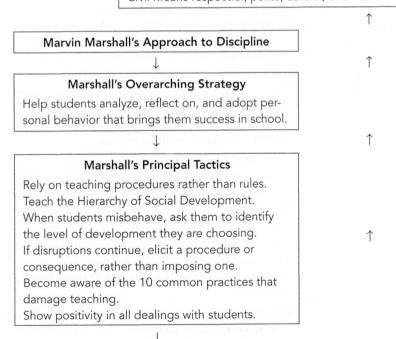

The Common Goal of All Approaches to Discipline
Responsible, Civil Classroom Behavior That Becomes Habitual and Lasts over Time
Responsible means paying attention, making a strong effort, and doing what is proper without being told.
Civil means respectful, polite, cordial, and well mannered.

Marvin Marshall's Approach to Discipline

Marshall's Overarching Strategy
Help students analyze, reflect on, and adopt personal behavior that brings them success in school.

Marshall's Principal Tactics
Rely on teaching procedures rather than rules.
Teach the Hierarchy of Social Development.
When students misbehave, ask them to identify the level of development they are choosing.
If disruptions continue, elicit a procedure or consequence, rather than imposing one.
Become aware of the 10 common practices that damage teaching.
Show positivity in all dealings with students.

SHALL WE BEGIN WITH WHAT *NOT* TO DO?

Marshall says virtually all teachers would like to organize meaningful, challenging lessons for their students, and they would like for students to control themselves and make reasonable efforts to learn. But in many classes, these results are rarely achieved. Why? One of the reasons, says Marshall (2008a), is that many teachers unknowingly engage in 10 practices that are counterproductive to success. He insists you can greatly improve your effectiveness if you avoid those damaging practices and replace them with alternatives that bring out the best in students. Here are the 10 damaging practices. Later we will see Marshall's suggestions for better approaches.

Damaging Practice 1: Being reactive rather than proactive. Reactive teachers are those who wait for misbehavior to occur and then react to it. They have not anticipated misbehavior or made plans for dealing with it. Consequently, their reactions are too often inappropriate and even counterproductive, especially when they are under stress.

Damaging Practice 2: Relying on rules of behavior. Rules are meant to control; they do not inspire. Rules are necessary in games, but when used between people, enforcement of rules automatically creates adversarial relationships. Instead of rules, *teach procedures.*

Damaging Practice 3: Aiming for obedience rather than responsibility. Obedience does not create desire. Successful teaching requires inspiration rather than obedience.

Damaging Practice 4: Creating negative images. You create the wrong image when you tell students what they should *not* do instead of what they *should* do. When people tell others what not to do, what follows the "don't" is what the brain visualizes. The reason is that the brain thinks in pictures, not words. To illustrate, if you say, "Don't run," you create an image of running. Instead when you say, "We walk in the hallway," the person visualizes walking.

Damaging Practice 5: Unknowingly alienating students. Even the poorest sales-person knows not to alienate a customer, but teachers often criticize students or talk to them in ways that prompt negative feelings. That dampens students' desire to cooperate with the teacher.

Damaging Practice 6: Confusing classroom management with discipline. Management has to do with *making instruction efficient* by classroom organiza-tion, procedures, and the efficient use of materials. It is the *teacher's* responsi-bility. Discipline has to do with self-control and appropriate behavior. It is the *student's* responsibility.

Damaging Practice 7: Assuming that students know what is expected of them. Too often, teachers assume students know how to do what is expected of them. Never assume students know. Teach them *how* to do what you would like them to do.

Damaging Practice 8: Employing coercion rather than influence. Although teach-ers can use coercion (meaning harsh or forceful means) to control students temporarily, this aiming at obedience does little to increase cooperation or motivate students to learn.

Damaging Practice 9: Imposing consequences rather than eliciting procedures or consequences. When you impose a consequence, you take away students' ownership of the problem and their desire for changing themselves. Anything imposed is weak or transitory.

Damaging Practice 10: Relying on external influences rather than internal processes. We make a serious mistake when we use reward and punishment to manipulate and coerce young people. Rewards and punishments come from outside the individual, rather than from inside. Behavior may temporarily change when external influences are applied, but the new behavior usually disappears when the teacher is not there to watch. Using *external* agents to foster *internal* responsibility is counterproductive.

SO WHAT SHOULD WE DO INSTEAD?

Marshall urges you to abandon the 10 negative practices just listed and replace them with the following:

Inspire responsible behavior. You will enjoy much better results if, instead of waiting for and reacting to misbehavior, you proactively inspire students at the outset to want to behave responsibly. This is accomplished by teaching his Hierarchy of Social Development, especially the difference between "internal" and "external" motivation. To inspire more effort in learning, the levels are visited *before* an activity and then students *reflect* on the level they had chosen *after* the activity. The nature of a hierarchy inspires achievement to the highest level.

Emphasize the importance of procedures. Rather than relying on rules that prompt an enforcement mentality, teach students the procedures and have students practice them so they know what is expected.

Promote responsibility rather than obedience. Rather than aiming at obedience, focus on promoting responsibility. Obedience then follows as a natural by-product. (Later you will see how Marshall's hierarchy of social development is used for this purpose.)

Create positive images in students' minds. To help students behave responsibly, have them create pictures of what you want—images that depict what they should do rather than what they should not do. For example, instead of saying, "Stop talking," it is more effective to say, "This is quiet time."

Cultivate a tone of positivity. People perform better when they feel positive, rather than negative. If you speak with students in a friendly and supportive manner, they are more likely to make an effort and cooperate with you willingly.

Clarify your expectations. Explain that you will provide a safe and supportive classroom in which students can learn comfortably. It is students' responsibility to conduct themselves in an acceptable manner. Let your students know you will not punish them. When they are not mature enough to act responsibly, you will show them how to control their inappropriate impulses.

Clarify the reasons for responsible behavior. After teaching procedures (the key to good classroom management) and expected standards of behavior, assure students that the positive feelings they receive for acting responsibly are more satisfying than any token given them.

Teach and inspire, rather than coerce. Recognize that people change themselves and will do so willingly when inspired and taught. Most students resist in some degree when *made* to do anything. Therefore, focus on inspiring and influencing students rather than trying to coerce them.

Elicit responsible ideas from students. When students misbehave or fail to meet expectations, **elicit** from the student involved a consequence or a procedure that he or she feels will improve the likelihood of responsible behavior. When you elicit, rather than impose, the student has ownership of the decision. People do not argue with their own decisions.

Help students build desirable behavior from within. Long-lasting change comes from self-satisfaction gained by one's own efforts, not from threats that induce fear or prizes that reinforce childish values. Therefore, do what you can to help students find pleasure in making personal improvements in learning and behavior. This is best accomplished by empowering them by communicating in positive terms, by offering choices, by prompting reflection, and by teaching the Hierarchy of Social Development.

WHAT IS INTERNAL MOTIVATION, AND WHY IS IT SO POWERFUL?

Marshall emphasizes that although humans are influenced by many external factors, all motivation emanates from *within* the person. Motivation can be stimulated from the outside, but the action emanates from within. Successful teachers tap into **internal motivation** so students *want* to become responsible. A way to begin is to resist thinking that students should automatically do what teachers want. Instead, we should create curiosity, interest, enjoyment, and challenge with activities that will have students *want* to put forth effort in their learning.

In working with students, teachers have traditionally relied on urging, directing, cajoling, admonishing, criticizing, and using rewards and punishments. These "external motivators" have little to do with motivation that activates long-term desire. Mainly what **external motivation** approaches do is bribe students to do something you want them to do. It uses rewards and punishments, which are two sides of the same coin. Rewards ask, "What will I get if I do what you want?" and punishments ask, "What will you do to me if I don't?" It is fair to say those external approaches are responsible for much of the stress and poor relations seen in many classrooms today.

WHAT ARE MOTIVATIONAL THEORIES X AND Y?

Marshall says if we are to get the best results in our classes, we must inspire students to achieve and ensure they find enjoyment in learning. He describes two opposite approaches to managing people, set forth by Douglas McGregor in 1960. McGregor called the approaches *Theory X* and *Theory Y.*

Theory X holds that people usually dislike their work, try to avoid it, and must be directed, coerced, controlled, or threatened with punishment before they will work as expected. (Does that sound familiar in your experience as a student?)

Theory Y holds that people work gladly if their jobs bring satisfaction and allow them to exercise self-direction, self-control, and personal responsibility.

Marshall's approach to discipline is concordant with Theory Y. He says that even though students are generally inclined to behave responsibly, they often don't—either because they don't know how or because peer pressure or lack of self-control overrides their better judgment. In keeping with Theory Y, Marshall (2005e) advises you to teach in ways that promote positive attitudes and good relationships that make school enjoyable for students and for you too. He suggests that using the three practices of *positivity, choice,* and *reflection* in your daily interactions with students produces these desired results.

Positivity leads to feelings of optimism. Being around optimistic people makes us feel better, whereas being around negative people has the opposite effect. Students will probably like you and be pleased to be in your class if they see you as positive in outlook and in your dealings with others, rather than being negative and demanding.

Unfortunately, students often perceive their teachers and schools in a negative light. That is because teachers unwittingly set themselves up as enforcers of rules rather than encouragers, mentors, and role models. They aim at promoting obedience, without realizing that obedience has no energizing effect on students, but instead promotes reluctance, resistance, resentment, and, in extreme cases, rebellion and retaliation.

Choice empowers students by offering them options. Marshall (2005b) reports the following comments about the **empowerment of choice** he received from a school administrator:

> I began to experiment with giving choices to students. When speaking to students about their behavior at recess, in the lunchroom, or on the bus, I would try to elicit from them what choices they had and how they could make better choices. If a consequence were needed, we would talk together about some of the choices. I would usually start with, "What do you think we should do about the situation?" When I was satisfied with the student's choice, I would say, "I can live with that." The process worked every time and I would wonder at its simplicity.

Reflection is a process of thinking about and evaluating one's choices. It is the most successful approach to having people change and improve. It is exemplified in what every super salesperson knows: *The art of influence is to induce people to influence themselves.* We can control students by aiming at obedience, making demands, or imposing consequences. But we cannot change anyone but ourselves. We cannot force change in how students think, want to behave, or will behave once our presence is no longer felt. Coercion is not long-lasting and pride cannot be mandated.

What we *can* do is establish expectations and empower students to attain them. This is done in a noncoercive manner by asking **reflective questions** that prompt students to think about their choices. Reflection often sets in motion a positive change in behavior. The way to jumpstart reflection is to prompt students to ask themselves questions such as, "If I wanted to be successful in this class right now, what would I be doing?" In most cases, the answer will be apparent and students begin behaving accordingly.

WHAT IS MARSHALL'S HIERARCHY OF SOCIAL DEVELOPMENT, AND HOW IS IT USED?

Marshall developed the **Hierarchy of Social Development** that many teachers now use in promoting responsible behavior in their classrooms. When students are taught the four levels of social development, they naturally begin moving upward on the hierarchy toward more responsible behavior. If students should slip and behave irresponsibly, teachers seldom have to do more than ask students to identify their chosen levels. This reflection prompts students to self-correct. Here is Marshall's Hierarchy:

Marshall's Hierarchy of Social Development

- *Level A—Anarchy (an unacceptable level of behavior).* This is the lowest level of social development. When students are functioning at this level, they are narcissistic, think only of themselves, and have little concern for others.
- *Level B—Bossing/bullying/bothering (also an unacceptable level of behavior).* When functioning at this level, students are bossing, bullying, or bothering others without considering the harm they are doing. They only obey the teacher when authority is used. In effect, they are saying to the teacher, "We are unable to control ourselves. We need you to boss us." Marshall says sharing this concept with students has a profound effect on how they behave.
- *Level C—Cooperation/conformity (an acceptable level of motivation).* When functioning at this level, students conform to, comply, and cooperate. The key to understanding is that, at this level, behavior comes from external influences. Discussing and thinking about the nature and effects of external motivation helps students understand how and why many people are motivated.
- *Level D—Democracy and taking the initiative to do the right thing (the highest and most desirable level of motivation).* When functioning at Level D, students take the initiative to do what is right and proper—they behave responsibly without having to be told to do so. Marshall advises teachers to explain to students that democracy and responsibility are inseparable. At this motivational level, people do the right thing because they understand it is best for themselves and for the people around them.

Marshall says that although Level C behavior is acceptable in school, teachers should have students aim for Level D, where students are motivated to make good decisions about their personal behavior regardless of circumstances, personal urges, or influence from others.

To illustrate how the Hierarchy of Social Development is used to help students reflect on their behavior, suppose two boys are talking audibly while another student is making a class report. The teacher quietly asks the disruptive boys, "At what level is that behavior?" They think for a moment and answer, "Level B." Their misbehavior typically ceases at that point and they return to behavior at a higher level.

How Does the Hierarchy Help Students Develop Self-Control?

Marshall says that once students understand the hierarchy, their attention turns away from compliance and toward self-control and social responsibility. This process is greatly helpful not only to teachers but to administrators as well (Marshall2005b). He describes the attributes that give the hierarchy its power, as follows:

- Enables teachers (and administrators) to separate the act from the actor, the deed from the doer. Without that separation, students become defensive when asked to change their behavior.
- Helps students realize they are constantly making choices, both consciously and unconsciously.
- Helps students understand and deal with negative or inappropriate peer pressure.
- Fosters internal motivation to behave responsibly and put forth effort in learning.
- Promotes good character development without calling attention to personal values, ethics, or morals.
- Serves as a vehicle for communication that uses the same conceptual vocabulary for youths and adults.
- Encourages students to keep their classroom conducive to learning, rather than relying solely on the teacher to do so.
- Raises awareness of individual responsibility.
- Empowers students by helping them analyze and correct their own behavior.
- Serves as an inspiration to improve.
- Encourages mature decision making.
- Fosters understanding about internal and external motivation.
- Promotes self-management and interest in doing the right thing, even when no adult is around or when no one else is watching.

Commentary from Anonymous Teacher 1

I've become a convert to Dr. Marshall's approach. My third graders can understand the levels and are showing the ability to take personal responsibility for their behavior. Previously I had been using a "card system" of three different colors, based on Canter's assertive discipline. That system worked all right, but I think my students responded to it more out of fear than anything else. The Marshall approach provides a number of additional benefits that help me and my students keep everything more positive and productive.

How Should I Teach the Hierarchy to My Students?

Marshall (2007) suggests a number of activities that are useful in teaching students the names and characteristics of the four levels in the hierarchy. Examples include visualizing each level and then drawing a picture of it, describing it in writing, describing it orally to others, and listening to others' examples of applying the levels to what goes on in school. Marshall explains that these various modalities help turn the levels into pictures students hold in their minds. He argues that it is the pictures in our minds that drive behavior—toward those activities we believe will bring satisfaction and away from those we believe will bring displeasure.

Marshall urges teachers to explain to students that the major difference between the acceptable levels of C and D is the nature of the motivation and where it comes from. Level C is motivation for behaving responsibly because of adult directions and may involve rewards and punishments. At that level, students are not really taking charge of themselves, and they remain overly susceptible to inappropriate peer influence. At Level D, students *take the initiative* to do the right thing because they consider it best for the class, the school, and themselves.

You might wonder how well students can understand these levels and relate them to real life. The brief excerpts from "A Letter Worth Reading" (Marshall, 2005a) presented in Figure 8.1 provide commentary on that question. The letter, sent to Dr. Marshall by a teacher using his system, is presented here with Dr. Marshall's permission.

For additional information on how the hierarchy promotes learning in reading, mathematics, spelling, physical education, and other areas, see "Samples of Hierarchies for Promoting Learning" (Marshall, 2005g).

WHAT OTHER TACTICS DOES MARSHALL SUGGEST FOR STIMULATING STUDENTS TO BEHAVE RESPONSIBLY?

Marshall suggests 25 specific tactics that stimulate responsibility in students and help them increase their reliance on internal motivation. Here, the tactics are grouped into clusters for easier consideration:

General Tactics

1. *Think and speak with positivity.*   If we approach students and situations in a positive manner, we enjoy ourselves more and bring greater pleasure to our students. Students are often put off if they perceive a negative tone in our communications with them. By helping students think in positive terms, we reduce stress, improve relationships, and help them become more successful.

2. *Use the power of choice.*   We all have the power to choose our responses to and attitudes toward situations, events, impulses, and urges. The optimists among us perceive that choices are available; the pessimists perceive a lack of choice. Optimistic thinking engenders responsibility and helps students move away from seeing themselves as victims of life events. All of us like to feel we have control over our lives. When we are encouraged to make choices, we become more aware of that control. Consider offering your students choices in school activities, including homework. Doing so noncoercively promotes optimism and desire to do what you ask.

3. *Emphasize the reflective process.*   Reflection increases positivity and choice and, when applied to one's own behavior, can lead to self-evaluation, correction, and gratitude (a major key to happiness). Ask students reflective questions and

Figure 8.1   A Letter Worth Reading.

Just this week we had a discussion with our students about how they could use their understanding of the four levels of development to help themselves become better readers. We talked about our 30-minute "Whole School Read" time that we participate in each morning. We had the children come up with scenarios of what it would look like if someone were operating at each of the four levels. Students were able to clearly describe conduct at each level.

At Level D, the students described that a person would be using reading time each morning to really practice reading. They wouldn't have to have an adult directly with them at all times; they would keep on task simply because they know what is expected of them. They would read and re-read sections of their book because they know that by doing so they will become better readers. The motivation would be INTERNAL. They wouldn't be wasting any time watching the teacher in hopes of being specially noticed as "someone who was reading," and they wouldn't rely on an adult to keep then on task. Instead they would be reading in an effort to become the best reader that they could be.

The children discussed further that Level D is where people take the initiative to do things that are truly going to pay off for them—what is right or appropriate. People at this level *motivate themselves* to work and achieve. The results are long lasting and powerful. These people put in the necessary effort to become good readers and therefore can get a lot of enjoyment from reading. Because they get enjoyment, they keep reading and therefore become even better readers. People behaving at this level feel good about themselves because they experience improvement and are aware that it is a result of choices that they have consciously made.

It is amazing to see the results of discussions such as these. That night, without any suggestion or prompting on my part, our poorest reader in the class went home and read his reader over and over again. Although his parents are kind people, they haven't understood the importance of nightly reading for their child despite many conversations with us. That night they watched as their little boy independently read and re-read his reader. Both the parents and little boy could see the dramatic improvement in his ability to read. They experienced the powerful impact that internal desire, coupled with one night of true effort, could have on someone's skill at reading. He came back to school the next day bursting with pride and determination to practice more and more so that he could move on to a new, more difficult reader. It only took one more night of practice, and he was able to do that.

Source: Marshall, M. (2005a). letter worth reading, retrieved from http://www.marvinmarshall.com/discipline/responsibility-system-letters/a-letter-worth-reading/.

encourage them to ask themselves questions, especially about behavior they have chosen. The questioning process activates the thinking process.

4. *Establish trust.*   Relationships with others are extremely important to students, especially students at risk or from low-income families. Students who do not value school will be motivated to put forward effort only for a teacher they trust and who they believe cares about them. Trust inside the classroom requires removing any sense of coercion and providing emotional and psychological safety. To promote trust, employ the three principles of positivity, choice, and reflection.

Tactics for Interacting with Students

5. *Use acknowledgment and recognition more than praise.*   Providing acknowledgment and recognition of students' efforts helps them feel affirmed and validated. Such a simple comment as, "I see you picked up the trash," fosters reflection and feelings of competence. In contrast, praise too often implies that the action was done to please someone else, as "I'm so pleased that you picked up the trash."

6. *Encourage students.*   One of the most effective techniques for stimulating students is to let them know you believe they can accomplish the assigned task. For many students, a word of encouragement following a mistake is worth more than a great deal of praise after a success. Emphasize that learning is a process and no one can learn and be perfect at the same time. Not being successful at a task is a valuable way of learning. It should be seen as a learning experience, not as failure (see Marshall, 2005f).

7. *Foster interpersonal relationships in the class.*   Connecting with your students one on one is extremely valuable, but helping them connect with each other one on one is also valuable. Relationships are extremely important to young people. At the end of a lesson, consider having students participate in *think, pair, and share,* in which they work in pairs and then share what they have learned with a partner.

8. *Control the conversation by asking questions.*   One way for teachers to remain in control of conversations is to ask questions. When you ask people questions, they have a natural inclination to answer them. If, in a discussion or argument, you find yourself in a reactive mode and want to move into a proactive mode, ask a question of your own. For example, a student asks you, "Why do we have to do this assignment?" Instead of answering, redirect the conversation by simply asking, "Why do you think this lesson is in the curriculum?"

Tactics for Motivating and Teaching

9. *Get yourself excited.*   You can't expect others to get excited about what you are teaching if you are not excited about it yourself. Relate a story or elicit one from students. When lecturing, use a little more animation than when you are conversing, facilitating, or reviewing.

10. *Raise your likeability level.*   Most teachers want students to like them. Many believe they can make that happen by trying to be friends with students and may decide, for example, to let students call them by their given name. There is much to be said for friendliness, but personal friendship is not what students need or even

want from teachers. If you provide encouragement and empowerment through positivity, choice, and reflection, your students will like you.

11. *Create curiosity.* Marshall says curiosity may be the greatest of all motivators for learning. He suggests presenting a problem or a challenge to students and allowing them to grapple with it at the beginning of a lesson.

12. *Create desire to know.* Allow some time at the beginning of each lesson to talk about what the lesson offers. Students like to know what's in it for them. Point out how new knowledge, skills, and insights can help them solve problems, make better decisions, get along better with others, and live life more effectively and enjoyably. A simple way to start is to ask yourself, "Why am I teaching this lesson?" and share your responses with your students.

13. *Use collaboration.* Generally speaking, allowing students to work together cooperatively promotes better learning than does competition. Competing with others is not effective for youngsters who never reach the winner's circle. Students who never feel successful would rather drop out or misbehave than compete and never win. Instead of competing, allow students to work together, preferably in pairs. Even a very shy student will usually participate with one other person (see Marshall, 2005d).

14. *Use variety.* Variety spices up topics that students might otherwise find tedious. A myriad of visual, auditory, and manipulative techniques can be employed in teaching, such as charts, cartoons, models, videos, PowerPoint creations, overhead transparencies, listening to music, recording music, rapping, creating verse, creating rhythms, physical movements, enacting the roles of characters in stories or events, large-group discussions, case studies, and working with small groups or buddies.

15. *Tutor a few students every day.* Tutoring students one on one is the easiest, quickest, and most effective way of establishing personal rapport with students.

Tactics for Influencing Positive Behavior

16. *See situations as challenges, not problems.* If we help students take a positive approach and view situations as *challenges*, rather than as problems, we help students feel they have more control. Emphasize to students that they can use adversity as a catalyst to becoming better, stronger, wiser, and more capable to deal with life's challenges.

17. *Use responsibility rather than rules.* Consider calling behaviors you expect in class *responsibilities* rather than *rules*. You will discover that rules are either procedures, in which case they should be taught, or they are expectations. Responsibilities should always be stated in positive terms—what you want, rather than what you do not want.

18. *Use listening to influence others.* It is surprising how strongly we can influence students simply by listening to them. The more students open to us, the greater our influence. Asking reflective and evaluative-type questions accomplishes this.

19. *Be careful when challenging students' ideas.* Very few people like to be put on the defensive. Instead of disagreeing with a student's idea, aim at clarification by probing, as in, "Tell me more."

20. *Think in terms of sharing, rather than telling.* When we tell someone to do something, the message is often perceived as criticism or an attempt to control, regardless of our intentions. Rather than telling, phrase your idea as a suggestion, such as, "You may want to consider doing that later and focusing on the current lesson now." Or use a reflective question stated as if you were curious, such as, "What would be the long-term effect of doing that?" Three more questions you will find useful are: "Is there any other way this could be handled?" "What would a responsible action look like?" and "What do you think a highly responsible person would do in this situation?"

Tactics for Empowering Students

21. *Empower by building on successes.* Great teachers know that learning is based on motivation, and students are best motivated when they can build on existing interests and strengths. That doesn't mean we should ignore the negative or disregard what needs improvement. But students are more likely to achieve success through their assets than through their shortcomings. The more they are successful, the more they are willing to put effort into areas that need improvement. This is especially true for students at risk who have negative perceptions of their success in school.

22. *Nurture students' brains.* Marshall refers often to Marian Diamond, an internationally known neuroscientist who has studied mammalian brains for decades and, with Janet Hopson, is the author of *Magic Trees of the Mind: How to Nurture Your Child's Intelligence, Creativity, and Healthy Emotions from Birth Through Adolescence.* In that book, Diamond and Hopson (1998) present some of the best advice on teaching you will ever receive, such as: Provide a steady source of positive emotional support for students, stimulate all the senses (though not necessarily all at the same time), maintain an atmosphere free of undue pressure and stress but suffused with a degree of pleasurable intensity, present a series of novel challenges that are neither too easy nor too difficult for the students, allow students to select many of their own instructional activities, offer opportunities for students to assess the results of their learning and modify it as they think best, provide an enjoyable learning atmosphere that promotes exploration and fun, and allow time for students to reflect and let their brains assimilate new information.

23. *Emphasize the **four** classical virtues.* The four classical virtues are prudence, temperance, justice, and fortitude. *Prudence* is making proper choices without doing anything rash. *Temperance* is remaining moderate in all things, including passions and emotions. *Justice* refers to ensuring fair outcomes based on honesty. *Fortitude* is showing courage, strength, and conviction in pursuit of the right path. Through the ages, philosophers have contended that these four virtues help people meet challenges effectively and find greater satisfaction in life.

Tactics for Addressing Problems (or Meeting Challenges)

24. *Hold frequent classroom meetings.* Classroom meetings provide excellent opportunities for all members of the class to think together. These meetings are valuable for resolving challenges that confront the whole class and for helping individual students deal with certain problems (see Marshall, 2005c).

25. *Resolve conflict in a constructive manner.* When people are involved in conflict, ask each of them what they are willing to do to resolve the situation. Get across the notion that we can't force other people to change, but we can *influence* them through our actions, including the changes we are willing to make in ourselves. This is a critically important understanding. Your students will come to your class as they always have. If students change, it will be a result from the change you make in yourself.

HOW SHOULD TEACHERS INTERVENE WHEN STUDENTS MISBEHAVE?

When considering any discipline plan, teachers always want to know the procedures for stopping misbehavior. You have seen how Marshall's Hierarchy of Social Development is used to empower students to move toward more responsible behavior. Let's suppose one of your students behaves inappropriately and you need to intervene. Here's how Marshall would have you proceed. (It is assumed that the hierarchy has been taught and students understand how it applies in the classroom.)

Step 1: Use an Unobtrusive Tactic. Suppose Syong is annoying Neri. Before saying anything to Syong, you would prompt her to stop by using an unobtrusive technique, such as facial expression, eye contact, a hand signal, moving near Syong, changing your voice tone, thanking other students for working, or saying, "Excuse me." Marshall (2001) lists 22 unobtrusive visual, verbal, and kinetic techniques that are useful at this juncture.

Step 2: Check for Understanding. Disruptions are handled by this second phase of the *Raise Responsibility System.* (Teaching the hierarchy is the first phase.) The strategy is to have the student identify their chosen level—not the action—thereby eliminating the natural desire to deny or self-defend. Spend no time quibbling if the behavior is on Level A or B; neither is acceptable. Most situations are handled using this simple two-step approach of teaching and having students reflect on their self-chosen level. Consider: When you tell, who does the thinking? When you ask, who does the thinking? Consistently asking students to reflect is the key for actuating change. For example, if the unobtrusive tactic doesn't stop Syong's misbehavior, check to see if she understands the level she had chosen. Use a neutral, unemotional tone of voice and phrase the question as, "Syong, which level are you choosing?" or "Syong, reflect on the level you have chosen." No mention is made of the nature of the behavior or what Syong is doing, only the level of chosen behavior. This helps prevent a natural self-defense and a possible confrontation. Without the hierarchy—which separates the student from the student's inappropriate behavior—a teacher may ask, "What are you doing?" This too often leads to a confrontational situation, especially if Syong responds, "Nothing." However, asking, "On what level is that behavior?" prompts not only acknowledgment but also self-evaluation. You are not attacking Syong; you are *separating* her as a person from the inappropriate behavior, something educators often talk about but find difficult to do.

Step 3: Use Guided Choice. If disruptions continue, the third phase of the *Raise Responsibility System* is employed. This final phase is used for students who have already acknowledged irresponsible behavior and continue to behave on an unacceptable level. Guided Choices stop the disruption by using authority without being coercive or punitive. Rather than imposing punishment, Marshall *elicits* a procedure or consequence to help the student prevent repetition of Level A/B behaviors. When something is imposed, the student feels like a victim and relationships between the teacher and student become adversarial. In contrast, *eliciting* allows for ownership because people do not argue with their own decisions. Marshall says this tactic allows you to use **authority without punishment**.

Another option is to use a variety of forms with upper grade students. If Syong continues to bother Neri, you can place an essay form on Syong's desk while quietly offering her three choices such as, "Do you prefer to fill out this form in your seat, in the rear of the room, or in the office?" The form, prepared in advance, contains the following headings Syong is to write about:

What did I do? (Acknowledgment)

What can I do to prevent it from happening again? (Choice)

What will I do? (Commitment)

Guided Choice should be adjusted in accordance with the grade level, the individual student, and the class. Before leaving class, the student is asked two questions: (1) "Do you know the reason the form was given to you?" and (2) "Do you think it is personal?" Students understand that the form was given because when the student behaves on an unacceptable level, the teacher needs to quickly resolve the disruption and return to the lesson. The second question is asked to assure the student that the teacher is only interested in the student's accepting responsibility and has no ill feelings against the student.

After the student responds to the second question, the teacher (of grades 4 and above) asks, "What would you like me to do with the form?" Students generally respond, "Throw it away." Although some teachers might wish to keep the forms, Marshall's approach is to tear up the form and place it in the wastepaper basket right then in front of the student, thus allowing the student to leave the class without negative feelings.

Guided Choice effectively stops the disruption, provide the student a responsibility-producing activity to encourage self-reflection, and allow the teacher to return promptly to the lesson. It is crucial to understand that when providing guided choices, the teacher does so by *asking* the student, not *telling*. This reduces confrontation, minimizes stress, and helps preserve student dignity.

It is very unlikely that Syong, having completed the essay form, will continue to bother others. If the teacher uses the forms, rather than eliciting a procedure or consequence, Marshall suggests using a *Self-Diagnostic Referral* as the next step.

Before moving to this more in-depth reflective form of using authority without punishment, Syong is given the essay form to complete a second time. If this procedure is not effective, then referral is given. This form contains items such as the following:

- Describe the problem that led to writing this.
- Identify the level of behavior.
- Explain why this level of behavior is not acceptable.

- On what level should a person act in order to be socially responsible?
- If you had acted on an acceptable level, what would have happened?
- List three solutions that would help you act more responsibly.

Marshall advises keeping the completed referrals on file for the entire year, as they might be used in discussions with caregivers or administrators.

If Syong continues to bother other students, assign an additional referral to complete, in the same manner as the first. Then mail a copy of the first and second referrals to Syong's caregiver, together with a brief note explaining the problem.

If Syong continues to behave on an unacceptable level, assign a third and final self-diagnostic referral. Mail a copy to her caregivers, along with copies of the first two referrals and both notes. The final note indicates to the caregivers that you have exhausted all positive means of fostering social responsibility and will refer future disruptions to the administration. Marshall points out that in all of these cases, it is the *student who has identified the problem and proposed positive solutions.* All the teacher does is write brief notes to caregivers and mail them copies of the student's self-diagnostic referrals. The student has done most of the thinking and planning, which gives ownership to the student—a necessary ingredient for lasting change. Marshall says the last few steps rarely, if ever, need to be used.

Marshall (2008a) goes on to emphasize that *having a system to rely on is superior to having a talent for teaching.* Even teachers with natural talent are challenged by student behaviors that teachers in former generations did not have to deal with. To retain the joy that the teaching profession offers and to reduce your stress, be proactive by teaching the Hierarchy of Social Development at the outset. Marshall advises explaining the system to caregivers when implementing the system. A form letter for this purpose is shown in Figure 8.2 in the section summarizing Marshall's teachings.

HOW DOES MARSHALL SUGGEST TEACHERS EVALUATE THEMSELVES?

If you wish to move in the direction Marshall advocates, the following questions will help you evaluate your progress:

- Are you teaching students the procedures you expect them to follow?
- Are you communicating with your students in a positive manner?
- Do you give your students choices (preferably three)?
- Do you ask questions that prompt reflection?

PERTINENT COMMENTS IN DR. MARSHALL'S WORDS

These statements are excerpted from a response Dr. Marshall (2010) made to a teacher who wrote to him. The original material is posted in *Promoting Responsibility & Learning,* Dr. Marshall's monthly newsletter, Vol. 10, No. 9, September 2010, available at www.MarvinMarshall.com.

- The difference between Level C (external motivation) and Level D (internal motivation) is not in the behavior; it is in the motivation. Level C is expected; Level D is voluntary.

- It is virtually impossible to know someone's motivation. And many kids have no idea how to articulate their motivation. (This is one reason that asking "Why?" leads to problems.)

- Someone behaving at Level B only understands a greater authority. So the students are saying to the teacher, "We are not mature enough to be responsible, so you need to boss us." The message to students is that they decide on the type of teacher they have. If they act on Level B, the teacher also needs to act on that level because the students will only behave responsibly when authority is used. (Notice the paradoxical approach: No one wants to be bossed.)

- *Discipline without Stress* (the official name of Marshall's total system) emphasizes that everyone always has a response to any situation, stimulation, or urge. He maintains that the only way to change an emotion is to change the thought because an emotion always follows cognition. For example, if a student gets angry with you, simply ask this question, "Are you angry at me or at the situation?" Reflection is engendered, the student is prompted to think, and the negative emotion immediately dissipates.

- Empower students by having them reflect on their motivational level—Level C or Level D—rather than on unacceptable behavior levels of A or B.

- The sooner you get in the habit of asking reflective questions, the more effective and easier it will be for you—and the better for your students.

Commentary from Anonymous Teacher 2

When considering Dr. Marshall's ideas, I immediately thought of Mrs. Mack, a colleague with whom I have taught for many years. Students love her, including those who have a hard time and seldom care much for their teachers. As I heard one boy say, "She doesn't hold it against us that we're just kids." Her classes are always packed, partly because of her reputation and partly because the school counselor recommends her classes as places where "challenging" students can fit in.

What Mrs. Mack seems to do naturally, I now realize, is quite similar to what Dr. Marshall suggests. I don't believe she knows about his hierarchy of social development, which I think can bring many "natural teacher" qualities easily within reach of all of us. Dr. Marshall's suggestions definitely prompt me to think in terms of positive messages and promoting student self-reflection. And they appear to help us teachers break away from ingrained habits of making rules, looking for mistakes, offering unbounded criticism, and all the while expecting student compliance. His procedures also show students that school need not be something that is done to them, but rather something that helps them increase self-control and assume responsibility for more enlightened behavior. In my opinion, students are always seeking those capabilities but often have the wrong idea about how to get them.

I very much like Dr. Marshall's approach to intervening when students misbehave. It relieves me from the frequent "policing" I do to make sure students don't get away with wantonly breaking rules. Guiding the student to pause and reflect on his or her own behavior and then describe solutions in writing seems to me more effective than repeatedly telling students how to behave and threatening punishment if they don't. I think students appreciate the opportunity to manage their behavior and, at the same time, understand how their behavior affects the way they are treated by others, including adults.

SUMMARY OF THE MARVIN MARSHALL TEACHING MODEL

A summary of Marshall's teaching model is provided in Figure 8.2.

Figure 8.2   The Marvin Marshall Teaching Model.

I. Classroom Management Versus Discipline

The key to effective classroom management is teaching and practicing procedures. This is the teacher's responsibility. Discipline, on the other hand, has to do with behavior and *is the student's responsibility.*

II. Three Principles to Practice

1) *Positivity.* Communicate in positive terms. This may often require changing negatives into positives. "No running!" becomes "We walk in the hallways." "Stop talking!" becomes "This is quiet time."

2) *Choice.* Give options whenever possible. Teach choice-response thinking—that regardless of the stimulation, situation, or urge, people always have a choice as to the response. Also, teach choice-response thinking and impulse control in order to redirect impulsive behavior.

3) *Reflection.* Although you can control someone, you cannot change anyone but yourself. The key to effectiveness is to hone the *skill of asking reflective questions* to prompt change.

III. The Raise Responsibility System

1) *Teaching the Hierarchy (Teaching).*

The hierarchy, by its very nature, engenders a desire to behave responsibly and put forth effort to learn. Students differentiate between internal and external motivation—and learn to rise above inappropriate peer influence.

2) *Checking for Understanding (Asking).*

When students act on an inappropriate level, they are prompted to reflect on their chosen level. This approach separates the person from the behavior, thereby negating the usual tendency toward self-defense that leads to confrontations between student and teacher.

3) *Guided Choices (Eliciting).*

If disruptions continue, a consequence or procedure is elicited to redirect the inappropriate behavior so it will not be repeated. This approach contrasts with the usual coercive approach of imposing consequences.

IV. Using the System to Increase Academic Performance

Using the hierarchy for review *before* a lesson and for *reflecting after a lesson* increases effort and raises academic achievement.

Source: Courtesy of Marvin Marshall.

Figure 8.3　Sample Letter to Caregivers.

Dear Parent(s) or Caretaker(s):　Our classroom houses a small society. Each student is a citizen who acts in accordance with expected standards of behavior. With this in mind, rewards are not given for expected behavior—just as society does not give rewards for behaving properly. Also, irresponsible behavior is seen as an opportunity for growth, rather than for punishment. Our approach encourages students to exercise self-discipline through reflection and self-evaluation. Students learn to control their own behavior, rather than always relying on the teacher for control. We want our classroom to be encouraging and conducive to learning at all times. In this way, young people develop positive attitudes and behavioral skills that are so necessary for successful lives.

Sincerely, (teacher)

Source: Courtesy of Marvin Marshall.

A sample letter Dr. Marshall suggests you send to caregivers to explain the discipline system is shown in Figure 8.3.

WHAT GUIDANCE DOES MARSHALL PROVIDE FOR APPLYING HIS SYSTEM IN THE CLASSROOM?

Marshall provides the following guidance for implementing his system:

- Carefully review the 10 practices that damage teaching.
- Clarify and differentiate Theory X and Theory Y and which mindset you will use.
- Understand the nature and power of internal motivation. Teach the difference between internal and external motivation.
- Evaluate yourself in terms of:
  - ✓ Have I carefully taught, and have my students adequately learned, the unacceptable behavior levels of A and B and the motivational levels of C and D of the Hierarchy of Social Development?
  - ✓ Do I use the hierarchy to promote a desire in students to put forth effort in learning?
  - ✓ When disruptions occur, do I ask questions in a noncoercive, nonthreatening manner that prompts student reflection and self-evaluation?
  - ✓ If disruptive behavior continues, do I elicit a procedure or consequence from the student for redirecting future impulsive behavior?
- Place a card on your desk with the following three reminders: *positivity, choice, reflection.*

■ Keep a list of reflective questions, even considering posting them around the room to help when an immediate response is called for. Remember that the person who asks the question controls the situation. Learn to respond by asking, rather than telling.

WHAT YOU HAVE LEARNED IN THIS CHAPTER

You have learned the *Discipline without Stress Teaching Model*, which includes teaching procedures, rather than relying on rules; the essential practices of communicating in positive terms, employing the empowerment of choice, and asking reflective questions to actuate change; and the three phases of the *Raise Responsibility System* of teaching, asking, and eliciting. You have reviewed 10 practices that are detrimental to teaching and have learned effective alternatives. You understand Theory X and Theory Y and how your choice of which you use determines how you will relate to your students. Finally, you have reviewed teaching practices that Dr. Marshall recommends as highly effective and compatible with his Discipline without Stress Teaching Model.

Activities

Self-Test: True/False

1. Marshall's hierarchy of social development consists of four levels, of which Level A is the highest and most desirable.

2. Marshall's hierarchy is aimed more at promoting responsibility than at student obedience to rules.

3. Marshall emphasizes that class management has to do with organizing and directing the class (the teacher's responsibility), whereas discipline has to do with behavior (the students' responsibility).

4. One of the main purposes of Marshall's hierarchy is to help teachers foster student self-control and sense of responsibility.

5. According to Marshall, Level C behavior is generally acceptable, although not optimal.

6. Marshall claims that allowing students to have a "choice" in how they behave is highly overrated and even a main contributor to misbehavior.

7. When a student misbehaves after being exposed to Marshall's hierarchy, the teacher's first step should be to "check for understanding" to make sure the student understands what is expected.

8. When it comes to discipline, Marshall would have teachers emphasize student responsibility even more than obedience to class rules.

9. Marshall says his hierarchy is very useful in motivating students, but not very useful in helping teachers evaluate their own performance.

10. Marshall urges teachers to plan how they will intervene when students misbehave, and then practice the intervention procedure until it becomes second nature.

Self-Test: Multiple Choice

1. The number of levels in Marshall's hierarchy of social development is
   (a) seven.
   (b) six.
   (c) five.
   (d) four.

2. The highest and most desirable level in Marshall's hierarchy is
   (a) Level A.
   (b) Level Y.
   (c) Level X.
   (d) Level D.

3. Marshall's hierarchy is used to help students raise their level of
   (a) obedience.
   (b) responsibility.
   (c) enthusiasm.
   (d) participation.

4. Marshall describes Level C as "expected," and Level D as
   (a) mandatory.
   (b) voluntary.
   (c) superfluous.
   (d) degrading.

5. Marshall says discipline is the responsibility of the
   (a) teacher.
   (b) site administrator.
   (c) caregivers.
   (d) students.

6. When teachers intervene in response to student misbehavior, they should
   (a) analyze.
   (b) elicit.
   (c) apply Theory X.
   (d) engage in dialog.

7. The best way to control conversations with students is by
   (a) setting an agenda.
   (b) asking questions.
   (c) reviewing the hierarchy.
   (d) following Theory Y.

8. Teachers sometimes unknowingly alienate students by the way they
   (a) smile.
   (b) criticize students.
   (c) try to befriend students.
   (d) provide helpful suggestions.

9. Bossing, bullying, and bothering are characteristics of behavior at
   (a) Level D.
   (b) Level C.
   (c) Level B.
   (d) Level D.

10. Of the following, which receives the most attention in Marshall's approach?
    (a) affirmation
    (b) reflection
    (c) analysis
    (d) reinforcement

Self-Test: Explain This

1. What is meant by McGregor's Theory X and Theory Y?
2. What does Marshall say about relying on classroom rules for behavior?
3. What does Marshall mean by "reflective questions," and what does he consider to be their benefits?
4. What does Marshall see as the difference between internal motivation and external motivation, concerning their nature and the results they promote?
5. What does Marshall mean by "eliciting responses" from students?

Additional Suggested Activities

1. In your journal, enter ideas from Marshall's *Discipline without Stress* you might want to incorporate into your personal system of discipline.
2. With a classmate or colleague, discuss the differences between Level A and Level B behaviors versus Level C and Level D behaviors in the Hierarchy of Social Development.
3. With a classmate or colleague, review two intervention approaches Marshall suggests you use when students misbehave.

Concept Cases

CASE 1   Kristina Will Not Work

Kristina, a student in Mr. Jake's class, is quite docile. She socializes little with other students and never disrupts lessons. However, despite Mr. Jake's best efforts, Kristina will not do her work. She rarely completes an assignment. She is simply there, putting forth no effort at all. *What would Marvin Marshall suggest to help Kristina and Mr. Jake?*

Marshall would classify this as a *learning challenge,* not as a *behavior problem.* He would tell Mr. Jake not to attempt to force Kristina to learn. Mr. Jake could not force her even if he wanted to: To learn or not to learn is Kristina's choice. Mr. Jake has seen that Kristina is capable of learning and would reassure her of this fact. If she chooses to put forward the effort to learn, she will feel more competent, enjoy herself more, and be happier. But this is her choice.

Accordingly, Mr. Jake would attempt to establish a positive relationship by sharing with her his belief in her competency. He would then find out what Kristina likes to do and weave into the assignments some activities that would capitalize on her interests. He would continually check with her to see how she is doing, and thereby communicate his interest in her. He would suggest that what she chooses to do or not do affects her more than anyone else and that she will not gain any satisfaction if no effort is put forth. Marshall also would encourage Mr. Jake to employ the hierarchy of social development as follows:

1. Ask Kristina to identify the level she is choosing.
2. Elicit from Kristina a few guided choices.
3. Ask her to start on one and see how it feels.
4. Reiterate the belief that Kristina is capable.
5. Ask her to reflect about her future decisions.

CASE 2   Sara Will Not Stop Talking

Sara is a pleasant girl who participates in class activities and does most, though not all, of her assigned work. She cannot seem to refrain from talking to classmates, however. Her teacher, Mr. Gonzales, speaks to her repeatedly during lessons, to the point that he often becomes exasperated and loses his temper. *What suggestions would Marvin Marshall give Mr. Gonzales for dealing with Sara?*

CASE 3   Joshua Clowns and Intimidates

Joshua, larger and louder than his classmates, always wants to be the center of attention, which he accomplishes through a combination of clowning and intimidation. He makes wisecrack remarks, talks back (smilingly) to the teacher, utters a variety of sound-effect noises such as automobile crashes and gunshots, and makes limitless sarcastic comments and put-downs of his classmates. Other students will not stand up to him, apparently fearing his size and verbal aggression. His teacher, Miss Pearl, has come to her wit's end. *Would Joshua's behavior be likely to improve if Marvin Marshall's noncoercion—but not permissive—approach were used in Miss Pearl's classroom? Explain.*

CASE 4   Tom Is Hostile and Defiant

Tom has appeared to be in his usual foul mood ever since arriving in class. On his way to sharpen his pencil, he bumps into Frank, who complains. Tom tells him loudly to shut up. Miss Baines, the teacher, says, "Tom, go back to your seat." Tom wheels around, swears loudly, and says heatedly, "I'll go when I'm _____ good and ready!" *How would Marvin Marshall have Miss Baines deal with Tom?*

You Are the Teacher

CLOWNING AROUND AND HORSEPLAY

Your new fifth-grade class consists of students from a small, stable community. Because the transiency rate is low, many of your students have been together since first grade, and during those years, they have developed certain patterns of interacting and assuming various roles, such as clowns and instigators. Unfortunately, their behavior often interferes with teaching and learning. During the first week of school, you notice that four or five students enjoy making smart-aleck remarks about most things you want them to do. When such remarks are made, the other students laugh and sometimes join in. Even when you attempt to hold class discussions about serious issues, many of the students make light of the topics and refuse to enter genuinely into an exploration of the issues. Instead of the productive discussion you have hoped for, you find that class behavior often degenerates into flippancy and horseplay.

A TYPICAL OCCURRENCE

You have begun a history lesson that contains a reference to Julius Caesar. You ask if anyone has ever heard of Julius Caesar. Ben shouts out, "Yeah, they named a salad after him!" The class laughs and calls out encouraging remarks such as "Good one, Ben!" You wait for some semblance of order, then say, "Let us go on." From the back of the classroom, Jeremy cries, "Lettuce and cabbage!" The class bursts into laughter and chatter. You ask for their cooperation and no more students call out or make remarks, but you know several continue to smirk and whisper, with a good deal of barely suppressed giggling. You try to ignore it, but because of the disruptions you are not able to complete the lesson on time or to get the results you hoped for.

CONCEPTUALIZING A STRATEGY

If you followed Marvin Marshall's suggestions, what would you conclude or do with regard to:

1. Preventing the problem from occurring in the first place.

2. Maintaining student dignity and good personal relations.

3. Using follow-up procedures to prevent the recurrence of the misbehavior.

9

William Glasser on Releasing the Power of Positive Choice

How Does William Glasser Use Noncoercive Choice to Promote Quality Learning and Student Self-Control?

Everybody wants students to behave responsibly in school, but educators have been unsuccessful in getting many of them to do so. William Glasser believes the problem lies in the approach teachers have used, one that ultimately relies on force. We face a losing battle, he says, when we try to *force* students to do anything. We get far better results when, instead of using force, we use *positive influence* to get students to behave more effectively. We do this by employing **noncoercive behaviors** in working with students—strategies such as relating personally with students, providing a curriculum that is genuinely attractive to students, and helping students understand how responsible choices lead to personal success. Glasser makes an additional strong suggestion—he urges us to emphasize quality in all aspects of teaching and learning. In this chapter you will see what he means and how he thinks we should proceed.

WHO IS WILLIAM GLASSER?

Psychiatrist William Glasser is one of the great educational thinkers of our time. He has made a number of important contributions to classroom management through his work with Quality Schools. Between 1965 and 1985, he introduced two major strategies that are still in vogue. The first focuses on helping students learn to *choose* more effective conduct, rather than trying to *force* it on them. As described in Chapter 3, that new strategy grew out of a psychiatric approach Glasser developed called *reality therapy,* in which clients are helped to deal with present-day reality instead of addressing matters that went wrong for them in the past.

Note 1: The author gratefully acknowledges the helpful review of this chapter by Jean Seville Suffield, Senior Faculty and International Communications Consultant, The William Glasser Institute, July 2012.

Note 2: Because the word "discipline" often implies the use of force, Dr. Glasser prefers to use the term "management" in regard to helping students make more effective choices.

At that same time, Glasser promoted the notion of eliminating *failure* from students' school experience. He believed the sense of failure was highly damaging to student motivation to work and learn. His remedy is to structure school learning, or what he calls "education" rather than "schooling," so that it leads to a genuine sense of accomplishment for virtually all students.

Glasser set forth those ideas and others in his 1969 book *Schools Without Failure*, which featured his assertion that all students choose to behave as they do—that they are not victims of circumstances that force them to do one thing or another. When given proper guidance, students can learn to make more effective choices and, in so doing, improve their lives overall.

The second period in which Glasser made major contributions began in 1986 and has continued to the present. In 1986 he published *Control Theory in the Classroom*, in which he provided new insights into how we can influence students to make more effective behavioral choices. In that book, he made two strong assertions. The first was that teacher forcefulness does not help students do better in school, but the use of noncoercive influence does. (He then explained how teachers can influence students noncoercively.) The second assertion was that we simply cannot expect students to work and behave properly unless they "believe that if they do some work, they will be able to satisfy their needs enough so that it makes sense to keep working" (Glasser, 1986, p. 15). Glasser insisted that teachers had the power to make school interesting and fulfilling for students, and that the key to doing so was to help students satisfy their needs for security, love and belonging, power, fun, and freedom in order to match their ideas of school as an important place that would bring quality to their lives (termed a **Quality World** picture).

In 1996, he changed the name of this approach from control theory to **Choice Theory**® in order to emphasize that student behavior is not controlled from the outside, but is the result of choices students make internally, motivated by their Quality World pictures, in order to satisfy one or more of their basic needs. It is up to teachers, he said, to interact with students in ways that influence them to make more effective choices, mainly by building relationships with them.

In 1998, Glasser published a succession of three books that greatly expanded his views about teaching and learning. Those books included the second edition of *The Quality School: Managing Students Without Coercion* (1998b), *Choice Theory in the Classroom* (1998a), and *The Quality School Teacher* (1998c). In 2001, he published *Every Student Can Succeed*, which he said wrapped up his conclusions about teaching and would be his last book in education.

In these later works, Glasser expresses his strong conviction that students will engage willingly in schoolwork if it offers interesting information that is accessed through activities that help students meet their needs. All of us, he says, continually make choices in trying to meet our needs, which are genetically encoded and cannot be denied. Some of our choices lead to success, whereas others lead to trouble or failure. Teachers' main obligation is to teach students how to make choices that lead to high-quality learning and socially acceptable behavior—and hence, success.

But what, exactly, can and should schools do? To repeat, Glasser would have us (1) provide a genuinely engaging curriculum, (2) emphasize quality in teaching and learning, and (3) influence students—in a noncoercive manner—to make choices that bring academic and social success.

Glasser says teachers will remain disappointed, and their students short-changed, if teachers continue to use the traditional teaching style he calls *boss management*. He describes boss management as follows: Teachers and schools select the curriculum, and then teachers deliver it to students, attempt to make students learn it, and attempt to make students behave acceptably in class. The results have always fallen well short of expectations.

Teachers do much better, he says, when they use a style he calls *lead management*. He describes lead management in education as follows: Students are helped to explore topics they find interesting or useful; teachers help students pose questions they would like to answer; teachers help students locate and use helpful resources; and teachers help students learn to do high-quality work.

Glasser also gives strong attention to how teachers relate with students. He identified what he considered to be some serious interactive mistakes teachers make, which he called *seven deadly habits*. He said teachers are far more effective when they replace the deadly habits with *seven connecting habits*. Later in this chapter, we will see what Glasser means by "deadly habits" and "connecting habits."

WHAT QUESTIONS WILL THIS CHAPTER ANSWER FOR ME?

- Why do so many students fail to do well in school, despite teachers' diligent efforts?
- What does Glasser mean by "noncoercive management?"
- What is "boss management," and why is it less effective in the classroom?
- What is "lead management," and why is it more effective than boss management in the classroom?
- What does Glasser mean by "deadly habits" and "connecting habits"?
- What are the basic premises of Choice Theory, and how are they used in teaching?
- What does Glasser mean by quality teaching, quality learning, and quality classrooms?
- How are quality teaching, quality learning, and quality classrooms achieved?
- How would Glasser have teachers respond to students who break class rules?

WHAT IS THE GLASSER MODEL OF CLASSROOM MANAGEMENT?

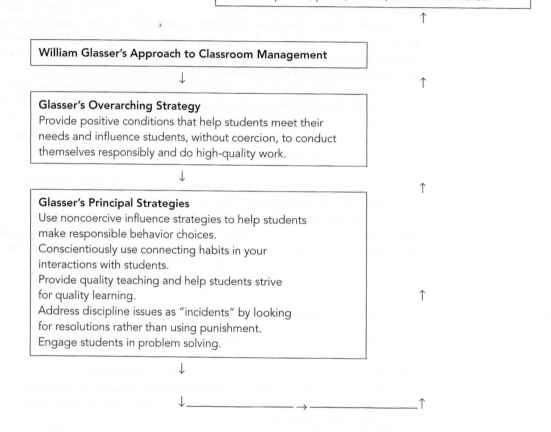

> **The Common Goal of All Approaches to Noncoercive Classroom Management** *Responsible, Civil Classroom Behavior That Becomes Habitual and Lasts over Time*
> Responsible means paying attention, making a strong effort, and doing what is proper without being told. Civil means respectful, polite, cordial, and well mannered.

↑

William Glasser's Approach to Classroom Management

↓   ↑

Glasser's Overarching Strategy
Provide positive conditions that help students meet their needs and influence students, without coercion, to conduct themselves responsibly and do high-quality work.

↓   ↑

Glasser's Principal Strategies
Use noncoercive influence strategies to help students make responsible behavior choices.
Conscientiously use connecting habits in your interactions with students.
Provide quality teaching and help students strive for quality learning.
Address discipline issues as "incidents" by looking for resolutions rather than using punishment.
Engage students in problem solving.

↑

↓

↓————————— → —————————↑

WHAT ARE GLASSER'S MAJOR ASSERTIONS ABOUT NONCOERCIVE CLASSROOM MANAGEMENT?

Noncoercive classroom management relies on the use of *positive influence* rather than forceful tactics to motivate student effort. It is based on long experience with the fact that, in schools, demands and other types of force seldom motivate students to want to learn or behave responsibly. Motivation comes from within the individual; accordingly, the teacher's role is to influence students, without coercion, to voluntarily make choices that bring success combined with pleasure, as fun is the natural payoff of learning. Here are some of Glasser's basic concepts:

- *All human behavior is purposeful.* Our behavior is never aimless or accidental. For the most part, it reflects our attempts to satisfy specific needs.

- *We are naturally disposed to be in charge of our own behavior.* Because our behavior is purposeful and self-chosen, we cannot ascribe it to circumstances, fate, or other people. Any credit for proper behavior, or blame for improper behavior, goes right back to us.
- *Our behavior can be thought of as our best attempts to meet our basic needs, five of which are for survival, love and belonging, power, fun, and freedom.* The school experience should be refined so that it helps students meet those five needs.
- *At least half of today's students will not commit themselves to learning if they find their school experience boring, frustrating, or otherwise dissatisfying.* There is no way teachers can "make" students commit to learning, although they can usually force behavioral compliance temporarily.
- *Few students in today's schools do their best work.* Most are apathetic about schoolwork. Many do no schoolwork at all.
- *If today's schools are to be successful, they must maintain quality conditions that ensure psychological comfort and reduce frustration for both students and teachers.* To be at their best, everyone must feel safe, feel they belong, have a degree of power, find fun in learning and teaching, and experience a degree of freedom in the process.
- *What schools require now is a new commitment to quality education—meaning education that promotes competence and behaviors that lead to success.* Quality education occurs naturally when the curriculum is made attractive to students and students are encouraged, supported, and helped to learn.
- *In order to be adequately attractive, the school curriculum must be comprised of learnings that are engaging, useful, or otherwise relevant to students' lives.* Usefulness and relevance are hallmarks of a quality curriculum, which is delivered through activities that attract student interest, involve students actively, provide enjoyment, and lead to meaningful accomplishments.
- *Students should be helped to acquire in-depth information about topics they consider useful or interesting.* Doing so increases the likelihood of quality learning.
- *Quality learning is evident when students become able to demonstrate or explain how, why, and where their learnings are valuable.* Opportunity and practice in making such explanations should be incorporated into the daily classroom activities.
- *Instead of scolding, coercing, or punishing, teachers should endeavor to befriend their students, build strong supportive relationships with them, provide encouragement and stimulation, and show unending willingness to help.*
- *Teachers who dictate procedures, order students to work, and berate them when they do not comply are increasingly less effective with today's students.* Glasser calls teachers who function in this way **boss managers.**
- *Teachers who provide a stimulating learning environment, encourage students, and help them as much as possible are most effective with today's learners.* Glasser calls teachers who function in this way lead teachers.
- *Motivation is the single most important factor in learning.* Students are motivated by what they find pleasurable or clearly part of their Quality World at any given time. It is up to teachers to ensure that the curriculum and instruction are pleasurable and/or worthwhile for students. When that is done, learning difficulties and behavior problems are seldom evident.

In summary, Glasser's convictions are as follows: Human behavior is purposeful. We are all driven to satisfy five basic needs that are set by our genetic code.

Behavior is compared to a car with the student as the driver; the driver has very strong beliefs about the direction the car should head, or pictures of the way the student wants things to be. Behaviors are chosen to match those pictures and, in so doing, students are able to satisfy one or more of their basic needs. Glasser calls all behavior **Total Behavior** because there are four components operating concurrently with each and every behavior, corresponding to the four wheels of the car on the ground: acting and thinking (front wheels) and feelings and physiology (back wheels). Behavior choices spring from our values, customs, information available to us, and the Quality World pictures we hold. Because we choose our behavior, we are personally responsible for it. All students can do competent work, and many can do very high-quality work in school.

WHY IS CLASSROOM BOSS MANAGEMENT CONSIDERED FUTILE?

Glasser repeatedly points to the futility of attempting to force students to behave in ways that are contrary to their natural inclinations. For example, when a student is not paying attention because the lesson is boring, it is a losing battle to try to force the student's attention. When lessons are interesting, students pay attention naturally and don't have to be continually cajoled. This fact is fundamental in Glasser's focus on what he calls *quality education*, in which students are seen to engage willingly in work that they perceive to be worthwhile (congruent with their Quality World pictures).

As mentioned, Glasser has concluded that many of today's students are content to do low-quality school work or even none at all. As he put it, "No more than half of our secondary school students are willing to make an effort to learn, and therefore cannot be taught" (Glasser, 1986, p. 3) and ". . . no more than 15 percent of high school students do quality work" (Glasser, 1990, p. 5). His solution is to offer instruction in a form that influences students to do at least some high-quality schoolwork. Nothing less, he says, will suffice.

Glasser says that meeting this goal requires only modest changes in curricula, materials, and physical facilities, but a significant change in the way teachers work with students. Glasser acknowledges that teaching is difficult, and he expresses sympathy for beleaguered teachers who yearn to work with dedicated, high-achieving students but are continually frustrated by students' lack of effort. Glasser says those teachers have told him that the main behavior problems they encounter do not involve defiance or disruption, but students' overwhelming apathy.

Students, for their part, tell Glasser that they dislike schoolwork not because it is too difficult, but because it is too boring. In Glasser's mind, that means schoolwork is not helping students meet their needs. If schooling is to be effective, he says, needs must be recognized and the curriculum organized to help students match their Quality World pictures of what school is all about and enable them to meet their needs.

Teachers, for their part, must move toward quality teaching and the implementation of Choice Theory, which holds that our actions are not determined by external causes, but by what goes on inside us. When we teach others, we cannot "make" them learn. All we can do is open possibilities, provide information, and expose them to the influence of good models (such as ourselves), and in so doing influence them to make more effective choices in what they do in school.

HOW CAN SCHOOLS HELP STUDENTS MEET THEIR BASIC NEEDS?

It is not difficult to manage the classroom to help students meet the needs Glasser identifies. He says students' **survival (safety)** needs are met when the school environment is kept safe and free from personal threat.

Students sense **belonging** when they receive attention from the teacher and others and are enabled to take part in class matters. In this regard, Glasser frequently mentions the value of cooperative learning teams (Glasser, 1998a) and the use of classroom meetings.

Students sense **power** when asked to participate in making decisions about topics to be studied and procedures for working in class, and also when given responsibility for classroom chores such as caring for class plants and animals, distributing and taking care of materials, keeping the classroom neat, being in charge of media equipment, and so forth.

Students experience **fun** when they are able to work and talk with others, engage in interesting activities, and share their accomplishments.

Finally, they sense **freedom** when the teacher encourages them to make responsible choices concerning what they will study, how they will learn the material, and how they will demonstrate their accomplishments.

HOW DOES GLASSER CHARACTERIZE A QUALITY CURRICULUM?

Glasser says that if schools are to be effective, they must provide a **quality curriculum** that helps students learn useful information and learn it well. He believes that the present-day curriculum focuses far too much on memorizing facts that are irrelevant to students' lives, while quality of teaching is judged by how many fragments of information students can retain long enough to be measured on written tests. Glasser (1992) advises that any part of the school curriculum that doesn't help students learn useful information and learn it well should be discarded as "nonsense."

Glasser says if students are old enough, you can ask for their input concerning what they would like to explore in depth. Once the topics have been selected, adequate time should be allocated for students to explore the topics thoroughly. Learning about a smaller number of topics in depth is always preferable to covering many superficially. Quality learning requires depth of understanding combined with clear awareness of its value. To ensure students recognize that value, they should always seek to explain why the material they are learning is valuable and how and where it can be used or make their lives better.

HOW DOES GLASSER CHARACTERIZE QUALITY TEACHING?

Glasser (1993, 1998c) stresses the importance of **quality teaching** and says it is reasonably easy to accomplish, although it requires a change in approach for many teachers. He recognizes that it is sometimes difficult for teachers to change their teaching style, but he nevertheless urges them to work toward the following:

1. *Provide a warm, supportive classroom climate.* This is done by helping students know and like you. Use natural occasions over time to tell students who you are, what you stand for, what you will ask them to do, what you will not ask

them to do, what you will do for them, and what you will not do for them. Show them you are always willing to help.

2. *Use lead management rather than boss management.* This means using methods that encourage students and draw them out, rather than trying to force information into them.

3. *Ask students only to do work that is useful.* **Useful work** consists of knowledge and skills that students will make use of in their lives. At times, teachers may have to point out the value of the new learnings, but if that value doesn't become quickly evident to students, they will not make a sustained effort to learn. Information to be taught and learned should meet one or more of the following criteria:

   ■ The information is directly related to an important skill.
   ■ The information is something that students express a desire to learn about.
   ■ The information is something the teacher believes to be especially useful.
   ■ The information is required for college entrance exams.

4. *Always ask students to do the best work they can.* The process of doing quality work occurs slowly and must be nurtured. Glasser suggests that a focus on quality can be initiated as follows:

   ■ First, discuss quality work so that students understand what it means.
   ■ Next, begin with an assignment that is clearly important enough for students to want do well.
   ■ Then ask students to do their best work on the assignment. Do not grade the work at this point because grades suggest to students that the work is finished.

5. *Ask students to evaluate work they have done and improve it.* Quality usually comes from modifications made through continued effort. Glasser suggests that when students feel they have completed work on an important topic, you should help them make **value judgments** about their work through the process of self-evaluation, as follows:

   ■ Ask students to explain why they think their work has high quality.
   ■ Ask students how they think they might improve their work still further. As students see the value of improving their work, higher quality will result naturally.
   ■ Progressively help students learn to use self-evaluation, improvement, and repetition (**SIR**) until high quality is achieved.

6. *Help students recognize that they feel good when doing quality work.* There is no better human feeling than that which comes from the satisfaction of doing something worthwhile that you believe is the very best you can do and finding that others agree. As students begin to sense this feeling, they will want more of it (Glasser, 1993).

7. *Help students see that quality work must never be destructive to oneself, others, or the environment.* Teachers should help students realize that it is not possible to achieve the good feeling of quality work if their efforts harm people, property, the environment, or other creatures.

WHAT ELSE DOES GLASSER SAY ABOUT BOSS MANAGEMENT AND LEAD MANAGEMENT?

We have seen Glasser's strong recommendation that teachers give up boss management and replace it with lead management. He asks teachers to recognize that they cannot force motivation into students and, in the long run, can seldom do high-quality teaching when using the boss approach. The following scenario depicting boss management illustrates Glasser's point:

Mr. Márquez (a boss teacher) introduces his unit of study on South American geography as follows: "Class, today we are going to begin our study of the geography of South America. You will be expected to do the following things:

1. Learn the names of the South American countries.
2. Locate those countries on a blank map.
3. Describe the types of terrain typical of each country.
4. Name two products associated with each country.
5. Describe the population of each country as to ethnic make-up and wealth.
6. Name and locate the most important river in each country.

You will learn this information from our textbooks and reference books. You will have two tests, one at . . . "

(Given these requirements, it is unlikely the students will pursue the work eagerly. Most will do only enough, and only well enough, to get by.)

Lead managers proceed differently. They attempt to activate the genuine motivation that resides within students. Therefore, they spend most of their time organizing interesting activities and providing assistance to students. They follow a regimen similar to the following:

- They lead the class into the discussion of several topics of interest.
- They encourage students to identify topics they would like to explore in depth.
- They discuss with students the nature of the schoolwork that might ensue, asking students what they would do to show evidence of quality.
- They explore with students resources that might be needed for quality work and anticipate the amount of time such work might require.
- They review ways in which the work can be done and, if possible, show or describe examples of finished work that reflect quality.
- They emphasize the importance of students continually self-evaluating their effort and progress.
- They clearly affirm that students will be provided good tools and a safe workplace.

To illustrate how lead teaching might proceed, consider this example of Mr. Garcia's introduction to a unit of study on the geography of South America.

"Class, have any of you ever lived in South America? You did, Samuel? Which country? Perú? Fantastic! What an interesting country! I lived for a while in Brazil. I traveled in the Amazon quite a bit and spent some time with jungle Indians.

Supposedly they were head hunters at one time. But not now. At least so they say. Tomorrow I'll show you a bow and arrow I brought from that tribe. Samuel, did you ever eat monkey when you were in Perú? I think Perú and Brazil are very alike in some ways but very different in others. What was Perú like compared to here? Did you get up into the Andes? They have fabulous ruins all over Perú, I hear, and those fantastic "Chariots of the Gods" lines and drawings on the landscape. Do you have any photographs or videos you could bring for us to see? What a resource you could be for us! You could teach us a lot! "

"Class, Samuel lived in Perú and traveled in the Andes. If we could get him to teach us about that country, what do you think you would most like to learn?" (The class discusses this option and identifies topics.)

"We have the opportunity in our class to learn a great deal about South America, its mountains and grasslands, its dense rain forests and huge rivers, and its interesting people and strange animals. Did you know there are groups of people originally from England, Wales, Italy, and Germany now living in many parts of South America, especially in Argentina? Did you know there are still thought to be tribes of Indians in the jungles that have had no contact with the outside world? Did you know that almost half of all the river water in the world is in the Amazon Basin, and that in some places the Amazon River is so wide that from the middle you can't see either shore?"

"Speaking of the Amazon jungle, I swam in a lake there that contained piranhas, and look, I still have my legs and arms. Surprised about that? If you wanted to learn more about living in the Amazon jungle, what would you be interested in knowing?" (Discussion ensues.)

"How about people of the high Andes? Those Incas, for example, and their ancestors who in some unknown way cut and placed enormous boulders to make gigantic, perfectly fitting fortress walls? Samuel might have seen them. The Incas were highly civilized and powerful, with an empire that stretched for three thousand miles. Yet they were conquered by a few Spaniards on horseback. How in the world could that have happened? If you could learn more about those amazing Incas and the area in which they lived, what would you like to know?"

(Discussion continues in this manner. Students identify topics about which they would be willing to make an effort to learn.)

"Now let me see what you think of this idea: I have written down the topics you said you were interested in, and I can help you with resources and materials. I have lots I can share with you, including photographs, South American music, and many cultural objects I have collected. I know people who lived in Argentina and Colombia that we could invite to talk with us. We can concentrate on what you have said you would like to learn about. But if we decide to work in that manner, I want to see if we can make this deal: We explore what interests you and I will help you all I can. For your part, you agree to explore some information I think you should know, and all along you agree to do the very best work you are capable of. We would need to discuss what you'd like to learn about and some things I want you to learn, and from that we could decide what you might do to show the quality of your learning. In addition, I hope I can persuade each of you to regularly evaluate yourselves as to how well you believe you are doing. Understand, this would not be my evaluation, it would be yours—not for a grade but so you can see what you are doing very well and what you think you might be able to do better. What do you think? Want to give it a try?"

HOW IS CHOICE THEORY APPLIED IN THE CLASSROOM?

Given a high level of motivation, students can learn almost anything taught in school, and when fully engrossed in learning, they seldom misbehave. This chapter has emphasized Glasser's contentions that educators too often assume that student motivation comes from teacher exhortation. You know Glasser's counterargument—that students are highly likely to do whatever is most satisfying to them at any point in time, if they can. That being the case, most students work hard and comply with expectations only when they get satisfaction from doing so. If natural satisfaction does not occur, they may work to please you, but usually not for long. To persevere, they must find satisfaction in the activity itself.

Glasser says one way to improve behavior in your class is to involve students in specifying what a quality existence in the classroom would be like—in other words, exploring students' Quality World pictures. Then, you plan for allowing the choices that would help bring about the realization or attainment those pictures. You can do the same with your manner of teaching. Try it: Begin by identifying one thing you could easily choose to change or add in your lessons that would make your classes more enjoyable for everyone—perhaps role-playing, enacting skits that verify learning, holding debates, working in small groups—things of that sort. What would you have to do to put the change into practice? Exchange ideas with fellow professionals if possible.

HOW DOES QUALITY TEACHING AFFECT DISCIPLINE?

Glasser acknowledges that no instructional approach can eliminate all less desirable or less effective behavior, but he maintains that such behavior can be reduced greatly if teachers do the following:

- Know your students and begin to build and maintain strong supportive relationships with them.
- Work with students to establish standards of conduct in the classroom.
- Begin with a discussion of the importance of quality work (to be given priority in the class) and explain that you will do everything possible to help students learn and enjoy themselves without using force.
- Lead the discussion on quality work by asking students about class behavior they believe will help them get their work done and truly help them learn. Glasser says that if teachers can get students to see the importance of courtesy, no other rules may be necessary.
- Solicit student input on what should happen when behavior agreements are broken. Glasser says students usually suggest punishment, even though they know punishment is not effective. If asked further, they will agree that behavior problems are best solved by looking for ways to remedy whatever is causing the rule to be broken.
- Once agreements and consequences are established, they should be put in writing and all students should sign the document, attesting that they understand

the agreements and that, if they break them, they will endeavor—with the teacher's help—to correct the underlying problem. Agreements established and dealt with in this way, says Glasser, show that the teacher's main concern lies in quality, not power, and that the teacher recognizes that power struggles usually damage the quality of learning.

- Show interest in students and, when appropriate, ask them, "What might I do to help?"
- Try to avoid adversarial encounters with students. Adversity dampens enthusiasm, damages cooperation, and reduces one's inclination to do quality work. When you have important disagreements with students, look for solutions without getting angry.
- Hold classroom meetings to explore what students like and dislike about the class. Show them you are willing to change what they dislike if you can.

> **?** You may recall that other authorities—such as Ron Morrish in Chapter 4 and Craig Seganti in Chapter 5— do not agree with Glasser on involving students in making class rules of behavior. They consider rule making to be the teacher's job, although they would have you explain to students why the rules exist and what they are intended to accomplish. At this point in time, which would be your preferred approach—making and explaining the rules yourself, or involving students in a total class effort to establish the rules? What is your rationale?

WHAT WOULD GLASSER HAVE ME DO WHEN STUDENTS BREAK CLASS RULES?

Glasser says you must intervene when a student breaks rules or class agreements, in order to help the student choose a more effective behavior and direct the student's mind back to productive class work. Suppose Jonathan comes into the room obviously upset. As the lesson begins, he turns heatedly and throws something at Michael. Glasser suggests you say the following:

"It looks like you have a problem, Jonathan. How can I help you solve it?"
[Jonathan frowns, still obviously upset, and says nothing.]
"If you will calm down, I will discuss it with you in a little while. I think we can work something out."

Glasser says that you should make it clear to Jonathan that you are unable to help him until he calms down. You should say this without emotion in your voice, recognizing that anger on your part will only put Jonathan on the defensive. If Jonathan doesn't calm down, there is no good way to deal with the problem. Glasser (1990) says to allow him 20 seconds, and if he isn't calm by then, admit that there is no way to solve the problem at that time. Give Jonathan a time-out from the lesson, but don't threaten or warn him. Say something like the following:

"Jonathan, I want to help you work this out. I am not interested in punishing you. Whatever the problem is, let's solve it. But for now you can go sit at the table. When you are calm, come back to your seat."

Later, at an opportune time, discuss the situation with Jonathan, approximately as follows:

> "What were you doing when the problem started? Was it against the rules? Can we work things out so it won't happen again? What could you and I do to keep it from happening?"

If the problem involves hostilities between Jonathan and Michael, the discussion should involve both boys and proceed along these lines:

> "What were you doing, Jonathan? What were you doing, Michael? How can the three of us work things out so this won't happen anymore?"

It is important to note that no time is spent trying to find out whose fault it was, and no blame is assigned to either Jonathan or Michael. You make clear to the boys that all you are looking for is a solution so that the problem won't occur again. Glasser says if you treat Jonathan and Michael with respect and courtesy, if you show you don't want to punish them or throw your weight around, and if you talk to them as a problem solver, their classroom behavior and the quality of their work will both improve. Glasser brings a third entity into the discussion with the boys, that of the relationship. He will encourage the boys to engage in behavior that helps them build or rebuild a friendly relationship and avoid behavior that might damage or break that relationship.

WHAT DOES GLASSER MEAN BY "QUALITY CLASSROOMS," AND HOW DO WE GET THEM?

Many educators avidly support Glasser's ideas concerning teaching and education. Numerous teachers have met the stringent requirements for earning the Choice Theory, Reality Therapy, and Lead Management (CTRTC) certification given by The William Glasser Institute. Several entire schools have done so as well, and when they meet the requirements, they declare themselves a Glasser Quality School and are officially recognized by The William Glasser Institute as such. Glasser (2001) describes them as schools that display the following (as updated on the Glasser website, www.wglasser.com) characteristics:

Criteria for a Glasser Quality School

- Relationships are based upon trust and respect, and all discipline problems, not incidents, have been eliminated.
- Total learning competency is stressed, and an evaluation that is below competence or what is now a "B" has been eliminated. All "schooling" as defined by Dr. William Glasser has been replaced by "useful education."
- All students do some quality work each year that is significantly beyond competence. All such work receives an "A" grade or higher, such as an "A+."
- Students and staff are taught to use Choice Theory in their lives and in their work in school. Parents are encouraged to participate in study groups to become familiar with the ideas of Dr. William Glasser.

■ Students do better on state proficiency tests and college entrance examinations (typically at the 80th percentile or better). The importance of these tests is emphasized in the school.

■ Staff, students, parents, and administrators view the school as a joyful place.

A Quality School rubric is available at www.wglasser.com.

In 2006, Therese Hinder conducted an independent review of seven Glasser Quality Schools in various states in America with enrollments that reflected a cross-section of the American school population. She found that all of the schools she reviewed adhered closely to Glasser's teachings and that student achievement in all of them ranked in the top category on their statewide student testing program.

WHAT ARE THE SEVEN DEADLY HABITS IN TEACHING, AND HOW DO I AVOID THEM?

A fundamental operating principle in Glasser's approach is that teachers and administrators must make school a happy place for students. Glasser asserts that if you are having trouble with a student, you can be absolutely sure the student is unhappy in your class and very likely unhappy in school. Glasser believes most problems between teachers and students are caused by unsatisfactory relationships; he therefore maintains that good relationships are of fundamental importance.

You can immediately improve relationships with and among students simply by avoiding what Glasser refers to as the *seven deadly habits* and replacing them with the *seven connecting habits.*

The **seven deadly habits** are actions or behaviors that prevent the establishment of caring relationships, specifically: *criticizing, blaming, complaining, nagging, threatening, punishing,* and *rewarding others to control them.* (These same deadly habits are equally detrimental to relationships with others outside of school.) If you are to establish good relationships with students and gain their willing cooperation, get rid of those habits immediately and help students do so as well.

In place of the deadly habits, find ways of promoting connections with others, as epitomized in the **seven connecting habits** Glasser identifies as *caring, listening, supporting, respecting, encouraging, trusting,* and *negotiating differences.* Glasser believes—and results at his Quality Schools support his contentions—that all students who come to school can do competent work. You make this possible when you strongly connect with your students on a personal level and show them how to maintain good connections as well. Glasser makes his point by describing how we relate with friends: We do not criticize, blame, or speak harshly to them. Instead, we build and maintain strong relationships and use the connecting habits Glasser has identified. Teachers who build strong relationships with their students discover that they have been added to their students' Quality World pictures, meaning that the teachers are important people in their lives.

Commentary from Anonymous Teacher 1

As a classroom teacher with 20 years of experience in a low-income neighborhood, I find myself in close agreement with Dr. Glasser's commentaries on the "seven deadly habits" and the "seven connecting habits." I try very hard to maintain a good personal relationship with my students, in the belief it helps them feel all right about school, want to be there, and in turn want to do good work to please me. I know for sure the younger students don't perform nearly as well when they are overly criticized. They seem to have a strong need for positive comments from me. That's human nature, I think. I tell my students that, and I try to exemplify it in how I treat my students. I also tell them it is difficult for me to teach well and it also makes me feel bad when my students misbehave and don't show any interest in school.

Realistically, no teacher is going to have perfectly behaving students 100% of the time, no matter what they do. And some classes are definitely more difficult than others. However, I find that Glasser's connecting habits win over most students' cooperation and loyalty before long and the result is a more pleasant classroom environment, fewer behavior problems, and a higher level of student engagement and competent work. I just try to treat my students as good friends. It's rather easy, actually.

IN SUMMARY, HOW CAN I MOVE TOWARD BUILDING A QUALITY CLASSROOM?

Here is a review of Glasser's main suggestions:

- *Replace deadly habits with connecting habits.* Determine that beginning today, you will assiduously avoid the seven deadly habits when working with your students, replace them with the seven connecting habits, and help your students do the same.
- *Make plain to students how you will work with them.* The message you want to get across to students is the following: "We are in this class together. I want to help you to become very competent. My job is to teach you and help you learn, not to find out what you don't know and punish you for not knowing it. If you have a question, ask me. If you need more time, I'll give it to you. If you have an idea how to do what we are trying to do better, tell me. I'll listen" (Glasser, 2001, p. 113).
- *Build strong relationships with your students.* Instead of telling students what they must do and not do, endeavor to befriend all of them. To begin, say something like, "I think an important part of my job is to do all I can to make sure you have a good time learning. You have to come to school and no one's going to pay you for doing schoolwork. So the least I can do is make this class fun for both you and me. I think we can learn a lot and still have a very good time" (Glasser, 2001, p. 54). Then implement a quality curriculum and steadfastly use the seven connecting habits.
- *Establish reasonable rules of class behavior.* Rely on one fundamental rule of behavior—the Golden Rule. Discuss the Golden Rule with students. A few other rules may occasionally be necessary, but the Golden Rule is fundamental to all.
- *Take the energy out of impending less-effective behavior.* Replace traditional discipline (external control) with talking and listening to students as soon as you

sense that undesirable behavior is likely to occur. Listen carefully. Inject humor into the situation if you can, but do not make light of students' concerns.

■ *Teach things that make a real difference in students' lives.* It is very important that students be able to make good use of what they learn in school. Therefore, ensure that your curriculum focuses on skills and knowledge that interest students and make them more knowledgeable and competent. Don't have them memorize anything just so they can repeat it back on tests. Explain to students that you will not ask them to learn anything that is not useful to them, and when there might be doubt, you will explain clearly how the new learning will benefit them.

■ *Help students learn to strive for quality.* Tell students you use a way of teaching that makes sure everyone can do competent work and everyone will make good grades (meaning a grade of B or better). Explain that you will ask students to work at any given assignment until they have achieved an acceptably high level of competence. Nobody will fail or receive a low grade. They can use any resources available to help them, including textbooks, caregivers, and other students. The primary objective is to do competent work. Beyond that, encourage students to work for even higher quality to help them learn what it feels like to do A-level work.

■ *Test students frequently, but productively.* Teach students using your best techniques, help them self-evaluate their work, and then test them regularly. Explain that the tests are for learning only and promise that no one will fail or receive a poor grade on them. When they have completed a test, have them go back over it and correct any incorrect or incomplete answers. Ask them to explain why each correction is better. Give them the time and help needed to achieve success.

■ *Emphasize understanding and making use of new learning.* Ask students always to focus on understanding and using the information and skills being taught. Ask them to share and discuss the learnings with caregivers.

■ *Provide options for students after competence is achieved.* Students who complete their work competently can then have the option of helping other students or moving ahead to doing something of yet higher quality. To experience the full sense of Glasser's ideas, consult his 2001 book entitled *Every Student Can Succeed* and/or visit his websites at www.wglasser.com and www.wglasserbooks.com.

Commentary from Anonymous Teacher 2

I cringed when I read Glasser's list of deadly habits, because I am guilty of all of them. I would like to believe I have been a positive model for my students, but am ashamed to admit I have criticized, blamed, complained about, nagged, threatened, punished, and rewarded students, with the intent of shaping their behavior and work habits. I can, of course, see the downside to blaming, complaining about, nagging, and threatening students or anyone else. I am a little confused about criticizing, though. Isn't it part of a teacher's function to offer a critique on student work in an effort to improve it? Most students have not had enough academic or life experience to know if their work is quality, and must depend upon the teacher for guidance. Feedback can be given gently.

I am conflicted (or possibly just lack complete understanding) about viewing punishing and rewarding as deadly habits. Every school in which I have taught has had a schoolwide discipline plan, and this plan has invariably included rewards (special activities, events, treats, recognition for good grades, awards, privileges) and punishment (exclusion from reward activities). I think most kids (and parents) expect this, and I am not sure what would take its place in individual classrooms or in schoolwide plans if the notion were abandoned.

I felt a little better about myself as a teacher when I reflected on the connecting habits. I have exhibited all of those behaviors at one time or another, as have most teachers. But before I pat myself on the back too vigorously I must add the caveat: with some students. And there's the rub, for it is easy to connect with students who are bright, cheerful, good-natured, respectful, and seem to like me and the subject. I have not always done everything possible to befriend the more difficult students. This is my own failing, and maybe I can rectify it.

I very much like Dr. Glasser's suggestions on creating interesting lessons and being friends with students as means of creating a joyful classroom where students achieve and don't misbehave. I like the notion of ditching the "boring" parts of the curriculum, because, frankly, those parts are harder to teach. But I'm struggling a bit with visualizing how it would all look in practice, with real teachers and real students. A series of webcasts offering observation of and discussion with lead teachers in Glasser Quality Schools would be very helpful.

HOW CAN I GO ABOUT IMPLEMENTING GLASSER'S IDEAS IN MY CLASSES?

Glasser's ideas for increasing quality in teaching and learning need not be implemented in one fell swoop. They can be introduced gradually, allowing you to evaluate each suggestion in terms of class climate and morale. Here are some of Glasser's suggestions:

- Remember that your students' behavior is internally motivated and purposeful, directed at matching their pictures to meet certain needs. Adjust your curriculum as necessary to help students share their pictures of what a classroom conducive to learning might be like so that students can meet those needs.
- Remember also that most of your students will not commit themselves to class activities they find boring, frustrating, or otherwise dissatisfying. Therefore, do what you can to eliminate those topics and replace them with alternatives that students like and find beneficial.
- Hold a discussion with your class on how school could be made more interesting and enjoyable. Identify a topic in which they show interest and

brainstorm ways to explore the topic, procedures for reporting or demonstrating accomplishment, personal conduct that would make the class function better, and how disruptions might be handled positively and effectively. The process is mainly for student input, but you might offer some of your opinions as well.

■ Following that, indicate that you will try to organize a few activities as students have suggested and that you will do all you can to help them learn and succeed. Meanwhile, give yourself a crash course on functioning as a lead teacher, eliminating the seven deadly habits and establishing the seven connecting habits in your relations with students.

■ As you get things under way, hold meetings with your class to discuss the new efforts and any results you see in effort and behavior. The meetings should focus only on improving learning and never be allowed to degenerate into fault finding, blaming, or criticizing.

■ Instead of coercing, scolding, and punishing your students to get them to learn and behave properly, build supportive relationships with them, provide encouragement and stimulation, and show unending willingness to help.

■ Ask students what kinds of class behavior will help them acquire quality learning. Ask them to reach class agreements that promote such behavior. Ask them what should happen when anyone breaks a behavior agreement. Ensure that all their suggestions are positive rather than negative.

■ When students choose a less-effective behavior, discuss this behavior and why it was not appropriate for the class. Refer to the agreement or class contract. Ask students what they can do to differently in the future. Remember that students have more direct control over acting and thinking (the front wheels of the Total Behavior car) and less control over feelings and physiology (the back wheels of the Total Behavior car). A student can replace a behavior that may be less effective with one that is more effective *only* if the more effective behavior is at least as need-satisfying as the original behavior, the one that teachers often call not appropriate or undesirable. So, just saying, "Stop it!" may work immediately as an external measure, but it does not help students develop new ways of dealing with situations that are not satisfying their needs. If the behavior is serious or chronic, make time to talk with those students privately. Some schools have set up the *Connecting Place* where students are taught Choice Theory and begin to understand why they behave the way they do, giving them more control over their own lives.

WHAT YOU HAVE LEARNED IN THIS CHAPTER

You have learned that Glasser strongly believes—and has evidence to back his beliefs—that student achievement and responsible behavior are fostered by teachers' organizing instruction to emphasize the following:

■ Quality curriculum consisting of useful and meaningful information that matches students' Quality World pictures in order for students to meet inborn needs (*survival, love and belonging, power, fun, and freedom*) and make life better for students.

- Quality teaching, meaning *lead teaching* and classroom lead-management strategies that energize students, as opposed to *boss teaching* and classroom boss management strategies that have a dampening effect on students.
- Application of *Choice Theory*, which emphasizes the value of positive influence and the understanding that all of us choose the behavior we display and are therefore responsible for it.
- Assiduous avoidance of the seven deadly habits in teaching (*criticizing, blaming, complaining, nagging, threatening, punishing,* and *rewarding students to control them*), which should be replaced with the seven connecting habits (*accepting, listening, supporting, respecting, encouraging, trusting,* and *negotiating differences*).
- Noncoercive classroom management practices (using positive influence) instead of coercive classroom management (using threat and force) to encourage students to conduct themselves responsibly.

Activities

Self-Test: True/False

1. According to Glasser, one of human beings' basic needs is to experience "fun."
2. Glasser concluded that about half of today's high school students make little effort to do well in school.
3. Glasser says it is immaterial whether students know how to use what they are learning because many of the things we need to know are not used until later in life.
4. "Lead teaching" attempts to draw students out so they become naturally engaged in learning information they find useful.
5. Glasser would not have teachers intervene when students break rules, but instead would let students learn from the consequences of their actions.
6. Glasser stresses that teachers and administrators must endeavor to help students be happy at school.
7. Among Glasser's seven deadly habits in teaching is one he calls "rewarding students in order to control them."
8. Glasser says schools should replace the seven deadly habits with the seven connecting habits, one of which is teachers' respecting their students.
9. Glasser says we can make education better for students if we ask them to clarify what a quality life in school would be like, and then plan the choices that would lead to it.

10. Because students are reluctant to commit themselves to class activities they find boring, you should always replace them with activities students find valuable and enjoyable.

Self-Test: Multiple Choice

1. Which was *not* included in Glasser's list of human needs?
   (a) freedom
   (b) fun
   (c) power
   (d) achievement
2. According to Glasser, the approximate percentage of high school students who do not make a reasonable effort to learn is
   (a) 25%.
   (b) 40%.
   (c) 50%.
   (d) 70%.
3. _____ is Glasser's term for teaching that opens many avenues and provides support.
   (a) Lead teaching
   (b) Expansion teaching
   (c) Discovery teaching
   (d) Guided teaching

4. For Glasser, frequently rewarding students as a means of controlling behavior is
   (a) beneficial.
   (b) counterproductive.
   (c) impossible in practice.
   (d) fine in theory.

5. Glasser's view of teachers' building relationships with their students is
   (a) wary.
   (b) lukewarm.
   (c) hot and cold.
   (d) positive.

6. Choice Theory would have teachers drop which of the following strategies in motivating students?
   (a) coercion
   (b) positive influence
   (c) encouragement
   (d) support

7. Choice Theory holds that motivation resides mainly
   (a) in the environment.
   (b) in the social group.
   (c) inside the individual.
   (d) in the collective imagination.

8. Glasser's level of enthusiasm about classroom meetings is
   (a) not enthusiastic.
   (b) lukewarm.
   (c) accepting.
   (d) very positive.

9. Glasser said this about class rules:
   (a) keep them to about 10 in number.
   (b) don't have them.
   (c) let students help make them.
   (d) leave them mainly to the teacher.

10. Which of the following is *not* a connecting habit?
    (a) accepting
    (b) listening
    (c) supporting
    (d) laying out a plan

Self-Test: Explain This

1. What does Glasser mean by "basic needs," and what are they specifically?
2. What does Glasser mean by "quality teaching"?
3. What are the main concepts that comprise Glasser's Choice Theory?
4. What does Glasser mean by "quality learning," and how can teachers promote it?

Additional Suggested Activities

1. Make notes in your journal concerning information from Glasser's teachings that you might like to incorporate into your personal system of classroom management.
2. Explain what Glasser means by each of the following terms: basic needs, boss teachers (boss management), Choice Theory, lead teachers (lead management), noncoercive classroom management, quality curriculum, quality teaching, seven connecting habits, seven deadly habits, SIR, useful work.
3. Give your appraisal of Glasser's system concerning the following: effectiveness in suppressing less-effective behavior, effectiveness in improving long-term behavior, ease of implementation, student willingness to cooperate and do the expected work, establishing trust between teacher and student.

Concept Cases

CASE 1   Kristina Will Not Work

Kristina, a student in Mr. Jake's class, is quite docile. She socializes little with other students and never disrupts lessons. However, despite Mr. Jake's best efforts, Kristina will not do her work. She rarely completes an assignment. She is simply there, putting forth no effort at all. *What would William Glasser suggest to help Kristina and Mr. Jake?*

Glasser would first suggest that Mr. Jake think carefully about the classroom and the program to try to determine whether they contain obstacles to Kristina's meeting her basic needs. He would then have Mr. Jake discuss the matter with Kristina, not blaming her but noting the problem of nonproductivity and asking what is at the root of the problem and what he might be able to do to help. In that discussion, Mr. Jake might ask Kristina questions such as the following:

- It appears that you may have a problem with this work. I believe the work is important and will help you in the future, but only you can decide whether or not to do it. Is there anything I can do to help you get started?
- Is there anything I could do to make the work more interesting for you?
- Is there anything in this class that you especially enjoy doing? Do you think that, for a while, you might like to do only those things? Is there anything we have discussed in class that you would like to learn very, very well? How could I help you do that?

Glasser would not want Mr. Jake to use a disapproving tone of voice with Kristina, but every day make a point of talking with her in a friendly and courteous way about nonschool matters such as trips, pets, and movies. He would do this casually, showing he is interested in her and willing to be her friend. Glasser would remind Mr. Jake that there is no magic formula for success with all students. Mr. Jake can only encourage and support Kristina. As Mr. Jake continues to build a relationship with Kristina, she is likely to begin to do more work of better quality.

CASE 2   Sara Will Not Stop Talking

Sara is a pleasant girl who participates in class activities and does most, though not all, of her assigned work. She cannot seem to refrain from talking to classmates, however. Her teacher, Mr. Gonzales, has to speak to her repeatedly during lessons, to the point that he often becomes exasperated and loses his temper. *What suggestions would Glasser give Mr. Gonzales for dealing with Sara?*

CASE 3   Joshua Clowns and Intimidates

Joshua, larger and louder than his classmates, always wants to be the center of attention, which he accomplishes through a combination of clowning and intimidation. He makes wise remarks, talks back (smilingly) to the teacher, utters a variety of sound-effect noises such as automobile crashes and gunshots, and makes limitless sarcastic comments and put-downs of his classmates. Other students will not stand up to him, apparently fearing his size and verbal aggression. His teacher, Miss Pearl, has come to her wit's end. *How do you think Glasser would have Miss Pearl deal with Joshua?*

CASE 4   Tom Is Hostile and Defiant

Tom has appeared to be in his usual foul mood ever since arriving in class. On his way to sharpen his pencil, he bumps into Frank, who complains. Tom tells him loudly to shut up. Miss Baines, the teacher, says, "Tom, go back to your seat." Tom wheels around, swears loudly, and says heatedly, "I'll go when I'm _____good and ready!" *What would Glasser advise?*

You Are the Teacher

MIDDLE SCHOOL WORLD HISTORY

Your third-period world history class is comprised of students whose achievement levels vary from high to well below average. You pace their work accordingly, ask them to work cooperatively, and make sure everyone understands what they are supposed to do. For the most part you enjoy the class, finding the students interesting and refreshing. Your lessons follow a consistent pattern. First, you ask the students to read in groups from the textbook, then you call on students at random to answer selected questions about the material. If a student, who is called on, is unable to answer a question, the group he or she represents loses a point. If able to answer correctly, the group gains a point. For partially correct answers, the group neither receives nor loses a point. For the second part of the period, the class groups do something productive or creative connected with the material they have read, such as making posters, writing a story, doing a skit, or the like. As appropriate, these efforts are shared with members of the class.

A TYPICAL OCCURRENCE

You call on Hillary to answer a question. Although she has been participating, she shakes her head. This has happened several times before. Not wanting to hurt Hillary's feelings, you simply say, "That costs the group a point," and you call on someone else. Unfortunately, Hillary's group gets upset at her. The other students make comments under their breath. Later, Clarisse also refuses to answer. When you speak with her about it, she says, "You didn't make Hillary do it."

You answer, "Look, we are talking about you, not Hillary." However, you let the matter lie and say no more. Just then, Deonne comes into the class late, appearing very angry. He slams his pack down on his desk

and sits without opening his textbook. Although you want to talk with Deonne, you don't know how to approach him at that time. Will is in the opposite mood.

Throughout the oral reading portion of the class, he continually giggles at every mispronounced word and at every reply students give to your questions. Will sits at the front of the class and turns around to laugh, seeing if he can get anyone else to laugh with him. He makes some *oooh* and *aaaah* sounds when Hillary and Clarisse decline to respond. Although most students either ignore him or give him disgusted looks, he keeps laughing. You finally ask him what is so funny.

He replies, "Nothing in particular," and looks back at the class and laughs. At the end of the period, there is time for sharing three posters students have made. Will makes comments and giggles about each of them. Clarisse, who has not participated, says, "Will, how about shutting up!" As the students leave the room, you take Deonne aside. "Is something wrong, Deonne?" you ask. "No," Deonne replies. His jaw is clenched as he strides past you.

CONCEPTUALIZING A STRATEGY

If you followed Glasser's suggestions, what would you do with regard to the following?

- Preventing the problems from occurring in the first place.
- Putting an immediate end to the less-effective behavior.
- Involving other or all students in addressing the situation.
- Maintaining student dignity and good personal relations.

Using follow-up procedures that would prevent the recurrence of the misbehavior.

10

Spencer Kagan on Working on the Same Side with Students

How Does Spencer Kagan Foster Good Behavior by Working in Tandem with Students?

Here's an abridged version of a little story told by Spencer Kagan:

> Two women are standing on a bank of a swift river. In the strong current, flailing about and desperately struggling to stay afloat, is a man being carried downstream toward them. The women both jump in and pull the man to safety. While the brave rescuers are tending to the victim, a second man, also desperate and screaming for help, is carried toward them by the current. Again the women jump to the rescue. As they are pulling out this second victim, they spot a third man flailing about as he is carried downstream toward them. One woman quickly jumps in to save him. As she does, she turns and sees the other woman resolutely walking upstream. "Why aren't you helping?" she cries. "I am," states the other. "I am going to see who is pushing them in!" (Kagan, 2001)

What do you think is the point of Kagan's story?

WHO IS SPENCER KAGAN?

Spencer Kagan, originator and principal disseminator of Win-Win Discipline, is a professor of psychology and head of Kagan Publishing and Professional Development. For several years, Dr. Kagan has been conducting research into how teachers can best establish harmonious classrooms, promote responsible behavior, and improve students' social skills, character qualities, and academic achievement. Kagan believes discipline is not something you do to a student, but rather something you help a student achieve. All disruptive behavior is an immature attempt to meet a need associated with a student position. For example, a student disrupts the class by acting like a clown. The student's position is attention-seeking. The job of the teacher, rather than disciplining the student, is to help the student learn responsible ways to meet the need for attention. When the student has responsible ways to meet her/his needs, the student is no longer disruptive. Thus, the focus in Win-Win Discipline is to help teachers recognize the seven positions from which disruptive behaviors spring, and to provide ways the teacher can help students learn responsible alternatives to their disruptive behaviors. It is a win-win. Disruptive students win: they learn responsible ways to meet their needs. The class and the teacher also win, as they have to deal with fewer disruptive behaviors. To help teachers teach students responsible behaviors, Kagan and his colleagues have developed many structures—step-by-step procedures to use to prevent disruptive behaviors, to deal with disruptive behaviors in the moment of disruption, and to help students learn responsible behaviors following a disruption. Thus, Win-Win is a *before*, *during*, and *after* approach to discipline.

Kagan believes discipline is established more satisfactorily when teachers and students work together from the *same side* to make decisions about behavior issues. Toward that end, he has developed a large number of *structures*—meaning sets of organized steps—that are applied to help students find greater success and to help teachers redirect irresponsible behavior when it occurs. The structures, which Kagan has aligned with the brain's multiple intelligences and ways of learning, are now being used internationally at levels from kindergarten through university, across a wide range of academic subjects.

Kagan is extremely enthusiastic about the value of structures in various aspects of teaching. To see what he has to say about them, you might take a few minutes to read his online article, "A Brief History of Kagan Structures," *Kagan Online Magazine*, Spring 2003, at www.kaganonline.com. You will find several other Kagan articles also available at that site.

WHAT QUESTIONS WILL THIS CHAPTER ANSWER FOR ME?

- How can students and teachers learn to work together on the same side to find solutions to behavior concerns?
- What are the primary goals of Win-Win Discipline, and how do those goals relate to students' lives in general?
- What four categories of irresponsible behavior are emphasized in Win-Win Discipline?
- What seven student positions (states of mind/body) can be identified in association with disruptive behavior?
- What is the nature of the structures (plans of action) teachers can use for interacting productively with misbehaving students?
- How do teachers apply Kagan's discipline tactics?
- What does Kagan say about befriending students and showing genuine fondness for them?

WHAT IS THE KAGAN MODEL OF DISCIPLINE?

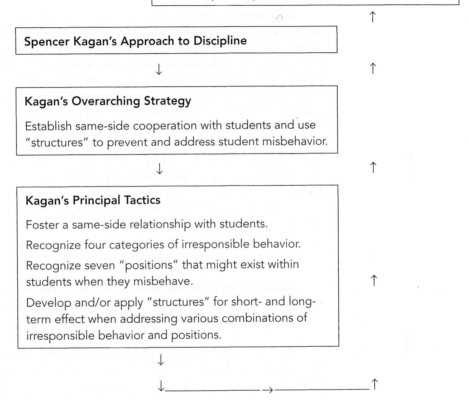

The Common Goal of All Approaches to Discipline *Responsible, Civil Classroom Behavior That Becomes Habitual and Lasts over Time.*

Responsible means paying attention, making a strong effort, and doing what is proper without being told. Civil means respectful, polite, cordial, and well mannered.

↑

Spencer Kagan's Approach to Discipline

↓ ↑

Kagan's Overarching Strategy

Establish same-side cooperation with students and use "structures" to prevent and address student misbehavior.

↓ ↑

Kagan's Principal Tactics

Foster a same-side relationship with students.

Recognize four categories of irresponsible behavior.

Recognize seven "positions" that might exist within students when they misbehave.

Develop and/or apply "structures" for short- and long-term effect when addressing various combinations of irresponsible behavior and positions.

↑

↓

↓————→————↑

WHAT IS THE FUNDAMENTAL PROPOSITION IN KAGAN'S APPROACH?

Discipline occurs best, Kagan maintains, when teachers do two things: (1) work on the same side with students to establish mutual agreements (rules) concerning acceptable and unacceptable behavior in the classroom, and (2) continue thereafter to work collaboratively with students by using "structures" to help them make good decisions that lead to responsible behavior.

We will now explore Kagan's ideas, beginning with a clarification of what he means by *irresponsible behavior, positions,* and *structures*. **Irresponsible behavior** means disruptive student behavior (i.e., misbehavior), which Kagan assigns to four categories: aggression, breaking rules, confrontations, and disengagement. He refers to the four categories as the **ABCD of disruptive behavior.**

Student positions refer to the physical and emotional states students are experiencing at the time they misbehave. In Kagan's terminology, misbehaving students are said to be "coming from" one or more of seven positions, which Kagan identifies as: attention-seeking, avoiding failure, angry, control-seeking, energetic, bored, and uninformed. By "coming from" he means the state of mind the student is experiencing at the time he or she misbehaves. When addressing misbehavior, the teacher acknowledges and accepts the student's emotional state (e.g., "I can see you are angry") but explicitly *does not* accept the inappropriate behavior (e.g., "But it is not all right to push anyone").

Structures are specific plans of action that teachers use for two purposes—to teach the curriculum and to address misbehavior. Here, we focus mainly on structures for addressing misbehavior. Kagan says all misbehavior is linked to one or more of the seven student positions. An example of a misbehavior-position combination, as indicated earlier, is a student behaving aggressively (the misbehavior) while being angry (the position). Another example is a student breaking a rule (the misbehavior) because he or she is attempting to avoid a sense of failure (the position the student is coming from).

Kagan says teachers master the skills of discipline by learning to select and apply a structure that deals effectively with a particular combination of misbehavior and student position. Kagan has developed a large number of structures, which he presents in *Win-Win Discipline* (Kagan, Kyle, & Scott, 2004, 2007) and in some of his website articles. Kagan shows teachers how to identify the category of misbehavior, identify the position the student is "coming from," and apply an appropriate structure to help the student contend with the situation in a positive manner. You can visualize the process as follows:

Teacher Identifies Misbehavior → Teacher Identifies Student Position → Teacher Selects and Applies a Structure That Addresses the Particular Combination of Misbehavior and Position

Up to this point, you have learned that Win-Win Discipline emphasizes same-side collaboration by teacher and students. It uses class rules of behavior, identifies types of misbehavior evident when students break rules, identifies students' states of mind when they display particular types of misbehavior, and applies structures that are appropriate for addressing various combinations of disruption and position. The Win-Win process is organized to accomplish two things: First, it helps students move away from misbehavior and return to appropriate behavior, and second, it promotes long-term improvement in behavior.

WHAT ELSE SHOULD WE KNOW ABOUT WIN-WIN DISCIPLINE?

Here is further information that will help you conceptualize Win-Win Discipline and how it is used:

1. *The name and goal of Win-Win Discipline.* The name—Win-Win Discipline—indicates that teachers and students both win, or benefit from using the approach. The goal is to help students develop *lifelong responsible behavior.*

2. *Three pillars of Win-Win Discipline.* **Three pillars** form the philosophical structure of Win-Win Discipline. They are (1) *same side,* meaning students, teachers, and sometimes others all work together on the same side to enhance the school experience for students; (2) *collaborative solutions,* meaning students and teachers cooperate in formulating workable solutions to discipline problems; and (3) *learned responsibility,* meaning students acquire the desire to behave appropriately as they practice self-management and the skills of getting along with others.

3. *Class rules.* Win-Win Discipline makes use of **class rules**, which are agreements worked out cooperatively by teacher and students. You can have the class begin by discussing what they believe to be responsible behavior—you might call the result "The Way We Want Our Class to Be." Rules (agreements) are then derived from statements about responsible behavior. They should be worded simply, limited to about five in number, posted in the room for easy reference, and reviewed periodically. Students are guided in practicing the behavior associated with each rule. All the while, teachers and other adults conduct themselves in a manner that is consistent with the class rules.

This process builds student involvement and cooperation. Students begin to behave responsibly without feeling that rules are being imposed on them. Although rules may vary somewhat from class to class, they usually turn out to be quite similar overall. Kagan suggests that the following rules are likely to emerge:

> *Ready rule:* Come to class ready to learn.
>
> *Respect rule:* Respect the rights and property of others.
>
> *Request rule:* Ask for help when needed.
>
> *Offer rule:* Offer help to others.
>
> *Responsibility rule:* Strive to act responsibly at all times.

Kagan says that some teachers prefer to condense rules into only one, such as: *In our class, we agree to foster our own learning, help others learn, and allow the teacher to teach.*

? If, at this point, you had to select one or two rules of behavior for your class, what would those rules be, and why?

---

4. *Attention to types of misbehavior.* In Win-Win Discipline, classroom misbehavior is categorized into four types—aggression, breaking rules, confrontations, and disengagement. As we noted, Kagan refers to these four types as the *ABCD of disruptive behavior.* In Win-Win Discipline, disruptive behavior is not referred to as "misbehavior," but is instead thought and spoken of as *ineffective behavior choices* students make when trying to meet specific needs. As George and Jaime come into the classroom, George shouts an obscenity at Jaime. Jaime responds in kind. Which category or categories of ineffective behavior choice do you think the boys' actions represent?

5. *Attention to student positions.* Student positions refer to the physical/emotional states that students are experiencing when they disrupt. We noted that Kagan identifies seven such positions: attention-seeking, avoiding failure, angry, control-seeking, energetic, bored, and uninformed. The positions are not considered to be right or wrong, good or bad. They simply indicate individual students' natural emotional and physical states at the time students misbehave. The positions provide teachers a starting point in addressing ineffective behavior choices. As we noted before, whenever a student makes ineffective choices, teachers should acknowledge the student's position as being normal, but should indicate that the behavior being exhibited is not acceptable. For example, "Jaime, we all get angry at times, but even when we do, it is not acceptable to swear at others." Once again, Jaime is "coming from" anger, his position, which is acceptable; his ineffective behavior choice is swearing, which is not acceptable.

6. *Structures.* When teachers recognize ineffective choices, they identify the position the student is coming from, as shown in the preceding example. At that time, they select and apply an appropriate structure (a procedure or set of steps) to help the student return to responsible behavior. Kagan provides over 200 such structures and shows how they are matched to the type of misbehavior and the student's position at the time of disruption. The structures do more than stifle disruptions; they help students learn to behave responsibly. Some of Kagan's structures are used proactively to prevent disruptions, whereas others are used reactively to address disruptions after they occur. Some are effective in the short term (e.g., stopping misbehavior), whereas others are effective in the long term (e.g., developing better self-control).

7. *Attention to needs.* Kagan asks us to think of disruptions as students' ineffective efforts to meet their needs. We saw in Chapter 9 that William Glasser lists five predominant needs of students in school: survival (safety), belonging, power, fun, and freedom. Students grow noticeably uncomfortable when any of those needs is not being met. Win-Win Discipline helps students meet those needs in acceptable ways that do not disrupt teaching or learning.

8. *Application of the process.* As suggested earlier, here is Kagan's paradigm for applying his approach when disruptions occur: For a given misbehavior, we quickly (1) identify the category of misbehavior, (2) identify the student's emotion or state of mind when disrupting, and (3) apply one or more helping structures that stop the disruption and direct the student back to appropriate behavior. Later we will examine some of the structures he suggests.

In order to be fully effective, the Win-Win process requires a classroom environment that consistently emphasizes and supports a "we" approach that gives teachers and students a joint interest in maintaining responsible behavior. Kagan refers to the "we approach" as **teacher–student same-side collaboration**. Now let's look at some of his suggestions in more detail.

HOW DOES KAGAN DESCRIBE THE ABCD OF DISRUPTIVE BEHAVIOR?

We saw that Kagan categorizes disruptive behavior as aggression, breaking rules, confrontation, and disengagement. He believes all misbehavior fits one or more of these categories. Here is what he says about them:

Aggression. Student aggression can be shown physically, verbally, and sometimes passively. Physical aggression includes hitting, kicking, biting, pinching, pulling, and slapping. Verbal aggression includes put-downs, swearing, ridiculing, and name-calling. Passive aggression involves stubbornly refusing to comply with reasonable requests.

Breaking Rules. When unable to meet certain needs satisfactorily, students often try to do so through behavior that violates class rules. Common examples of rule-breaking behavior are talking without permission, making weird noises, chewing gum, passing notes, being out of seat, and not turning in work. Sometimes students break rules just to see what it feels like or to see what happens when they do.

Confrontation. Confrontations occur among students or between student and teacher when the parties involved try to get their way, vie for control, or attempt to show dominance. Examples of confrontational behavior are refusing to comply, complaining, arguing, calling names, and giving myriad reasons why things are no good or should be done differently. When students don't get their way in confrontations, they often pout or make disparaging remarks about the task, teacher, or fellow students.

Disengagement. Students may disengage from lessons for a variety of reasons. They may have something more interesting on their minds, feel incapable of performing the task, or find the task boring or meaningless. Passive disengagement includes inattention, being off task, not finishing work, and pretending to be incapable. Active disengagement includes put-downs, excessive requests for help, and comments such as, "This stuff is stupid."

WHAT ELSE DOES KAGAN SAY ABOUT STRUCTURES?

Kagan, Kyle, and Scott (2007) explain that teachers continually use structures without recognizing them as such. They explain that structures are simply plans of action and ways of reacting. For example, one of the most frequently used (and least effective) structures in discipline is posing the *why* question, which proceeds as follows:

[Teacher hears and sees Anthony talking abusively to Jason during silent work time.]

Teacher asks: "Anthony, why are you talking?"
Anthony replies: "Just answering a question for Jason."
Teacher replies: "Well it didn't sound like it. You both know better than that."

In *Win-Win Discipline* (2007) Kagan, Kyle, and Scott describe in detail a large number of structures for dealing with types of disruption and student positions. These structures are similar, but not identical, to the "procedures" emphasized by Harry and Rosemary Wong, indicating steps and the order in which they occur. Some of those structures are designed to *prevent disruptions.* Examples of such preventive structures are reviewing class rules, having students practice complying with rules, and having students familiarize themselves with class routines.

Other structures are designed for *responding to disruptions* when they occur. These responsive structures are applied at three different points in time: (1) at *the moment of disruption*, to stop the behavior and rechannel it into responsible behavior; (2) during *follow-up*, when students require further assistance in moving beyond a particular disruptive behavior; and (3) repeatedly over the *long-term*, to help students develop and maintain effective life skills such as positive self-direction and getting along with others.

Once the Win-Win philosophy of same-side collaboration has been internalized, students who disrupt usually need only a reminder to get back on track. Teachers can refer to the chart of rules posted in the room and ask, "Are we living up to the way we want our class to be?" If more is required, the teacher might use a structure such as *Picture It Right,* which asks students to picture how they would like the class to be and verbalize what they need to do to make it that way.

More on Structures for the Moment of Disruption

At the moment of disruption, you should intervene in a way that ends the disruption and quickly refocuses attention on the lesson. You might acknowledge the student's position, communicate that the disruptive behavior is not acceptable, request cooperation, or involve the student in specifying a satisfactory alternative. Here are three examples of structures designed for use at the moment of disruption:

- *Picture It Right.* "If we were at our very best right now, how would we look?"
- *Make a Better Choice.* "Try to think of a better choice to make right now."
- *To You . . . To Me.* "To you, this lesson may be boring; to me, it is important because . . ."

More on Structures for Follow-Up

Follow-up structures are used when students need additional assistance in behaving responsibly. They are applied when moment-of-disruption structures do not bring about a complete or lasting result. Typical follow-up structures include the following:

- Establish a new preventive procedure or reestablish an existing preventive procedure.
- Select a new moment-of-disruption procedure for use the next time the student disrupts.
- Implement a follow-up structure, such as a "same-side chat," or explore ways in which students might behave responsibly.
- Provide training in a life skill such as self-control or relating well with others.

Follow-up structures often involve highly prescriptive activities such as directly practicing appropriate behavior. They may even call on students to make apologies and restitution, or endure time away from the lesson. If still stronger measures are needed, students may be required to develop a *personal improvement plan* that specifies behavior changes the student intends to make and how those changes will be accomplished.

If it is necessary to administer consequences to control disruptive behavior, they should be applied in the following sequence:

1. The student is given a warning.
2. If that doesn't work, the student is given reflection time to sit alone and think about the disruptive behavior and how to improve it.
3. If that doesn't work, a personal improvement plan is formulated by the disruptive student to help develop responsible ways of meeting needs in the classroom.
4. If that doesn't work, the student's parent or guardian is contacted.
5. If that doesn't work, the student is assigned to make a visit to the principal's office.

More on Structures for Long-Term Success

Long-term structures are intended to help students get along with others, become more self-directing, and control their volatile emotions. They fortify proper behavior after preventive and moment-of-disruption structures have begun producing their desired results. Keep in mind that the major goal of Win-Win Discipline is to help students learn to control themselves responsibly over time in various situations. Thus, when opportunities present themselves, teachers should allow students to try to resolve problems on their own and display responsible behavior. Different long-term goals come into play for various student positions. For example:

- Students who continually seek attention need help with self-validation.
- Students who avoid failure or embarrassment need help with self-confidence.
- Students who are often angry need help with self-control.
- Students who seek control need help with recognizing others' capabilities.
- Students who are overly energetic need help with self-direction.
- Students who are frequently bored need help with self-motivation.
- Students who are frequently uninformed need help in obtaining information for themselves or from others.

Win-Win Discipline offers a progression of follow-up structures to help students move toward these long-term goals. Here are a few such structures, ranging from less directive to more directive:

Same-Side Chat. Teacher and student talk together in a friendly manner. In so doing, they get to know each other better and come to see themselves as working on the same side toward better conditions for all.

Responsible Thinking. Discussions are used to prompt students to reflect on three considerations: (1) their own and others' needs, (2) how they treat others, and (3) how they conduct themselves. Applied to a specific misbehavior, students can be asked to consider the following three questions in relation to their own behavior:

- What if everyone acted that way? (How would our class be if everyone acted that way?)

- How would I like to be treated? (Did I treat others the way I would like to be treated?)
- What would be a win-win solution? (What would meet everyone's needs?)

Reestablishing Expectations. Discuss and, if necessary, reteach expectations concerning rules, procedures, and routines.

Identifying Replacement Behavior. Guide students to generate, accept, and practice responsible behavior they can use in place of disruptive behavior.

Agreeing on Contracts. Make written contracts in which teacher and individual students clarify and formalize agreements they have reached. Contracts sometimes increase the likelihood that the student will remember, identify with, and honor the agreement.

Establishing Consequences. Agree on actions the teacher will take when students chronically disrupt. These consequences are held as a last resort and are used only when all other follow-up efforts have failed. Consequences should be aligned with the three pillars of Win-Win Discipline—they begin with same-side orientation, are established through teacher–student collaboration, and are instructive and aimed at helping students learn to conduct themselves with greater personal responsibility.

When disruptions harm others and responsible thinking is not enough, students may need to *apologize* to those they have offended or make *restitution* of some sort. Genuine apologies have three parts: a statement of regret, a statement of appropriate future behavior, and the request for acceptance of the apology. *Restitution* means making amends for emotional damage that was done or repairing or replacing physical damage or damaged materials. Restitution is a tangible way of taking responsibility and dealing with the consequences of inappropriate choices. It also has the potential to "heal the violator."

More on Structures for Promoting Life Skills

One of the major goals of Win-Win Discipline is to promote the progressive development of a number of *life skills* that help students live more successfully. Examples of life skills are self-control, anger management, good judgment, impulse control, perseverance, and empathy. Teachers are urged to teach these skills as part of the curriculum and exhibit them at all times, especially when responding to misbehavior. Kagan says that when teachers foster life skills, they move beyond interventions that simply end disruptions while leaving students likely to disrupt again. He illustrates his points in this manner (2007):

A student puts down another student. The recipient of the put-down, having been publicly belittled, has the impulse to retaliate by giving back a put-down or even initiating a fight. If the recipient has developed adequate self-control and/or anger management, he might smile and rise above the affront.

A student is finding an assignment difficult. She is tempted to avoid a sense of failure by saying to herself and others, "This assignment is stupid." But if she has acquired adequate self-motivation and pride in her work, she may decide to persevere.

A student is placed on a team with another student he does not like. He is tempted to mutter, "Oh no! Look who we are stuck with!" If the student has developed sufficient empathy and kindness, he might dispose himself to working with the other student.

HOW DO I MATCH INTERVENTION STRUCTURES TO VARIOUS TYPES OF DISRUPTION?

Interventions are the actions teachers take to deal with disruptions. They usually involve a structure the teacher applies to stop the disruption and help students return to appropriate behavior that lasts over time. Kagan provides many suggestions for such interventions. Following are some examples.

Interventions for Attention-Seeking Behavior

Most individuals have a strong need for attention. They want to know others care about them or at least take notice of them. When they feel left out or not cared for, they often behave undesirably in trying to get the attention they crave. They may interrupt, show off, annoy others, work more slowly than others, ask for extra help, or simply goof off. These acts seldom bring the results students would like—in fact, they are likely to lead to further disruption and increased teacher annoyance.

What You Can Do

For the moment of disruption, you can use physical proximity and hand or facial signals to stop the disruption, or provide additional personal attention, appreciation, and affirmation. If attention seeking becomes chronic, ask students to identify other positive ways they can get attention, such as helping others or doing exemplary work. You can follow up by meeting with disruptive students and discussing the need for attention and how it can often be obtained in a positive manner. Strategies for long-term solutions include helping students strengthen their self-concepts and acquire the skills involved in self-validation.

Interventions for Attempts to Avoid Failure or Embarrassment

We have all been in situations where we rationalize our inadequacies in order to soften the embarrassment of failure. No one likes to appear inept. The student who says, "I don't care about the stupid math quiz," knows it is more painful to fail, especially in front of others, than not to try at all, and therefore will rationalize failure as lack of caring.

What You Can Do

Win-win teachers help students find ways to persist and continue to perform without feeling bad if they aren't first or best. For the moment of disruption, you can encourage students to try to complete the task, assign them partners or helpers, or reorganize the task into smaller pieces. For follow-up and long-term strategies, ask students how they think responsible people might deal with fear of failure. You can also provide for peer support, review the fact that mistakes are always part of the learning process as people move toward excellence, and use "team–pair–solo," a structure in which students practice first as a team and then in pairs before doing the assigned activities by themselves.

Interventions for Anger

Anger is a natural reaction many students have to situations that involve frustration, humiliation, loss, or pain. Angry students may act out in unacceptable ways because they do not know to deal effectively with the emotions they are experiencing.

What You Can Do

Teachers don't enjoy interacting with angry students. They sometimes experience hurt or indignation. Often, because they feel personally attacked, their immediate reaction is to retaliate against the students, which does little to help students manage their anger. Win-Win Discipline provides several structures to help you respond positively to angry disruptions. Three of those structures are teaching responsible ways of handling anger, allowing students to cool down and have time to think, and tabling the matter for attention at a later time. *Long-term interventions* include having students practice the skills of self-control and teaching them how to resolve conflicts in a positive manner.

Interventions for Control-Seeking Behavior

All of us want to feel we are at least partly in charge of ourselves and able to make our own decisions. In our efforts to exercise self-direction, we sometimes try to control others as well. At times, students display this take-charge attitude by disregarding or defying directions from the teacher. Doing so often leads to power struggles between student and teacher. Teachers don't take kindly to noncompliance, arguing, or making excuses, and they often counter in ways that show their dominance, which does little to help the student.

What You Can Do

At the *moment of disruption,* acknowledge the student's power, use language of choice (a structure in which the teacher provides students with a choice such as, "You may either . . . or . . ."), or provide options for how and when work is to be done. For *follow-up* you might schedule a conference or class meeting at a later time to discuss the situation, ask the class why they think students often struggle against the teacher, and consider how such struggles can be avoided. *Long-term strategies* include involving students in the decision-making process and requesting their help in establishing class agreements about showing respect for the teacher and fellow students.

Interventions for the Overly Energetic

At times, humans experience periods of high energy, so strong they cannot sit still or concentrate. Some students are in this state a good deal of the time, moving and talking incessantly.

What You Can Do

If overly energetic behavior becomes troublesome, at the *moment of disruption* take a brief class break or switch to another activity that allows energy to dissipate. You might also provide time for progressive relaxation, remove distracting elements and objects, and channel energy productively. *Follow-up strategies* include teaching a variety of calming strategies and providing activities that allow students to work off energy in positive ways. *Long-term solutions* include managing energy levels during instruction and helping students learn how to channel their energy in ways that bring positive results.

Interventions for Boredom

To say that students are bored is to say they are no longer enjoying particular activities sufficiently to continue in them willingly. Their boredom will be evident in their body language, disengagement, and disinclination to participate.

What You Can Do

To help bored students at the *moment of disruption,* you can restructure the learning task, involve students more actively, and inject short activities that energize the students. As *follow-up,* you might talk privately with the students and assign them helping roles such as caretakers for the classroom, materials assistants, or coaches to assist other students. For *long-term solutions,* you can provide a rich, relevant, and developmentally appropriate curriculum that actively involves students in the learning process, emphasizes cooperative learning, and calls on students to use their multiple intelligences.

Interventions for the Uninformed

Sometimes students respond or react disruptively because they simply don't know what to do or how to behave responsibly. Disruptions stemming from being uninformed do not occur because of strong emotions, but because of lack of information, skill, or appropriate habit. Even when these disruptions are not emotionally volatile, they are nonetheless frustrating to teachers.

What You Can Do

To determine whether students know what is expected of them, at the *moment of disruption* gently ask students to say or do what is expected of them. If they are unable to do so, you can reteach them at that time. If they only need support, let them work with a buddy. *Follow-up strategies* include more careful attention to giving directions, modeling desired responses, and providing practice in responsible behavior. *Long-term solutions* include encouragement and focusing on student strengths.

WHAT DOES KAGAN SAY ABOUT PARENT AND COMMUNITY ALLIANCES AND SCHOOLWIDE PROGRAMS?

Kagan, more than most other authorities in discipline, urges teachers to establish partnerships with caregivers and the wider community to assist students in making responsible behavior choices. Caregivers and community citizens usually appreciate and support teachers who handle disruptive behavior in a positive manner. Input, support, follow-through, and backup from caregivers and other adults strengthen the likelihood of success. Teacher–parent–community cooperation depends largely on teachers reaching out to make contacts. Kagan urges you not to give up when caregivers or community members seem reluctant to participate. Continue inviting them to become actively involved.

Win-Win Discipline provides many helpful suggestions for teacher–parent–community communication and interaction. Contact with potential participants should be made during the first week of school. Phone calls, letters, class newsletters, class websites, and emails are efficient ways to connect with caregivers. Parent nights and open houses offer opportunities for person-to-person communication, showing caregivers and others they are valued as allies and possibly mentors and tutors. The broader community can become involved through field trips, guest speakers, apprenticeships, and having students work with day-care and senior centers. Schoolwide efforts in this endeavor usually bring good results.

> **?** The school principal is urging teachers to make better connections with parents and the community, but is leaving it up to teachers to decide how they will do so. Miss Able sets up a class website describing class activities that interested people can access. Mr. Beeson sends out personalized invitations to attend a class performance at school. Mrs. Calipari calls 10 parents on the phone and tells them how pleased she is to have their child in class and describes something each child has done especially well. How do you assess the impact and value of these three different attempts to reach out for support?

Commentary from Anonymous Teacher 1

Several of the principles Dr. Kagan teaches have worked effectively for me over the years, although I tweak some of them so they are better suited to my students (third grade, lower performing). For example, I regularly review class rules and expectations when it seems students are not complying with them. This is helpful not only in the beginning weeks of school, but throughout the year. At the time I am writing this, there are only 3 weeks left in our school year. Yet, only last week, as a class we reviewed our expectations and rules, not only for the classroom but for the playground, as well, helping students remember that expectations last right up through the last day of school.

One of our expectations has to do with "responsible thinking," which many of my students do not learn at home very well. For this reminder, I use role-playing (a favorite activity of my students) to help get the meaning across.

My students also respond very well to same-side chats, in which I often ask students privately if they have ideas on how we might cut down on interruptions during learning time. If no one overhears them, students usually tell me honestly what they can do to help. But if peers can hear, their responses are not so honest or helpful. I also find the "to you . . . to me" structure effective with individuals, groups, and the class as a whole. When more serious misbehavior occurs, such as name-calling or hitting, I sometimes ask students to write apology notes to the person or persons they have offended. Just last week, I asked a student to write such a note for continually teasing a girl about liking a certain boy. The unwanted behavior stopped and everyone seemed to feel okay. In that case, I kept the matter private to the persons involved.

HOW DO I IMPLEMENT WIN-WIN DISCIPLINE IN MY CLASSROOM?

The Three Essentials

In order to implement Win-Win Discipline as intended, you must do three things. The *first* is to commit yourself to complying with what Kagan calls teaching's **Big Three**:

- Establish an interesting and challenging *curriculum*.
- Provide *cooperative activities* that allow students to work together meaningfully.
- Be an *interesting, stimulating teacher* who adapts the curriculum to student interests and needs.

The *second* is to familiarize yourself with the seven student positions and relate them to the types of misbehavior you are likely to encounter. Remember, you are to accept and validate the seven positions, but not accept the disruptive behavior associated with them.

The *third* is to select or design structures that help disruptive students return to responsible conduct. You will put some of these structures in place as preventive measures before classes begin; you will use others to help redirect misbehavior; and you will use still others to help students develop long-term responsibility.

Introducing Win-Win Discipline

When you introduce Win-Win Discipline, begin by setting the tone for the class. Let the students know that the class will be built on the three pillars of Win-Win Discipline—same side, collaborative solutions, and learned responsibility. You might say something like the following:

> This is our class, and with all of us working together we will create a place where each person feels comfortable and all of us can enjoy the process of learning. As your teacher, I have a responsibility to create an environment where this can happen, but I need your help to make it work. I want each of you to realize you are an important member of this class, with important responsibilities, and that you can help make the class a pleasant place for all of us. One of your main responsibilities is to help create and maintain a positive learning atmosphere where everybody's needs are met. To accomplish this, we all must work together. I suggest that we begin by creating an agreement about how we will treat each other in this class.

Next, consider creating class agreements as follows: Begin by constructing a chart with the headings *Disruptive Behavior* and *Responsible Behavior*. Under each heading write two subheadings, *Say* and *Do*. Ask the students to name some of the disruptive things people say and do when they want attention. Record their responses under *Disruptive Behavior*. Then ask the class to name some of the responsible things people say and do for attention. Record their responses under *Responsible Behavior*. Continue this process for each of the seven positions.

When you have reasonable lists, ask students, "How do you feel about these lists? Would you be willing to adopt the responsible behaviors as our class agreement? Can we agree to avoid the disruptive behaviors?" It is essential that students believe their opinions and cooperation are valued. Tell them,

> You and I need to be on the same side and work together to create a classroom we all enjoy and where everyone can learn. You will always be included in the decision-making process. You will be able to have your say. We will learn and practice skills that are important for being citizens in a democratic society. Choosing responsible behavior will be one of the most important things you will learn.

During the first weeks, use activities that strengthen the concept of the three pillars. This reassures students that discipline will not be done *to* them, but will happen *with* them. In collaboration with the class, you might discuss discipline structures and their purposes, develop logical consequences and follow-ups, and solicit student input on some curriculum decisions.

You can also show students how you will help them turn disruptive behavior into good learning situations, where reflection, follow-up, and long-term structures come into play. You can do these things in a series of class meetings. Kagan adds that very early in the school year, you should begin establishing alliances with caregivers and interested members of the community.

REMINDERS AND SUGGESTIONS

Review with your class the four types of disruptive behavior and the seven student positions associated with them. Explain that (1) disruptive behavior (which is unacceptable) consists of inappropriate actions people take in trying to meet their needs; (2) when students disrupt, they are "coming from" a particular emotional state that is natural and identifiable; and (3) for the various emotional states, there are procedures for helping students meet their needs and return to acceptable behavior.

Continuing to stress collaboration, ask students to think along with you about what could be done to help them behave more appropriately, should they misbehave. You might discuss an example such as the following:

> During a cooperative group situation, Samuel, a new boy in class, disrupts the class by standing up and calling over to Duwahn in another group. Samuel may or may not know that this behavior is inappropriate, but his action violates one of the class rules that class members have agreed on. What should be done?

In accordance with advice from Kagan, Kyle, and Scott (2007), you might describe the following approach and ask for your students' reactions to it:

- Identify the category of disruption. Using Kagan's ABCD categories, we see Samuel's behavior is category B (breaking rules).
- Look beyond the behavior to identify the position Samuel is coming from. (Let's suppose you determine that Samuel's position is "being uninformed.")
- Apply a structure for the moment of disruption that is consistent with Samuel's position. You might say, "Samuel, because you are a new member of our class, you may not know, or may not remember, our rule against calling out in class. Do you remember that rule? No? Let's take just a moment to review it so you will remember it in the future."
- It is not likely you will need to say more, but if necessary you could use a follow-up structure to help Samuel make better decisions in the future. For example, you and Samuel might, in private, have a friendly same-side chat to help Samuel understand the rule against calling out and help him identify an alternative behavior that would be acceptable.

Ideally, implementation of Win-Win Discipline should begin before the school year starts, with advance preparation for procedures, routines, and materials associated with each of the seven student positions. But teachers who want to try the approach after the year has begun will find they can put Win-Win Discipline in place at any time. You will need to teach the fundamental concepts and procedures thoroughly, but once your students are comfortable with them, the program is relatively easy to maintain.

Commentary from Anonymous Teacher 2

My first student-teaching assignment was with an eighth-grade class taught by a cool, calm, and collected master teacher. She made everything look so easy. I was young and very green and really thought if I were kind to the students they would behave nicely. As luck would have it, most of them did, but not Stevie and Nickie, twin sisters who wanted to rule the world, or at least the class. They did whatever they could to mess up my lessons and my composure, and they were very successful at both. My master teacher invited me over for dinner and gently let me know that my students didn't need another friend, they needed a Teacher, and it was up to me to become one. I learned there must be a system in place to define the "society" of the classroom. I wish I had had the insight of Win-Win to help me and the students.

In staff lounges and workrooms, or anywhere teachers congregate, you will hear some lamenting, "In addition to teaching, we have to civilize them, too!" It is true; many students come to us not really knowing how to work respectfully with others or how to be responsible for their own behavior. What I like about Kagan's plan is it doesn't overlook the power that we teachers do have: the power to create interesting lessons; the power to organize meaningful cooperative activities; the power to be a dynamic teacher. But in addition, he gives us "handles" to help us grasp how disruptions and emotions can get in the way of a peaceful and productive classroom. For me, personally, Win-Win provides a way that I can be more objective about misbehavior, more understanding of students and their emotions, and best of all, have access to a plan to help them. I really wish I could have a second chance to work with Stevie and Nickie. I know I could do better now.

Activities

Self-Test: True/False

1. By "structure," Kagan means a series of steps designed to help students experience success in a particular situation.
2. Kagan would have you use structures, but not accept the student's inappropriate behavior or his or her internal "position."
3. Kagan identifies seven positions that disruptive students are said to be "coming from."
4. "Same side" refers to teachers and students working together, including how the class goes about correcting misbehavior.
5. The four categories of student disruptions are defiance, dishonesty, lack of courtesy, and offensiveness.
6. Structures, when used to redirect misbehavior, are organized to address particular combinations of disruptions and student positions.
7. Kagan warns teachers against trying to be friends with students, as friendships damage the normal lines of authority in the classroom.
8. Kagan advises teachers to keep caregivers and the community informed about discipline problems that are occurring in the class.
9. The three pillars of Win-Win Discipline are same side, collaborative solutions, and learned responsibility.
10. Kagan says teachers should validate (acknowledge as normal) students' positions of anger and desire to control.

Self-Test: Multiple Choice

1. Kagan says students "come from"
   (a) structures.
   (b) positions.
   (c) frames of reference.
   (d) interpersonal events.
2. At how many main points in time are responsive structures applied?
   (a) 3
   (b) 6
   (c) 9
   (d) 12
3. "Impulse control" is an example of a
   (a) reactive structure.
   (b) long-term success structure.
   (c) imposed structure.
   (d) moment-of-disruption structure.
4. Structures can most properly be thought of as
   (a) student needs.
   (b) teacher needs.
   (c) involvement of caregivers.
   (d) teacher plans of action.
5. Which of the following is a "pillar" of Win-Win Discipline?
   (a) rules specificity
   (b) learned responsibility
   (c) classroom meetings
   (d) conflict resolution

6. Which of the following is *not* an ABCD of disruptive behavior?
   (a) aggression
   (b) breaking rules
   (c) confrontation
   (d) disrespect
7. What should teachers do first when addressing disruptive behavior?
   (a) acknowledge
   (b) identify
   (c) prescribe
   (d) apply
8. When students disrupt, they are coming from an emotional state that is
   (a) overwrought.
   (b) contrived.
   (c) natural.
   (d) short-lived.
9. When students disrupt, you should accept their
   (a) positions.
   (b) attitude.
   (c) behaviors.
   (d) structures.
10. The ultimate goal of Win-Win Discipline is
   (a) good citizenship.
   (b) high achievement.
   (c) class energy.
   (d) responsible self-control.

Self-Test: Explain This

1. What does Kagan identify as comprising the "three pillars" of Win-Win Discipline?

2. What categories of disruptive behavior does Kagan identify?
3. Explain what Kagan means by disruptions, positions, and structures.
4. Explain the relation or interplay between disruptive behavior, position, and structure.
5. As Kagan explains it, what does "same side" mean, and how do you get there?

Additional Suggested Activities

1. In your journal, enter ideas from Win-Win Discipline that you might wish to include in your own system of discipline.
2. Working with a partner, check yourselves to make sure you understand the following elements and ideas in Win-Win Discipline: ABCD of disruptive behavior; Big Three; class rules; student positions; structures; follow-up structures; long-term structures; the three pillars.
3. Win-Win Discipline rests on three pillars—same side, collaborative solutions, and learned responsibility. How would you go about communicating these key principles to students?
4. To what extent do you feel you could put Win-Win Discipline into effect in your classroom? What portions do you believe you could implement easily? What portions do you believe might present difficulty?

<hr>

Concept Cases

CASE 1   Kristina Will Not Work

Kristina, a student in Mr. Jake's class, is quite docile. She socializes little with other students and never disrupts lessons. However, despite Mr. Jake's best efforts, Kristina will not do her work. She rarely completes an assignment. She is simply there, putting forth no effort at all. *What would Spencer Kagan suggest to help Kristina and Mr. Jake?*

Kagan would advise Mr. Jake to do the following: Mr. Jake would identify Kristina's problematic behavior and ask behavior-specific questions. He also would identify and help Kristina acknowledge her position. Mr. Jake might ask Kristina how she feels about the work, determining if it is too difficult for her (leading to avoidance of failure), or not interesting (leading to boredom). If the work is too difficult for Kristina, and her position is avoiding, or if she doesn't know how to do the work, he might say quietly, "I really want to help you be successful, Kristina. I see this work is not getting finished. None of us wants to tackle something we know will be too hard for us. The best thing to do if something is too hard is to break it into smaller pieces, mastering a part at a time. Another good strategy is to work on the difficult pieces with someone else. What suggestions do you have that will help you be successful?"

Together they come up with possible solutions and then, if they agree that Kristina could benefit by working with a partner on smaller pieces, Mr. Jake may ask, "Would you like to work on this section with Danielle before moving on?" Throughout the interaction, Mr. Jake is attempting to help Kristina find a nondisruptive way to meet her needs. But more important, Mr. Jake is helping Kristina internalize a process of validating her own needs and seeking responsible rather than disruptive ways to fulfill them. As follow-up, Mr. Jake might focus on her success by saying something like "Kristina, I knew you could do this if we tried making the pieces smaller." His long-term solutions will include further encouragement and individual attention to Kristina's strengths.

CASE 2   Sara Will Not Stop Talking

Sara is a pleasant girl who participates in class activities and does most, though not all, of her assigned work. She cannot seem to refrain from talking to classmates, however. Her teacher, Mr. Gonzales, has to speak to her repeatedly during lessons, to the point that he often becomes exasperated and loses his temper. *What suggestions would Spencer Kagan give Mr. Gonzales for dealing with Sara?*

CASE 3   Joshua Clowns and Intimidates

Joshua, larger and louder than his classmates, always wants to be the center of attention, which he accomplishes through a combination of clowning and intimidation. He makes wise remarks, talks back (smilingly) to the teacher, utters a variety of sound-effect noises such as automobile crashes and gunshots, and makes limitless sarcastic comments and put-downs of his classmates. Other students will not stand up to him, apparently fearing his size and verbal aggression. His teacher, Miss Pearl, has come to her wit's end. *Would Joshua's behavior be likely to improve if Win-Win Discipline were used in Miss Pearl's classroom? Explain.*

CASE 4   Tom Is Hostile and Defiant

Tom has appeared to be in his usual foul mood ever since arriving in class. On his way to sharpen his pencil, he bumps into Frank, who complains. Tom tells him loudly to shut up. Miss Baines, the teacher, says, "Tom, go back to your seat." Tom wheels around, swears loudly, and says heatedly, "I'll go when I'm _____ good and ready!" *How would Tom's behavior be handled in a Win-Win classroom?*

You Are the Teacher

MIDDLE SCHOOL WORLD HISTORY

Your third-period world history class is comprised of students whose achievement levels vary from high to well below average. You pace their work accordingly, ask them to work cooperatively, and make sure everyone understands what they are supposed to do. For the most part, you enjoy the class, finding the students interesting and refreshing. Your lessons follow a consistent pattern. First, you ask the students to read in groups from the textbook, then you call on students at random to answer selected questions about the material. If a student who is called on is unable to answer a question, the group he or she represents loses a point.

If able to answer correctly, the group gains a point. For partially correct answers, the group neither receives nor loses a point. For the second part of the period, the class groups do something productive or creative connected with the material they have read, such as making posters, writing a story, doing a skit, or the like. As appropriate, these efforts are shared with members of the class.

A TYPICAL OCCURRENCE

You call on Hillary to answer a question. Although she has been participating, she shakes her head. This has happened several times before. Not wanting to hurt Hillary's feelings, you simply say, "That costs the group a point," and you call on someone else. Unfortunately, Hillary's group gets upset at her. The other students make comments under their breath. Later, Clarisse also refuses to answer. When you speak with her about it, she says, "You didn't make Hillary do it."

You answer, "Look, we are talking about you, not Hillary." However, you let the matter lie and say no more. Just then, Deonne comes into the class late, appearing very angry. He slams his pack down on his desk and sits without opening his textbook. Although you

want to talk with Deonne, you don't know how to approach him at that time. Will is in the opposite mood.

Throughout the oral reading portion of the class, he continually giggles at every mispronounced word and at every reply students give to your questions. Will sits at the front of the class and turns around to laugh, seeing if he can get anyone else to laugh with him. He makes some *oooh* and *aaaah* sounds when Hillary and Clarisse decline to respond. Although most students either ignore him or give him disgusted looks, he keeps laughing. You finally ask him what is so funny.

He replies, "Nothing in particular," and looks back at the class and laughs. At the end of the period, there is time for sharing three posters students have made. Will makes comments and giggles about each of them. Clarisse, who has not participated, says, "Will, how about shutting up!" As the students leave the room, you take Deonne aside. "Is something wrong, Deonne?" you ask. "No," he replies. His jaw is clenched as he strides past you.

CONCEPTUALIZING A STRATEGY

If you followed Kagan's suggestions, what would you do with regard to the following?

- Preventing the problems from occurring in the first place?
- Putting an immediate end to the misbehavior?
- Involving other or all students in addressing the situation?
- Maintaining student dignity and good personal relations?
- Using follow-up procedures to prevent the recurrence of the misbehavior?
- Helping the students involved develop increased responsibility and self-control?

11

Paula Cook on Helping Students Who Exhibit Neurological-Based Behavior

What Is Neurological-Based Behavior, How Does It Impact Your Students and You, and How Can You Help Students Who Have It?

The information you explored in previous chapters pertained primarily to students who are able to control their behavior, whether acceptable or unacceptable. But unfortunately, not all students can reliably control themselves. Some students—estimated at about 1 in 10—are at times notably erratic in what they say and do. This behavior that is not always under one's self-control is referred to as neurological-based behavior (NBB). In most cases, the brain's informational processing capability has been compromised. As you can imagine, NBB poses special challenges for both teachers and students.

WHO IS PAULA COOK?

The lead author of this chapter is Paula Cook, a specialist in teaching students who display NBB. Many of the students with whom she works have average or above-average intelligence, but are challenged by behavioral manifestations occasioned by emotional or other psychiatric disorders. Dr. Cook's responsibilities have to do with curriculum modifications and adaptations, individualized educational planning, advocacy, behavior management, and social and life skills education. She also teaches at Red River Community College and the University of Manitoba. She has made numerous presentations at regional, national, and international conferences, and in 2003 received the Council for Exceptional Children's Outstanding Educator of the Year award.

WHAT IS COOK'S MODEL OF DISCIPLINE FOR STUDENTS WITH NBB?

The Common Goal of All Approaches to Discipline
Responsible, Civil Classroom Behavior That
Becomes Habitual and Lasts over Time.
Responsible means paying attention, making a strong effort,
and doing what is proper without being told.
Civil means respectful, polite, cordial, and well mannered.

↑

Paula Cook's Approach to Discipline

↓   ↑

Cook's Overarching Strategy
Provide conditions and support that allow
each student to feel secure and have the
best possible access to learning.

↓   ↑

Cook's Principal Tactics
Attempt to provide each and every student the
best learning opportunities possible. Assess each
student's particular needs and provide the specific
support he or she requires.
Work toward helping each student develop
the self-control needed for successful
participation in group settings.
Reduce or eliminate distractive conditions
in the classroom environment.
Celebrate every student's progress
and never give up.

↓   ↑

↓ —————— → —————— ↑

WHAT QUESTIONS WILL THIS CHAPTER ANSWER FOR ME?

- What is neurological-based behavior (NBB), and how is it manifested?
- What kinds of behavior might indicate that a student has NBB?
- What two diagnoses within NBB are you almost certain to encounter?
- What are the additional diagnoses within NBB that you are likely to encounter?

■ How might you work more effectively with students with NBB?
■ What is the nature of rage, and how does one deal with it?

WHAT IS NEUROLOGICAL-BASED BEHAVIOR (NBB)?

Neurological-based behavior refers to the erratic behavior that sometimes occurs when one's cerebral processes do not function in a "normal" manner (Kranowitz, 2005). In school, almost all classes contain one or more students with NBB. Most teachers find NBB a special challenge because it is difficult to understand and does not respond reliably to ordinary discipline tactics.

Scenario 1 Tyler

Tyler began the morning by refusing to participate in opening activities. He chose instead to make beeping sounds. After the opening activities, the class was to read quietly on their own for 10 minutes, but Tyler decided to sing loudly. When asked to stop, he began to hoot. He was belligerent and noisy for some time. He poked Jackie with a pencil, chewed the eraser off his pencil and swallowed it, and insisted on writing on his math sheet with a tiny piece of pencil lead moistened with spittle. He refused to comply with academic instructions until it was almost time for recess. During recess, Tyler pushed, poked, hit, and tried to choke other students. He laughed when they protested. He engaged in violent play fantasies and was extremely argumentative with the teachers on duty, swearing at them and insisting they could not make him do anything he didn't want to do. Finally, Tyler had to be led physically back to the classroom. He screamed that his rights were being violated and that he would sue the school and kill the teachers.

Tyler worked the rest of the morning alone in the resource room with the resource teacher. In the afternoon, he was well behaved, compliant, and willing and able to participate and learn.

Application: After you have read this chapter, you will be asked in the Activities section to return to this scenario and, with a fellow teacher or classmate, discuss Tyler's behavior and reflect on how one might address it.

Students such as Tyler behave erratically or inconsistently for reasons that are mysterious to teachers, sometimes even to those who have been specially trained. The behavior in question is believed to result from a compromised ability to process information correctly, a condition that can be caused by chemical imbalances in the brain, congenital brain differences, brain injuries, or brain diseases (Cook, 2004a; Greene, 2001; Hall & Hall, 2003; Kranowitz, 1998; Papolos & Papolos, 2002).

*Note: This chapter contains seven scenarios describing episodes of behavior of real students with whom Dr. Cook has worked. The students' names have been changed to protect anonymity.

Because **neurological differences** are not easily diagnosed, the affected students often do not receive the help they need for several years after their symptoms first appear.

Please remember that students with NBB are not abstractions, but real people struggling to deal with life. When ordinary discipline procedures do not help them behave productively in the classroom, it is not because the students are "bad" or "too far gone" or come from "horrible families." Rather, they behave as they do because of the way their brains work, and their brains cannot always control their behavior in ways that serve them best.

Indicators: What Would Suggest That a Student Might Have NBB?

Three indicators—behavior difficulties, language difficulties, and academic difficulties—can each signal the strong possibility that a student might be exhibiting NBB.

Behavior difficulties are frequently the first indication that something unusual is occurring in the student, especially if the behavior is atypical, inconsistent, compulsive, or immune to normal behavior management. Such behavior may result from a neurological event that is promoting confusion, uncertainty, fear, or frustration. Later in the chapter you will find suggestions to help you manage the behavior of students with NBB.

Language difficulties include problems in understanding, processing, and expressing information verbally. Classroom interactions operate on the assumption that language is understood in more or less the same way by all students and teachers. But such is not the case for students with NBB, who often do not interpret, understand, process, respond to, or use language in a normal manner (Cook, 2004a; Cook, Kellie, Jones, & Goossen, 2000; Greene, 2001; Hall & Hall, 2003).

Suggestions: If you notice students who seem to have difficulty understanding, or who are not complying with expectations or requests, try using fewer words and increase the wait time for compliance. Make your directions clear, concrete, and consistent. You may need to show directions physically as well as explain them verbally. Ask students to repeat the directions or show you they understand what they are supposed to do.

Academic difficulties vary among students with NBB. Some of those difficulties are easily recognized and dealt with. Some are not. Memory is often compromised in students with NBB, resulting in variable gaps in learning. Difficulties with fine and gross motor skills, comprehension, language, and mathematics are often evident.

Suggestions: If you have a student with NBB who has been approved for special services, take note of what the special education teachers do. You can adapt and use some of their strategies in your normal teaching. Doing so will benefit not only students with NBB, but may benefit other students as well. One example involves providing differentiated instruction that is in keeping with Howard Gardner's (1999) theory of multiple intelligences, which involves teaching concepts in various ways. That approach provides support for students by helping with comprehension while pinpointing specific strengths and weaknesses.

THE TWO MOST COMMON DIAGNOSES IN NBB: WHAT ARE THEY?

The two most prevalent diagnoses within NBB are learning disabilities (LD) and attention-deficit hyperactivity disorder (ADHD). **Learning disabilities** are associated with particular areas of the school curriculum, such as reading or mathematics. **Attention-deficit hyperactivity disorder** is characterized by student restlessness and short attention span. Let's go into a bit more detail about these two frequently encountered diagnoses.

Learning Disabilities: How Are They Manifested, and How Can I Help?

Learning disabilities (LD) are neurobiological disorders that interfere with learning in specific subjects or topics. They are categorized by the academic areas in which difficulties are identified. Some of the common learning disabilities are *dyslexia*, which is difficulty in processing language; *dyscalculia*, difficulty with basic mathematics; *dysgraphia*, difficulty with handwriting and spelling; and *dyspraxia*, difficulty with fine motor skills (National Council for Learning Disabilities [NCLD], 2005).

Because LD is so often confused with other diagnoses, it is useful to note that learning disabilities are *not* the same as attention disorders, although the two may occur together. Nor are learning disabilities the same as mental retardation, autism, auditory or visual impairment, physical disabilities, or emotional disorders. Learning disabilities are *not* caused by lack of educational opportunities, frequent changes of schools, poor school attendance, or lack of instruction in basic skills.

Learning disabilities *are* difficulties in learning in certain areas, especially reading, writing, and mathematics. They appear to be inherited, and they affect girls and boys equally. Students never outgrow their particular LD, but with support and intervention, they can be successful in learning and life.

What Are Indicators of LD?

At various stages, individuals with average or above-average intelligence may display characteristics that indicate learning disabilities. Such indicators include the following (NCLD, 2005):

- Inability to discriminate between/among letters, numerals, or sounds.
- Difficulty sounding out words; reluctance to read aloud; avoidance of reading and/or writing tasks.
- Poor grasp of abstract concepts; poor memory; difficulty telling time.
- Confusion between right and left.
- Distractibility, restlessness, impulsiveness; trouble following directions.
- Saying one thing but meaning another; responding inappropriately.
- Slow work pace; short attention span; difficulty listening and remembering.
- Eye–hand coordination problems; poor organizational skills.

Specialized psychological and academic testing is needed to confirm a suspected LD. In some countries, the law requires that the diagnosis be made by a multidisciplinary group, including the teacher, student, other school staff, family members, and professionals such as psychologists, reading clinicians, and speech and language therapists. Based on their assessment and on the availability of resources, special services may be provided to the student at school.

Scenario 2 Justin

The class had just finished a discussion of a chapter in the book they were reading. Justin actively participated in the discussion, making correct and well-thought-out responses. Mr. Gatta, the teacher, then instructed the class to complete a chapter summary sheet at their desks. Justin needed to be told a second time to get started. Justin put his feet up on his desk and began to belch loudly. The students laughed. Mr. Gatta asked Justin to stop belching and take his feet off his desk, whereupon Justin put his feet down and wrapped his legs around the legs of his desk. He then leaned back and made himself fall backwards, pulling his desk on top of him.

When Mr. Gatta came to help disentangle Justin from the furniture, Justin grabbed the desk, wrapped his legs tighter around it, squealed loudly, and laughed uncontrollably.

Commentary: Justin shows great reluctance to write down answers, even though he can say them correctly. His behavior may be linked to a learning disability, and there may also be other neural issues involved.

What Is Dyslexia?

Dyslexia is the most widespread and commonly diagnosed of all learning disabilities, affecting over 40 million American children and adults (Dolphin Education, 2006). It is characterized by difficulties in word recognition, spelling, word decoding, and occasionally the phonological (sound) component of language.

From a young age, students with dyslexia show deficits in coordination, attention, and reading, which often damage their self-concept and sense of competence. The other cognitive faculties of people who have dyslexia are believed to function properly.

Examinations of thousands of students with reading disabilities revealed that while none showed evidence of a brain or linguistic impairment, over 95% had clear-cut balance, coordination, and rhythmic difficulties that are indicators of an inner ear/cerebellar dysfunction (Levinson, 2000). Although dyslexia makes learning difficult, many people with dyslexia are very high achievers, as exemplified by Albert Einstein, Thomas Edison, and Winston Churchill.

Attention-Deficit Hyperactivity Disorder: How Can I Help Students Who Have This Diagnosis?

Attention-deficit hyperactivity disorder (ADHD) is the second most common diagnosis in NBB. It affects about 10% of the school population (Kahn & Faraone, 2006) and is characterized by short attention span, weak impulse control, and hyperactivity, all of which inhibit learning and often promote misbehavior. ADHD can begin in infancy and extend into adulthood, with negative effects on the individual's life at home, in school, and in the community.

The cause of ADHD is not known. Maternal alcohol consumption or drug use during pregnancy is often associated with ADHD, as are childhood maladies such as viral infections, meningitis, encephalitis, head injury, and epilepsy (Millichap, 2008). The role of heredity is not as significant as once thought. More males than females have the condition. Among students with attention-deficit disorder (ADD), males typically have ADD with hyperactivity, whereas females typically have ADD without hyperactivity (Amen, 2001). ADHD often occurs in combination with other diagnoses.

Suggestions: You can do a number of things to promote success among students with ADHD, such as:

- Maintain a highly structured classroom. Use a written schedule augmented with pictures to support the structure. Keep assignment folders and equipment in specific and consistent places with specific locations for all materials (pencil pouches, tabs in notebooks, etc).
- Build small sequential steps into the classroom routine.
- Examine the class environment when the student is on-task, and when the student is off-task. Look for differences that might help or hinder the student.
- Keep at hand extra pencils, texts, and other materials for students to use when they cannot find their own.
- Give written/pictorial directions whenever possible rather than auditory prompting.
- Give fewer problems/questions on worksheets and consider using "window boxes," which are pieces of paper with a hole cut in them. The hole exposes only the question the student is to work on, but covers the rest of the questions on the page.
- Use a visual timer to help the student understand time constraints.
- Limit distractions as much as possible.
- Color code materials. Cover the textbook for one course in the same color as the notebook for that subject.
- Be aware of where the student is seated. Sit in the child's desk and observe the environment. Understand that stimulation and variety in the classroom often adversely affect students with ADHD or ADD. You may also wish to seat the child at an individual desk rather than a table and have separate work areas for different activities, which seems to help students with ADHD work better.
- Give advance warning of when a transition is going to take place (now we are completing the worksheet, next we will . . .) and the expectation for the transition (and you will need . . .). Visual timers are good for transitions.
- Allow students to doodle or manipulate quiet fidget items, such as stress or foam balls, or small plastic items; this can improve their attention level. If students begin to tap their pencils on their desks, ask them to tap their thighs instead.
- Tape a large piece of coarse sandpaper on the top inside of the student's desk, for the student to rub when he or she needs to pay attention.

- Decrease auditory and visual distractions during difficult or new tasks. Study carrels or corners away from the group can be beneficial.
- Specifically say and display lists of materials needed. List steps necessary to complete each assignment.
- Allow the student to get into a comfortable position while learning.
- Have lists, calendars, charts, pictures, and finished products in the classroom for students to refer to.
- Provide short movement breaks, such as allowing the student with ADHD to pass out papers, run errands, or go for a drink of water.

WHAT OTHER DIAGNOSES IN NBB AM I LIKELY TO ENCOUNTER?

It is very likely you will find among your students some who have other diagnoses in NBB. You can expect at one time or another to work with students who have sensory integration dysfunction (SID), bipolar disorder, oppositional defiant disorder (ODD), autism spectrum disorder (ASD), fetal alcohol spectrum disorder (FASD), and brain injuries. These diagnoses, along with LD and ADHD, are considered to be **mental health conditions** (American Academy of Child and Adolescent Psychiatry [AACAP], 2004a). Information is presented here to alert you to these diagnoses and their implications.

It is important to recognize that students with mental health disorders cannot overcome their difficulties through willpower. Their conditions are not related to their character or intelligence. Most of their disorders can be treated successfully with medication, but in some cases, the medication adversely affects attention, concentration, and stamina (National Institute of Mental Health, 2008). Psychosocial support, provided in part by schools, can also be helpful.

Sensory Integration Dysfunction: How Can I Help Students Who Have This Diagnosis?

Sensory integration dysfunction (SID)—also called **sensory processing disorder**—reflects abnormalities in organizing, interpreting, and responding to information taken in through the senses. Sensory integration occurs automatically to keep us informed, ready to act, and able to protect ourselves. At times and for some people, flaws in the process result in incorrect perception and interpretation of information. Impaired processing of information may lead in turn to inappropriate behavior and poor learning.

Most teachers know little about SID, even though it is suspected of being a major cause of hyperactivity, inattention, fidgety movements, inability to calm down, impulsivity, lack of self-control, disorganization, language difficulties, and learning difficulties (Cook, 2008; Kranowitz, 1998; Kranowitz, Szkut, Balzer-Martin, Haber, & Sava, 2003). Some students' sensory processing systems seem to be easily overwhelmed by excess visual and auditory stimulation.

Suggestions: You can help those students by keeping the classroom neat and tidy, removing sources of loud or unpredictable noise, enlarging printed questions or directions, and standing in front of a solid white overhead screen when giving instructions and directing lessons, all of which reduce distractions from extraneous sources. You should also give directions slowly and distinctly, check that students have understood correctly, and maintain a sense of calm.

Scenario 3 Jimmy

Jimmy entered kindergarten in September. By January, his behavior was worse than when he began school. Every day he had a series of tantrums, usually beginning when he arrived at school. He sometimes complied with directions, but more often, especially during changes of activity, he might scream, cry, kick, flail his arms, fall to the floor, or run out of the classroom.

During his "episodes," he had kicked and hit staff members and assaulted students who were in his way. Jimmy's home life was unremarkable. He had an older sibling, both parents, and lived in a quiet neighborhood. His family environment was loving and stable. His parents were very concerned about his behavior. Jimmy did not have any diagnosed neurological conditions. His mother did not drink or use illicit substances during her pregnancy. The pregnancy and his birth were deemed typical.

Commentary: This child, with no diagnosis other than his behavior to suggest neurological dysfunction, was having a terrible experience in school. His teacher ultimately changed the classroom environment to cut down sensory stimulation, after which Jimmy's behavior improved considerably.

Bipolar Disorder: How Can I Help Students Who Have This Diagnosis?

Bipolar is an affective disorder characterized by severe mood swings that occur in cycles of mania and depression, or highs and lows. Individuals with bipolar disorder can change abruptly from irritable, angry, and easily annoyed, to silly, goofy, giddy, and disruptive, after which they return again to low-energy periods of boredom, depression, and social withdrawal (AACAP, 2004c). The abrupt swings of mood and energy, which in some individuals occur several times a day, are often accompanied by poor frustration tolerance, outbursts of temper, and oppositional defiant behavior. Students with bipolar disorder are also frequently diagnosed with sensory integration dysfunction (Papolos & Papolos, 2002).

The cause of bipolar disorder is not known. The disorder was once thought to be rare in children, but recent research shows it can begin very early in life and is much more common than previously believed. Proper drugs can stabilize mood swings, and cognitive therapy and counseling can often help. Indicators of bipolar disorder in school students include the following (Papolos & Papolos, 2002):

- Episodes of hysterical laughing and infectious happiness for no evident reason, followed by periods of lethargy.
- Belligerence and argumentation, often followed by self-recrimination.
- Jumping from topic to topic in rapid succession when speaking.

Oppositional Defiant Disorder: How Can I Help Students Who Have This Diagnosis?

You expect some of your students to talk back to you now and then, argue, and disregard your directives. You don't enjoy such behavior, but probably realize it is a normal occurrence in human development. However, an occasional student will behave in a manner so uncooperative and hostile that it not only drives you to distraction but also damages the student's social, academic, and family life. That sort of behavior is characteristic of oppositional defiant disorder (ODD).

The American Academy of Child and Adolescent Psychiatry (2004b) lists the following as symptoms of ODD:

- Frequent temper tantrums
- Excessive arguing with adults
- Active defiance and refusal to comply with adult requests and rules
- Belligerent and sarcastic remarks, made when directly praised
- Deliberate attempts to annoy or upset people
- Blaming others for one's own mistakes or misbehavior
- Being touchy or easily annoyed by others
- Speaking hatefully when upset
- Seeking revenge

The AACAP (2004b) reports that 5 to 15% of all school-age children have ODD. Its cause is not known.

Suggestions: If you have a student who displays the characteristics of ODD, you might consider using positive reinforcement when the student shows flexibility or cooperation. Indirect or earshot praise sometimes works well, such as when the student "overhears" two adults talking positively about him or her (intending to be overheard).

It is also helpful to reduce the number of words you use when speaking to a student with ODD (Hall & Hall, 2003). A suggested procedure is to say and show what you mean, just once, and then do not explain yourself further. Students will ask for more information if they need it, and then you can provide what they need. If you feel your responses are about to make the conflict worse, take a personal time-out. This allows you to calm down, and it also presents a good model for the student.

Autism Spectrum Disorder: How Can I Help Students Who Have This Diagnosis?

Autism spectrum disorder (ASD) includes various diagnoses of abnormal development in verbal and nonverbal communication, along with impaired social development and restricted, repetitive, and stereotyped behaviors and interests (Faraone, 2003). It also includes delays in the development of socialization and communication skills and Asperger syndrome, which is a pattern of behavior among students of normal intelligence and language development who also exhibit autistic-like behaviors and marked deficiencies in social and communication skills.

At present, about 1 in every 110 children is diagnosed with autism. However, that proportion is increasing (Autism Speaks, 2010). It affects four times as many males as females. Students with ASD may show extreme hyperactivity or extreme passivity in relating to people around them. In its milder form, autism resembles a learning disability. Indicators of ASD include the following:

- Self-stimulation, spinning, rocking, and hand flapping
- Obsessive compulsive behaviors such as lining objects up evenly
- Repetitive odd play for extended periods of time
- Insistence on routine and sameness
- Difficulty dealing with interruption of routine schedule and change
- Monotone voice and difficulty carrying on social conversations
- Inflexibility of thought and language (e.g., one student with autism refused to wear his winter jacket during subzero weather in early December because he had learned winter did not officially begin until December 21)

Manifestations of autism vary enormously in severity. Sensory integration dysfunction is also common in students with ASD, and sensory overload can lead to behavior problems in school.

Suggestions: Modifying the physical environment can do much to improve behavior and academic achievement of students with ASD. Some people with autism never develop language and need full-time care, whereas others become fully functioning, independent members of society, as exemplified by Temple Grandin, perhaps the world's most accomplished and well-known adult with autism. Dr. Grandin has appeared on major television programs such as *Today, Larry King Live, 48 Hours,* and *20/20,* and has been featured in publications such as *Time, People, Forbes, U.S. News and World Report,* and the *New York Times* (see www.templegrandin.org).

Scenario 4 Tay

Tay is extremely noisy. Even during quiet work time, she taps, hums, or makes other noises. When the teacher asks her to stop, she denies doing anything. She talks very loudly. When classmates ask her to be quiet, she ignores them.

Tay wears three pairs of socks all the time and adjusts the cuffs on each pair a number of times a day. She cannot settle down and focus until her socks are just right. She will not change shoes for gym class. When the gym teacher tried to make her do so, Tay swore at her and ran out of the gym and away from school, crying hysterically. When dashing across the street, Tay ran into the side of a parked car, then fell to the road and sobbed until a teacher came to get her.

Commentary: Tay is diagnosed with ASD with extreme SID. Outside noise bothers her greatly, so she makes her own noise to drown it out. It is speculated that she wears the three pairs of socks to put extra pressure on her feet, which would be an indicator of SID, as is her continual cuff adjustment. Things that have been done to help her benefit more from school include (a) providing ear covers to block outside noise, (b) using a portable radio/CD player with headphones to drown out other noise, (c) giving her chewing gum or mints to help keep her mouth quiet, (d) overlooking her sock rituals, which are not a major issue, and (e) compromising by allowing Tay to decide whether she will change shoes for gym class or move to an alternate activity arranged for her, which includes instruction in social skills in her individualized education program.

Fetal Alcohol Spectrum Disorder: How Can I Help Students Who Have This Diagnosis?

FASD is a group of neurobehavioral and developmental abnormalities that includes fetal alcohol syndrome (FAS), alcohol-related neurodevelopmental disorder (ARND), and partial fetal alcohol syndrome (pFAS). The spectrum affects about 1% of the population in the United States (Clark, Lutke, Minnes, & Ouellette-Kuntz, 2004).

The disorder results from the fetus being exposed to alcohol from the mother's blood. Ingestion of even small amounts of alcohol by the mother, as little as 1 ounce per week, has been linked to delinquent and aggressive behavior in the child. The Centers for Disease Control and Prevention (CDC) contend that alcohol consumption by pregnant mothers is a significant contributor to brain impairment and that no level of alcohol consumption during pregnancy is considered to be safe (CDC, 2004). This conclusion was challenged, however, by findings in a large study in the UK that showed no ill effects in offspring whose mothers were "light drinkers" during pregnancy (Brooks, 2010).

Most individuals with FAS and other diagnoses on the FASD continuum have normal intelligence (Streissguth, Barr, Kogan, & Bookstein, 1997). At the same time, many of them have compromised adaptive and social skills, including poor impulse control, poor judgment, tendency to miss social cues, lack of common sense, learning difficulties, and difficulty with the tasks of daily living. ADHD usually occurs in association with FASD, and behavior difficulties are common (Kellerman, 2003).

Scenario 5 Sam

Sam, age 10, never sits still in class. He is always talking and calling out answers in class even though they are usually wrong. Yesterday he pushed a classmate when they were coming in from recess. The teacher spoke to him, reminded him of the rules, and told him he could not go out for recess that afternoon.

This morning, Sam was reminded to keep his hands to himself or he would lose recess again. Sam repeated word for word what he was told: "I will keep my hands to myself and if I don't I won't be able to go out for recess this afternoon." Fifteen minutes later Sam pushed Jonathan. When the teacher spoke to him, Sam claimed he didn't do anything and it wasn't his fault.

Commentary: Sam has been diagnosed with FASD and ADHD. His repeating back the words and consequences indicates language-processing difficulties common to FASD. Like other students with the condition, he reacts automatically to situations without always remembering what he did. Calling out and inability to sit still indicate ADHD.

Brain Injuries: What Are They?

Brain injuries, traumatic and nontraumatic, often inhibit the brain's ability to function in a normal manner. Traumatic injuries result from blows to the head incurred during events such as accidents, sporting events, or assaults. Nontraumatic injuries result from disrupted blood flow to the brain (as in strokes), or from tumors, infections, drug overdoses, and certain medical conditions (Brain Injury Society of Virginia, 2012.). The effects of severe injuries are readily apparent, but mild injuries may go unrecognized even when they have a significant effect on behavior. Because brain injuries affect behavior in so many different ways, students' resultant limitations must be diagnosed and special instruction devised to help with particular difficulties.

Rage: How Can I Recognize and Respond to It?

You may never experience an episode of rage in your classroom, but the following information will help you if you do.

Rage is not normally listed as a type of neurological disorder, but rather is an extreme kind of behavior sometimes exhibited by students with NBB. Puzzling and frightening, it displays as an explosion of temper that occurs suddenly, with little warning, and may turn violent (Packer, 2005). The process is traumatic for everyone and should be understood as a neurological event that involves behavior over which the student has little control.

Rage differs from tantrums, which are goal-directed with the purpose of getting something or getting somebody to do something. Rage is not goal-oriented. Rather, it is a release of built-up tension or frustration. (Tantrums sometimes evolve into rage.) Once a rage episode has begun, there is little one can do to stop it. It may only last for a few minutes, or may continue for hours. Although it usually has to run its course, it can be softened and controlled somewhat by teachers and other adults.

Four phases comprise the **rage cycle**: (1) triggering, (2) escalation, (3) rage, and (4) post-rage. These phases, their characteristics, and how you can help in each of them are described in the following observations and suggestions (Cook, 2008b; Echternach & Cook, 2004; Greene, 2001; Hill, 2005; Packer, 2005).

Phase 1: Triggering

Triggers are precipitating events that provoke or set in motion episodes of rage, apparently by initiating neurochemical changes in the brain that greatly heighten the self-protective responses commonly called fight/flight/freeze reactions. In classrooms, triggering conditions seem to be associated at times with work transitions, sensory overload, being told "No," fatigue, frustration, confusion, hunger, anxiety, and mood swings. For children with ADHD, triggers tend to be related to sensory and/or emotional overstimulation. For children with bipolar disorder, triggers are often related to having limits set on their behavior (Papolos & Papolos, 2002). In the triggering phase, students may appear angry, confused, frustrated, dazed, tense, or flushed, and they may swear and use other rude language.

Suggestions: When a student is in this phase:

■ Recognize that a rage episode has begun and you may not be able to prevent it.
■ Understand that this is a neurological event. The student's flight/fight/freeze responses are strongly activated.

- Understand that the rage is not intentional or personal toward you.
- Stay calm. Use a quiet tone of voice. Do not become adversarial.
- Use nonthreatening body language. Stand at an angle off-center to the student, at least a long stride away. Make sure the student can see your hands.
- Use empathic verbal support ("It sounds like you're upset." "That would upset me too.").
- Deflect control elsewhere ("The clock says it's time to clean up." "The big rule book in the office says . . .").
- Calmly, quietly, and succinctly use logical persuasion to provide the student an alternative behavior.

Phase 2: Escalation

Following the triggering, the rage may escalate mildly or rapidly. In *mild escalations*, the student may begin to get angry, call names, swear, exhibit startled verbal or physical responses, talk rapidly, increase the volume and cadence of speech, and show tension in the arms, hands, and body. *Rapid escalations* are characterized by violent temper, hostility, aggressive comments ("Leave me alone!" "I'm going to kill you!"), profanity, flushed face, and clammy body. The student may show fists and throw objects or furniture.

Suggestions: When a student is in this phase:

- Remain calm.
- Ensure the safety of others by clearing them from the room or supporting them to ignore the escalation.
- If the student threatens you, walk away.
- Calmly direct the student to a safe place (e.g., Quiet Room or designated area) to allow the energy to dissipate.
- Continue to use short and direct phrases, nonemotional language, and body language that is nonthreatening and nonconfrontational.
- Praise the student as soon as he or she begins to respond to your direction.
- Do not address the student's inappropriate language, threats, or other behavior at this time. The student cannot process the information and may only become further inflamed.

Phase 3: Rage or Meltdown

Here, the student is fully caught up in the rage.
Suggestions: When a student is in this phase:

- Allow the student space to go through the physical manifestations.
- Do not restrain the student unless there is an immediate threat to physical safety.
- Do not question, make sarcastic comments, or try to talk the student out of the rage.
- Do not try to make the student understand instructions.
- While the student is going through the cycle of reactions, support others in the room and help ensure that their interpretations of the rage event are correct.

Phase 4: Post-Rage or Post-Meltdown

After a rage event, the student may or may not remember the behavior or the triggering causes. This is a low point for the student because he or she has expended a great amount of energy and is left confused and often embarrassed. The student will now be tired, passive, headachy, and sometimes remorseful and apologetic. He or she may need sleep.

Suggestions: When a student is in this phase:

- Reassure the student that he or she is all right now.
- When the student is ready, help him or her put language to the event.
- Help him or her plan what to do the next time a rage occurs—such as finding a sensory-friendly refuge (a safe place or room in which to rage), using words to get what he or she needs, and remaining in a safe place until able to calm down.
- After the rage event and when the student is calm, take care of yourself. Relax, drink water, and remind yourself that it was not personal and that you did the best you could. Meanwhile, document your observations, hold debriefing conversations with a colleague, and listen to reflections made by anyone involved.
- Note any evident triggers, sensory influences, or other environmental characteristics that may have precipitated the rage.

MEDICATION: WHAT DO I NEED TO KNOW ABOUT MEDICATION FOR STUDENTS WITH BEHAVIORAL ISSUES?

The U.S. National Institute of Mental Health (2006) affirms that most childhood mental health problems are treatable with medication. However, because the use of medication is controversial, the decision to use it is ultimately made by the parents. If the parents give approval for medication at school, established policies stipulate where the medicine must be stored, who is to administer it, and what teachers and other educators are allowed to say about it. It is important that you familiarize yourself with the medication policies at your school and your attendant responsibilities.

Monitoring the effects of medication is usually a shared responsibility among caregivers, school, and the medical practitioner, with school personnel asked to watch for any unusual behavior or symptoms during the school day. If teachers are asked to give reports of how the child behaved, they are to state them in the following manner: "During the math lesson, Jason got up five times without permission. On one occasion he berated another student." Teachers should not make emotionally charged commentary such as, "Jason was badly out of control and seriously disrupted the class with his antics." In other words, teachers should make sure they avoid vocabulary that reflects their own emotional reactions to the student's behavior.

Managing the Behavior of Students with NBB: What Specifically Can I Do?

Scenario 6 Michael

Teacher sees Michael begin to scribble all over his math worksheet. Teacher calls out from across the room, "Stop that, you're making a mess." Or says in an accusatory tone of voice, "And what do you think you are doing, young man?"

Those accusatory statements attract attention of all students in class and thereby set up a power struggle between Teacher and Michael.

Michael begins to scream, "I hate this f----- s-----! I'm going to kill myself!" His screaming threatens the teacher and affects the functioning of the class.

Teacher responds, "Michael, you cannot swear in this classroom. As for killing yourself, don't be ridiculous." Michael thinks Teacher has called him ridiculous, which further inflames him. Other students in the class are now alert and waiting to see what happens.

A *more effective response* would be for Teacher to walk calmly to Michael, bend down, and quietly ask, "Do you need some help?" When Teacher stoops down, she is not vulnerable to being kicked and is not physically intimidating to Michael. Teacher knows never to scold students for swearing at the time they swear. The time to deal with profanity is after the student has settled down, not in the middle of the incident.

Effective Teacher suggests to Michael that the two of them talk in the private area of the classroom. She says, "It is nobody else's business, so let's talk privately about this." Teacher may say, pointing to Michael's scribbles, "Boy, Michael, I used to have a dress that looked like that." The issue of profanity is then dealt with privately, and Michael apologizes later to the class for swearing. Teacher might further defuse the situation by asking Michael to go to the photocopy room to get more paper.

What Are Some Specific Suggestions for Preventing Misbehavior?

When working with students with NBB, do what you can to increase the likelihood of student success, such as:

- Establish a positive and nurturing rapport with the students. Warmly greet them when they arrive at class. Show interest in them and talk about pop culture or something they are interested in.
- Modify the classroom to make it sensory friendly. Sit in the student's seat and look at the room from the student's perspective. See if there are things that might be distracting or annoying. It is far more productive to change the classroom than try to change the student.
- Add structure to time periods that are ordinarily unstructured, such as recess and free time. Students with NBB often have difficulty with unstructured time.
- Make appropriate use of humor, which is effective with all students.
- Keep in mind that students with NBB are not predestined to fail. Look for their many qualities and strengths that can be nurtured and built into important life competencies.
- All small improvements by students with NBB should be celebrated as important steps to a better-quality life, now and in the future.

What Are Suggested Ways of Redirecting Misbehavior?

When misbehavior does occur, keep your reactions as positive as possible. Here are some suggestions:

- Be careful about eye contact. It can stimulate upper-cortex activity, which is good for academic thinking, but can at times trigger episodes of misbehavior. Eye contact combined with a stern tone of voice is often interpreted as a threat.

- Be careful how you use your voice. If you raise your voice, students with NBB will often raise their voices in return.
- When giving students a choice of behaviors, provide two alternatives you can live with and let the students select the one they prefer.
- Remain positive. Your positive attitude can greatly improve the quality of service you provide to students with NBB and their families. Remember that students experiencing difficulties in neurological processing are human beings first and foremost, and you have the opportunity to help them.

As to what you can say, specifically, to individual students who break class rules of conduct:

- Tell them in nonemotional language that the rule was broken.
- Using very few words, tell them what to do to fix the mistake. Stand close to shield them from the view of others.
- Congratulate them when they begin to comply.
- If they begin to argue, say, "Wrong tone of voice . . . you're not ready to fix your mistake . . . I'll wait." Then wait, not staring at them and not making eye contact. You may have to wait a few seconds or even a few minutes.
- When they have calmed down, tell them what to do to begin to "fix the mistake." Start the statement with them to ensure they know what to do, then let them finish it. Quietly congratulate them as soon as they begin the task.
- End with congratulations for taking care of the problem so well.

Scenario 7 Abraham

Abraham, a 10-year-old student with severe behavior issues, was brought back from gym class. An educational assistant had Abraham by his wrist, escorting him to a private area in the back of the classroom as Abraham loudly spewed a tirade of profanities and death threats. To ensure everyone's safety, we used the "separate and supervise" strategy to isolate Abraham from his peers. He was put in a back room off the side of the classroom where he continued to scream profanities and threats. As the other staff members helped the other students carry on the daily classroom routine, I walked toward the back area of the room where a staff member stood in front of the closed door. Abraham had a history of running away. I opened the door just a fraction and saw Abraham standing with a chair over his head in a threatening pose.

I quietly called in, "You sound angry at me, Abraham." I was deliberately trying to deflect and divert his attention to me in an attempt to engage another part of his brain.

Abraham shrieked, "I'm not f---ing angry at you, I'm angry at Billy!"

"Excellent, Abraham! You put other words to this, way to go!" I said this in an encouraging, sincere, but soft tone. "Why are you angry at Billy?"

Abraham was still shouting and still had the chair over his head. "Because Conrad is my friend!" he screamed.

"Oh, I'm glad Conrad is your friend, but what does Billy have to do with this?" I gently put my index finger to my lips in a shhhing motion.

"Billy told Conrad to f--- off, and that's not nice," Abraham replied indignantly, at a lower volume but still with the chair over his head.

"Great, Abraham, you put words to this! Hey, Abraham, let's add other words to this so you can respectfully tell Billy why you're upset. Billy doesn't even know you are mad at him, and he and Conrad are already eating lunch together. Put the chair down so I can come in."

"NOOOOO!" Abraham screamed. "You'll try to put me in the Quiet Room if I put the chair down."

I answered quietly, "Abraham, as long as you are safe, I'm safe, and the class is safe, you don't need to go to the Quiet Room. Put the chair down so we can plan to get out of here."

Abraham put the chair down, but removed the detachable plastic seat, holding it ready to strike anyone who came close.

"Great, Abraham, you put down the chair, good for you! Now let me help you fix the chair where the seat has come off." I slowly approached from his left, walking on an angle and off-center from him, so he could see me coming and not be startled by any sudden movements I made. I positioned myself between the chair and Abraham, with him on the inside of the room, and myself near the door. Although the screaming had subsided, I was still concerned about my safety.

Together, we snapped the seat back on the chair and Abraham quickly sat down. "Thanks, Abraham," I said. "I always have trouble getting those blasted seats back on those chairs."

Abraham was now calm. He had been able to articulate why he was upset, without using profanity, and he found a way to let Billy know he was upset and tell Conrad that he was his friend. Within 4 minutes, Abraham had "fixed things up," made amends, and was with his peers having lunch. Abraham did not have any more big explosions after this. Perhaps he began to understand he had other options when he was confused or upset. This situation appeared to provide an invaluable learning experience.

Success! It does happen.

Commentary from Anonymous Teacher 1

When I first began teaching, I knew nothing about NBB. To my knowledge it was never mentioned in my teacher education program. I learned no special techniques or strategies for helping students with NBB. I learned from whomever I could and just did my best.

One of my students I remember well was a boy who had fallen from a balcony at age 2 and suffered a traumatic brain injury. He exhibited the signs of NBB I read about in this chapter. He was frequently off task, wouldn't stay in his seat, made noises, scribbled on his desk, and hit, slapped, and pushed kids on the playground. For some time, no form of discipline I tried helped change his behavior.

Finally, after much collaboration with the principal and the school psychologist, I did the following: Each day, if my student failed twice to control himself, I would send him to a special desk in the classroom separated from the others. There he would work until the completion of activities in a particular subject area. After that, he could return to the "group," as we called it. The process would start all over at that point. This young man did not like the isolation from the group, and generally his disruptive behavior would stop. As the year progressed, I came to realize that oftentimes this boy could not fully control his behavior.

In this chapter, I found the scenarios especially helpful. They gave me a new perspective on the behavior I sometimes encountered. I think all prospective teachers should be aware of NBB and recognize that the number of students with NBB is increasing. Such is certainly the case at my school. New teachers need to be able to recognize the conditions of NBB and have techniques in place to help those students with NBB.

Commentary from Anonymous Teacher 2

I must confess I was unaware of the term "neurological-based behavior" before I read this chapter. I had received no pre-service training in recognizing, identifying, understanding, or helping students with any of the diagnoses in NBB. I knew my subject matter and the basics of curriculum design but very little about working with the amazing variety of students I would encounter. I wasn't far into my first year when it became evident I needed help if I were going to survive.

I didn't like admitting my ignorance, but I had to go to colleagues for help. The special education teachers opened their trove of ideas, techniques, and strategies to help me. My fellow teachers offered tips that had worked for them. Often I just asked the students directly, "What can I do to help you succeed?" I attended inservice sessions when appropriate and researched when necessary. I spoke with parents about my hopes for their child. I learned by experience, sometimes the hard way.

Now, many years later, I have had my share of successes in helping students and regret that I never could find the key for others. Although I have taught many students with ADD/ADHD, learning disabilities, and other diagnoses, I never had to deal with violent, threatening, profane, or raging students, although I know many teachers who have.

As we all know, overcoming strong challenges does not happen quickly or easily. We all want to prepare our students to live successful lives. I think I got better at it as I learned to do the following: (1) *Retain patience* to allow students to think, make mistakes, and be patient with themselves and others; (2) *show persistence* in going the distance with students and doing what it takes to help them keep trying and not give up; (3) *keep a positive attitude,* expect good things, maintain hope, and help students look on the bright side; and (4) *search for strengths* by helping students recognize that we all have our strengths and weaknesses and can find many strengths in ourselves and others.

WHAT YOU HAVE LEARNED IN THIS CHAPTER

You have accomplished a great deal in what must have seemed a blizzard of information. You have learned the meaning of NBB and have an idea of how often you will encounter it. You recognize the two major diagnoses within NBB, along with some of the diagnoses that occur less frequently. You know the indicators of ADHD and learning disabilities, especially dyslexia. You know that many of these diagnoses are successfully treated with medication and you know how the medication is to be handled. You realize that NBB is not uncommon and that you will have students with various NBB diagnoses in your classes of "regular" students. You have learned that you can be successful in helping students with NBB even though the discipline tactics that work well with most students may not be so effective in their case. The keys are doing the best you can and never giving up.

Activities

Self-Test: True/False

1. NBB is a condition noted in students who are able to control their behavior but often choose not to do so.
2. Students with NBB do not usually respond very well to higher levels of structure in the classroom.
3. Learning disabilities are one of the most frequently encountered diagnoses within NBB.
4. Students with various kinds of learning disabilities often have poor eye–hand coordination.
5. Students with ADHD may at times have difficulty learning, but on the whole, they present few behavior problems for teachers.
6. Dyslexia is a condition that affects students' performance in mathematics and handwriting.
7. Some authorities say that pregnant women who drink even very small amounts of alcohol put their unborn children in danger of having fetal alcohol spectrum disorder (FASD).
8. "Rage" is the technical name for what we normally call "temper tantrums."
9. Normally, schools cannot provide medication to help students with NBB unless the students' caregivers agree to it.
10. When teaching, it is not likely you will encounter students with NBB, but it is best to be prepared in case you do.

Self-Test: Multiple Choice

1. In neurological-based behavior, students have notably low levels of
   (a) parental affection.
   (b) teacher attention.
   (c) self-control.
   (d) amino acids.
2. Which of the following is the most common diagnosis within NBB?
   (a) learning disabilities
   (b) ADHD
   (c) autism
   (d) bipolar disorder
3. Dyslexia involves special difficulties students experience in
   (a) reading.
   (b) mathematics.
   (c) memory.
   (d) personal relationships.
4. Classroom success for students with ADHD is increased through use of
   (a) self-direction.
   (b) physical exercise.
   (c) memory exercises.
   (d) structure.

5. Students with sensory integration dysfunction (SID) are helped by
   (a) reducing sensory input.
   (b) increasing sensory input.
   (c) visual and auditory checkups.
   (d) reducing structure.

6. Fetal alcohol spectrum disorder (FASD) is linked to
   (a) fathers who drink.
   (b) mothers who drink while pregnant.
   (c) family history of alcoholism.
   (d) family history of various addictions.

7. Many students with NBB do not respond well to
   (a) eye contact.
   (b) quiet voice.
   (c) medication.
   (d) the physical presence of adults.

8. The final decision concerning whether or not to use medication for students with NBB is made by
   (a) teachers.
   (b) trained nurses.
   (c) mental health professionals.
   (d) parents.

9. When an episode of rage begins, you should
   (a) let it run its cycle.
   (b) stop its escalation.
   (c) intervene by reasoning with the student.
   (d) call the parent immediately.

10. On average, what percentage of students is probably adversely affected by NBB?
   (a) 2%
   (b) 10%
   (c) 20%
   (d) 30%

Self-Test: Explain This

1. What is "neurological-based behavior," and why is it given a special name?

2. What are the most common symptoms of ADHD, and how can teachers respond to them?

3. What indicators would suggest that a student might have dyslexia?

4. Why is the word "spectrum" used in some diagnoses, such as fetal alcohol spectrum disorder and autism spectrum disorder?

5. In general, what can you do to reduce misbehavior among students with NBB?

Additional Suggested Activities

1. Working with a fellow student, if possible, explain what each of the following terms refers to: affective disorders, anxiety disorders, attention-deficit hyperactivity disorder (ADHD), autism spectrum disorder, behavior difficulties, bipolar disorder, brain injuries, conduct disorder, dyslexia, fetal alcohol spectrum disorder (FASD), learning disabilities (LD), neurological-based behavior (NBB), neurological differences, oppositional defiant disorder, rage, rage cycle, sensory integration dysfunction (SID), sensory processing disorder.

2. For discussion: Teachers in regular classrooms are often evaluated on how well they "maintain a rich learning environment." Yet an abundance of materials might adversely affect some students with neurological-based behavior. How might teachers organize a classroom environment that would be supportive of all students?

3. With one or more classmates or fellow teachers, go back to Scenario 1 at the beginning of the chapter. Discuss how you might help Tyler move past his inappropriate behavior. The commentary from Tay's teacher in Scenario 4 might help your organize your thoughts. Share your conclusions with peers.

PHASE FOUR

Perfecting and Personalizing Your Approach to Discipline

In Which You Bring Your Conclusions Together, Strive for Excellence, and Organize a Discipline Approach That Is Optimized for You and Your Students

CHAPTERS IN PHASE IV

CHAPTER 12 Revisiting the Eight Fundamental Questions in Discipline and Reviewing Related Authoritative Conclusions

Here we review the eight fundamental questions in discipline and the authoritative answers to those questions, and then call on you to answer those questions in your own words.

CHAPTER 13 How Can I Assess My Capabilities and Reach for Mastery in Discipline?

This chapter guides you toward mastery in discipline by assessing and strengthening your knowledge and capabilities.

CHAPTER 14 How Do I Organize Effective Discipline That Meets My Needs and Those of My Students?

This chapter guides you in composing a customized approach to discipline designed to meet your needs and those of your students.

Aligning Authoritative Views with the Eight Fundamental Questions in Discipline

Revisiting the Eight Fundamental Questions in Discipline and Reviewing Related Authoritative Conclusions

This chapter revisits the eight fundamental questions in discipline and summarizes authoritative conclusions related to them. The ultimate purpose of this effort is to enable you to answer those eight questions and expand on them convincingly in your own words. The eight questions are reiterated in Figure 12.1. Later, in Chapter 13, you will be helped to assess and strengthen your knowledge of ideas and tactics related to those questions that lead to the threshold of excellence in discipline.

WHAT AUTHORITIES SAY ABOUT QUESTION 1: HOW CAN I EXPECT MY STUDENTS TO BEHAVE, AND WHAT IS *MISBEHAVIOR*?

Jean Piaget (1951) on developmental stages: Intellectual development in children occurs through a series of identifiable stages. In each stage, children display particular ways of thinking and behaving. The stages with greatest implications for education are the *preoperational stage* (from age 4 up to approximate age of 7), the *concrete operational stage* (from approximately age 7 to age 11), and the *formal operational stage* (from approximately age 11 into adulthood). To review depictions of students' reasoning and behavior in primary grades, intermediate grades, middle school, and high school, please refer back to "How Can I Expect My Students to Behave?" in Chapter 1.

C. M. Charles (2010): Behavior is the sum total of all human actions. *Classroom misbehavior* is narrower in scope: It is student (and sometimes teacher) actions that disrupt teaching, interfere with learning, demean others, or otherwise violate the moral codes of society. It is manifested in the following forms, sequenced from less serious to more serious:

- *Inattention.* Daydreaming, doodling, looking out the window, and so on.
- *Apathy.* Sulking, not caring, fearing failure, simply not wanting or trying to do well.
- *Needless talk.* Chatting during instructional time about things unrelated to the lesson.

Figure 12.1   The Eight Fundamental Questions in Discipline.

The Eight Fundamental Questions in Classroom Discipline

These first four questions touch on realities of discipline that teachers face:	1. How can I expect my students to behave, and what is *misbehavior*? 2. How does misbehavior *damage* teaching and learning? 3. What is the *purpose and nature* of classroom discipline? 4. What does discipline *require of me* legally, professionally, and ethically?
These last four questions are about attitude and tactics:	1. What attitude serves me best in *ensuring* good discipline? 2. How can I proactively *prevent or reduce* student misbehavior? 3. How can I best provide *ongoing support* for proper student behavior? 4. How can I best *redirect misbehavior* humanely and effectively?

- *Moving about the room.* Getting up, wandering around, congregating.
- *Annoying others.* Provoking, teasing, picking on, demeaning by calling names.
- *Disrupting.* Shouting out, talking and laughing inappropriately, using vulgar language.
- *Lying.* Falsifying for personal gain.
- *Stealing.* Taking things that belong to others.
- *Cheating.* Making false representations or wrongly taking advantage of others.
- *Sexual harassment.* Sexual innuendo, inappropriate remarks, sex-related language.
- *Aggression and fighting.* Showing hostility, threatening, shoving, hitting, bullying.
- *Malicious mischief.* Intentionally damaging school property or belongings of others.
- *Defiance of authority.* Talking back, ignoring directions, refusing to do as requested.

Teacher misbehavior is sometimes manifested as the following:

- Lack of commitment and effort.
- Inattention to students and insensitivity to their needs.
- Demeanor that is unduly lax or overly harsh, demanding, or psychologically punitive.
- Being poor models of good behavior.

WHAT AUTHORITIES SAY ABOUT QUESTION 2: HOW DOES MISBEHAVIOR *DAMAGE* TEACHING AND LEARNING?

Consensus of authorities: Misbehavior disrupts teaching, inhibits student attention and participation, and often demeans and threatens students, leaving them fearful and hesitant, aimless and dissatisfied. These effects dampen learning and lead to poor class morale. For these reasons, student misbehavior is considered to be the most serious challenge in teaching.

WHAT AUTHORITIES SAY ABOUT QUESTION 3: WHAT IS *CLASSROOM DISCIPLINE?*

Charles (2010): Classroom discipline includes everything teachers do to limit misbehavior and foster responsible behavior. It relies on a substantial number of specific tactics that can be categorized according to the purposes they serve, which are: (1) to prevent misbehavior, (2) to support responsible behavior, and (3) to provide helpful and respectful redirection when misbehavior occurs. These three categories are sometimes called the **three facets of discipline** and are labeled *preventive discipline, supportive discipline,* and *redirective discipline.*

WHAT AUTHORITIES SAY ABOUT QUESTION 4: WHAT DOES DISCIPLINE *REQUIRE OF ME* LEGALLY, PROFESSIONALLY, AND ETHICALLY?

Regarding Legal Restrictions and Requirements

It is inadvisable and often illegal for you to date your students. It is illegal for you to engage in immoral activities that might in any way affect your teaching, although the meaning of "immoral activities" is not clearly defined in law. In all cases, it is far better to be safe than sorry.

Other legal requirements have to do with due diligence, avoidance of negligence, breach of duty, and teachers' service *in loco parentis* (in place of parents), meaning teachers must watch over students and safeguard them just as students' parents would do. *Due diligence* refers to paying close and reasonable attention to students who are under your supervision. *Negligence* is the failure to maintain careful watch over students under your supervision; it is considered to be a serious *breach of duty,* meaning a failure to comply with one of your legal obligations at school. You can protect yourself against litigation for negligence and breach of duty by adhering to the following guidelines that will put you in a defensible position should questions arise:

- Perform your assigned duties as directed by school policy and common sense, even duties that seem boring and unnecessary.
- Carefully oversee your students at all times.

* Note: The legalities noted here are not all-inclusive. They may be discussed in greater detail in your school district handbook. Please check that source, if possible.

- For activities that involve physical risk, provide thorough instructions and teach your students the necessary safety procedures before undertaking the activities.
- Be vigilant for signs that students might be inclined to harm themselves.
- Be alert to any signs that a student is being abused. Follow your school guidelines to familiarize yourself with signs of abuse.
- Exercise special caution regarding physical contact with students. Don't allow yourself to be alone in the classroom with a student, unless you are in plain sight of others. Refrain from touching students, other than on the hands or arms or with pats to the shoulders or head. Never strike students or grab any part of their bodies in anger. Never throw pencils, pens, erasers, books, desks, or chairs, no matter how strongly you are provoked.

Regarding Professional Expectations

Professionalism refers to displaying the best and most ethical ways of fulfilling one's duties in any given profession. In discipline, the teacher's primary professional duty is to establish and maintain a safe and productive learning environment. That means keeping students physically and emotionally safe, keeping them on task, stopping unwarranted disruptions, establishing positive relationships among members of the class, and minimizing behavior that interferes with teaching or learning. Please take the following suggestions seriously:

- *Regarding Effort.* You must give your genuine best effort to the profession.
- *Regarding Teaching.* You must teach in a manner that is conducive to success for each and every one of your students.
- *Regarding Helpfulness.* Always do what you can to help students, collectively and individually.
- *Regarding Respect.* Show genuine respect for your students. Treat all of them as your social equals, worthy of your time and attention.
- *Regarding Cooperation.* Help your students understand that you and they must accept each other and work together in order to achieve expectations in a satisfying manner.
- *Regarding Communication.* Make sure students know what is expected of them. When speaking with them, be positive, helpful, and encouraging. Avoid criticizing and making demands.
- *Regarding Style of Dress.* Dress professionally, as an adult in a professional situation.
- *Regarding Style of Speech.* Use appropriate language for the educational setting, with correct speech patterns and complete avoidance of obscenities.

Regarding Ethical Expectations

The line between professional expectations and ethical expectations is not sharply defined. Think of ethics as general principles of doing things the right way. Ethical expectations held for you as a teacher include: Always treat students and colleagues fairly, kindly, and supportively. Do the best you can for students. Be honest with students, colleagues, and students' caregivers, but at the same time, avoid saying or doing things that hurt feelings or dampen the desire to learn or cooperate. And of course, you must be circumspect in your personal behavior.

WHAT AUTHORITIES SAY ABOUT QUESTION 5: WHAT *ATTITUDE* SERVES ME BEST IN ENSURING GOOD DISCIPLINE?

Composite of authoritative opinion: Your attitude toward discipline reflects your feelings and beliefs about (1) the nature and value of discipline and (2) how discipline is best established and maintained. The following comments describe the teacher attitude or mindset that is generally considered most effective in discipline:

- The conviction that you can influence students to behave positively and are grateful for the opportunity to do so.
- The confidence that you can acquire and refine the best tactics for exerting positive influence on students from all backgrounds.
- The belief that student success, in school and later, depends strongly on students' making a positive effort to learn in school.
- The determination that even when setbacks occur, you will persevere in doing all you can to help your students become the best and most successful persons they can be.

Authoritative opinion suggests that the following efforts are effective in exerting positive influence on students and demonstrating your gratitude for the opportunity to help:

- Befriending students and showing personal interest in them.
- Willingly going the "extra mile" for students whenever you can.
- Chatting with students informally and showing concern for their difficulties.
- Reflecting frequently on your good fortune in being able to make genuine contributions to students' quality of life.
- Behaving toward students and others in a manner that is *civil* (polite, considerate).
- Conducting yourself in a manner that is highly *responsible* (always doing what you believe is the right thing to do).
- Avoiding negativity by making sure you do not use admonition, criticism, or coercion when trying to help students or others.
- Displaying positivity as you make efforts to connect with students personally, suggest possibilities and choices, ask for opinions, offer encouragement, and provide help as needed.
- Endeavoring to connect personally with students by talking with them individually, commenting occasionally on the incredible value of a good education, and mentioning from time to time people of high character and how they exhibit self-control and responsibility.
- Asking students' opinions about their educational program, the efforts they are making, the obstacles they are encountering, what they think of topics and activities in their lessons, what they like best and least in school, how you might make things better for them, and incidentally how they might make things easier for you.

WHAT AUTHORITIES SAY ABOUT QUESTION 6: HOW CAN I PROACTIVELY *PREVENT OR REDUCE* STUDENT MISBEHAVIOR?

For Prevention, Take These Proactive Steps

Charles (2010): Soften or eliminate the known causes of misbehavior. Address in advance a number of factors that seem to lead to, or "cause," misbehavior in school. Suspected causative factors are noted here, grouped according to where they seem to originate or "reside." They include:

- *Resident in Individual Students.* Thwarted desires, expediency, urge to transgress, temptation, inappropriate habits, poor behavior choices, avoidance, egocentric personality, and neurological-based behavior (NBB).
- *Resident in Peer Groups.* Contagious group behavior, provocation, bullying.
- *Resident in Instructional Environments.* Physical discomfort, tedium, meaninglessness, lack of stimulation.
- *Resident in Teachers and Other School Personnel.* Being poor models of behavior, showing little interest in or appreciation for students, succumbing easily to personal frustration, reacting badly to provocation, providing ineffective guidance or feedback, using ineffective personal communication, failing to plan proactively, and relying on coercion, threat, and punishment.

For suggestions in attending to the foregoing potential causes, please refer back to Chapter 1.

For Prevention, Make Sure Students Know What Is Expected of Them

Wong and Wong, 2007; Morrish, 2005; Ginott, 1972; Golubtchik, 2008; Forni, 2006; and others: There are a number of things you can do during the first 2 weeks of class to reduce misbehavior over the long run. They include:

- Clarify *class roles, expectations, and rules,* and teach students to abide by them.
- Begin establishing *personal rapport* with students.
- Teach *routines* thoroughly so students can follow them automatically.
- From the outset, add *interest* to your lessons and direct them effectively.
- Communicate with students in ways that *encourage cooperation* and *preserve dignity.* Teach your students to do the same.
- Teach *civility* and work to activate students' *internal motivation* to do the right thing.

The Wongs (2007) put great emphasis on how teachers should conduct their first day of class. Here's what they say:

- Have your classroom ready for instruction and make it inviting.
- Prepare a written script to follow that states exactly what you will say and do throughout the class or day.
- Stand at the door and greet students as they enter.
- Give each student a seating assignment and a seating chart.
- Position yourself in the room near the students, remembering that behavior problems are proportional to distance.

- Post an assignment in a consistent location for students to begin when they enter the room.
- Display your diploma and credentials with pride. Dress in a professional manner that models success and shows you expect achievement.

The Wongs (2007) also suggest clarifying the teacher's responsibilities and the students' responsibilities as follows:

My Responsibilities as Your Teacher

- To treat you with respect and care as an individual
- To provide you an orderly classroom environment
- To provide the necessary discipline
- To provide the appropriate motivation
- To teach you the required content

Your Responsibilities as My Students

- To treat me with respect and care as an individual
- To attend class regularly
- To be cooperative and not disruptive
- To study and do your work well.

Morrish (1997) gives this advice: Explain to students that your job is to provide a classroom in which they can learn easily, without threat or put-downs, and where everyone behaves courteously and willingly undertakes the tasks expected of them. Explain why it is necessary that students follow your directions every time. Show them how you will teach the directions for activities. Emphasize that their job is to follow your directions, perform the routines as you have taught them, make the best effort they can to learn, and treat everyone with respect and courtesy.

Marvin Marshall (2007): Explain to your students that it is your job to provide them a classroom in which they can learn comfortably and efficiently. Reassure them you will keep them safe and will always help and encourage them.

Further explain that the students' job is to conduct themselves in a responsible manner in keeping with class rules, and that you will teach them how to do so. Tell them they can learn to control their behavior by asking themselves, "If I wanted to be successful in this class right now, what would I be doing?" In most cases, the answer will be apparent.

For Prevention, Make Sure to Meet Students' Needs

Dreikurs (1995): All students have a *primary need* to feel they "belong"—that they are an important part of the class and the school. When that need is not being met, students often turn to the "mistaken goals" of seeking attention, seeking power, seeking revenge, or displaying inadequacy.

Glasser (1986): All students share five basic needs—for survival (security), belonging, power, fun, and freedom. If those needs are not met in school, students often become resistive, resistant, and disobedient, and turn to inappropriate ways to meet their needs.

Charles (2010): You might find it helpful to expand Glasser's list of needs to eight in number, with the following labels:

- *Security.* To feel safe, without worry.
- *Association.* To associate and interact with others.
- *Belonging.* To feel a part of things, valued, with a sense of place in the class.
- *Dignity.* To be respected and made to feel worthwhile.
- *Hope.* To believe that school is worthwhile and success is possible.
- *Power.* To exert some control over and provide input into events in the class.
- *Enjoyment.* To participate in activities that are interesting, pleasurable, or rewarding.
- *Competence.* Growth in capability to do many things well, including schoolwork.

For Prevention, Streamline the Classroom Environment

Charles (2000): You can promote good behavior by making the class environment attractive, inviting, and efficient to use. You can be welcoming and supportive. Materials can be kept readily available. Items of special interest can be prominently displayed. A variety of media can be featured. The environment can be neat and tidy, and students can be involved in keeping it so. These conditions suggest school is for learning and they predispose students to participate.

Checklist of Useful Preventive Tactics

- ✓ Remain mindful of students' needs for security, belonging, enjoyment, and competence.
- ✓ In advance, reduce or eliminate conditions that are known to promote misbehavior.
- ✓ Set up your classroom for efficiency, helpfulness, convenience, and attractiveness.
- ✓ Ensure you teach in an interactive manner that attracts and involves students.
- ✓ Quickly learn the names of your students and interact with each of them personally.
- ✓ Carefully teach students the roles, responsibilities, and rules of behavior in your classes.
- ✓ Communicate convincingly that the class is organized to promote student success.

WHAT AUTHORITIES SAY ABOUT QUESTION 7: HOW CAN I BEST PROVIDE *ONGOING SUPPORT* FOR PROPER STUDENT BEHAVIOR?

Supportive discipline exerts ongoing influence to help students willingly participate, follow the rules, do their work, remain on task, and treat each other civilly. Here are some suggestions.

For Support, Establish Personal Rapport with Students

Rapport with others involves being on the same wavelength with them, enjoying their presence, exchanging ideas easily, and building trust and confidence. Various authorities assign it high importance in maintaining good relationships. Following are some of their very helpful observations.

Haim Ginott (1971): Teachers "at their worst" label students, belittle them, preach at them, impose guilt, and denigrate their character. Those tactics are counterproductive. You get much better results when, "at your best," you listen to students, confer dignity on them, invite their cooperation, and treat them as social equals capable of making good decisions.

Glasser (2001, p. 54): When you first meet your students, tell them: "We are in this class together. I want to help you to be competent or go beyond. My job is to teach you and help you learn, not to find out what you don't know and punish you for not knowing it. If you have a question, ask me. If you need more time, I'll give it to you. If you have an idea how to do what we are trying to do better, tell me. I'll listen."

Glasser also advises you to befriend your students and refrain from telling them what to do and not do. You might say something like, "I think an important part of my job is to do all I can to make sure you have a good time learning. I will try to make this class fun for both you and me. I think we can learn a lot and still have a very good time." Then right away continue focusing on the *seven connecting habits* of caring, listening, supporting, contributing, encouraging, trusting, and befriending.

Marshall (2001): There is much to be said for friendliness, but students respond even better to encouragement and empowerment, which you provide through positivity, choice, and reflection. Give them those things, and your students will like and support you.

Charles (2000): Students love charismatic teachers. You acquire charisma by making yourself interesting to students, being upbeat and pleasant, and sharing with them some of your interests, experiences, and talents. Let students know a bit about your family life and what you like to do outside of school. Use humor, without being silly. Avoid sarcasm—you may think it clever, but it is too easily misinterpreted.

Seganti (2008a): You will be seen as a good teacher if you give something back to students in the form of sparkle and enthusiasm. Just teach students useful information in an engaging manner. Combine that with tight but reasonable boundaries on behavior and students will see you care about them and are willing to work hard for their benefit. They will reciprocate.

Morrish (2000): Work hard at helping your students learn the "Great Skills" of courtesy, self-discipline, concentration, concern for others, and perseverance.

For Support, Communicate with Students in Ways That Invite Cooperation and Preserve Dignity

Several authorities urge teachers to give careful attention to how they communicate with students. They note that certain types of communication attract cooperation and increase motivation, whereas other types alienate students and stifle enthusiasm.

Ginott (1971): Confer dignity on your students by treating them as social equals. When they behave inappropriately, focus on the situation rather than students' character or past history. Simply state the problem and ask students if they can help correct it. Use laconic language (short and to the point) with no sarcasm. Avoid *why* questions, the kind in which you ask students why they have behaved inappropriately. *Why* questions put students on the defensive and do not motivate them to find better ways of behaving.

Dreikurs (1972): Always speak with students in positive terms and make mention of their strengths rather than their weaknesses. Encourage them to strive for improvement. Be optimistic, enthusiastic, and show faith in students and pride in their accomplishments.

Morrish (2000): Maintain focus on the positive—on what students do right instead of what they do wrong. We get along with students much better and have more influence on them when, instead of finding fault, we show them how to improve. When students do something wrong, simply have them correctly repeat the act, or display a positive alternative if the first act is undesirable. If they don't know how to do so, teach them.

Jones (2007a): Teachers nag students too much. They tell them over and over and over what they should do and how they should behave. Nagging does not solve behavior problems. It is counterproductive, and after a while it makes students "deaf" to suggestions. You can communicate that you mean business much better through body language such as eye contact, physical proximity, and posture.

Glasser (1998c): Ask your students to do the best they can in class and, when appropriate, ask them, "What can I do to help?" Be mindful of the "seven deadly habits" that teachers fall into when interacting with students—criticizing, blaming, complaining, nagging, threatening, punishing, and rewarding students to control them. Make a concerted effort to replace those habits with the "seven connecting habits" of caring, listening, supporting, contributing, encouraging, trusting, and befriending.

Marshall (2007): Make frequent use of "reflective questions" when helping students improve their behavior. Recognize that we cannot control students simply by asking for obedience. What we can do is clarify expectations of proper behavior and then empower students to reach those expectations. We can do this noncoercively by asking reflective questions that prompt students to think about their actions and then allow them to choose, from acceptable alternatives, how they will follow up. One of the most effective reflective questions is to have students ask themselves, "If I wanted to be successful in this class right now, what would I be doing?"

For Support, Present Interesting Lessons and Direct Them Effectively

When students are involved in lessons they truly enjoy, they don't misbehave much (except sometimes they get overly exuberant and noisy). The problem with most lessons in school is not excessive exuberance—it is excessive boredom and passivity.

Glasser (1998c): Most discipline problems arise because students find school unduly boring. Here is how to avoid that problem: Provide a class environment that is warm and receptive and teach students things they truly want to learn about. Present most lessons in a "lead-teacher" style, featuring much interaction by drawing out students' ideas and helping them pursue topics they find appealing.

Jones (2007a): In typical classes, students are passive rather than active most of the time. When passive, they tend to disengage from the lesson and turn to talking, daydreaming, or looking out the window. This disconnection is most likely to occur when instruction is teacher-dominated and fails to involve students or otherwise engage them intellectually.

Here are three things you can do to replace this pattern: (1) Use body language to demonstrate leadership and move about the room so as to be close to all students during seat work. (2) Use Say, See, Do teaching that keeps students actively responding through the lesson. (3) Post visual instructional plans in the room to help students remember procedures to be followed.

Charles (2000): Although there are exceptions, students usually don't like to sit still, keep quiet, or work by themselves for long. They don't like to memorize facts and regurgitate them on tests. They don't like lengthy writing assignments. They don't like to do repetitive work. They don't like long reading assignments, although many spend hours reading material that interests them. Most do not like individual competition in which they have little chance of winning.

On the other hand, most students do like to talk, work together, move about, and do productive and creative work with their hands. They like variety. They enjoy team competition and trying to surpass their previous levels of achievement. They like to use computers and other media. They like to hear and learn language that has rhythm, rhyme, and metaphor. They like to tell and listen to stories. They like to do role-playing, perform skits, and give performances. They like rhythmic activities that involve repetition, music, chanting, clapping, and dancing.

To almost any activity you can add movement, novelty, mystery, adventure, drama, storytelling, challenge, role-playing, acting out, and music and rhythm. Primary teachers sometimes have students clap, hop, and chant when learning new words and number combinations. They tell stories that highlight new vocabulary words. Teachers of older students can use challenges such as, "I bet you can't get this work done in less than 10 minutes." They can have students act out the functions of parts of speech or let them role-play the duties of government officials or take field trips to businesses to learn how they function.

Golubtchik (2008): Students like activities that bring multiple senses into play. Examples are making and labeling three-dimensional models, physically acting things out, drawing and painting, pantomiming, writing and performing original raps and jingles, creating imaginary correspondence between historical figures, writing a class newspaper, using cameras to create pictorial reports, and the like.

Marshall (2001): Use a variety of visual, auditory, and manipulative techniques to attract and hold students' attention, such as charts, cartoons, models, parts of films, videos, PowerPoint creations, projected materials, listening to music, recording music, rapping, creating verse, creating rhythms, physical movements, enacting the roles of characters in stories or events, large-group discussions, case studies, and working with small groups or buddies.

For Support, Teach Civility and Call on Students' Internal Motivation to Do the Right Thing

Borba (2001): Schools are about the only places today that are likely to teach students how to conduct themselves civilly and morally. You do students a great favor when you teach them about the importance of the "seven essential virtues of goodness"—empathy, conscience, self-control, respect, kindness, tolerance, and fairness. Help them learn good manners, too.

Gossen (2004): Call on students to evaluate their behavior in terms of the positive values emphasized by their families and communities and to strive to conduct themselves accordingly.

Marshall (2007): Use the Hierarchy of Social Development to help students understand how one behaves when functioning at the hierarchy's highest level—Level D. Calling on students to identify the level at which they are behaving helps them develop a sense of what is right and proper, and when you tap into that sense you help them regulate their own behavior. Just ask them reflective questions such as: "At what level is your behavior now?" "What might you do to move to a higher level?" "If you wanted to be very successful right now, how might you act?"

For Support, Maintain Awareness, Presence, and Physical Proximity

Kounin (1971): The best teachers remain constantly aware of what is going on in all parts of the classroom and are able to attend to two or more situations simultaneously. Effective teachers also conduct their lessons very efficiently and keep students occupied, with very little dead time that might encourage misbehavior.

Jones (2007a): Arrange seating in the classroom so you can quickly move alongside any student in the room. The "interior loop" seating arrangement facilitates mobility and makes it easier for you to "work the crowd," interacting with many students in short periods of time. Use body language such as eye contact and physical proximity to connect personally with students and keep them on task.

For Support, Reiterate Your Expectations and Inspire Student Cooperation

Marshall (2007): Although human behavior is influenced by many factors, all genuine motivation takes place *within* the person. It is not something you can push into students from outside. Therefore, you should stop thinking of yourself as a "motivator," and instead serve as a *stimulator* who activates students' internal motivation. To get the best results in your classes, inspire students to achieve by ensuring they find pleasure in school.

Seganti (2008a): Convey the following messages to your students clearly:

- This classroom is for academic learning. Everything we do in class will be aimed at learning. I will make it as interesting for you as I can, but you must also do your part, which is to focus and learn.
- Students who disrupt the class are not only cheating themselves but are interfering with other students' constitutional rights to a good public education.
- I know you want to feel good about yourselves and I will help you do that. But you need to understand that self-esteem doesn't come from messing around in the classroom. It comes from doing hard work and learning knowledge and skills that will help you achieve a quality life.

Seganti also gives this advice:

- *Rely on actions rather than words.* It is worse than useless to spend time cajoling, arguing, and continually trying to justify your decisions to students. Just make good rules and enforce them without fail. No explanations are needed. If you don't enforce your rules, students will act as though your rules don't exist.

■ *Forget warnings.* Giving students warnings wastes time and is utterly useless. Students know when they are misbehaving. If you don't want students to manipulate you, forget the warnings and simply enforce the rules.

■ *Forget rewards, too.* Don't give students rewards for learning. Provide activities they enjoy, if you can, but help students understand that the reward they get for making an effort in school is a good education, which is priceless and the only reward that really counts.

For Support, Interact Personally and Work Together with Students

Authorities are virtually unanimous in urging teachers to give every one of their students some personal attention every day, if only a smile or a wink. Speak to them in a friendly manner. Only a few words are necessary.

> *Glasser (2001).* Employ much teacher–student interaction as a part of quality teaching.
> *Marshall (2007).* Use interaction with students to tap into their internal motivation.
> *Seganti (2008a).* Personal interactions make you more effective with difficult students.
> *Daly (2004); Cook (2004a).* Include personal interaction in your routine of working with students with ADHD and other NBB disorders.

These suggestions all have one thing in common—they acknowledge students in a friendly manner. A good time to interact briefly with students is when they are entering the classroom.

For Support, Use Body Language Effectively

Jones (2007a): All of us can learn to use body language to help students control their behavior. Body language is easier to use and far more effective than verbally reminding students how they should behave.

Your body carriage, eye contact, and tone of voice can stop most student backtalk and arguing. Body language has the additional advantage of being non-adversarial. With a little self-training in using body language, you can increase achievement for the bottom half of a class (those who typically disengage) by as much as 50% and eliminate most disruptions.

Further, you should also practice effective breathing that is slow, deep, and calm; body carriage with good posture that conveys confidence; and facial expressions that indicate enthusiasm, seriousness, enjoyment, and appreciation. Winks, smiles, and thumbs-up demonstrate a sense of humor and personal connection that students appreciate.

For Support, Give Students Choices and Ask for Their Cooperation

Glasser (1986): We cannot control anybody except ourselves, and we cannot force students to learn. All we can do is open up possibilities and encourage students to pursue them. In school, we need to articulate acceptable alternatives from which students may choose. Doing so gives students a sense of power and keeps them involved.

Marshall (2007): We cannot make students learn or even try to learn, but we can allow (and show we expect) them to select from positive options for behaving and engaging in learning. For example, when Mary fails to complete her essay in the time allowed, you might ask her, "Would you rather sit in the back of the room and complete your essay now, or would you rather take it home to complete and bring it back to me tomorrow?"

For Support, Conduct an Occasional Discussion on Ethics, Trust, and What Makes a Person Likeable

If you address this topic (only occasionally) it can cause students to reflect seriously on their personal behavior. You can begin by saying, "Class, there is something I've been thinking about that I'd like to get your opinions on. It is what is called 'ethics,' which has to do with right and wrong ways of conducting oneself and treating others. Over the centuries, it has been a favorite topic of philosophers, some of whom have spent much of their lives thinking about it and trying to communicate their ideas.

"The average person seldom thinks twice about ethics as a topic, and yet our lives are strongly affected by our sense of right, wrong, and the proper ways of behaving. We hear about people who behave ethically and people who behave unethically. What does it mean to behave ethically or unethically? Who has an idea?" And so you proceed with questions such as:

> How does an ethical salesperson treat customers?
>
> How does an ethical lawyer treat clients?
>
> What does an ethical teacher do?
>
> What does an ethical student do?
>
> What causes us to trust someone?
>
> Does ethics have anything to do with trust or friendship?
>
> Does ethics affect the strength of friendships?
>
> If you believe a person is unethical, how do you feel toward him or her?
>
> If you want people to think of you as ethical, what must you do?

By asking students their views on these matters, you get them thinking more deeply about correct and honorable behavior in various contexts.

Checklist of Useful Supportive Tactics

✓ Practice expectations, rules, and roles so students abide by them automatically.
✓ Use personal charisma to strengthen rapport with and cooperation from students.

✓ Use effective communication tactics and discard those that are counterproductive.
✓ Continue teaching students how to conduct themselves civilly and use good manners.
✓ Use intrigue and sensory activities to make your lessons as interesting as possible.
✓ Increase personal contact with students during lessons and independent work.
✓ Make effective use of body language such as facial expressions and physical proximity.
✓ Frequently give students choices and ask them to follow up responsibly.
✓ Occasionally discuss ethics, responsibility, and natural motivation to do the right thing.

WHAT AUTHORITIES SAY ABOUT QUESTION 8: HOW CAN I BEST *REDIRECT MISBEHAVIOR* HUMANELY AND EFFECTIVELY?

This question takes us into the *redirective facet* of discipline, which is brought into play when students misbehave. Although this facet is no more important than preventive or supportive discipline, it addresses the question teachers most often ask: "What do I do when James (misbehaves in one way or another)?" Here are some authoritative suggestions for redirecting misbehavior.

For Redirection, Refer to a Rule and Talk with Offenders, Without Threatening

Redl and Wattenberg (1951): Student behavior is best controlled by using "influence techniques" such as encouragement and support, rather than demands and reprimands.

Ginott (1971): When redirecting misbehavior, simply indicate what needs to be done correctly. Don't comment on the student's character or past behavior. Instead, provide support without preaching, moralizing, imposing guilt, or demanding promises.

Glasser (1969): When there's a problem, focus on the present. Don't waste time dwelling on the past or complaining or listening to excuses. Just determine what might be done here and now to resolve or improve the situation.

For Redirection, Teach or Reteach Students How to Abide by a Rule

Charles (2000): Even though you teach students how to perform procedures and comply with class rules, over time they forget or get careless or follow someone's bad example. Even students whom you would expect to know better may break a rule because they don't understand it or don't know how to comply. When that is the case, simply stop what you are doing and, in a kindly manner, reteach the rule or manner of compliance. You won't have to do it often. Occasional reminders are good for the entire class.

For Redirection, Have Students Redo the Misbehavior Properly

Morrish (1997), *the Wongs* (2007), and *Marshall* (2007): When students misbehave, have them repeat their behavior properly, with no scolding or punishment. If students don't know how to behave appropriately, then reteach them and have them perform the behavior correctly.

For Redirection, Help Students Identify Their Misbehavior and Then Select from Acceptable Options You Provide

Marshall (2007): Use the hierarchy of social development when asking misbehaving students to reflect on their behavior. Suppose two boys are talking together audibly while another student is making a class report. The teacher quietly asks the disruptive boys, "At what level is that behavior?" They think for a moment and answer, "Level B." Their misbehavior typically ceases at that point and they turn to behavior at a higher level.

Or if two students get into a heated argument, you might say, "I think we need to give this matter some attention. Would you rather iron out the problem between yourselves or meet with me later today for the three of us to discuss it?"

Coloroso (1994/2002): The best way to help students correct mistakes or resolve problems is, first, to have them acknowledge what they have done wrong, thus giving them ownership of the problem. Then, assign them the responsibility for resolving it. On occasion, you may have to suggest some acceptable steps or alternatives from which they may choose. All the while, make sure their personal dignity remains intact.

For Redirection, Have Students Self-Evaluate and Make a Plan for Improving Their Behavior

Coloroso (1994/2002): See the previous comment just above.

Ford (2004): When students have difficulty getting along with others, or when they disrupt in class or other school settings, you should teach them how to get what they want *without infringing on the rights of others,* an approach that is rarely mentioned in education. You can do this by asking the following questions in a matter-of-fact way, with no hint of anger, exasperation, or disappointment:

> *Question 1:* "What are you doing?" This question should be asked first, but always in conjunction with question 2, which follows. When students hear this first question, they look within themselves and identify their behavior. If you tell them what they are doing wrong, you do not help them develop the skill of self-reflection. Also, avoid asking them why they are behaving as they are—that only encourages them to make excuses.

> *Question 2:* "What are the rules?" When asked this question, students quickly tie the rules to what they are currently doing and assess their actions *in terms of the rights of others.*

> *Question 3:* "What do you want to do now?" This question helps students formulate a plan of action that resolves the conflict between their behavior and the rights of others.

For Redirection, Apply Redirective Structures as Suggested by Spencer Kagan

Kagan (Kagan, Kyle, & Scott, 2007): Use the following process to redirect misbehavior:

- First, identify the student position (state of mind) at the time the misbehavior occurred. For example, James heatedly calls Martin "stupid." Teacher says, "James, you appear angry, is that right?" James mutters.
- Second, communicate *acceptance* of the position while *refusing to accept* the disruptive behavior associated with it. Teacher says, "We all get angry at times. That's natural. But it is not all right to call people names."
- Third, apply a structure (procedure) to redirect the behavior appropriately. Teacher: "See if you can think of a better choice than calling names. You can tell me later."

As reminders, here are three examples of Kagan structures. These structures are for use at the moment of disruption:

- *Picture It Right.* If you were at your very best right now, what would you be doing?
- *Make a Better Choice.* Try to think of a better choice you could make right now.
- *To You . . . to Me.* To you, this lesson may be boring; to me, it is important because . . . .

For Redirection, Apply Legitimate Teacher Leverage When Necessary

Teacher leverage refers to the power teachers have to insist that students behave themselves properly. In most of today's approaches to discipline it is considered a last resort—it is what you do when persuasive tactics fail to stop the misbehavior.

The Canters (1976) used leverage as a key component in assertive discipline, which was immensely popular for many years. Their leverage embodied a hierarchy of consequences that could be invoked to stop misbehavior. The Canters' approach included:

- A clear set of rules for class behavior.
- Positive consequences such as recognition and praise that were applied when students complied with the rules.
- Negative consequences that were applied when students broke the rules. The negative consequences became progressively more unpleasant if students continued to break rules. When teachers applied a consequence of sufficient strength, students would choose to comply with class rules rather than endure the consequence.

Jones (2007a), whose discipline approach is eminently positive, also makes provisions for leverage, in the form of backup responses. *Small backup responses* are conveyed privately or semi-privately to the student: "I expect you to stop talking so we can get on with our work." Such low-keyed messages show that the teacher means business. Whispering privately helps preserve student dignity.

Medium backup responses are delivered publicly in the classroom: "Emily, sit in the thinking chair for 3 minutes and think about what you have done that caused me to send you there." Or, "Brian, you have disrupted again. You'll have detention with me tomorrow after school." Other medium backup responses include loss of privilege and parent conferences.

Seganti (2008a): Class rules are useless unless you can enforce them. You must create the mindset in every student that breaking the rules in your class is just not worth it. To do so you must have some kind of leverage that makes students decide to follow the rules. (Seganti has determined that the most effective leverage for his classes is "Mr. Seganti's famous 15-minute detention after school." This detention is only slightly inconvenient for students; nevertheless, they dislike it. And because they can't get out of it, it works all the better.)

Seganti calls his detention the "lever that can move boulders." It promotes compliance while causing little resentment. It doesn't punish teachers, either—they have to stay after school for a while anyway. A student who comes to your detention is tacitly agreeing that you are the primary authority. Once you have established that point, behavior problems dwindle.

For Redirection of More Serious Misbehavior, Help Students Learn to Make Amends for Their Offenses to the Environment, Others, and Themselves

Coloroso (1994/2002): When students misbehave seriously, guide them through a process of restitution, resolution, and reconciliation. *Restitution* means doing what is necessary to repair the damage that was done. *Resolution* means identifying and correcting whatever caused the misbehavior so it won't happen again. *Reconciliation* establishes healing relationships with people who were hurt or offended by the misbehavior. Ask the offending student(s) to make decisions concerning future behavior and follow up accordingly.

Gossen (2004): Consider teaching students to use "self-restitution" following their misbehavior. The student is to do three things: (1) reflect on the misbehavior, (2) identify the need or condition that prompted the misbehavior, and (3) create new ways of behaving that are *in keeping with the kind of person he or she wants to be.*

This process helps restore the individual. It does not dwell on faults or mistakes, but instead helps students learn how to make things right *within themselves* and with whomever they have offended. The process helps students learn to conduct themselves in harmony with their needs and inner sense of morality, and also helps them deal with their behavioral shortcomings while committing themselves to better behavior in the future.

For Redirection of Neurological-Based Behavior, Are There Special Considerations?

Yes. Paula Cook (see Chapter 11) advises that when redirecting students with NBB, you should:

- Be careful about eye contact. It can stimulate upper-cortex activity, which is good for academic thinking, but can at times trigger episodes of misbehavior. Eye contact combined with a stern tone of voice is often interpreted as a threat.

- Be careful how you use your voice. If you raise your voice, students with NBB will often raise their voices in return.
- When giving students a choice of behaviors, provide two alternatives you can live with and let the students select the one they prefer.
- Remain positive, which improves the quality of service you provide to students and their families. Remember that students experiencing difficulties in neurological processing are human beings first and foremost, and you have the opportunity to help them Cook (2004).

Here are some things you can say to individual students with NBB who break class rules:

- First, tell them in nonemotional language that the rule was broken.
- Second, in very few words, tell them what to do to fix the mistake. Stand close to shield them from the view of others.
- Third, congratulate them when they begin to comply.
- If they begin to argue, say, "Wrong tone of voice . . . you're not ready to fix your mistake . . . I'll wait." Then wait, not staring at them and not making eye contact. You may have to wait a few seconds or even a few minutes.
- When they have calmed down, start the statement with them to ensure they know what to do, then let them finish it. Quietly encourage them as soon as they begin the task.
- End with congratulations for taking care of the problem so well.

Checklist of Useful Redirective Tactics

- ✓ Without attacking the student, indicate what needs to be done and wait for compliance.
- ✓ Calmly ask students to repeat the behavior, correctly this time.
- ✓ Ask the student to identify his or her level of behavior on Marshall's hierarchy.
- ✓ Ask the student to choose from positive options you provide for responsible behavior.
- ✓ Ask students to self-evaluate and make a plan for responsible behavior in the future.
- ✓ Apply redirective structures in the manner suggested by Spencer Kagan.
- ✓ When other tactics fail, apply legitimate teacher authority to enforce the rules.
- ✓ Use special tactics when redirecting the behavior of students with NBB.

Activities

1. Do the following to strengthen your abilities in redirective discipline: Working with one or more colleagues, identify and explain five tactics you would prefer using when you wish to (1) prevent misbehavior, (2) support proper behavior, and (3) redirect inappropriate behavior.

2. If you are enrolled in a university or inservice class, select your two favorite tactics in each facet of discipline and share those selections with the class. Explain why the tactics are your favorites.

3. In small groups, conduct practice sessions in using the redirective tactics you think are most useful.

13

Striving for Personal Excellence in Discipline

How Can I Assess My Capabilities and Reach for Mastery in Discipline?

You are now on the verge of achieving every teacher's dream, which is to be able to turn ordinary classes into groups of students who are cooperative, courteous, and nondisruptive. The previous chapters in this book have described the best available information and skills for doing so, and you have seen much of that information summarized in Chapter 12.

As you internalize the information and further perfect your discipline skills, your classes become highly likely to reflect the marvels of group energy, quality learning, and high morale. Those qualities make teaching a wonderful profession, but the skills upon which they depend do not appear automatically. For great numbers of teachers, they remain tantalizingly out of reach until and unless those teachers learn to exert positive influence on students and tap into their innate desire to succeed.

Now a very important task lies just ahead, and that is for you to make absolutely sure you possess an array of discipline skills that are best suited to your personality and the needs of your students. This chapter will help you do so by guiding you through self-assessment in a representative number of skills. It will also direct you to information for strengthening those skills about which you are not fully confident.

AREAS INCLUDED IN THIS SELF-ASSESSMENT

The four areas included in the self-assessment are as follows:

Knowledge of Terminology and Contributions: (Assesses your level of informational grounding.)

- Confirms ability to explain misbehavior and how it affects teaching and learning.
- Confirms ability to explain the purpose and nature of modern discipline.
- Confirms knowledge of legal, professional, and ethical obligations within discipline.

- Confirms familiarity with the major ideas, concepts, and terminology in discipline.
- Confirms knowledge of major authorities and their contributions to discipline.
- Confirms knowledge of student behavior at various stages of development.
- Confirms knowledge of effects of culture and economics on students' behavior.

Skills in Preventing Misbehavior: (Indicates you know what to do, before class begins and during the first 2 weeks of class, in order to reduce potential misbehavior to a minimum.)

- Verifies you understand students' needs, capabilities, and behavior patterns at various age levels.
- Ensures you can make plans for meeting students' needs for security, belonging, enjoyment, and competence.
- Verifies you know how to eliminate or soften factors known to lead to misbehavior.
- Verifies you have the capability to explain what you and the class will do for students and what they must do.
- Verifies your capability to explain and demonstrate expectations and rules of behavior for the class.
- Ensures you can explain and demonstrate how students are to comply with class expectations.
- Ensures you know how to give personal attention to students and develop rapport with them.

Skills in Supporting Proper Behavior: (Identifies what you are able to do on an ongoing basis to promote responsible student behavior.)

- You can reiterate as necessary what you expect of students regarding effort and conduct.
- You know how to teach students the routines they are to follow.
- You know how to use communication, helpfulness, and charisma to develop rapport with students.
- You possess adequate knowledge of how to enhance the quality of classroom communication.
- You know how to provide high-quality instruction.
- You understand tactics and methods for building character, ethics, civility, and responsibility among your students.

Skills in Redirecting Misbehavior: (Specifies what you will do when dealing with misbehavior.)

- Verifies your ability to redirect misbehavior in different ways that preserve student dignity.
- Shows you know how to help students evaluate their behavior and make responsible choices.
- Shows you know how to help students take ownership of misbehavior and make plans for improvement.

- Shows you are able to help students with restitution and self-restitution following misbehavior.
- Shows you possess tactics for redirecting misbehavior of students with neurological-based behavior.

HOW THESE SKILLS WILL BE ASSESSED

In the remainder of the chapter, you will be asked to judge yourself on your knowledge and skills in discipline. You will encounter seven clusters of self-assessment items and will be asked to appraise yourself in each of them. Some of the longer assessment areas are divided into smaller parts for easier management. It would be unrealistic to expect that on your first attempt you will earn the highest rating on every item. However, you should make that capability a priority. Information is provided in association with each set of items for your review when you need it.

SELF-ASSESSMENT AREA 1: PROFESSIONAL GROUNDING IN KNOWLEDGE OF EXPECTATIONS, TRAITS, TERMS, CONCEPTS, AND CONTRIBUTIONS IN DISCIPLINE

This assessment reviews and strengthens your familiarity with students' behavioral traits and expectations and fundamental terminology, goals, concepts, and contributions in discipline. Using the scale of 1 to 4, enter the numeral of your self-rating.

1. (weak)   2. (borderline)   3. (adequate)   4. (strong)

Part 1a.	Rating
How would students at age 6 and age 15 differ in how they relate to teachers?	
How might students at age 6 explain the reason for seasons of the year?	
What is meant by the term "living in poverty"?	
Name two effects poverty seems to have on student behavior, according to Ruby Payne.	
What is meant by "psychological needs"?	
Name four psychological needs that affect behavior in almost all students.	
In what ways, if any, do teachers' psychological needs differ from those of students?	

Part 1a.   Rating

What is meant by "misbehavior" in school? Can misbehavior occur
   unintentionally?

Explain three ways in which misbehavior seriously damages the
   educational process.

Which is the more serious misbehavior—daydreaming or bullying?
   Why?

What is the defining characteristic of neurological-based behavior
   (NBB)?

Part 1b.   Rating

Explain what is meant by "classroom discipline."

In what main way does "today's discipline" differ from
   "old-fashioned discipline"?

Name three legal requirements (related to discipline) with which
   teachers must comply.

Explain what is meant by "*in loco parentis.*"

Name three teacher professional responsibilities in discipline.

Explain the nature and purpose of "preventive discipline."

Explain the nature and purpose of "supportive discipline."

Explain the nature and purpose of "redirective discipline."

Explain the meaning of "discipline with dignity" and why
   dignity must be safeguarded.

Explain the difference between (1) coercion and (2) exerting
   positive influence.

Give three examples of how one exerts strong positive influence
   in discipline.

Part 1c.   Rating

Name two major contributions Fritz Redl and William Wattenberg
   made to discipline.

Describe two of Jacob Kounin's major contributions to discipline.

Describe three ideas Haim Ginott contributed to discipline.

Name three ideas William Glasser contributed to discipline.

Part 1c.	Rating

What did Rudolf Dreikurs identify as students' prime need in school?

Explain why Harry and Rosemary Wong emphasize class routines.

Name the four levels in Marvin Marshall's Hierarchy of Social Development.

Explain how Marshall's hierarchy is used in redirecting misbehavior.

Explain the purported value of Fred Jones's "working the crowd."

Explain the nature and value of Fred Jones's Say, See, Do teaching.

Explain the nature and use of Fred Jones's "interior loop."

Explain why Craig Seganti places primary emphasis on class rules.

Describe the two fundamental tenets in William Glasser's "choice theory."

Explain what Spencer Kagan means by "same side" and "structures."

Explain the general meaning of a "personalized system of discipline."

Explain why the author of this text advocates personalized systems of discipline.

Suggestions for Review in Assessment Area 1

1. Check this book's glossary for definitions of terms that may not be entirely clear in your mind.
2. Turn back to Chapter 12 and review commentaries on the eight questions in discipline.
3. Consult the "Timeline of Developments in Modern Discipline" presented in Chapter 3 to review major discipline contributions in the 20th century.

SELF-ASSESSMENT AREA 2: PREVENTING MISBEHAVIOR BY PROACTIVELY ADDRESSING ITS KNOWN CAUSES

As you prepare to work with a new class, you should anticipate a number of conditions you can address in advance and during the first 2 weeks of class to promote better behavior and learning. Please rate yourself on the following items using the scale:

1. (weak)   2. (borderline)   3. (adequate)   4. (strong)

Part 2	Rating
Differentiate between physical and psychological factors that influence class behavior.	
Why do we want children to be free from fearfulness and insecurity in the classroom?	
Identify three ways in which teachers inadvertently promote student misbehavior.	
How would you improve the behavior of students who are overly "egocentric"?	
How would you provide students the comforts of attention, affirmation, and success?	
In your classes, how would you eradicate threat, verbal put-downs, and intimidation?	
How would you provide students a strong sense of belonging in your classes?	
What does it mean to address a matter "proactively"?	
According to Tom Daly, what one thing do misbehaving students really want from you?	
How does Daly say you can best provide that main thing students want from you?	
What does William Glasser identify as the primary cause of misbehavior in school?	
How would Glasser have you address the primary cause of misbehavior?	
For discipline, what would the Wongs have you do before you first meet your students?	
For discipline, what would Craig Seganti have you do before you first meet your students?	

Suggestions for Review in Assessment Area 2

1. Check the commentaries from Kohn, Glasser, and Daly that appear later in this chapter.
2. Turn back to Chapter 1 to review the 26 factors that can foment misbehavior and the suggestions for eliminating or softening their effects.

3. Turn back to Chapter 12 to review suggestions on:

- Needs, provocation, bullying, and contagious misbehavior.
- Physical discomfort, tedium, meaninglessness, lack of stimulation.
- Teachers and other school personnel being poor models of behavior, show-ing little interest in or appreciation for students, succumbing to personal frustration, reacting badly to provocation, providing ineffective guidance or feedback, using ineffective personal communication, failing to plan proac-tively, and using coercion, threat, and punishment.

Paraphrasing Alfie Kohn (1996/2001) on Building Communities of Learners

We must learn to transform our classes into "learning communities," which are places where students feel safe and cared about and are encouraged to care about each other, where they come to experience a sense of being valued and respected, and where they feel connected to each other—are part of an "us." When that hap-pens, students truly sense they "belong" and at the same time feel safe in their classes.

Paraphrasing William Glasser (2001) on Making Students Happy

If students misbehave in school, it is mostly because they are unhappy there, either with a particular class or teacher or with school in general. Therefore, the main question for teachers is, "How do I make my students happy?"

Here is how to do so: Give students a useful curriculum they find enjoyable and establish personal relationships with them. Those two things work wonders in improving student behavior.

You also quickly improve relations with students if you assiduously avoid the *seven deadly habits in teaching* that damage or destroy relations with students: *criticizing, blaming, complaining, nagging, threatening, punishing,* and *rewarding stu-dents to control them.* You improve relations still further by making regular use of the *seven connecting habits* of *caring, listening, supporting, contributing, encouraging, trusting,* and *befriending.* The success of the Glasser Quality Schools shows that virtually all students who come to school can do competent work. To make sure this happens in your classroom, you must strongly connect with your students. The connection is fairly quickly accomplished when you use the connecting hab-its and give up trying to use external controls to make students behave as you would like.

Paraphrasing Tom Daly (2004) on What Misbehaving Students Want

It is very important to realize that students who misbehave the most are often sending teachers a coded message that says, "Reach me," meaning they are asking for attention or personal connection. If you can reach your students in a likeable way while holding their respect, you will quickly accomplish significant reductions in misbehavior. To reach out effectively to misbehaving students, stop thinking of confronting or controlling their behavior and help them turn their attention to acceptable behavior. That replacement is best accomplished in a process akin to coaching or personal training—you first establish a personal connection with students and then progressively coach them in how to behave appropriately.

SELF-ASSESSMENT AREA 3: PREVENTING MISBEHAVIOR BY IMPROVING COMMUNICATION AND TEACHING CLASS ROUTINES

Several authorities contend that misbehavior can be reduced significantly by improving communication and thoroughly teaching students the routines they are to follow. Here you are asked to assess your capabilities regarding: (1) improving communication with and among students, in ways that increase willingness to learn and cooperate, and (2) teaching students to follow the routines that are important in most class activities. Please rate your ability to do the following, using the numerical scale:

1. *(weak)*   2. *(borderline)*   3. *(adequate)*   4. *(strong)*

Part 3	Rating

Explain with examples how you would speak with students "as your social equals."

How would you go about listening to your students in an "empathic" manner?

Describe how you would teach students to listen to each other empathically.

How would you ensure what you say is compatible with a student's frame of reference?

How can you teach students to disagree with you and each other without being offensive?

Give examples of how you would or would not use "sane messages" and "*why* questions."

How would you teach students to use Glasser's "connecting habits"?

How would you teach students to avoid Glasser's "deadly habits"?

Why do various authorities place so much emphasis on teaching class routines?

What procedure would you use in teaching students to follow a particular routine?

What behaviors would you teach students for the routine of turning in completed work?

How would scripting help you in preparing to teach routines to students?

How might you use Marshall's "positive choices" in communicating with students?

Describe three nonverbal communication tactics you would use when presenting lessons.

Suggestions for Review in Assessment Area 3

Read the following commentaries.

Regarding "Social Equality" in Communication

When teachers speak with students they should do so as "social equals," meaning they speak with students as they do with friends in a manner that is neither bossy nor subservient. They treat students as intelligent people who are able to understand and make decisions, and they use expressions that do not give offense, such as: "I may be wrong, but my opinion is . . ." or "I understand your point of view. Have you considered the alternative point of view that . . . ?"

Paraphrasing Stephen Covey (2004) on Empathic Listening

The key to communicating effectively and establishing productive relationships lies in empathic listening, meaning listening sensitively to others with attention to their emotions. It is helpful if we (1) clarify for ourselves our own frame of reference (our perspectives, values, beliefs, preferences, and so forth) relating to the matter at hand and at the same time (2) try to grasp and adapt to the frame of reference being used by the person with whom we are communicating.

When working with students, try to move from your frame of reference into theirs and communicate from that perspective. That will help you know not just their thoughts but what those thoughts mean in light of their deeper hopes, fears, realities, and difficulties. When you obtain that understanding, you can adjust what you wish to communicate so it fits into the student's frame of reference as child or adolescent.

SELF-ASSESSMENT AREA 4: SUPPORTING PROPER BEHAVIOR BY ESTABLISHING RAPPORT, BUILDING CHARACTER, AND ATTENDING TO STUDENTS

Expert teachers are notably adept at relating to students easily and positively, bringing out the best in students, and providing ongoing support for proper behavior. They normally play an active role in promoting good character, and they help students abide by rules, pay attention, stay on task, complete their work, and do high-quality work.

Please rate yourself on the following competencies using the scale:

1. (weak)   2. (borderline)   3. (adequate)   4. (strong)

Part 4a.	Rating

What did Haim Ginott say about teachers "at their best" and teachers "at their worst"?

If you adopted three of Ginott's suggestions on talking with students, what would they be?

What did Ginott identify as teachers' "hidden asset"?

Part 4a.	**Rating**

What is the meaning of "laconic language," and how does it support proper behavior?

What did Dreikurs say about teachers making positive versus negative comments?

What did Stephen Covey say about students' and teachers' "frames of reference"?

Explain how you would seek to understand a student's frame of reference.

List five of the "seven connecting habits" William Glasser urges teachers to use.

Which two of Glasser's connecting habits do you consider most important, and why?

List five of Glasser's "seven deadly habits" you should carefully avoid.

Which two of Glasser's deadly habits do you believe teachers use most often?

What did Marvin Marshall say was even more valuable than befriending your students?

What did Dale Carnegie say was the great danger in arguing? What was his solution?

Why did Marshall put so much emphasis on "giving students positive choices"?

Which do you consider the more important teacher quality—trustworthiness or charisma?

Part 4b.	**Rating**

How did Tom Daly advise building rapport with "difficult" students?

What are the pros and cons of using humor and sarcasm in building rapport?

What is meant by "character," and why do schools feel they should deal with it?

Name three character traits you would value above others in the students you teach.

What do you see as the relation between "character" and "civility"?

How highly do you value civility, and how would you try to promote it in your classes?

Part 4b.   Rating
_____

Name four things you will teach students about your roles and re-
    sponsibilities in class.

Name four things you will teach students about their roles and re-
    sponsibilities in class.

Describe what you will say to students concerning how you will treat
    them.

Describe what you will say to students about how they must treat
    fellow class members.

Describe and give your rationale for how you expect students to
    address and relate to you.

Part 4c.   Rating
_____

State five rules of behavior that you might expect students to follow in
    your classes.

Explain how you would teach students to follow each of those
    rules.

Name three important class procedures and explain why they should
    be taught well.

Describe how, in general, you would teach students to follow
    procedures.

Name three qualities you will build into lessons to increase and hold
    student attention.

Describe three things you will do while presenting lessons to keep
    students involved.

Describe two things you will do during independent seat work to
    keep students on task.

What would Glasser have students do to strongly improve the quality
    of their work?

What did Glasser say tests should be used for, and how frequently you
    should use them?

What did the Wongs say about the nature and frequency of tests?

Why do some authorities want students to assemble "portfolios" of
    their best work?

Describe instruction that would integrate the ideas of Jones, Glasser,
    and the Wongs.
_____

Suggestions for Review in Assessment Area 4

1. Read the commentaries from Michele Borba and Dale Carnegie that follow.
2. Turn back to Chapter 12 and scan the extensive commentaries on supportive discipline.

Paraphrasing Michele Borba (2004) on Building Character

Let your students know that you will continually emphasize—and expect them to show— "good character" in your classes. You accomplish this by creating a moral learning community in the classroom, where students feel safe and cared about. In such a community, you will be better able to connect with students, show care for them, and model the core traits of solid character. Without such a community, no approach to discipline is going to work well. If students persistently misbehave in school, their character invariably diminishes. You must therefore target and address the specific behaviors that damage respectful classrooms and student character—behaviors such as vulgarity, cruelty, bullying, and disrespect. You must replace those negative behaviors with positive ones, by teaching the desired behaviors explicitly and having students practice them. When students misbehave, have them review their behavior, reflect on it, and make things right with anyone who has been offended. This intervention process works over time; it is not a quick fix, but it transforms the student. Patience is required, and you must persist in giving help over and over while tolerating repeated mistakes.

Paraphrasing Dale Carnegie (1981) on the Pitfalls of Arguing with Students

It is self-defeating to argue with students about any matter. It is worse than a waste of time, because telling them (or anyone) they are wrong doesn't change their mind. It often makes them even more resistant to your point of view. What's more, you can't win an argument. It is impossible. If you make the weaker case, you lose. If you make the stronger case, you also lose, because you have made the other person feel inferior and have wounded his or her pride. Wounded pride does not seek to cooperate. Therefore, it is best to avoid arguments as you would avoid rattlesnakes.

So how do you manage disagreements? First, control your temper, listen, look for areas of agreement, and promise to think carefully about what the other person has said. Then, when you express your view of the situation, say, "I may be wrong. I often am. Let's see if we can examine the facts together." Never tell the other person he or she is wrong. If it turns out you are wrong, admit it quickly and sincerely.

SELF-ASSESSMENT AREA 5: SUPPORTING PROPER BEHAVIOR BY PROVIDING HIGH-QUALITY INSTRUCTION

The overall quality of your instruction has a strong bearing on your students' behavior. In this assessment, you are asked to (1) show you know how to *organize and direct instruction* in a manner that engages students, keeps them actively involved, and promotes understanding and competence; and (2) show you know how to *instill excitement about learning* through involving students in activities they enjoy; incorporating mystery, intrigue, and sense of wonder; helping students apply what they have learned; and helping them see evidence of genuine progress.

Please rate yourself on the following competencies using the numerical scale:

1. (weak)   2. (borderline)   3. (adequate)   4. (strong)

Part 5a.	**Rating**

Describe four things excellent teachers often build into lessons to help students learn.

How capable are you in doing the four things you listed in the item above?

How will you make your learning environment attractive, functional, and efficient?

What will you say and do when you introduce a new lesson?

What will you tell students, in advance, about the lesson?

How will you make sure students know clearly what they are to do in the lesson?

Part 5b.	**Rating**

Describe how you would teach a lesson using Jones's Say, See, Do teaching.

Describe how you would teach a lesson functioning as a "lead teacher."

Are "boss teachers" necessarily ineffective? Have you had good ones? Explain.

Describe, with examples, what you would do to instill interest and excitement in lessons.

Describe how you would interact with students when they are doing independent work.

To what extent and for what purpose would you use cooperative learning activities?

Describe four things you will do to ensure that students remain engaged in your lessons.

Describe how you will provide students the help they need during independent seat work.

Explain how, when, and for what purposes you will communicate through body language.

Name two things you will do to help students increase the quality of their work.

Part 5b.	Rating
How would you arrange for students to practice applying what they have just learned?	
Why does Benna Golubtchik extol multisensory learning experiences?	
Name two things you will do to help students recognize their genuine improvement.	
How would you go about teaching your students to behave civilly?	
How (if at all) would you go about teaching students to be more likeable?	
In teaching, how would you blend seriousness, structure, and personal charisma?	
Glasser and Morrish disagree on whether we can "make" students learn. What is your opinion?	
How often, and for what purpose, would you use tests/quizzes in your classes?	

Suggestions for Review in Assessment Area 5

1. Turn back to Chapter 12 and review the section on presenting interesting lessons and directing them effectively.
2. Read the following commentaries.

C. M. Charles (2000) on Charismatic Teachers

The most memorable teachers in our lives (those we remember favorably, that is) are those who showed us personal attention and made learning fun and exciting. You can do those things for your students by attending to their needs for security, association, belonging, dignity, hope, power, enjoyment, and competence. Here is how you will appear when doing so:

- Personally, you are friendly, interesting, helpful, and supportive.
- You encourage students to engage in topics you believe they will find stimulating and worthwhile.
- You provide clear explanations of what, why, and how students are being asked to learn.
- You provide for camaraderie, meaning enjoyable cooperation and associations among members of the class.
- You add to all your lessons an element of interest or intrigue.
- You provide abundant opportunity for success, improvement, and accomplishment.

- You clearly indicate you are always willing to help.
- You draw attention tactfully to students' personal and group accomplishments.

Benna Golubtchik (2008) on Energizing Lessons

Multisensory activities allow students to use various sensory modalities to enrich the learning experience, and they help students recognize their individual learning strengths and weaknesses. Suppose, for example, you have had your students build and color a tabletop three-dimensional model of the state in which they live. Afterward, ask them to describe and evaluate the activity, the senses they used in making the model, and which parts of the activity they enjoyed most. Help them explore further by asking them to reflect on the following questions:

- What did I learn?
- What did I like best about the assignment?
- What senses did I enjoy using the most (e.g., touch, sight, hearing)?
- What part did I find most difficult?

Here are a number of other activities that call upon various sensory modalities:

Tactual/Kinesthetic Activities

- Demonstrate any given process by physically acting it out.
- Create designs, shapes, and patterns to illustrate a scene from history or nature.
- Construct a timeline and fill in details.
- Draw or paint a picture, poster, chart, or sketch of what you learn.
- Construct props and costumes to dramatize or role-play a historical event.
- Build a shadow box or diorama that reflects something learned.
- Create a dance or movement to tell a story.
- Use whole-body learning by acting out vocabulary words or a sequence of events.
- Construct projects and make diagrams, models, or replicas of systems or procedures.
- Build puppets and put on a show related to content.
- Pantomime a sequence.

Auditory Processing Activities

- Identify rhythmic patterns in music or poetry.
- Perform a rap or song that summarizes information.
- Write an original play, rap, jingle, cheer, or song.
- Compose music to convey the theme or mood of the lesson.

Visual Processing Activities

- Write a journal of activities and events in class.
- Create imagined correspondence between historical or contemporary characters.
- Write newspaper accounts of the news, fashion, entertainment, and features of an earlier time.

- Research, compare, and contrast art of different cultures or time periods.
- Rewrite difficult information in a simpler form for an audience of younger students.
- Write poetry, stories, ideas, or thoughts.
- Compose scripts to depict historical events.
- Utilize a camera or video camera to create a pictorial report.
- Create a Venn diagram or concept map to convey information to others.
- Develop color-coding systems to categorize information.

SELF-ASSESSMENT AREA 6: SUPPORTING PROPER BEHAVIOR BY PROMOTING CIVILITY, RESPONSIBILITY, AND POSITIVE PERSONAL RELATIONS

We have noted that when most people speak of discipline, they envision two things—first, student misbehavior and, second, what the teacher does to correct it. Certainly "corrective" redirection is essential in discipline, but you can greatly reduce the need for it by helping students learn to conduct themselves civilly, ethically, and responsibly in the classroom. Here you are asked to assess your capabilities in promoting these valuable qualities in your classes. Please rate yourself on the following, using the numerical scale:

1. (weak)   2. (borderline)   3. (adequate)   4. (strong)

Part 6	Rating
Explain, with three examples, what is meant by "civility."	
Describe five things you would do to increase the level of civility in your classes.	
Explain, with three examples, the nature and value of ethical behavior.	
Describe two things you would do to increase ethical behavior in your classes.	
Explain, with one or more realistic examples, the nature and value of trust.	
Explain how trust develops, and how it can be damaged.	
Describe two things you would do to promote trust in your classes.	
Indicate two ways you would show you are always ready to help your students.	
Name three things you would do to refine and project your personal charisma.	

Part 6	Rating

Describe two things you would do to help students increase their level of likeability.

List six things you consider to be major student obligations in school.

Describe three things you could do to help students meet their obligations responsibly.

How might you use Marshall's hierarchy to help students develop responsibility?

How might you use Gossen's self-restitution to help students develop responsibility?

How might you use rules as proposed by Seganti to increase student responsibility?

Describe three things you would do to show your personal responsibility in teaching.

Explain how you might document student growth in responsibility over time.

Suggestions for Review in Assessment Area 6

Following are selected commentaries related to items in the foregoing assessment.

A Composite of Opinion on Civility, Ethical Behavior, Trust, and Likeability

If you are to shape your classes into communities of learners, you must endeavor to establish a prevailing sense of civility, ethics, and trust among the members of your class, including yourself. *Civility* refers to politeness and consideration for the feelings of others. *Ethics* refers to doing the correct and honorable thing in all situations. *Trust* is the belief that we can count on others to support us and not harm us in any way.

Civility, ethics, and trust are interrelated and are at the core of high-quality learning environments. We are open to trusting and cooperating with people we like and who seem to like us. We cannot trust others who treat us inconsiderately and who we fear might treat us unethically. (Our initial openness to trust is provisional and can be quickly lost.) If we want others to trust us, we must make ourselves likeable. We can do this by giving attention to others, treating them civilly and ethically, providing help when they need it, and always keeping our word. To ensure quality education, teachers need to be consistently likeable and trustworthy, and so do students.

Paraphrasing Michele Borba (2004) on Moral Intelligence and Responsibility

Schools offer one of the few remaining places where many of the young can learn the value of responsibility, caring, respect, and cooperation and where they can observe adults displaying those traits consistently. When students persistently misbehave, their character diminishes. To counter detrimental misbehavior, we should do what we can to eliminate vulgarity, cruelty, bullying, and disrespect. When these behaviors occur, take time to have those involved reflect on the impact of such behavior. Then show them how to make things right with those they have offended. Do this seriously but pleasantly and over time you will see those hurtful behaviors disappear from your classes.

Paraphrasing P. M. Forni (2006) on the Nature and Value of Civility

Civility shows respect for others and their opinions. It incorporates the concepts of courtesy, the "Golden Rule," niceness, politeness, kindness, good manners, fairness, decency, concern for others, justice, tolerance, equality, sincerity, morality, honesty, awareness, trustworthiness, moderation, compassion, friendliness, helpfulness, good citizenship, and abiding by rules.

Here are some *rules of considerate conduct* to help us understand better ways of relating to and connecting with others. By employing these rules, we are able to establish more enjoyable, companionable, and rewarding relationships with the people we meet. Each rule provides a fruitful topic for class discussions and role-playing:

- Acknowledge others in a positive way.
- Think the best of others.
- Listen.
- Speak kindly.
- Accept and give praise.
- Respect others' opinions.
- Respect other people's time.
- Apologize earnestly.
- Refrain from idle complaints.

Civility, politeness, and good manners help improve our relations with others. We are social beings, and our happiness and overall well-being depend, in large measure, on the quality of our relationships. Conducting ourselves in a kindly manner allows us to connect more meaningfully with others, and the more considerately we behave, the more likely we are to establish harmonious relationships that improve the quality of our lives.

We all need social support. To obtain it, we must treat others with kindness and consideration, showing we value them as persons. When we do that, others usually want to remain connected to us, sometimes resulting in long continuing relationships.

If we are considerate toward others, they will tend to like and trust us; if they like and trust us, they will let us help them; and by helping them, we help ourselves. Good social skills strengthen social bonds and are therefore invaluable in promoting a good quality of life.

Paraphrasing Craig Seganti (2008a) on Rules and Responsibility

A good complete set of rules will make students' class obligations plain. Make the rules yourself and give students copies. Spend the first 2 or 3 days teaching the rules very thoroughly, with both you and the students role-playing the actions involved. Once you have done that, there should be no question in students' minds concerning the rules, what they are for, and how one complies with them.

Paraphrasing Marvin Marshall (2001, 2007) on Options and Responsibility

Most students resist in some degree being *made* to do anything. Therefore, do what you can to *inspire and influence* students to learn and conduct themselves responsibly. There is ample evidence that choice empowers students by offering them options. Therefore, teachers should establish expectations and then empower students to reach them. This process occurs in a noncoercive manner when you ask *reflective questions* that prompt students to think about how they are behaving. The reflection often sets in motion a positive change in behavior. One way to start the reflection process is to prompt students to ask themselves questions such as, "If I wanted to be responsible in this class right now, what would I be doing?" In most cases, the answer will be apparent and they will begin behaving accordingly.

Ask students questions and encourage them to ask themselves questions about behavior they have chosen. The questioning process activates the thinking process. Make your students aware that they continually make choices, knowingly and unknowingly, that largely determine their happiness and success in school and life.

Consider spending a bit of time teaching students the Hierarchy of Social Development. Once students have internalized the four levels, when they misbehave, you only have to ask them to identify the level of their behavior. That will cause them to reflect and choose to behave responsibly.

SELF-ASSESSMENT AREA 7: REDIRECTING STUDENT MISBEHAVIOR, WITH DIGNITY

You must redirect student behavior when it is disruptive or otherwise unacceptable. But if you are to be fully effective as a teacher, you must redirect the misbehavior in a positive, helpful manner that does not alienate students. In this book, you have encountered a number of redirective tactics which return students to appropriate behavior, maintain their dignity (self-respect), and promote immediate and long-term improvement. Please assess your capabilities in the following, using the scale:

1. (weak)   *2. (borderline)*   *3. (adequate)*   *4. (strong)*

Part 7	Rating
Clarify the nature of misbehavior and how it damages teaching and learning.	
How would you help students differentiate between proper and improper behavior?	
How could you help students understand how misbehavior cheats them personally?	

Part 7   **Rating**

What does "with dignity" mean in the context of redirecting misbehavior?

Clarify why and how you will stress positivity and dignity when redirecting misbehavior.

List three redirective tactics you would feel good about using when misbehavior occurs.

What does "taking responsibility" mean in association with redirecting misbehavior?

What are the first three things you'd say to students whose behavior needs redirecting?

In what cases might you ask misbehaving students to choose among positive alternatives?

Describe two positive tactics for redirecting less serious misbehavior such as inattention.

Describe two positive tactics for redirecting students whose noise disrupts the class.

Describe tactics you would use to redirect more serious misbehavior such as bullying.

Explain how you would preserve student dignity when you redirect serious misbehavior.

Describe the personal conduct you would show when redirecting misbehavior.

Explain how you might help students recognize and redirect their own misbehavior.

George intimidates Harry: How might you use Barbara Coloroso's redirective tactics?

George intimidates Harry: How might you use Marvin Marshall's redirective tactics?

George intimidates Harry: How might you use Ron Morrish's redirective tactics?

George intimidates Harry: How might you use Ed Ford's redirective tactics?

George intimidates Harry: How might you use Diane Gossen's redirective tactics?

Part 7	Rating
George intimidates Harry: How might you use William Glasser's redirective tactics?	
George intimidates Harry: How might you use Spencer Kagan's redirective tactics?	
George intimidates Harry: How might you use Craig Seganti's redirective tactics?	

Suggestions for Review in Assessment Area 7

Read the following authoritative opinions on how you should go about redirecting student misbehavior.

Paraphrasing William Glasser (1990) on What to Say to Misbehaving Students

Teachers must intervene when students break rules or class agreements. The interventions (nonpunitive) should serve two purposes: stop the misbehavior and get the student's mind back on class work. If a student misbehaves, you might say, "It looks like you have a problem. I want to help you. I'm not interested in punishing you. Let's see if we can solve the problem. Is what you are doing against the rules? What can you and I do together to make sure it won't happen again?"

Paraphrasing Ronald Morrish (2005) on Having Students Repeat Behavior Correctly

When students misbehave, have them repeat the behavior in an acceptable manner. Do this every time they misbehave. They usually know how to behave acceptably, but if necessary, show them what you expect and advise them you will insist on proper behavior.

Paraphrasing Barbara Coloroso (1994/2002) on Redirecting by Giving Students Ownership

When students misbehave, have them acknowledge what they have done. This gives them ownership of the problem. Then, in a kindly manner, show you expect them, as owners, to resolve the problem. You may need to suggest some positive choices to help them do so. All this makes students realize that when they behave inappropriately, it is up to them to correct the problem. You give them the responsibility, opportunity, and guidance to do so.

Paraphrasing Diane Gossen (2004) on Rules Assessment and Self-Restitution

When students disrupt or fail to do their work, it is suggested that the teacher ask, "What's the rule?" or "What's your job?" Doing so moves attention from the problem to the solution and avoids debate and excuses.

If the student doesn't know the rule or won't say it, state it yourself and ask, "Can you do that?" When the student complies, say "Thank you, I appreciate it." This type of exchange involves monitoring and redirection of behavior, and is vastly preferable to lecturing or moralizing.

Self-restitution is an effective process of restoring oneself to correct ways of behaving. When students misbehave, help them select responsible behavior through (1) reflecting on their misbehavior, (2) identifying the need or condition that prompted it, and (3) creating new ways of behaving that are *in keeping with the kinds of persons they want to be.* This process does not dwell on faults or mistakes, but instead helps students learn how to make things right *within themselves* and with whomever they have offended or whatever they have damaged.

Paraphrasing Marvin Marshall (2007) on Redirecting Misbehavior with the Hierarchy

(In order to use Marshall's approach, you would have already taught students the four levels of behavior in the Hierarchy of Social Development.) Let's say Heather and Julie are talking aloud during quiet time of independent work. You say, "Heather, Julie, at what level is your behavior?" The girls answer honestly and return at once to appropriate behavior.

Paraphrasing Spencer Kagan (Kagan, Kyle, & Scott, 2007) on Redirecting by Applying Structures

When students misbehave, you should identify the misbehavior, identify the position (internal feelings "from which the student is coming"), show acceptance of the position but not the behavior, and apply a structure (set of steps) that brings students back to acceptable behavior. If possible, use a structure that has long-term positive effects.

For example, suppose Juan heatedly swears at Armando. You say, "I know you are angry, Juan, and perhaps with good reason. But you know swearing is not allowed in our class. I want you to write out for me two ways you could have replied better to Armando to show your displeasure, and also explain how you will make sure you don't swear again in class."

Ed Ford's (2004) Advice on Redirecting Through Student Self-Appraisal

When a student misbehaves, ask the following questions, with a pleasant, matter-of-fact demeanor and no sign of anger, exasperation, or disappointment:

Question 1: "What are you doing?"   When students hear this question, they look within themselves and identify their behavior. Telling or asking them what they are doing wrong doesn't help them develop the skill of self-reflection—that only encourages students to make excuses.

Question 2: "What are the rules?"   When asked this question, students quickly tie the rules to what they are currently doing and assess their actions in terms of the rights of others.

Ford says the foregoing two questions are usually all you need to ask, but in the early stages of learning this protocol, you might also need to ask if the behavior is against the rules, what happens when rules are broken, and what do you want to do now?

CONCLUSION

This concludes the self-appraisal portion of your development toward excellence in discipline. It would be very unusual, on your first attempt, to reach level 4 on a majority of the items. It is now up to you to do what is necessary to strengthen yourself in areas of uncertainty, so that over time you can give yourself the highest ratings on all items. When you've accomplished that goal, you will have reached the mastery level in knowledge of classroom discipline and how it is best managed in classrooms.

In the next chapter, you move ahead to the final step in your preparation for establishing and maintaining excellent discipline in your classes. There, you will be guided in constructing a personalized system of discipline that is fully attuned to your preferences and to the traits and needs of your students. Quite an achievement that will be, and it is now at your fingertips.

14

Building Your Personalized Approach to Discipline

How Do I Organize Effective Discipline That Meets My Needs and Those of My Students?

You are now ready to finalize a system of discipline you strongly believe will best serve you and your students. Three ways in which you might approach this task will be discussed momentarily. As you weigh the options, make sure to select or develop a plan that meets the following criteria:

- It is suited to the age level and sociocultural background of the students you teach or expect to teach. (See Chapter 2 for guidance.)
- It is consistent with your philosophy, preferences, and personality.
- It is balanced in its ability to prevent misbehavior, support proper behavior, and redirect misbehavior.
- The tactics it involves are sensible, positive, and easy to apply.
- You believe your students will react to it positively and will have little difficulty abiding by its stipulations.

THREE OPTIONS

Regarding the options, the first is to select *in toto* one of the exemplary discipline programs described in Chapters 4 through 10. All of those programs have loyal followers and attract considerable attention. Using one of them would be the easiest thing to do if the approach is well matched to the traits, needs, and realities of your students and to your preferences as well.

The second option is to adopt one of the exemplary programs, but modify it to meet your specific needs, your students' needs, or your personal preferences. You might add something to the program, leave something out, or change some of the procedures. For example (these are not suggestions, but simply illustrations), you might want to use Craig Seganti's structured approach in combination with the active teaching style and body language advocated by Fred Jones. Or you might want to use Marvin Marshall's Hierarchy of Social Development in combination with the emphasis on procedures advocated by Harry and Rosemary Wong. If you make such modifications, you must be sure the changes you make do not render the overall approach ineffective.

The third option—and one for which this book has prepared you—is to select discipline principles and tactics from various sources and organize them into a balanced program of preventive, supportive, and redirective discipline. This option would, in most cases, provide the greatest likelihood of meeting the needs of both you and your students. If you have kept a journal of entries from the various chapters, you already have at hand the information you need for organizing such a plan.

FORMULATING YOUR PERSONALIZED APPROACH TO DISCIPLINE: RUBRIC, REMINDERS, AND SUGGESTIONS

Now let's look once again at the planning rubric that was introduced in Chapter 2. Suggestions have been added that you might find useful. By referring back to your journal notes, you can easily complete a well-designed system of discipline that meets the needs of your students in a manner consistent with your personal views and preferences. You can also use the rubric to ensure balance if you decide to modify an existing approach.

Rubric Topic 1. Stating My Philosophy of Discipline

A philosophy of any topic summarizes one's beliefs concerning the overall nature and value of that topic.

Reminders for philosophy of discipline: Classroom discipline refers to teachers' efforts to help students conduct themselves responsibly. Discipline is used to forestall misbehavior, support acceptable behavior, and deal positively with misbehavior. Misbehavior is defined as any behavior that, through *intent or thoughtlessness*, interferes with teaching or learning, threatens or intimidates others, or oversteps society's standards of moral, ethical, or legal behavior. Misbehavior, when left unchecked, makes classroom life chaotic, hinders teaching, suppresses learning, harms personal relationships, and fosters self-defeating habits.

> **Your turn:**   Now state your philosophy of discipline in your own words, including your definition of discipline, its primary purpose, your main duties in discipline, and students' main duties. Suggested length of response: one-half to one page. ■

Rubric Topic 2. Stating My Theory of Discipline

Theories are attempts to describe the processes and relationships inherent in given events or efforts. You can express your **theory of discipline** by identifying discipline's necessary components and explaining how they work independently and/or in conjunction to produce the results you desire.

Reminders for theory of discipline: A well-rounded system of discipline must give attention to preventing misbehavior, supporting proper behavior, and redirecting inappropriate behavior in a manner that maintains student dignity.

A good system of discipline will specify class rules or explicit understandings that set limits on behavior, indicate how students are to relate to you and to each other, and clearly help students improve their self-control, responsibility, and relations with others.

Preventive tactics are put in place to stop or reduce misbehavior before it occurs. Some are done before you meet your students; others are done during the first 2 weeks of class and periodically thereafter. They include such things as planning to meet student needs, working to eliminate factors known to lead to misbehavior, teaching students how to conduct themselves, and teaching procedures for carrying out a number of class routines.

Supportive tactics are used on an ongoing basis to engage students, inspire them, keep them on task, help them persevere, and ensure they enjoy their learning experiences. These tactics include such things as providing learning experiences of interest to students, using an engaging instructional approach that calls for frequent student responses, and circulating among students and interacting with them in a positive manner.

Redirective tactics are applied when misbehavior occurs. Their purpose is to stop the misbehavior and help students regain self-control and return to responsible behavior. To be most effective, redirective tactics must not damage students' personal sense of dignity. Examples of recommended tactics are having students redo inappropriate behavior in a correct manner, speaking personally with individual students about inappropriate behavior, and influencing students to make behavior choices that lead to success in school.

Your turn: Now state your theory of discipline in your own words. Suggested length of response: one-half to one page. ∎

Rubric Topic 3. The Professional and Ethical Demeanor I Will Display

You must make sure you comply with legal, professional, and ethical expectations in teaching, and also work to develop positive relations and trust with students and others.

Reminders for professional demeanor: Your legal requirements relate to due diligence (keeping close watch on students under your care), breach of duty (failure to comply with legal requirements of teachers), and service *in loco parentis* (taking the place of parents while in charge of students). You might wish to refer back to Chapter 2, where these topics are discussed.

Also very important to your success is your ability to quickly develop a trusting relationship with your students, their families, and your fellow professionals. Present yourself as friendly but business-like, enthusiastic (but not maniacal), and eager to help. Learn names quickly and chat with individuals as often as feasible. Always speak in a respectful manner, using the *connecting habits* of *caring, listening, supporting, contributing, encouraging, trusting,* and *befriending*. Treat students and colleagues as you treat your friends. Be constantly mindful of everyone's need for security, hope, appreciation, and competence. And finally, do your best to make sure you conduct yourself ethically in all situations, especially in the school setting.

> **Your turn:** Now provide a brief statement describing the professional demeanor you will display and what you will do to develop trust with students, families of students, and colleagues. Suggested length: one-half to one page. ■

Rubric Topic 4. The Student Behavior I Will Endeavor to Promote and the Rules That Support It

Think carefully about the behavior you want your students to display in class. You might recognize that different kinds of activities promote or require different kinds of behavior. Here you can clarify your preferences and the rules to support them.

Reminders for class behavior: Effective teachers strive to help their students engage actively in learning and routinely exhibit behavior that is civil, respectful, purposeful, and responsible. They discuss these behaviors with students and formalize class rules that promote them. Some teachers establish rules in advance and then explain everything to their students. Other teachers involve students in helping formulate expectations and set the rules.

Students don't always know how to comply with rules and therefore must sometimes be taught. In teaching a rule, you should describe it and its purpose, demonstrate the behavior involved, ask students to act it out, and then call on students to follow the rule during class activities. Most discipline authorities suggest you use approximately five rules. Others say you only need one—such as "Always treat others the way you would like to be treated"—whereas still others say you need a larger number that apply to various activities and procedures. Review the notes you have taken while reading various chapters in the text.

> **Your turn:** Now write out the rules you want students to follow, along with your rationales for selecting those particular rules. Suggested length of response: one-half page. ■

Rubric Topic 5. What I Will Do Proactively to Prevent or Reduce Misbehavior

Good discipline depends more on preventing misbehavior than on correcting it, although both are necessary. Prevention has the additional advantage of not consuming instructional time.

Reminders on preventing misbehavior: You might wish to turn back to Chapter 1 and review the section entitled "What Causes Students to Misbehave?" That section reviews 26 conditions that tend to promote misbehavior and suggests how you can eliminate or soften their effects. Perhaps you have already made notes in your journal concerning causes and prevention of misbehavior. Keep your response to this item relatively short. You might mention what you will or will not do as concerns the following:

- How you will address, in advance, various causes of misbehavior;
- How you will make learning more enjoyable for students while reducing factors that produce frustration;

- How you will inform students when you first meet them about class expectations and rules;
- How you will interact with students regularly and show appreciation for them and their efforts;
- How you will communicate with students in ways that influence them positively.

Your turn: Now, without going into too much detail, indicate what you will do, in advance, to prevent or reduce factors that are known to promote misbehavior in the classroom. Suggested length of response: one to two pages. ■

Rubric Topic 6. How I Will Support My Students' Efforts to Participate and Persevere

In former times, teachers seemed to assume that right-minded students would work assiduously at their assigned tasks. When students failed to do so, teachers considered their actions to be misbehavior, and so they would give students stern looks or words of disapproval or direct commands to get back to work. Today's discipline recognizes the value of tactics that keep students actively engaged, productive, and constantly improving. Teachers who are very good at their jobs use such tactics in a manner that seems effortless.

Reminders on providing support: Students will work and stick with lessons very well when they find the instructional activities interesting, enjoyable, valuable, and perhaps even intriguing. If you provide those conditions, you won't see much misbehavior. But it would be ingenuous to imply that you can always provide lessons that prevent students from becoming tired, bored, restless, or inattentive. When, despite your efforts, you see students begin to yawn, talk, look out the window, and so forth, you must have alternatives to which you can turn, such as:

- Circulate among students and give them personal attention.
- Use body language in a positive, supportive manner.
- Refer to visual instructional plans—illustrated series of steps you have posted that remind students how to proceed without getting stalled.
- Show interest in student work, cheerfully ask questions, make favorable comments, and provide hints.
- If the activity is overly boring or difficult, restructure it or change to another activity.

Your turn: Now indicate what you will normally do to help students remain engaged in lessons and refrain from misbehaving. Suggested length of response: one page. ■

Rubric Topic 7. How I Will Redirect Students When They Misbehave

You know that developments over the past 60 years have led teachers to a new approach to discipline that relies on positive influence rather than threat and punishment. The advantage of positivity is that it reduces students' fear and prompts them to work in collaboration with teachers rather than resisting them. In earlier chapters, you encountered a number of influence tactics that are effective in helping students behave responsibly.

Reminders on providing redirection: When students misbehave, you should respond in a manner that (1) stops the misbehavior, (2) helps students return to behavior that is appropriate for the situation, and (3) allows the students' dignity to remain intact. Students usually know when they are misbehaving and know what they should do instead, but occasionally you might have to suggest two or three acceptable alternatives from which students may choose. At times, you only have to ask students to accept responsibility for correcting their behavior. In all cases, you should interact with students in a manner that does not attack them personally. Suggestions include the following.

For minor misbehavior:

■ Move alongside students and show interest in their work.
■ Catch students' eyes, send private signals, or move closer to students.
■ Provide a light challenge: "Can you get two more problems done before we stop?"
■ Ask students if they are having difficulty. Ask what you might to do help.

For more serious or disruptive behavior: Follow intervention procedures that have been established and practiced in advance, such as:

■ Ask the student to repeat the behavior in an acceptable manner.
■ Stop and reteach the proper behavior.
■ Have students show you they understand how to behave responsibly.
■ Calmly ask offending students to identify their level or type of behavior.
■ Allow students to choose among two or three acceptable alternative behaviors you stipulate.
■ Help students accept ownership of the problem and decide how they will correct it.
■ Ask students (perhaps privately) to accept personal responsibility for conducting themselves properly in class.
■ Ask the student to engage in a process of self-restitution, as described by Diane Gossen (2004).
■ Talk with offending students calmly and respectfully, without lecturing or threatening. Remain pleasant and composed. Don't argue. Ask them how they can (and will) conduct themselves responsibly in the future. Make notes of what they say. Assure them they can now make a fresh start and everything will be all right as long as they show responsibility and follow the class rules. Remain friendly with offending students and thank them privately when they comply with expectations.

Your turn: Describe how you will stop misbehavior of different degrees of seriousness when it occurs and what you will do to help students willingly return to appropriate behavior. Suggested length of response: one to two pages. ■

Rubric Topic 8. How and When I Will Communicate My Discipline Approach to Students, Administrators, and Students' Caregivers

You should communicate your discipline plan very clearly to students, administrators, and caregivers. Your purpose in doing so is to inform and obtain support.

Reminder of sequence to follow:

- First, compose your plan in writing (which is what you are doing now).
- Second, take a neat copy to leave with your principal and ask if he or she will examine and support your plan (they almost always do, but may make a suggestion or two).
- Third, review your plan thoroughly with students: Explain what is required, the reasoning behind it, and their responsibilities within the plan.
- Fourth, send condensed copies to students' caregivers. Do this via the school website if possible, or send copies home with students for caregivers to read and then sign, indicating they have reviewed, understand, and agree to the plan. Have the signed copies returned to you. You may want your students to sign the plan, as well.

It is usually well worth your time to explain the following to students, caregivers, and others:

- How and why you will establish and maintain a classroom in which students feel safe, physically and emotionally.
- How you will communicate with and relate to students.
- How you expect students to relate to you and each other.
- In what ways the relations you desire are beneficial to learning and student well-being.
- Your roles and the students' roles in class, perhaps shown on a "My Job—Your Job" chart.
- How you will respond when students fail to comply with class rules, and what you will expect of noncompliant students.

Your turn: Briefly describe how you will communicate your plan to your administrator, your students, and your students' caregivers. Suggested length of response: one-half page. ■

TWO ILLUSTRATIVE DISCIPLINE PLANS

For your perusal, here are two discipline approaches constructed and used by experienced teachers. One is for use at the primary-grade level, and the other is for the secondary level. It is not suggested you emulate either of these approaches, but you might enjoy reading the teachers' efforts in organizing discipline for their classes. You, of course, will have your own way of doing things.

Example 1. An Approach That Emphasizes Rules and Consequences

Many teachers use discipline plans built around rules and consequences. They feel this approach provides maximum clarity and allows students to learn in a supportive environment. Discipline plans of this type involve good teaching combined with (1) a set of *rules* concerning what students are allowed and not allowed to do in class; (2) *consequences*— what happens when students follow the rules and when they violate them; and (3) *procedures* for invoking consequences. This approach has served hundreds of thousands of teachers for many years and is still popular. To see how a present-day teacher uses the rules-consequences-procedures protocol, examine the following program developed by third-grade teacher Deborah Sund.

Deborah Sund's Third-Grade Discipline Plan

Deborah Sund, who had been teaching for 2 years when she devised this program, wanted a discipline approach that provided structure for class members while meeting the needs of all concerned. Here is her plan.

My Philosophy of Discipline.   *Purpose of Discipline*: I believe the purpose of discipline is to provide a safe, supportive, calm environment in which students are able to learn to the best of their abilities. To make that possible, I believe teachers should strive to meet the needs of everyone in the class, students and teacher alike.

Students' needs I will keep foremost in mind are:

- To feel safe and personally valued in the group.
- To learn interesting and useful information, especially skills in reading, math, and language.
- A learning environment that is attractive, stimulating, and conducive to productive work.
- A teacher who is helpful, attentive, and kind.
- The opportunity to interact and work cooperatively with other students.
- To learn how to relate to others humanely and helpfully.
- To have the opportunity to excel.

My own needs that I hope will be met are:

- To be respected and valued as a teacher.
- To be able to teach without unwarranted disruptions.
- To have an orderly classroom appearance: good room arrangement; materials neatly stored; interesting, well-thought-out displays.
- To have structure and routines that provide comfort and security with flexibility.
- To have students who are considerate of others, attentive, and willing to participate and follow directions.
- A class sense of warmth, enthusiasm, responsibility, and mutual regard.

My Particular Dislikes: I want to be upfront with my students about my particular dislikes, which are:

- Inattention to speaker, teacher, other adult, or class member.
- Excessive noise: loud voices, inappropriate talking and laughing.
- Distractions such as toys, unnecessary movement, poking, teasing.
- Abuse of instructional materials: misusing, wasting, or destroying.
- Unkind and rude conduct: ridicule, sarcasm, bad manners, and physical abuse.

My Theory of Discipline.   I believe good discipline must maintain a focus on learning, which in turn is supported by persistent helpfulness and kindness by all class members. I believe the desired behavior is best promoted through preventing misbehavior, supporting proper behavior, practicing class rules, responsibly fulfilling roles and requirements, and relying on instructional tactics that assist students in abiding by the rules.

What I Will Do Proactively to Limit Misbehavior.   I will familiarize myself further with the known causes of misbehavior and try to attend to all of them in advance. I will make sure to maintain proper lighting, temperature, traffic patterns, and room attractiveness so students won't feel strained, tired, or inconvenienced. I will endeavor to meet students' needs for safety, belonging, and interesting activities. I will plan carefully for modeling, teaching, and practicing good manners and courtesy. I will discuss with my students the meaning and practice of responsibility and why it is so important in learning. And I will carefully plan out an active curriculum that includes interesting activities, physical movement, and singing, along with times of quiet listening and resting.

What I Will Do to Support Proper Behavior.   *Establish Class Rules.* On the first day of school I will ask my students to tell me how they would like to be treated by others in the room. I will also ask them what kinds of behavior they especially dislike. We will discuss their contributions at length, making sure through examples that we have a clear understanding of everyone's wishes. By the next day, I will have written out some statements that summarize what they have said. I'll then ask if these ideas seem good ones to live by in the class. I anticipate students' agreeing with the ideas, which we will then call our class rules.

Practice Abiding by Rules. We will spend time practicing how we will conduct ourselves in accordance with the rules. I will demonstrate the prompts, cues, hints, and other assistance I will give to help students abide by the behaviors we have agreed on. I expect the following to emerge as class rules:

- Be considerate of others at all times. (We will discuss and practice speaking kindly, behaving helpfully, and not bothering others.)
- Do our best work. (We will discuss the importance of getting as much done as possible, not wasting time, and doing neat work we are proud of.)
- Use quiet voices in the classroom. We will discuss and practice using regular speaking voices during class discussions, speaking quietly during cooperative work, and whispering at other times. I will inform students which volume of voice is appropriate until they learn to use the proper volume automatically.
- Use signals to request permission or receive help. I will explain and have students practice the signals for assistance, movement, and restroom pass.

Recognize and Comply with Roles and Responsibilities. We will identify and practice the "job descriptions" expected of both teacher and students.

I will describe my role, with examples, as including:

- Having main responsibility for what we will learn and making sure we learn it.
- Being as helpful as I can to each and every student, without exception.
- Always treating everyone with kindness and consideration.

I will describe students' roles, with examples, as:

- Paying attention, participating, and doing one's best to learn.
- Always being polite and behaving the way you know is best.
- Helping keep the classroom neat and orderly.

Help Students Learn to Behave Responsibly. To support students' efforts to behave responsibly, I will routinely do many of the things suggested by Fred Jones, such as:

- Circulate among class members to remind them I am attentive and available.
- Interact with individual students to provide acknowledgment and support.
- Provide help immediately as it is needed.
- Show I am genuinely pleased when students follow the rules and behave responsibly. I will make use of winks, nods, and pats. Sometimes I will say aloud how pleased I am with the way they are working or behaving toward each other.
- Keep their caregivers informed about the class activities and their child's progress, and invite them to be involved with the class.
- Begin and end each day on a positive note, with fond greetings or good-byes and expectations of happy and productive days in class.

How I Will Redirect Students When They Break Rules.   Earlier, when first discussing the class rules, I will ask students what they think should happen when someone breaks a rule. I expect them to suggest punishment, but I will tell them that instead of punishment, I will probably do one of the following:

- Look at them with "pirate eyes" (a stern glance with disappointed or puzzled expression) that lets them know they need to behave properly.
- Point out that a rule is being broken by saying: "I hear noise." "Some people are not listening."
- Tell them exactly what they have done wrong and ask them to do it properly: "Gordon, you did not use the signal. Try again and use the signal this time."
- Have them take "time out" from the group until they can conduct themselves properly.

My Attention to Professionalism.   I believe the established standards of the teaching profession provide reliable guidance and safeguards for working effectively with colleagues and young learners. I take those standards seriously, none more so than those affecting the physical and psychological safety of the students in my care. I will also check continually to make sure I am complying with the ethical standards of the profession and with normal human decency as well. It is very important to me to present myself as a good teacher, a valued colleague, and a good person.

Example 2: An Approach That Combines Prevention of Misbehavior and Cooperation Between Teacher and Students

The following approach emphasizes preventing misbehavior by meeting students' needs and building personal relationships. It is designed to gain student cooperation and reduce student inclination to disregard or try to outwit the teacher. It emphasizes the following:

- Attending continually to students' needs for security, hope, acceptance, dignity, power, enjoyment, and competence.
- Making class activities consistently enjoyable and worthwhile, with abundant attention, encouragement, and support for students.
- Discussing and practicing manners, courtesy, and responsibility.
- Reducing misbehavior by attending to its causes.

Gail Charles's Discipline Plan for Her English Classes

My Philosophy of Discipline.   I think discipline in a school setting should focus on responsibility and respect for others. I will emphasize to my students why we benefit from getting along with others, why we need to limit some of our personal actions for the good of the group, and why and how classmates and school personnel should be treated with respect and civility. I also believe students can benefit greatly by learning how to speak respectfully with adults, including making eye contact, using a pleasant tone of voice, and making use of courteous expressions such as "please" and "thank you." I agree with Tom Daly that it is beneficial for students to behave in ways that cause teachers to like them. It is highly desirable that students learn to relate respectfully with classmates, as well.

My Theory of Discipline.   I consider there to be four necessary components of an effective system of discipline. The first component is a set of class rules or agreements that places limits on behavior and informs students how they are to manage their behavior and interact with each other. The second, third, and fourth components are, respectively, preventive tactics that forestall misbehavior, supportive tactics that reinforce proper behavior and help students persevere, and redirective tactics that cause misbehaving students to return to proper behavior. My preventive tactics will include providing a suitable learning environment and preparing lessons with student needs in mind. My supportive tactics will feature positive interactions with students, much student participation in lessons, and quick attention and help to students when they need it. My redirective tactics for most misbehavior will involve body language, physical proximity, and asking students to redo misbehavior correctly. I believe these efforts will maintain good interpersonal relations, increase student self-control, and increase student productivity.

The Professional and Ethical Behavior I Will Display.   Here are matters of professionalism I will endeavor to live by:

First, I will give my best to my students and the profession. I will provide the best learning environment I can and will teach using the best methods known to me. I will show the high value I place on education. I will model responsibility and self-control. I will laud effort and accept mistakes as a natural part of learning.

Second, I will supervise and safeguard the well-being of my students at all times. I will always be mindful of due diligence and my obligations associated with *in loco parentis*.

Third, I will value and respect my students as social equals and friends. I will keep my promises and commitments to them, be helpful in all situations, and strive to be fair and consistent. I will do my best to remain positive and optimistic. And as William Glasser suggests, I will do my best to replace my "deadly habits" of blaming, complaining, criticizing, nagging, punishing, rewarding to control, and threatening with the "connecting habits" of befriending, caring, contributing, encouraging, listening, supporting, and trusting in all of my interactions with students, their families, and my colleagues.

Fourth, I will treat my students' families as valued partners. I will maintain a class website to inform families of class policies, assignments, and upcoming events. I will update students' grades weekly. I will support PTA projects and keep lines of communication open.

Fifth, I will maintain a network of mutual support with my colleagues. I will express interest in their personal lives. I will show myself as open to new ideas and suggestions, and will offer support by sharing supplies, experiences, ideas, and lessons when asked. I will contribute to the school by volunteering to help with extracurricular activities and programs.

And sixth, I will show I am trustworthy by keeping confidences, following through on commitments, and not gossiping. I will behave in a way that reflects well on me, my family, my school, my district, and the profession. I will comply with state and federal regulations and school district policies, and I will do my best to be truthful, compassionate, and kind in my dealings with others.

The Behavior I Will Endeavor to Promote and the Rules That Support It.   Here's what I will try to promote in my students:

I want them to share my enthusiasm for learning. I want them to show self-discipline and persistence in learning. And I want them to be respectful, patient, and tolerant in their dealings with others.

I will use the following rules to support proper behavior:

- Treat others in this classroom the way you would like to be treated.
- Pay attention and complete assignments on time.
- Do your best. When you make mistakes, learn from them, and don't give up.
- Do your part to keep the classroom running smoothly.
- Always behave in a way that shows the kind of person you want to be.

What I Will Do Proactively to Prevent or Reduce Misbehavior.   I will do my best to address, in advance, conditions that are likely to promote misbehavior. I will do the following:

First, I will ensure that the classroom is comfortable and conducive to learning, as concerns lighting, ventilation, temperature, seating, and the availability of ample textbooks and materials for various lessons.

Second, I will endeavor to devise lessons that keep students involved, including topics of interest to students, skills that have value and relevance, and activities that call for much student participation.

Third, I will teach in an engaging style. I will bring energy and enthusiasm to the classroom. I will inject humor, novelty, challenge, and fun to keep things lively. And I will personally interact a great deal with students in all phases of the lesson.

Fourth, I will be continually mindful of meeting students' needs, ensure they experience a sense of belonging, and find ways for them to makes choices and participate in class decisions.

Fifth, I will do my best to create routines and procedures that facilitate a highly functional classroom. I will teach the routines to students, have students rehearse them, and re-teach the routines as needed until all students become familiar with them.

How I Will Support My Students' Efforts to Participate and Persevere.   I will support my students' efforts to learn through my physical presence and the ways I speak.

Physical presence: I will be conspicuous in the classroom rather than inconspicuous. I will circulate, use proximity, and be quickly alongside students who seem to need help. I will use eye contact, facial expressions, gestures, and posture to show I am attentive to them.

Manner of speaking: I will speak to students in ways that show caring, appreciation, kindness, and encouragement. I will notice and comment on new hairstyles, clothing, braces on/off, and so forth. I will ask students how they are feeling and listen to their responses. I will acknowledge accomplishment, and I will offer help and hope. I will speak with kindness, as I would speak to a friend and, if necessary, teach students to speak to me in the same way.

At the same time, I will avoid speaking to students in ways that nag, threaten, intimidate, criticize, humiliate, or belittle. I will not ask them "why" they did something. I will not raise my voice to them or pronounce judgments on them.

How I Will Make Sure Students Know What They Are Expected to Do.   As indicated previously, I will establish procedures for classroom routines and carefully teach the procedures and provide practice. I will make plain what students are to do at the beginning of the class period, how to put headings on their papers, how papers will be collected, how students are to prepare for dismissal, and what they are to do when they hear the fire alarm.

Further, I will provide oral and written instructions for each assignment and check to make sure students understand. I will monitor students as they begin independent work. When necessary, I will provide visual instructional plans for students to follow as Fred Jones suggests. I will also post assignment directions on my classroom website for student reference.

Finally, I will teach students how to engage and participate in various types of exercises I like to emphasize, such as those that call upon a variety of learning modalities, involve teamwork, and permit choices and creative thinking.

How I Will Engage Students Actively When I Am Providing Instruction.   Any time I use large-group instruction, I want to keep my students actively engaged. Here are some things I will use toward that end: I will use Fred Jones's Say, See, Do teaching. I will frequently check for understanding. I will build novelty and fun into the lesson. I will relate the lesson to the students' lives. I will incorporate media when possible. I will pace the lesson carefully and make adjustments to keep it moving forward.

How I Will Monitor Students During Independent Work.   I will use Fred Jones's "interior loop" seating arrangement for quick access to all students. I will circulate among students to help them stay on task and to provide help as needed. I will use body language such as proximity, posture, eye contact, gestures, and facial expressions. I will use smiles, nods, winks, and thumbs-up, but will refrain from head shaking, eye rolling, and scowls. I will attempt to show confidence and energy.

How I Will Influence Students to Do High-Quality Work.   I will provide students specific examples of high-quality work by former students and explain why it is good. I will also provide rubrics for guidance and self-evaluation. I will have students keep portfolios of their work and compile a "showcase portfolio" of their best work over a given grading period.

How I Will Redirect Students When They Misbehave.   When students misbehave, here's what I will do:

In a positive manner, I will stop the misbehavior and take an appropriate action to help students return to appropriate behavior. Here are some of the tactics I will use:

Low-key options: (1) Eye contact, facial expression, body language, and proximity. (2) Using Marshall's Hierarchy, ask the student to describe the current level of behavior. (3) Mention to the class that a rule is being broken and ask them to behave as they know they should.

Mid-level options: (1) Ask the student to repeat the behavior correctly. (2) Choose a technique such as "picture it right" as suggested by Spencer Kagan. (3) Ask the student to reflect on the misbehavior and take responsibility for finding a solution, as suggested by Barbara Coloroso.

Stronger options: (1) Engage the student in thinking responsibly as suggested by Ed Ford (2004) who asks students, when necessary, in a calm voice (a) What are you doing? (b) Is that against the rules? (c) What could you do that would be better?. (2) Apply leverage such as after-school detention as suggested by Craig Seganti to ensure compliance. (3) Have the student take "time out" and sit alone in a designated area or in a colleague's classroom. (4) In cases of absolute refusal to comply with my directions, I will very calmly tell the student I know I can't make him or her comply, but it is absolutely necessary that students follow my directions; those who are unwilling to do so will have to be placed elsewhere. I will tell the student that I am genuinely sorry we could not work this out, but I will ask the principal to proceed with finding another placement for the student (for this, I will have previously made sure of the principal's approval and support).

How and When I Will Communicate My Discipline Approach to Students, Administrators, and Students' Caregivers.   Here are some of the things I am considering for explaining my discipline plan to students. I will cover the plan thoroughly at the beginning of a term and review it periodically thereafter.

- Create a PowerPoint presentation to share with students.
- Prepare note-taking sheets for students to use during my initial presentation for later feedback.

- Print rules and "My Job—Your Job" lists on a single sheet of paper to distribute to students.
- Post discipline plan and rules sheet on the class website.
- Post charts of rules in the classroom.
- Review, rehearse, and reteach as many times as necessary.
- Ask students to sign a form indicating they understand and will abide by the discipline plan.

I will share this plan in its entirety with my principal before the year or term begins. I will ask for feedback, suggestions, and support. I will make suggested modifications if needed.

Once the principal has approved my plan, I will post it on the classroom website. I will print out rules and "My Job—Your Job" on single sheets of paper and send them home for families to review. I will request that caregivers sign a form indicating they have read and understood the plan and support it. I will cover the plan again with them on Back to School Night.

END WORD

That's it, ladies and gentlemen. Having completed the tasks outlined in this chapter you now have at your command an effective system of discipline that is compatible with your personality and optimized for attracting students' cooperation, meeting their needs, supporting their efforts, and helping them become better and more successful people.

As you put your plan into effect, you can expect to make some mistakes. That's nothing to worry about because mistakes, when corrected, enhance quality, and those corrections or improvements are long remembered. Ask your students forthrightly to work with you, and assure them you will work on their behalf to the best of your ability. Show you mean what you say, and before long, a sense of cooperation, pleasure, and success will permeate your classes. You'll like it, and so will your students.

Bon voyage.

The following terms are given special emphasis in this book. When appropriate, authorities who originated and/or helped popularize a given term are indicated.

ABCD of disruptive behavior (Kagan): Aggression, breaking rules, confrontations, disengagement.

Academic difficulties: Problems with learning that may be associated with compromised memory, fine and gross motor skills, comprehension, and language or mathematics abilities.

Acceptable behavior: Student conduct that is consistent with class expectations. It does not interfere with learning, demean others, or violate moral codes of society.

Accountability: Showing responsibility is discharging expected tasks.

ADHD: Attention-deficit hyperactivity disorder. The second most common diagnosis in NBB, characterized by short attention span, weak impulse control, restlessness.

Affective disorders: Disorders that affect mood or feeling, such as bipolar disorder.

Aggression (Kagan; others): Behavior in which hostility or unwanted attention is directed toward others.

Appraising reality (Redl & Wattenberg): Having students acknowledge what they are doing wrong.

Appreciative praise (Ginott): Praise that expresses gratitude or admiration for effort.

Appropriate behavior: Student conduct that is consistent with class expectations. It does not interfere with learning, demean others, or violate moral codes of society.

Assertive response style (Canter & Canter): Responding to student behavior in a helpful manner while insisting that class rules be followed.

Assertive teachers (Canter & Canter): Teachers who clearly, confidently, and consistently reiterate class expectations and attempt to build trust with students.

At-risk, behaviorally: Refers to students who are likely to fail in school because of unacceptable behavior.

Attention-seeking (Dreikurs): A mistaken goal of student behavior, involving disruption and showing off, to gain attention from the teacher and other students.

Authority without punishment (Marshall): Methods of exerting authority in the classroom without resorting to threat or punishment.

Autism spectrum disorder (ASD): A range of disorders in which individuals fail to develop normal speech patterns or personal relationships.

Autocratic classrooms (Dreikurs): Classrooms in which the teacher makes all decisions and imposes them upon students.

Autocratic teachers (Dreikurs): Teachers who command, demand cooperation, dominate, and criticize.

Backup system (Jones): The planned action teachers take when students misbehave seriously and refuse to comply with positive teacher requests—often involves being sent to the principal's office.

Basic needs: Psychological requirements for normal functioning.

Basic student needs:
(Charles): Security, association belonging, hope, dignity, power, enjoyment, and competence.
(Dreikurs): Belonging.
(Glasser): Security, belonging, power, freedom, fun.

Behavior: The totality of one's physical and mental activities.

Behavior as choice (Glasser; others): The contention that students choose their behavior at any given time.

Behavior difficulties: Generally, student behavior that breaks rules or disrupts learning.

Behavior management: Organized efforts to influence students to behave in particular ways.

Behavior modification (Skinner's followers): The use of Skinnerian principles of reinforcement to control or shape behavior.

Behavior shaping (Skinner): The process of gradually modifying behavior through application, or withdrawal, of reinforcement.

Bell work (Jones; Wong & Wong): Work students do to begin a class period that does not require instruction from the teacher, such as reading, writing in journals, or completing warm-up activities.

Belonging (Dreikurs; Glasser; others): A basic human need for legitimate membership in groups, with attendant security and comfort. For Dreikurs, the primary need that motivates social behavior in school.

Big Three of discipline (Kagan): (1) Establish an interesting curriculum. (2) Provide meaningful cooperative activities. (3) Be an interesting teacher; adapt curriculum to student needs.

Bipolar disorder: A mental health diagnosis characterized by alternating cycles of euphoria and depression.

Body carriage (Jones): Posture and movement—can indicate to students whether the teacher is well, ill, in charge, tired, disinterested, or intimidated.

Body language (Jones): Nonverbal communication transmitted through posture, eye contact, gestures, and facial expressions.

Boss managers (Glasser): Teachers who set the tasks, direct the learning activities, ask for little student input, and grade student work. (Contrasted with *lead managers*.)

Brain injuries, nontraumatic: Cerebral injuries resulting from disrupted blood flow to the brain (as in strokes), or from tumors, infections, drug overdoses, and certain medical conditions.

Brain injuries, traumatic: Cerebral injuries resulting from blows or other physical damage to the brain, incurred during events such as accidents, sporting events, assaults, or birth.

Breach of duty: A teacher's failure to comply with one or more legal obligations at school.

Breaking rules: Student behavior that violates class agreements.

Causes of misbehavior (Charles): Factors known to foster misbehavior, such as boredom and threat to personal dignity. Charles identifies 26 such factors, most of which can be minimized or eliminated in the classroom.

Charisma, teacher (Charles): Teacher personal allure that attracts student attention and cooperation.

Choice theory (Glasser): Theory that we all choose how to behave at any time, cannot control anyone's behavior but our own, and that all behavior is purposeful in meeting basic needs.

Class agreements: Agreements or codes formalized by teachers and students that indicate how class behavior, instruction, and other matters are to occur.

Class code of conduct: See **Class agreements**.

Class roles: Roles that students play in the classroom, either unintentionally (Dreikurs) or because they are stipulated as "jobs" in the class agreements (Gossen; others).

Class rules: Written statements that specify acceptable and unacceptable behavior in the classroom.

Classroom discipline: Everything teachers do to establish and maintain conditions wherein teachers can teach, students can learn, students cooperate with one another, and teacher and students experience satisfaction.

Classroom meetings (Glasser; others): Planned, regularly scheduled sessions for all class members and teacher to promote communication, allow for feedback on activities and policies, and for addressing and solving problems.

Communities, classroom (Kohn): Classrooms and schools where students feel cared about and care about each other, are valued and respected, are involved in decision making, and have a sense of "we" rather than "I."

Community building: Intentional efforts to develop and communicate a sense of belonging, trust, and respect among class members.

Compliance training (Morrish): Efforts to cause students routinely to abide by teacher requests and directions—an important element in Morrish's approach to discipline.

Conferring dignity (Ginott; Curwin & Mendler; others): Showing respect for students by putting aside their past history, treating them considerately, and being concerned only with the present situation.

Confrontation (Kagan): One of four basic types of classroom misbehavior featured in Win-Win Discipline; occurs when parties involved vie for control and/or attempt to show dominance.

Congruent communication (Ginott): A style of communication in which teachers acknowledge and accept students' feelings about situations and themselves.

Correcting by directing (Ginott; others): Teachers correcting student misbehavior simply by telling or showing students respectfully what they should be doing, rather than dwelling on what they are doing wrong.

Democratic classrooms (Dreikurs): Classrooms in which teachers give students responsibility and involve them in making decisions.

Democratic teachers (Dreikurs): Teachers who show friendly guidance and encourage students to take on responsibility, cooperate, and participate in making decisions.

Discipline: (Charles): What teachers do to help students conduct themselves appropriately in class. (Jones): Efforts to engage students in learning, with teachers using the most positive, unobtrusive tactics possible.

Discipline, preventive (Charles): Steps teachers take in advance to prevent or reduce the occurrence of misbehavior.

Discipline, redirective (Charles): Steps teachers take to stop misbehavior and redirect it in a positive manner.

Discipline, supportive (Charles): Tactics teachers use in an ongoing manner to help students remain attentive and on-task.

Discipline structures (Kagan): Discipline tactics that are designed for addressing types of disruptive behavior.

Disengagement: Withdrawing from an activity or not paying attention; "D" of Kagan's ABCD of disruptive behavior.

Displaying inadequacy (Dreikurs): Student withdrawal and failure to try.

Disruptive behavior: Actions that disrupt teaching or learning. Often used interchangeably with "misbehavior."

Doorway tactics (Seganti): Tactics teachers use as students enter the room to help ensure that students do not misbehave.

Do-over (Morrish): A tactic in which teachers ask students to repeat, in a correct manner, a behavior that has not been acceptable.

Due diligence: A responsibility of all school personnel to pay close and reasonable attention to students under supervision; reasonable care must be taken to protect students from harm.

Dyslexia: The most commonly diagnosed of all learning difficulties; characterized by difficulties in word recognition, spelling, word decoding, and occasionally with the phonological (sound) component of language.

Eight fundamental questions of discipline (Charles):

1. What is misbehavior?
2. How does it damage teaching and learning?
3. What is classroom discipline?
4. What does discipline require of a teacher?
5. What attitude toward discipline serves teachers best?
6. How can teachers prevent misbehavior?
7. How can teachers support proper behavior?
8. How can a teacher redirect misbehavior and maintain student dignity?

Elicit (Marshall): Asking offending students to suggest positive options that might replace misbehavior.

Empowerment of choice (Marshall): Allowing students to select from acceptable choices how they will conduct themselves—a tactic that empowers students to succeed.

Essential virtues, seven (Borba): empathy, conscience, self-control, respect, kindness, tolerance, and fairness, all of which can and should be taught in school.

Ethical concerns: The professional requirement that teachers conduct themselves in accordance with moral and legal codes of conduct.

Ethics: Behavior considered in terms of what is right and what is wrong.

Ethics in the classroom (Charles): A principle of behavior management that stresses morally correct behavior as part of developing trust in the classroom.

Evaluative praise (Ginott): Praise that expresses judgment about students' character or quality of work. Considered to be detrimental by Ginott and various other authorities.

External motivation: Synonymous with *extrinsic motivation*—that which comes from outside the individual.

Extinction (Skinner): In behavior management, the gradual removal of a given behavior, accomplished by withholding reinforcement.

Fetal alcohol spectrum disorder (FASD): A mental health diagnosis in which students show poor impulse control, poor judgment, lack of common sense, and learning difficulties; caused by alcohol consumption by the mother during pregnancy.

15-minute detention (Seganti): The requirement that misbehaving students must attend after-school detention for 15 minutes; provides strong leverage in ensuring that students comply with class rules.

Five A's (Albert): Acceptance, attention, appreciation, affirmation, and affection. Used for establishing and strengthening interpersonal connections.

Follow-up structures (Kagan): A discipline tactic used to help students develop proper behavior over the long run; used when students need additional assistance in behaving responsibly.

Four classical virtues (Marshall): Prudence, temperance, justice, and fortitude. Should be emphasized in the process of helping students develop desirable behavior.

Four essential skills (Nelson & Lott): 1. Intrapersonal. (I understand my emotions and can control myself.) 2. interpersonal. (I can communicate, cooperate, and work well with others.) 3. Strategic. (I am flexible, adaptable, and responsible.) 4. Judgmental. (I can use my wisdom to evaluate situations.)

Frame of reference (Covey): Point of view. To communicate effectively, it is important to understand the other's perception of reality.

Freedom (Glasser): A basic student need that can be met when teacher allows choices in subject matter and in methods of study.

Fun (Glasser): A basic student need that can be met when the teacher provides opportunities for students to work and talk with others, engage in interesting activities, and share accomplishments.

General rules (Jones): Rules that define class standards and expectations that apply at all times, as distinct from specific rules related to certain activities.

Genuine discipline (Ginott and others): Personal self-discipline.

Genuine goal of class behavior (Dreikurs): Belonging—a fundamental desire to acquire a sense of place and value in a group.

Genuine incentives: (Jones) Incentives that truly motivate students to work or behave appropriately, as contrasted with vague incentives such as "become a better person."

Grandma's rule (Jones): "First eat your vegetables, then you can have your dessert," or, "First finish your work, then you can do something you especially enjoy."

Group alerting (Kounin): Quickly getting students' attention to advise them of what they should be doing or do next.

Group behavior (Redl & Wattenberg): Behavior occurring in groups that is different from the ways individuals typically behave—more conforming in some ways, combined with more risk-taking.

Group concern (Jones): A condition in which every student has a stake in the behavior the group uses to earn preferred activity time.

Group dynamics (Redl & Wattenberg): Psychological forces that occur within groups and influence the behavior of group members.

Guided choices (Marshall): Eliciting from students a consequence or procedure to help redirect inappropriate or impulsive behaviors.

Habits: Patterns of willful behavior ingrained to the point that we repeat them without having to think.

Helpless handraisers (Jones): Those students who sit with hands raised, not working unless the teacher is hovering nearby.

Hidden asset, the teacher's (Ginott): Sincerely asking students, "How can I help you?"

Hidden rules (Payne): Seldom-recognized values and guidelines that strongly affect behavior in various ethnic and socio-economic groups.

Hierarchy of Social Development (Marshall): A hierarchy of four levels used to help students reflect on their chosen behaviors. From lowest to highest, the four levels are: (A) anarchy, (B) bossing/bullying, (C) cooperation/conformity, and (D) democracy (inseparable from responsibility). Levels A and B are unacceptable in the classroom. Level C is the expected level of behavior and is essential for a civil society. Level D connotes taking the initiative to do the right thing without supervision.

Hostile teachers: In an effort to exert control over students, these teachers treat students like enemies and rely on strict commands and stern facial expressions to maintain order.

I-messages (Ginott): Teachers' expressing their personal feelings and reactions to situations without addressing student behavior or character: Example, "I have trouble teaching when there is so much noise in the room."

Inappropriate behavior: Any behavior that through intent or thoughtlessness interferes with teaching or learning, threatens or intimidates others, or oversteps society's standards of moral, ethical, or legal behavior.

In loco parentis: Teachers' exercising care over students as if they were the students' parents—in place of parents.

In poverty: Any member of a family that has to spend more than one-third of its disposable income for food adequate to meet the family's nutritional needs is said to be living in poverty.

Incentive (Jones): Something outside of the individual that can be anticipated and that entices the individual to act.

Incentive, genuine (Jones): An incentive that motivates all members of the class rather than just a few.

Influence techniques (Redl & Wattenberg; others): Helping students behave properly by providing attention and support, rather than punishment.

Insistence (Morrish): A discipline tactic teachers should use when students show reluctance to comply with directions.

InTASC: The Interstate New Teacher Assessment and Support Consortium that has described competencies teachers require for professional teaching.

Interior loop (Jones): A classroom seating arrangement with wide aisles that allows teachers to move easily among students at work.

Internal motivation (Marshall): The desire to behave responsibly without having to be told to do so, because of innate needs or beliefs rooted in ethics and values.

Interventions (Kagan & others): What teachers do to deal with misbehavior at the moment of disruption, for follow-up, and for the long term.

Inviting cooperation (Ginott): Encouraging and enticing students into activities and giving them choices, rather than demanding their participation.

Irresponsible behavior (Kagan & others): Synonymous with *misbehavior.*

Laconic language (Ginott): Brevity of teacher's comments about misbehavior. Example: "This is work time."

Language difficulties: Problems in understanding, processing, and expressing information verbally.

Lead managers (Glasser): Teachers who involve students in exploring topics and activities for learning. Lead teachers also provide necessary help and encourage students to do quality work. (Contrasted with *boss managers*.)

Learning communities (Kohn): See **communities, classroom**.

Learning disabilities (LD): Unusual difficulties students exhibit in learning certain subjects in school. A mental health diagnosis, not simply a teacher observation.

Level A, Level B, Level C, Level D (Marshall): Levels in Marshall's hierarchy of social development, useful in promoting desired behavior and acceptance of responsibility.

Leverage (Seganti): Something that teachers can use to ensure student compliance with rules. In Seganti's approach, leverage exists in the form of the 15-minute detention after school.

Limits: The imaginary boundaries that separate acceptable/appropriate behavior from misbehavior/inappropriate behavior.

Living in poverty: Any member of a family that has to spend more than one-third of its disposable income for food adequate to meet the family's nutritional needs is said to be living in poverty.

Long-term structures (Kagan): Plans for helping students get along with others, become more self-directing, and control their behavior.

Massive time wasting (Jones): A condition Jones found prevalent in classrooms where discipline was not done efficiently.

Mental health conditions: Diagnoses in NBB, such as learning disabilities and attention-deficit hyperactivity disorder.

Misbehavior: Behavior that is considered inappropriate for the setting or situation in which it occurs. Any behavior that, through intent or thoughtlessness, interferes with teaching or learning, threatens or intimidates others, or oversteps society's standards of moral, ethical, or legal behavior.

Misbehavior, causes of (Charles): Factors that reside in students, the class environment, school personnel, and elsewhere, that tend to promote student misbehavior. (Charles identifies 26 such factors).

Misbehavior, teacher (Charles): Anything teachers do in the classroom that adversely affects learning or human relations, or that is unprofessional in any way.

Misbehavior, types of:

(Charles): Inattention, apathy, needless talk, moving about the room, annoying others, disruption, lying, stealing, cheating, sexual harassment, aggression and fighting, malicious mischief, and defiance of authority.

(Coloroso): Mistakes (unintentional), mischief (intentional light misbehavior), and mayhem (more serious misbehavior).

(Dreikurs): Attention-seeking, power-seeking, revenge-seeking behaviors, and feigned helplessness.

(Kagan): Aggression, breaking rules, confrontation, and disengagement.

Mistaken goals (Dreikurs): Goals of attention, power, revenge, and avoidance of failure that students seek in the mistaken belief they will bring positive recognition and sense of belonging.

Momentum (Kounin): Refers to teachers' getting activities started promptly, keeping them moving ahead, and bringing them to efficient transition or closure.

Moral intelligence (Borba): The ability to distinguish right from wrong, the establishment and maintenance of strong ethical convictions, and the willingness to act on those convictions in an honorable way.

Need: A mental construct (an imaginary "something") we use to explain motivation and behavior; a desire that is long-lasting and recurrent.

Needs of students, basic:

(Charles): Security, association, belonging, hope, dignity, power, enjoyment, competence.

(Dreikurs): Belonging.

(Glasser): Security, love and belonging, power, freedom, fun.

Neglected 50% (Charles): The aspect of teaching that exerts positive influence on students to cooperate and make an effort in class. Tactics involve persuasion, personal charisma, skilful communication, intriguing questions, personal attention, helpfulness.

Negligence: A teacher's failure to maintain a careful watch over students under supervision.

Neurological-based behavior (NBB) (Cook): Somewhat erratic behavior associated with compromised neurological functioning, often outside the control of the student.

Neurological differences: Notable variations in student behavior, believed to be the result of differences in cerebral functioning.

Nonassertive teachers (Canter & Canter): Teachers who fail to take charge and instead assume a passive, hands-off approach in dealing with students.

noncoercive behaviors (Glasser; Marshall; many others): Discipline in which teachers invite, encourage, and otherwise influence students to behave properly, without using demands or threats.

Omission training (Jones): An incentive plan for an individual student who, by cutting down on undesired behavior, can earn preferred activity time for the entire class.

Oppositional defiant disorder: A mental health diagnosis in which students regularly oppose and defy the teacher and others.

Overlapping (Kounin): Refers to teachers' attending to two or more issues in the classroom at the same time.

Ownership of behavior problem (Coloroso; Ford): Students taking responsibility for their improper actions in advance of working out appropriate solutions.

Permissive classrooms (Dreikurs): Classrooms in which teachers overlook students' failure to comply with rules, which suggests teacher acceptance of misbehavior.

Permissive teachers (Dreikurs): Teachers who put few if any limits on student behavior and do not invoke consequences for disruptive behavior.

Personal style of behavior management (Charles): The contention that each teacher, in order to be optimally authentic and effective, must develop a personal style of working with students.

Perspective taking (Kohn): Doing one's best to see and understand a situation from another person's point of view.

Philosophy of discipline: The beliefs one has about the nature, purpose, and value of discipline.

Physical proximity (Redl & Wattenberg; others): The teacher's moving close to a student who is becoming restive or is misbehaving.

Picture it right (Kagan): A tactic in which students are asked to picture how they would like the class to be and verbalize what they need to do to make it that way.

Positive influence: What teachers do to invite or entice students to cooperate, through providing helpful assistance rather than criticism.

Positivity (Marshall): Maintaining an inclination toward optimism.

Poverty, living in: Any member of a family that has to spend more than one-third of its disposable income for food adequate to meet the family's nutritional needs is living in poverty.

Power (Glasser): A basic student need for control, satisfied when students are given significant duties in the class and are allowed to participate in making decisions about class matters.

Power-seeking behavior (Dreikurs): Behaviors such as temper tantrums, backtalk, disrespect, and defiance that students use to try to show they have power over the teacher.

Practice of discipline (Charles): How discipline is put into effect and conducted in the classroom—follows from one's philosophy and theory of discipline.

Praxis: A series of tests published by the Educational Testing Service for assessing the competency of teachers.

Preferred activity time, or **PAT** (Jones): Time allocated for students to engage in activities of their preference; used as an incentive to encourage responsible behavior.

Prevention of misbehavior: Same as *preventive discipline*.

Preventive discipline (Charles): The aspect of discipline in which one removes or otherwise controls factors likely to lead to misbehavior.

Procedures (Wong & Wong): Detailed instructions that show students how to perform all activities in class—effective use can eliminate a number of discipline problems.

Professionalism: For teachers, displaying the fairest, most considerate, and most ethical ways of fulfilling the duties of the teaching profession.

Providing help efficiently (Jones): A technique in which the teacher quickly provides enough help to get a student working again, then moves away. To be accomplished in 20 seconds or less.

Proximity: Moving close to a student who is misbehaving.

Quality curriculum (Glasser): A program of study that emphasizes excellence in learning in topics that students consider useful.

Quality teaching (Glasser): Instruction in which teachers help students become proficient in knowledge and skills the students consider important. This is usually done via "lead teaching."

Rage: Extreme behavior, sometimes exhibited by students with NBB, manifested as an explosion of temper that occurs suddenly with no real warning and may turn violent.

Rage cycle (Cook): Progression of rage episode through four phases—triggering, escalation, rage (or meltdown), and post-rage (or post-meltdown).

Real Discipline (Morrish): An approach to discipline that makes use of teacher insistence and careful teaching of expectations and procedures.

Real Discipline, three phases of (Morrish): Training, teaching, and management.

Reconciliation (Coloroso): A human relations skill in which individuals who have been in a dispute take steps to resolve and smooth over their differences.

Reflective questions (Marshall): Questions posed to students to help them make better behavioral choices and assume responsibility.

Reinforcing stimuli (Skinner): Stimuli received by an organism immediately following a behavior that increase the likelihood the behavior will be repeated.

Resolution (Coloroso): Identifying and correcting whatever caused a behavior problem—one of the follow-up steps in dealing with misbehavior.

Responsible behavior: Student behavior consistent with class expectations—does not interfere with learning, demean others, or violate the moral codes of society. Synonymous with *proper behavior*.

Restitution (Gossen; Coloroso): Repairing or replacing damage done when one behaves irresponsibly—one of the steps in resolving the problem.

Right to learn (Canter & Canter): The contention that students have a right to learn in classrooms that are safe and free from threat.

Right to teach (Canter & Canter): The contention that teachers have a right to teach in classrooms that are free from disruptions, with backing from administrators and caregivers.

Sane messages (Ginott): Teacher messages that address situations rather than students' character.

Satiation (Kounin): Getting all one can tolerate of a given activity, resulting in frustration, boredom, or listlessness.

Say, See, Do teaching (Jones): A teaching method of repeated short cycles of teacher input, each followed by student response. Keeps students attentive and involved.

Self-diagnostic referral (Marshall): A self-diagnosis done by a student who has violated class rules and submitted as a plan for improvement—includes description of what was done wrong and the steps that will be taken to improve.

Self-discipline, for teachers (Ginott): When working with students, being careful to not display behaviors that should be eradicated in students, such as raising the voice to end noise and reacting rudely to impolite students.

Self-restitution (Gossen): An activity in which students who have behaved inappropriately are encouraged to reflect on their behavior, identify the need that prompted it, and create a new way of behaving as the responsible person they want to be. This was the first system to ask misbehaving students to make things right within themselves and improve from the experience.

Sense of community (Kohn): A condition in classrooms where students feel safe and are continually brought into making judgments, expressing their opinions, and working cooperatively toward solutions that affect themselves and the class.

Sensory integration dysfunction (SID): Irregularities in the process we use to take in information from our senses, organize it, interpret it, and respond to it.

Sensory processing disorder: Same as *sensory integration dysfunction*.

Setting limits: Clarifying with the class exactly what is expected of them.

Seven connecting habits vs. seven deadly habits (Glasser): Seven habits that help teachers connect with students are *caring, listening, supporting, contributing, encouraging, trusting,* and *befriending*. They should replace the seven deadly habits of *criticizing, blaming, complaining, nagging, threatening, punishing,* and *rewarding students to control them*.

Shaping behavior (Skinner): The process of using reinforcement to produce desired behavior in students.

Significant seven (Nelsen & Lott): Within a positive classroom environment, students develop three empowering perceptions about themselves: (1) personal capability, (2) significance in primary relationships, (3) personal power. They develop four essential skills: (1) intrapersonal, (2) interpersonal, (3) strategic, (4) judgmental.

SIR (Glasser): An acronym standing for the process of self-evaluation, improvement, and repetition, used to promote quality.

Smoothness (Kounin): Absence of abrupt changes or interruptions by the teacher that interfere with students' activities or thought processes.

Social interest (Dreikurs): The concept that one's personal well-being is dependent on the well-being of the group. This encourages individuals to behave in ways that benefit the group.

Specific rules (Jones): Rules relating to procedures and routines that detail exactly what students are to do in various learning activities.

Structures (Kagan): Discipline approaches designed for use with particular combinations of disruptions and student needs; specific plans of action that teachers use to teach the curriculum and to address misbehavior.

Student dislikes (Charles): Activities, situations, topics, people, and the like that students do not enjoy. They should be avoided, to the extent feasible.

Student likes (Charles): Activities, situations, topics, people, and the like that students typically enjoy. They should be emphasized in the educational program.

Student needs:

(Charles): Security, association belonging, hope, dignity, power, enjoyment, competence.

(Dreikurs): Belonging.

(Glasser): Security, love and belonging, control, freedom, fun.

Student positions (Kagan): Conglomerates of factors that leave students uninformed or dispose them to seek attention, show anger, avoid failure, become bored, seek control, or be overly energetic.

Student responsibility (Jones; Glasser; Marshall; others): The contention that students have the obligation to reflect on their behavior choices, recognize how they effect themselves and others, and deal with whatever consequences occur.

Student roles (Redl & Wattenberg): Roles students assume in the classroom, such as instigator, clown, leader, and scapegoat.

Successive approximations (Skinner): Behavior that, through reinforcement, moves progressively closer to the desired goal.

Support buddies (Wong & Wong): Students assigned to help or support each other; members of cooperative learning groups.

Support groups (Wong & Wong): Groups of students who help and support each other; cooperative learning groups.

Survival (Glasser): A basic need that motivates self-protective behavior.

Synergetic teaching (Charles): Teaching in a manner that energizes the class. Done by putting in place combinations of elements known to produce heightened classroom energy.

Teacher misbehavior (Charles): Anything teachers do in the classroom that adversely affects learning or human relations, or that is unprofessional in any way.

Teacher roles (Redl & Wattenberg): Various roles students expect teachers to play, such as surrogate parent, arbitrator, disciplinarian, and moral authority.

Teacher self-discipline (Ginott): Teacher self-control, of paramount importance in helping students conduct themselves appropriately.

Teacher–student same-side collaboration (Kagan): A "we" approach that gives teachers and students a joint interest in maintaining responsible behavior.

Teachers at their best (Ginott): Teachers, when using congruent communication that addresses situations rather than students' character, invites student cooperation, and accepts students as they are.

Teachers at their worst (Ginott): Teachers, when they name-call, label students, ask rhetorical *why* questions, give long moralistic lectures, and make caustic remarks to their students.

Teachers' hidden asset (Ginott): Showing willingness to help any given student at any given moment.

Theory of discipline: An overall explanation of the elements that comprise discipline and how they work together to produce particular outcomes.

Theory X and Theory Y (Marshall): Theories of managing people. Theory X holds that people must be directed and controlled, whereas Theory Y holds that people should be encouraged and given responsibility.

Three C's (Albert): To help students feel that they have an important place in class; focus on helping students (1) feel capable, (2) connect with others, (3) make contributions to class and to others.

Three facets of discipline (Charles): (1) Preventive discipline, to forestall misbehavior. (2) Supportive discipline, to encourage appropriate behavior. (3) Redirective discipline, to stop misbehavior and help students move to appropriate behavior.

Three perceptions (Nelson & Lott) 1. Perception of *personal capability.* (I have ability; I can do this.) 2. Perception of *significance in primary relationships.* (I am needed; I belong.) 3. Perception of *personal power* to influence one's own life. (I have control over how I respond to what happens to me.)

Three phases of Real Discipline (Morrish): (1) Training for compliance, (2) teaching students how to behave, and (3) managing student choice.

Three pillars of Win-Win Discipline (Kagan): (1) Same side—students and teachers work together for benefit of students. (2) Collaborative solutions—teachers and students work together to solve discipline problems. (3) Learned responsibility—students develop desire to behave appropriately, practice self-management, and get along with others.

Traditional teaching (Glasser): Teaching in which the teacher states expectations, strives for student compliance, makes and enforces rules of conduct, directs almost all aspects of lessons, and evaluates student performance.

Types of classroom misbehavior:

(Charles): Inattention, apathy, needless talk, moving about the room, annoying others, disruption, lying, stealing, cheating, sexual harassment, aggression and fighting, malicious mischief, and defiance of authority.

(Coloroso): Mistakes (unintentional), mischief (intentional light misbehavior), and mayhem (more serious misbehavior).

(Dreikurs): Attention-seeking, power-seeking, revenge-seeking, and feigned helplessness.

(Kagan): Aggression, breaking rules, confrontation, and disengagement.

Unobtrusive tactic (Jones): A discipline tactic directed at a particular student that is unnoticed by most of the class members, such as facial expression, eye contact, hand signal, or physical proximity.

Useful work (Glasser): Schoolwork that deals with skills and information that students deem valuable in their lives.

Value judgments (Glasser): Students evaluate their own work in terms of quality—a step in moving toward high-quality work.

Value systems: Overall, what members of particular cultures and segments of society believe to be right, proper, and worthwhile, and, conversely, what they believe to be wrong, improper, and of no worth.

Visual instructional plans (VIPs) (Jones): Graphic prompts that guide students through the process of the task or performance at hand.

Why **questions** (Ginott): Counterproductive questions that teachers put to students, asking them to explain or justify their behavior, e.g., "Why did you . . . ?"

Win-Win Discipline (Kagan): A "together, same-side" approach to discipline in which teachers and students work collaboratively to promote good classroom behavior—both teachers and students are deemed to "win."

Withitness (Kounin): The teacher's knowing what is going on in all parts of the classroom at all times.

Work the crowd (Jones): Moving about the class while teaching and interacting with students.

You-messages (Ginott): Teacher messages that attack students' character, such as "You are acting like barbarians." These messages are put-downs that can convey heavy blame and guilt.

Amen, D. (2001). *Healing ADD: The breakthrough program that allows you to see and heal the six types of attention deficit disorder.* New York: G. P. Putnam's Sons.

American Academy of Child and Adolescent Psychiatry. (2004a). Child psychiatry facts for families: Recommendations, help and guidance from the AACAP. Retrieved from http://pediatrics.about.com/library/bl_psych_policy_statements.htm

American Academy of Child and Adolescent Psychiatry. (2004b). Children with oppositional defiant disorder. Retrieved from http://www.aacap.org/publications/factsfam/72.htm

American Academy of Child and Adolescent Psychiatry. (2004c). Bipolar disorder in children and teens. Retrieved from www.aacap.org/publications/factsfam/72.htm

Autism speaks. (2010). Retrieved from http://www.autismspeaks.org/

Borba, M. (2001). Building moral intelligence: The seven essential virtues that teach kids to do the right thing. San Francisco: Jossey-Bass.

Borba, M. (2004). Don't give me that attitude! 24 rude, selfish, insensitive things kids do and how to stop them. San Francisco: Jossey-Bass.

Borba, M. (n.d.). [See various articles, from 2005–2009, posted on the Borba website: http://www.michele-borba.com]

Brain Injury Association of Virginia. 2012. *Brain Injury 101* http://www.biav.net/brain-injury-101.htm

Canter, L., & Canter, M. (1976). *Assertive discipline: A take-charge approach for today's educator.* Seal Beach, CA: Lee Canter & Associates. [The second and third editions of the book, published in 1992 and 2001, are entitled *Assertive discipline: Positive behavior management for today's classroom.*]

Carnegie, D. (1981 revision). *How to win friends and influence people.* New York: Pocket Books.

Centers for Disease Control and Prevention (CDC). (2004). Alcohol consumption among women who are pregnant or who might become pregnant—United States, 2002. Retrieved from http://www.acbr.com/fas/

Charles, C. (1974). *Teachers' petit Piaget.* San Francisco: Fearon.

Charles, C. (2000). *The synergetic classroom.* Boston: Allyn and Bacon.

Charles, C. (2008). *Today's best classroom management strategies: Paths to positive discipline.* Boston: Allyn & Bacon.

Charles, C. (2010). *Building classroom discipline.* Boston: Pearson.

Clark, E., , Lutke, J., Minnes, P., & Ouellette-Kuntz, H. (2004). Secondary disabilities among adults with fetal alcohol spectrum disorder in British Columbia. *Journal of FAS International, 2,* 1–12.

Collaborative for Academic, Social, and Emotional Learning, Chicago. (n.d.) [This organization has a goal to make social and emotional learning an essential part of education. Numerous resources are provided at its website: http://www.casel.org/]

Coloroso, B. (1994/2002). Kids are worth It!: Giving your child the gift of inner discipline. New York: Quill.

Cook, P. (2004). Behaviour, learning and teaching: Applied studies in FAS/FAE [Distance education curricula]. Winnipeg, Canada: Red River College.

Cook, P. (2008a). Sensory integration dysfunction: A layperson's guide (2nd ed.) [Booklet]. Available from the author, Paula Cook. Internet contact: pcook59@shaw.ca

Cook, P. (2008b). A layperson's guide to what to do when someone begins to rage (2nd ed.) [Booklet]. Available from the author, Paula Cook. Internet contact: pcook59@shaw.ca

Cook, P., Kellie, R., Jones, K., & Goossen, L. (2000). *Tough kids and substance abuse.* Winnipeg, MB, Canada: Addictions Foundation of Manitoba.

Council of Chief State School Officers. (2003/2011). Model standards for beginning teacher licensing, assessment, and development. Retrieved from http://www.ccsso.org/projects/Interstate_New_Teacher_Assessment_and_Support_Consortium

Covey, R. (1989). *The 7 habits of highly effective people.* New York: Simon and Schuster.

Covey, R. (2004). *The 7 habits of highly effective people: Restoring the character ethic.* New York: Free Press.

Daly, T. (2004). The ADHD solution for teachers: *How to turn any disruptive child into your best student.* San Diego: Smarty Pants Publications.

Diamond, M., & Hopson, J. (1998). *Magic trees of the mind: How to nurture your child's intelligence, creativity, and healthy emotions from birth through adolescence.* New York: Dutton.

Dolphin Education. (2006). Dyslexia research: 4. The incidence of dyslexia. Retrieved from http://www.dolphinuk.co.uk/education/case_studies/dyslexia_research.htm

Dreikurs, R., & Cassel, P. (1995). *Discipline without tears*. New York: Penguin-NAL. (Originally published in 1972.)

Drye, J. (2000). *Tort liability 101: When are teachers liable?* Atlanta, GA: Educator Resources. Retrieved from http://www.Educator-Resources.com

Echternach, C., & Cook, P. (2004). The rage cycle [Paper]. Available from the author, Paula Cook. Internet contact: pcook59@shaw.ca

EduBlogs. (n.d.). [This site hosts numerous free blogs for teachers, students, librarians, researchers, and administrators: http://edublogs.org/]

Faraone, S. (2003). *Straight talk about your child's mental health*. New York: The Guilford Press.

Feng, J. (1994). Asian-American children: What teachers should know. (ERIC Document Reproduction Service No. EDO-PS-94-4).

Ford, E. (1999). *Discipline for home and school, Book Two* (revised and expanded). Scottsdale, AZ: Brandt Publishing.

Ford, E. (2004). *Discipline for home and school, fundamentals*. Scottsdale, AZ: Brandt Publishing.

Forni, P. (2006). The other side of civility. Retrieved from http://www.jhu.edu

Gardner, H. (1999). Intelligence reframed: Multiple intelligences for the 21st century. New York: Basic Books.

Ginott, H. (1971). *Teacher and child*. New York: Macmillan.

Ginott, H. (1972). I am angry! I am appalled! I am furious! *Today's Education, 61*, 23–24.

Glasser, W. (1965). *Reality therapy*. New York: Harper & Row.

Glasser, W. (1969). *Schools without failure*. New York: Harper & Row.

Glasser, W. (1977). 10 steps to good discipline. *Today's Education, 66*, 60–63.

Glasser, W. (1986). *Control theory in the classroom*. New York: HarperCollins.

Glasser, W. (1990). *The quality school: Managing students without coercion*. New York: HarperCollins.

Glasser, W. (1992). The quality school curriculum. *Phi Delta Kappan, 73*(9), 690–694.

Glasser, W. (1993). *The quality school teacher*. New York: HarperCollins.

Glasser, W. (1998a). *Choice theory in the classroom*. New York: HarperCollins.

Glasser, W. (1998b). *The quality school: Managing students without coercion*. New York: HarperCollins.

Glasser, W. (1998c). *The quality school teacher*. New York: HarperCollins.

Glasser, W. (2001). *Every student can succeed*. Chatsworth, CA: William Glasser Incorporated.

Glavac, M., (2005). Summary of major concepts covered by Harry K. Wong. The Busy Educator's Newsletter. Retrieved from http://www.glavac.com/

Golubtchik, B. (2008). Create a multi-sensory classroom. Retrieved from http://www.teachersnetwork.org/ntol/howto/energize/c13472,.htm

Google for Educators. (n.d.). [This site has many free resources for teachers, including GoogleDocs (a wiki used for collaborative writing): http://www.google.com/educators/index.html]

Goorian, B., & Brown, K. (2002). Trends and issues: School Law. ERIC Clearinghouse on Educational Management. Retrieved from http://eric.uoregon.edu/trends_issues/law/index.html

Gossen, D. (2002). What do you want? Student behavior. *γA! Magazine for Middle Level Educators, 3*(3).

Gossen, D. (2004). It's all about we: Rethinking discipline using restitution. Saskatoon, SK, Canada: Chelsom Consultants Limited.

Grandin, T. (2005). [See website on Temple Grandin for information on her life and struggle with autism: http://www.templegrandin.org]

Greene, R. (2001). *The explosive child*. New York: Harper Collins.

Hall, P., & Hall, N. (2003). *Educating oppositional and defiant children*. Alexandria, VA: Association for Supervision and Curriculum Development.

Hill, P. (2005). Pharmacological treatment of rage. Retrieved from http://www.focusproject.org.uk/SITE/UPLOAD/DOCUMENT/Hill

Hinder, T. (2006). An overview of seven Glasser Quality Schools in the USA. NSW Department of Education and Training Leadership Fellowship 2005–2006. A Report of a Study Tour to the USA—April 2006. Therese Hinder. Principal. Epping West Public School. 96 Carlingford Road. Epping NSW 2121. Australia. [Use title of the article for browser to locate this report on the Internet.]

How Stuff Works. (n.d.). ["How Stuff Works" was founded by North Carolina State University President Marshall Brain in 1998. It includes easy-to-understand explanations of how the world actually works, including many technology tools: http://www.howstuffworks.com/]

Interstate New Teacher Assessment and Support Consortium (InTASC). (2003/2011). [See InTASC's website at: http://www.ccsso.org/intascst.html#preface]

Jensen, B., Hunter, A., Sonnemann, J., and Burns, T. (2012). Catching up: Learning from the best school systems in East Asia. Retrieved from http://www.Grattan.edu.au/pub_page/129_report_learning_from_the_best.html

Jones, F. (1987a). *Positive classroom discipline.* New York: McGraw-Hill.

Jones, F. (1987b). *Positive classroom instruction.* New York: McGraw-Hill.

Jones, F. (2007a). *Tools for teaching.* Santa Cruz, CA: Fredric H. Jones & Associates.

Jones, P. (2007b). *The video toolbox.* Santa Cruz, CA: Fredric H. Jones & Associates.

Jones, F. (n.d.). PAT Bank. [Jones's and various teachers' suggestions for PAT activities.] Retrieved from http://www.fredjones.com/PAT/index.html

Kagan, S. (2001). Teaching for character and community. *Educational Leadership, 59*(2), 50–55.

Kagan, S. (2003, Spring). A brief history of Kagan structures. *Kagan Online Magazine.* Retrieved from http://www.kaganonline.com [Other articles on structures are posted on this site as well.]

Kagan, S., Kyle, P., & Scott, S. (2004/2007). *Win-Win Discipline.* San Clemente, CA: Kagan Publishing.

Khan S. & Faraone, S. 2006. The genetics of attention-deficit/hyperactivity disorder: A literature review of. 2005. *Current Psychiatry Reports,* 2006 Oct; 8:393-397.

Kellerman, T. (2003). The FAS community resource center. Retrieved from http://www.come-over.to/FASCRC/

Kohn, A. (1993/1999). *Punished by rewards: The trouble with gold stars, incentive plans, A's, praise, and other bribes.* Boston: Houghton Mifflin.

Kohn, A. (1999). *The schools our children deserve: Moving beyond traditional classrooms and "tougher standards."* Boston: Houghton Mifflin.

Kohn, A. (1996/2001). *Beyond discipline: From compliance to community.* Upper Saddle River, NJ: Merrill/Prentice Hall. [1996 edition—Alexandria, VA: Association for Supervision and Curriculum Development.]

Kounin, J. (1971). *Discipline and group management in classrooms.* New York: Holt, Rinehart & Winston. (Reissued in 1977.)

Kranowitz, C. (1998). *The out-of-sync child.* New York: Skylight Press.

Kranowitz, C., Szkut, S., Balzer-Martin, L., Haber, E., & Sava, D. (2003). *Answers to questions teachers ask about sensory integration.* Las Vegas, NV: Sensory Resources LLC.

Levinson, H. (2000). The discovery of cerebellar-vestibular syndromes and therapies: A solution to the riddle—dyslexia (2nd ed.). Lake Success, NY: Stonebridge Publishing, Ltd.

Looking at Student Work. (n.d.). [This website provides protocols and resources for teachers committed to studying and working together to examine and learn from examples of student work: http://www.lasw.org/]

Marshall, M. (2001). *Discipline without stress® punishments, or rewards: How teachers and parents promote responsibility & learning.* Los Alamitos, CA: Piper Press.

Marshall, M. (2005a). A letter worth reading. Retrieved from http://www.marvinmarshall.com/aletter-worthreading.html

Marshall, M. (2005b). A principal's experience. Retrieved from http://www.marvinmarshall.com/principal.htm

Marshall, M. (2005c. Classroom meetings. Retrieved from http://www.disciplinewithoutstress.com/sample_chapters.html

Marshall, M. (2005d). Collaboration for quality learning. Retrieved from http://www.disciplinewithoutstress.com/sample_chapters.html

Marshall, M. (2005e). Promoting positivity, choice, and reflection. Retrieved from http://www.MarvinMarshall.com/promoting_positivity.htm

Marshall, M. (2005f). Reducing perfectionism. Retrieved from http://www.disciplinewithoutstress.com/sample_chapters.html

Marshall, M. (2005g). Samples of hierarchies for promoting learning. Retrieved from http://www.marvinmarshall.com/hierarchy.htm

Marshall, M. (2007). *Discipline without stress® punishments, or rewards: How teachers and parents promote responsibility & learning* (2nd ed.). Los Alamitos, CA: Piper Press.

Marshall, M. (2008a). A system is superior to talent. Retrieved from http://teachers.net/gazette/MAR08/marshall/

Marshall, M. (2008b). *Promoting Responsibility & Learning, the Monthly Newsletter by Marvin Marshall, 8*(6) [Entire issue]. Retrieved from http://www.DisciplineWithout-Stress.com

Marshall, M. (2008c). *Promoting Responsibility & Learning, the Monthly Newsletter by Marvin Marshall, 8*(3) [Entire issue]. Retrieved from http://www.marvinmarshall.com/newsletter/

Marshall, M. (2010, September). A response from Dr. Marshall to a letter received. *Promoting Responsibility & Learning, the Monthly Newsletter by Marvin Marshall, 10*(9). Retrieved from http://www.marvinmarshall.com

Marshall, M. (n.d.). [*Promoting Responsibility & Learning, the Monthly Newsletter of Marvin Marshall* has been published monthly since August 2001. Check out past issues at: http://www.MarvinMarshall.com]

Maslow, A. (1954). *Motivation and personality*. New York: Harper.

McGregor, D. (1960). *The human side of enterprise*. New York: McGraw-Hill.

Millichap, G. (2008, February). Etiologic classification of attention deficit/hyperactivity disorder. *Pediatrics, 121*, e358–e365.

Morrish, R. (1997). *Secrets of discipline: 12 keys for raising responsible children*. Fonthill, Ontario, Canada: Woodstream Publishing.

Morrish, R. (2000). *With all due respect: Keys for building effective school discipline*. Fonthill, Ontario, Canada: Woodstream Publishing.

Morrish, R. (2003). *FlipTips*. Fonthill, Ontario, Canada: Woodstream Publishing.

Morrish, R. (2005). What is Real Discipline? Retrieved from http://www.realdiscipline.com

National Council for Learning Disabilities. (2005). The ABCs of learning disabilities. Retrieved from http://www.ncld.org/

National Education Association. (1975). Code of Ethics of the Education Profession. Retrieved from www.nea.org/aboutnea/code.html

National Institute of Mental Health. (2006). Medications. Retrieved from http://www.nimh.nih.gov/publicat/medicate.cfm#ptdep1

National Institute of Mental Health. (2008). Health information quick links. www.nimh.nih.gov.

Nelsen, J., & Lott, L. (2000). *Positive discipline in the classroom*. Rocklin, CA: Prima.

Packer, L. (2005). Overview of rage attacks. Retrieved from http://www.tourettesyndrome.net/rage_overview.htm

Papolos, D., & Papolos, J. (2002). *The bipolar child*. New York: Broadway Books.

Payne, R. (2001). *A framework for understanding poverty*. Highlands, TX: Aha! Process, Inc.

Payne, R. (2003). [Quoted in] Claitor, D. (2003). Breaking through: Interview of Ruby Payne. Retrieved from http://www.hopemag.com/issues/2003/septOct/breakingThrough.pdf

Pellegrino, K. (2005). The effects of poverty on teaching and learning. Retrieved from http://www.teach-nology.com/tutorials/teaching/poverty/

Piaget, J. (1951). *Judgment and reasoning in the child*. London: Routledge & Kegan Paul.

Redl, F., & Wattenberg, W. (1951). *Mental hygiene in teaching*. New York: Harcourt, Brace & World. (Revised and reissued in 1959.)

Seganti, C. (2008a). Classroom discipline 101: How to get control in any classroom. Retrieved from http://www.classroomdiscipline101.com

Seganti, C. (2008b). *Ezine*. [See articles on the Seganti approach to discipline.] Retrieved from http://ezinearticles.com/?expert=Craig_Seganti

Skinner, B. (1953). *Science and human behavior*. New York: Macmillan.

Skinner, B. (1954). The science of learning and the art of teaching. *Harvard Educational Review, 24*, 86–97.

Starr, L. (1999). Speaking of classroom management—an interview with Harry K. Wong. *Education World*. Retrieved from http://www.educationworld.com/a_curr/curr161.shtml

Streissguth, A., Barr, H., Kogan, J., & Bookstein, F. (1997). Primary and secondary disabilities in fetal alcohol syndrome. In A. Streissguth & J. Kanter (Eds.), *The challenge of fetal alcohol syndrome. Overcoming secondary disabilities* (pp. 23–39). Seattle: University of Washington Press.

William Glasser Institute. (2005). Control theory. Retrieved from http://www.wglasser.com/whatisct.htm

Wong, H., & Wong, R. (2000a). The first five minutes are critical. *Teachers.net Gazette*. Retrieved from http://teachers.net/gazette/NOV00/wong.html

Wong, H., and Wong, R. (2000b). The Problem is Not Discipline. *Teachers.net Gazette*. http://teachers.net/gazette/SEP00/wong.html

Wong, H., & Wong, R. (2000c). Your first day. *Teachers.net Gazette*. Retrieved from http://teachers.net/gazette/JUN00/covera.html

Wong, H., & Wong, R. (2004a). A well-oiled learning machine. *Teachers.net Gazette*. Retrieved from http://teachers.net/wong/MAR04/

Wong, H., & Wong, R. (2004b). *The first days of school: How to be an effective teacher*. Mountain View, CA: Harry K. Wong Publications.

Wong, H., & Wong, R. (2005). The first ten days of school. *Teachers.net Gazette*. Retrieved from http://teachers.net/wong/JAN05/

Wong, H., & Wong, R. (2007). *The first days of school: How to be an effective teacher* (2nd ed.). Mountain View, CA: Harry K. Wong Publications.

Wong, H., & Wong, R. (2009b). *The first days of school: How to be an effective teacher* (3rd ed.). Mountain View, CA: Harry K. Wong Publications.

Wong, H., & Wong, R. (n.d.). [*Teachers.net Gazette* articles from 2000–2009 are available at this site: http://teachers.net/wong/]